ABC and United Paramount Theaters agreed to merge.
CBS color halted by Korean wartime shortages.

1952   FCC ended the TV Freeze and gave assignments to educators.

1953   FCC approved NTSC system of color television.
First ETV stations came on the air.
Ford Foundation funded NET as a program source for ETV.
Congress approved the United States Information Agency.

1954   FCC changed multiple-ownership rules to help UHF.
Edward R. Murrow attacked Senator McCarthy in "See It Now."
NBC evicted the Voice of Firestone.
British Parliament formed Independent Television Authority.

1955   NBC bought UHF station in Buffalo, N.Y.
FCC announced deintermixture proposals.
CBS achieved parity with NBC in television ratings.

1956   Ampex demonstrated videotape recorder.
Stations petitioned FCC to regulate CATV.

1957   FCC awarded Channel 5 in Boston to Herald Traveler.

1958   FCC refused to assert jurisdiction over CATV.
Carroll case decision on economic injury and service to public.

1959   Quiz scandals over rigged television programs.
Payola scandals over payments to disc jockeys.
WDAY case said station not liable for political speech.
Congress amended Section 315 to exempt news.
NET bicycle network started circulating programs on videotape.
FCC asked Congress for authority to regulate cable.

1960   FCC deintermixed Fresno, Calif., removing active VHF channel.
Presidential candidates Kennedy and Nixon held "Great Debates."
Senate failed to pass bill so FCC could regulate cable.
FCC issued Programming Policy Statement.

1961   FCC Chairman Newton Minow made "vast wasteland" speech.

1962   FCC imposed partial freeze on new AM stations.
FCC ruled all new television sets must have UHF capacity.
FCC denied Carter Mountain application for microwave relays.
Congress passed the Educational Television Facilities Act.

1963   FCC ruled broadcasters must give free response to paid comment.
Networks expanded evening news programs to half hour.

1964   WGCB refusal of time to Fred Cook was beginning of *Red Lion* case.
UCC opposed renewal of WLBT in Jackson, Miss.
FCC issued Fairness Doctrine Primer.

1965   FCC limited duplication of AM schedules on FM.
Research report led to color breakthrough.
FCC renewed WLBT for one year.
FCC issued rules for cable systems engaged in importation.

1966   FCC extended cable rules to all systems.
Ford Foundation proposed domestic television satellite.

UNDERSTANDING BROADCASTING

SECOND EDITION

EUGENE S. FOSTER

BROOKLYN COLLEGE OF THE CITY UNIVERSITY OF NEW YORK

UNDERSTANDING BROADCASTING

SECOND EDITION

**ADDISON-WESLEY
PUBLISHING COMPANY**

Reading, Massachusetts ▪ Menlo Park, California
London ▪ Amsterdam ▪ Don Mills, Ontario ▪ Sydney

Sponsoring Editor: *Brian Walker*
Production Editor: *Elydia Siegel*
Designer: *Vanessa Piñeiro*
Cover Design: *Nason Design Associates*

This book is in the Addison-Wesley Series in Mass Communication

Library of Congress Cataloging in Publication Data

Foster, Eugene S.
    Understanding broadcasting.

    (Addison-Wesley series in mass communication)
    Bibliography: p.
    Includes indexes.
    1. Broadcasting—United States.   I. Title.
II. Series.
HE8689.8.F67   1982   384.54′0973   81-3539
ISBN 0-201-10106-8   AACR2
Reprinted with corrections, July 1982

ISBN 0-201-10106-8
    0-201-23487-4
BCDEFGHIJ-DO-898765432

PREFACE

There have been several dramatic and significant four-year periods in the history of broadcasting. From 1924 to 1928 there was the beginning of commercial radio; chaos, caused by the breakdown of the 1912 law; the beginning of modern regulations and the formation of the national networks. From 1948 to 1952 network radio almost died but individual stations developed format programming which was to be highly successful; the FCC devoted its attention to long-range planning for television and the new medium became solidly entrenched in American life. In the late 1960s the Supreme Court upheld the FCC's Fairness Doctrine in the *Red Lion* case and its authority to regulate cable in the *Southwestern* case; the Appeals Court in the *WLBT(TV)* case opened FCC proceedings to the public, marking the start of minority access to programming decisions and to employment; the Carnegie Commission report on public television paved the way for the Public Broadcasting Act of 1967, and Americans watched live coverage of a man walking on the moon. Still, none of these periods had more impact than the four years following final writing of this book's first edition in 1977.

By far the greatest changes have occurred in cable which four years ago was desperately searching for program material. In 1977 Ted Turner's first superstation was just getting started. Now there are four. In 1977 Home Box Office (HBO) was practically the only national pay cable service. Now there is not only strong competition from "Showtime" and others, but there is also the promise of developing a per-program pay service through interactive cable pioneered by Warner's Qube in Columbus, Ohio. In 1977 the only origination services were those offered by individual systems. Two years later satellite usage made possible the Cable Satellite Public Affairs Network (C-SPAN) and the Entertainment and Sports Programming Network (ESPN). In June of 1980 Ted Turner's Cable News Network (CNN) started and within a year Warner-Amex was using its "Kaleidoscope" transponder to originate cultural programming by ABC's Alpha Network in the evenings. There are now more competitors for available cable channels than can be easily listed or accommodated on most systems. As services have expanded, cable penetration has mushroomed.

In 1977 subscription television (STV) was written off as an idea whose time had come and gone. A handful of stations had tried it and failed. In 1981 up to a dozen STV stations are on the air, healthy and looking to future growth and the FCC is entertaining a COMSAT petition to start work on satellite subscription television (SSTV). $700 million have been committed to the effort to deliver a satellite pay service directly to homes.

A host of technical innovations have not only made possible the above developments in cable and STV but also promise other variations in making the home television set a communications center. There has been dramatic growth in video games, home videotape recorders, and video discs. Closed captioning (CC) offers an important service for viewing by the hard-of-hearing. Teletext is on the horizon. Combining interactive cable with computer technology may revolutionize personal banking and other commercial services along with home security.

In 1977 the Carter administration was starting a drive to increase minority ownership of broadcast stations. The FCC introduced distress sales and tax certificates to encourage owners to sell to minorities. To increase the number of stations for which minorities might apply the FCC approved low-power television (LPTV), VHF dropins, reduction of protection for clear channel radio stations and the squeezing of more FM stations into the table of allocations. The FCC is also considering narrowing the AM channels to 9 kHz. While these measures have not yet had substantial impact, there is reason to hope that minority representation in ownership will improve in the 1980s.

Underlying progress in cable, STV and minority ownership has been a significant attempt to deregulate radio and television. As the number of stations has increased, there is a feeling that the public interest can best be served by marketplace forces. Although one major effort to rewrite the Communications Act failed, the broadcasters think they have reason to hope that in the near future their licenses will cover longer periods and be easier to renew, that the Fairness Doctrine and Section 315 will be eliminated or watered down.

Although National Public Radio (NPR) flourished in the past four years and the Public Broadcasting Service (PBS) saw a significant increase in its audiences, there is little cause for optimism about the future of public television. The report of a second Carnegie Commission spelled out the weaknesses of the system but failed to provide useful alternatives. The Reagan administration has proposed drastic cuts in federal subsidies and PBS faces serious threats from competition in cultural programming by cable origination and pay service.

The purpose of this second edition is to place these and other recent developments in perspective by incorporating them into the overall study of broadcasting.

Understanding Broadcasting was designed as a text for a one-semester beginning course in broadcasting. Its purposes are:

1. To describe American broadcasting as it currently exists with emphasis on interrelationships among its structural elements.

2. To examine the processes by which current principles and practices evolved so there can be a better understanding of the present and an intelligent anticipation of events which might occur in the future.

3. To serve as a basis for evaluation and criticism of broadcasting in our society.

It is assumed that the great majority of Americans have an intimate relationship with radio and television. Some are participants in the broadcasting industry; most are consumers; and a few are or may become advocates for the interests of parents, minority groups, and others seeking improvement in broadcasting through public criticism and pressure brought to bear on the leaders of broadcasting and government. Perhaps the most common characteristic (one which applies to many participants in the industry as well as the general public) is a failure to understand fully how the various elements of the media operate and interrelate and to appreciate sufficiently the points of view of others. Until such understanding and appreciation are gained, participants will find it more difficult to achieve success in the field and advocates of change will find it impossible to engage in the kind of meaningful dialogue which can result in constructive changes.

This book has been written and organized to provide this understanding and to prepare you for meaningful analysis and dialogue. As such, it attempts to combine factual and theoretical essentials with pedagogical soundness.

Topical/Conceptual Integration

The organization of the text provides an integration of concepts and topics within an historical, practical, and descriptive framework. Most instructors hope that by the end of the course, students will have a grasp of concepts like "the public interest," "freedom of speech," and "the role of broadcasting in our society." It has been observed that most beginning students more easily comprehend and learn how to apply such concepts if they are treated as they naturally arise in the discussion of different specific topics. For example, the concept of freedom of speech is first discussed in the Prologue as one of the national priorities which shaped the media. It is then related to Secretary Hoover's regulatory philosophy in the early 1920s on which the Radio Act of 1927 was based. It is still a key issue in the FCC's regulatory problems in radio. The concept also is discussed in the chapter on Section 315 and the Fairness Doctrine, which highlights the conflict between the literalist and functionalist approaches to free speech. The functionalist right of the public to hear was a key point in the controversy over the Commission's antisiphoning rules on pay cable. When discussing the systems of broadcasting around the world, the differences are related to the concept of what various governments wish their people to see and hear. In the Epilogue the need to accommodate conflicting interpretations of freedom of speech is considered critical to the improvement of the media.

Historical Perspective

Closely tied to the framework of a topical/conceptual integration is the historical perspective that looks at the interrelatedness of developments, issues, and concepts within society and broadcasting. This perspective helps students understand how broadcasting arrived at its present philosophy, complexity, and methods of operation. The book attempts, therefore, to place the institution, concept, or situation in its historical framework and then to weave its development throughout the book. Economics, politics, social trends and structures, technological developments, personalities and tastes—all have contributed to the growth of the industry and to the processes in which broadcasters, regulators, and the public seek solutions to problems.

Descriptive Approach

This approach seeks to enable students first to understand the history, development, and current operations of broadcasting in order to understand the issues and controversies surrounding the field. Such an approach follows not only the historical trends of a developing industry but the critical issues of a maturing industry. Certainly there is room for controversy and criticism. If the criticism is to be constructive, it must be based on a solid knowledge of what is being criticized. Hence, the priority is on description with the expectation that students will subsequently see for themselves the criticisms which are most important to them and that they will have acquired the significant grounds on which to base their arguments.

To assist the student in mastering the material in this text, the author has included a number of special features.

1. At the beginning of each chapter is a one-paragraph *preview* of the material to be covered in the following pages. It will alert the reader to certain key points which are critical to understanding.

2. For those chapters where the historical approach is most obvious, there are *chronologs* listing key events which occurred in given years. They will be helpful in summarizing the sequence of changes.

3. At the end of most chapters is a list of words and phrases which are defined in the *glossary* following the body of the text. As students encounter a word or phrase for the first time, they will find it helpful to look it up in the glossary to be sure they know precisely what it means.

4. To personalize the development of broadcasting there are *biographical sketches* of a dozen persons who were singularly important to some aspect of the media.

5. Because broadcasters are inclined to refer to various concepts and groups by initials and rarely use the full names, the text includes an *index of initials* which are frequently used.

6. *Marginal notes* identify important concepts and topics and can be used for previewing and reviewing a section or chapter.

At the same time it must be emphasized that, in light of rapid changes in the field, the reader must take note of current developments if he is to have an understanding of current broadcasting.

Brooklyn, New York   E.S.F.
May 1981

CONTENTS

CHAPTER

HISTORICAL PERSPECTIVES II 1945–1980 with Emphasis on RADIO   87

CHAPTER

HISTORICAL PERSPECTIVES III 1920–1980 with Emphasis on TELEVISION   119

CHAPTER 8   THE STATION AND LOCAL ADVERTISING   229

CHAPTER 9   THE NETWORKS   253

CHAPTER 10

NATIONAL SPOT ADVERTISING AND PROGRAM SYNDICATION   295

CHAPTER 11

RATINGS   317

CHAPTER 12   SECTION 315 AND THE FAIRNESS DOCTRINE   347

CHAPTER 13   PUBLIC (EDUCATIONAL) BROADCASTING   389

CHAPTER **14**

AMERICA AND BROADCASTING AROUND THE WORLD   425

PREVIEW

The goal of this book is to help the student "understand broadcasting" —what it is, how it works, and how it interacts with society. An important first step is realizing that broadcasting has evolved as part of society and that its structure and purposes are determined by such national priorities as:

1. Free enterprise.

2. Regulation of scarce resources.

3. Free speech.

4. The use of compromise to resolve differences.

It will help if the reader seeks the logic of the media today by seeing responses to problems and circumstances in various historical periods. Especially important are the interrelationships among the units of broadcasting and how people perceive what they encounter. Finally, one must make allowance for the fact that in any controversy both sides tend to exaggerate and one must expect to find the truth between the extremes.

CHAPTER 1

PROLOGUE

At 10:50 on the evening of December 8, 1980 a limousine drew up to the Dakota, a luxury apartment building on West 72nd Street, just off Central Park in New York City. From it descended a forty-year-old man and his wife. Following her to the door, he heard someone call his name. As he half turned, he was struck by four bullets fired from only five feet away. Gasping "I'm shot," he staggered to the doorman's office, where he collapsed in a pool of blood. The police arrived within minutes and rushed him fifteen blocks to Roosevelt Hospital, where he was pronounced dead in spite of a desperate struggle by seven surgeons to revive him.

Just another entry in the grim crime statistics of a big city? Consider the following: within minutes radio and television had spread word across the country and to all the continents that John Lennon had been shot and was dead. Two hours later more than a thousand mourners had gathered at the Dakota, singing his songs and adorning the gate with flowers and pictures of him and his wife. Not since the assassination of President John Kennedy seventeen years before had there been such a spontaneous outpouring of love and grief.

The response to this tragedy had a special character because John Lennon was a child of broadcasting being mourned by the first generation to have known television from its infancy. Television was an intimate family member for this generation from the first moments they could focus their eyes. It had been their babysitter; the set had been on in the morning while they had breakfast and prepared for school. They had rushed home from school to see the afternoon programs, stayed inside on Saturday mornings to watch cartoons, and pled with their parents to stay up just a little longer to see one more evening program. By the time they were sixteen or seventeen years old this generation had spent more hours with television than they had going to school or doing anything else but sleeping.

It was through television that they first met John Lennon and the Beatles, on the Ed Sullivan Show in 1964. It was through radio's constant repetition that this generation came to know the new popular music so well that they bought great numbers of recordings for their own libraries. It was through broadcasting that they followed the career of John Lennon and the Beatles and were induced to make concerts and movies very successful by their attendance. It was through television that his fans followed the career of John Lennon after the Beatles disbanded. Through radio and television they followed his re-emergence as a personification of the desire for peace and as an important influence on modern music. The many tributes to Lennon were seen through broadcasting by those who could not be present in person. It was fitting that so many of the radio stations that had contributed to his popularity should, at the suggestion of his widow, stay silent for ten minutes. Even Radio Moscow devoted a special ninety minutes to his music.

What is this thing called "broadcasting"? Ask a random sample of people and any individual answer will be determined by the perspective of the respondent, as with the responses of the men in this poem:

> There were six men of Indostan
>   To learning much inclined
> Who went to see the elephant
>   (Though all of them were blind)
> That each by observation
>   Might satisfy his mind.

As each of the six feels a portion of the elephant, he "sees" the animal is a wall, or a spear, or a snake, or a tree, or a fan or a rope. The fable concludes:

> And so these men of Indostan
>   Disputed loud and long
> Each in his own opinion

Exceeding stiff and strong
Though each was partly in the right
And all were in the wrong.*

John Godfrey Saxe, "The Blind Men and the Elephant"

In our sympathy for the blind men, it is easy to overlook the fact that the sighted, also, are greatly limited in comprehending what they encounter. When it comes to "understanding" the elephant as opposed to simply "seeing" it, there can be as much confusion among those with twenty-twenty vision as there was among the blind men.

Even the mahout who spends a lifetime in the teak forest with his Indian elephant is limited in "understanding." He may know nothing about the prehistoric ancestor to his elephant and the characteristics that enabled it to survive while other species perished. He cannot visualize the intricate musculature of his animal and how it is applied to provide leverage to move not only his own bulk but also the load he is asked to carry. He probably knows little of the economic impact of elephant labor and does not understand the role the elephant plays in his country's cultural heritage. In short, even the mahout (like the blind man) is limited in understanding his elephant despite his intensive experience with it.

There is a parallel between the blind men (or the mahout) and the elephant and the failure of many Americans to understand their most ubiquitous medium of communication. All of us have "seen" television and know enough about it for our particular interests, but few understand either its inner workings or how it has sought to solve its problems.

1.1 "SEEING" VS. "UNDERSTANDING" BROADCASTING

For the average viewer, an evening with television is a rather uncomplicated experience. We know that when we turn on the set we can receive a number of stations that we identify by channel numbers and call letters, by the names of favorite programs, and, possibly, by the network with which each may be affiliated. We assume stations receive their revenues from advertisers. We are so accustomed to have a program pause "for this important message" that it seems normal to us and commercials are a source of little or no irritation. We may know a great deal about the talent on the programs and we have expectations about the story lines we will see. Beyond that we have little interest in or information about American broadcasting. It is a very complex system that has many different facets, depending on your perspective. What you "see" when you consider broadcasting is related to where you stand in relation to it, and probably is only a part of the whole.

* Verses one and eight, in *Poems*. Courtesy of Houghton Mifflin Company.

The Stockholders

For the stockholders, broadcasting is an investment from which they hope to earn a high annual yield and an increase in the value of the stock for possible future sale. Some stockholders may be extremely wealthy while others may have invested part of their limited life savings in broadcasting because a broker or friend so advised. They may watch the ratings, since the fortunes of networks and stations reflect viewing popularity, but know little about the details of government regulation that may have an important bearing on their stocks.

The Station Manager

For the station manager, broadcasting is economics. Success is determined by the profit-and-loss statement furnished by the accountants. The manager is at the center of an intricate pattern of program purveyors, sales efforts, and personnel decisions as well as regulatory activities that each year seem to require more of his or her attention. The manager has little time to be critical of the program schedule and may fail to grasp the philosophical grounds on which the Federal Communications Commission (FCC) and the courts stand when insisting that the public has a stake in the station's business.

The Network Executive

For the network executive, broadcasting is a chain of some 200 stations through which programs are circulated. The schedule is designed to compete with the other networks for the attention of the audience and for advertising dollars. Tools of the trade are ratings figures and budgets showing above-the-line and below-the-line costs. The executive knows that most station managers are concerned with "ascertaining" in preparation for license renewal but has probably had no experience with it.

The Advertiser

For the advertiser who pays the bills, broadcasting is a highly efficient medium for delivering sales messages into nearly every American home. It incorporates both sight and sound, an ideal combination for many products. It may be used as a primary advertising vehicle or as a supplement to advertising in print or direct mail. Television time may be purchased simultaneously on 200 network stations or it may be spread among 500 stations in a national spot campaign. The small retailer will often buy time on a single station to inform local residents about services and products offered for sale. Whether national or local, the advertiser is not concerned with and may not understand Section 315 of the Communications Act or the FCC's Fairness Doctrine.

The Talent

For people seen on the air (the talent), broadcasting is an opportunity to receive good pay to perform for more people at one moment than traditional stage actors could have reached in a lifetime. They know broadcasting is a high-risk field where the supply of talent is greater than the demand. For many it can be a long time between jobs, and they know the experience of waiting on tables or washing dishes to tide them over. In their search for successful auditions, these people have little time to worry about the details of a network's contract with affiliates.

The Program Syndicator

For the program syndicator, broadcasting is 700 commercial stations throughout the country that need more programming than they can produce for themselves or want to obtain from networks and Hollywood movie companies. The program syndicator is constantly on the road dealing with station managers and program directors, wining and dining them and preparing brochures that, it is hoped, will be on the right desks at the moment program-purchasing decisions are made. Income is earned only as programs are sold, and the syndicator is unconcerned about the relationship between station managers and their congressional representatives.

The Time Salesperson

For the time salesperson, broadcasting is a business where one seeks to sell in a profitable transaction bits of time available for commercials. The salesperson needs to be thoroughly conversant with ratings and demographic data detailing the breakdown of the audience by age, sex, education, and other characteristics, but has no need to know or care about the science of electromagnetic propagation or the problems of the FCC in interpreting freedom of speech.

The News Reporter

For the news reporter, broadcasting is our most important news medium because it is the source from which most people get most of their information about what is going on in the world. He or she is working in a long tradition of press freedom and journalistic integrity. The news reporter knows well the intricacies of the complex organization whereby news comes into homes with incredible speed from all corners of the globe. It is no reflection on the news person that he or she knows little about the workings of syndicated programming (off-network, original, or barter) that may adjoin the news or the function of the station rep through whom the advertiser may be paying the reporter's salary.

The Federal Communications Commissioners

For members of the FCC, broadcasting is a medium for which they have regulatory responsibility. It is a focal point of pressures applied by people seeking to influence the development of the medium. Commissioners are expected to be responsive to legitimate needs and demands of broadcasters, legislators, viewers, and representatives of those aggrieved by lack of programming or employment opportunities. Television is so ubiquitous and so controversial that there is no hope of pleasing everyone. Most members of the FCC have no occasion to become conversant with the efforts of the many people who are involved in the sale of television time.

The Parents

To some parents, television is the ideal "babysitter" that makes it possible to work around the house without interference from the youngsters. To other parents, television is a monster that inculcates violence and exploits children with commercials against which they have no defenses. They little realize how low ratings for a single time segment can affect sales for a whole morning, afternoon, or evening.

The Minorities

To members of ethnic and other minorities, broadcasting is a highly visible and discriminatory medium. Their goal is to get "a piece of the action" in better employment opportunities and programming addressed to their particular needs. In the 1980s the major emphasis of minority groups has been on achieving a more equitable share in the ownership of stations. Until they get their own licenses it is of little importance to them that managers traditionally try to keep a healthy balance among local, network, and national spot business.

Ask any of those listed or others who have a more or less intimate association with television to explain the American system of broadcasting and its important interrelationships and we return to our opening analogy of the blind men and the elephant where "each is partly in the right and all are in the wrong."

1.2 THE NATIONAL CONTEXT OF AMERICAN BROADCASTING

Broadcasting is "as American as apple pie." Its financing is consistent with American economic principles, its regulation is an outgrowth of American political philosophy, and its programming is a reflection of American values and desires. American broadcasting has been shaped by four elements of American tradition:

1. Free enterprise.
2. Regulation of scarce resources.
3. Free speech.
4. The use of compromise to resolve differences.

Free Enterprise

It is the American tradition to depend on the private sector, motivated by free enterprise incentives (profits), for everything it is able to accomplish satisfactorily. We have turned to government only when private companies have proven inadequate to a given task. For example, at one time postal companies were private enterprises with each competing for business. As the nation grew, it was necessary to have a postal service that would reach every section and serve every community and hamlet. Since no private company had the resources for such expansion or the incentive to serve where it was unprofitable, the government had to take over. At one time, fire-fighting companies were also privately run. The spectacle of competing companies watching homes burn with no attempt to help owners who had not signed up for protection made it obvious we needed a better way to cope with fire hazards. We started our social security system when it became clear that Americans were unable through private insurance companies to provide adequately for their retirement needs.

It was natural in this country that broadcasting should develop in the free enterprise tradition and that stations that are licensed by the FCC should remain privately owned in the absence of a clear need to change the system. We have about 8,500 commercial stations—some 4,600 AM radio, 3,200 FM radio, and 750 TV—in the early 1980s. All are privately owned by companies and individuals hoping to make a profit on their operations. Because there are needs that commercial stations cannot meet, we also have over 1,350 noncommercial or public stations—1,100 FM and 270 TV.

The 8,500 commercial stations are the heart of the American system. Associated with them are networks, advertising agencies, station representatives, program packagers, and others. As one seeks to understand why certain principles and practices dominate the system, one should consider what is most likely to be profitable. This is most obvious in an analysis of the commercial program schedules. A characteristic of free enterprise is that each member tries to achieve maximum profit; this frequently means appealing to the largest number of potential customers. Airlines schedule the largest number of flights where most people want to travel. Stores stock the goods which most people will want to buy. Manufacturers produce the cars which will be in the greatest demand. It can be difficult to find plane schedules to places visited by few or to buy products desired only by a small minority.

Similarly, most television stations schedule the programs they think most people want to see and they subscribe to ratings organizations to learn what is most popular. Since the majority of Americans are fairly homogeneous in their entertainment tastes, this means the schedules of most stations and networks appear to be copies of each other. This is a source of concern to some critics. They feel that the networks have somehow achieved the power to dominate the stations and to control their schedules against their wishes. But networks exist and prosper only because some 600 of the most powerful stations have decided that a network affiliation is good business just as a dealer in any product might decide it would be profitable to become associated with one of the big manufacturers. This may appear paradoxical when it is shown that affiliated stations carry network programs for well over half of their schedules but receive less than ten percent of their income from their affiliation. However, it will also be clear that the affiliation is more profitable than being an "independent."

As with the rest of our free enterprise economy, there are prohibitions against monopolistic practices that would take away the independence of the individual stations. By FCC rules no more than twenty-one stations (seven AM, seven FM, and seven TV) can be owned by a single licensee. In practice, most group owners have fewer than the maximum and each gives the managers of individual stations leeway to make decisions in responding to local problems and conditions. In addition, the FCC requires each licensee to demonstrate familiarity with his or her community and relate the program schedule to the needs and interests of the local audiences. When it appeared from time to time that networks were in a contractual position to force their wills upon the affiliated stations, the FCC passed various regulations removing that power. The fact that the stations frequently continued the same practices on a voluntary basis is an indication that the free enterprise system with its emphasis on profits is the dominating factor in most broadcasting decisions.

Service to small groups in the population is provided by the free enterprise system at that point where the large number of suppliers makes it unprofitable for all to seek a fraction of the majority of people who form a homogeneous center of the population. For example, there were fewer than 1,000 radio stations in the late 1930s and early 1940s and the medium was subject to the same criticism leveled at television today—too little variety in programming. As the number of radio stations rose into the thousands and as viewing largely supplanted listening in the majority of homes, AM and FM broadcasters started specializing in programming for smaller segments of the audience. There is now programming (music, news, and dialogue) on the radio dial for almost everyone who seeks it. There seems to be little possibility that the number of television stations can increase to the degree seen in radio. Some who would like to see as much diversity in television look to cable with its potential of bringing twenty or forty or more channels into each home. They feel that after a handful of channels are devoted to majority interests, the minorities will have a chance to see what they want, and events of the late 1970s seem to bear out this view. Whether or not it is correct will depend upon the workings of the free enterprise system and whether it is profitable to spend the money for programs that only a few will want to see.

Regulation of Scarce Resources

So long as our natural resources appeared to be inexhaustible, private companies were free to exploit them without regulation. But when it became clear that a vital resource was or soon would be in short supply, the government assumed a degree of control over its use. For example, private individuals or companies have never been permitted to own or control vital and limited means of transportation. In each area of the country there are only a few rivers and streams, and it has been assumed that they belonged to the people. Even ownership of the land on both banks of a river at a given point did not give one the automatic right to build a dam that would interfere with navigation. When the government granted a franchise to operate a ferry across the river, there were limitations with respect to the rates that might be charged and a requirement that it be a common carrier offering service to all without discrimination.

When the first legislation broadly regulating radio was passed in 1912, there was a realization that the airwaves were limited in extent and that their ownership should not pass to private individuals. The need for radio frequencies has surpassed the number available even as over the years knowledge and technology have expanded our capacity to use them. It was the limitation or scarcity of the airwaves that provided the underpinning for all radio (and television) regulation.

Since the start of modern radio regulation in 1927, broadcasters have complained because they were subject to more restrictions than were newspaper publishers. In response it was pointed out that there were many more daily papers than there were stations. After World War II, when the number of stations far exceeded the number of papers, broadcasters claimed that the scarcity-of-the-airwaves argument was no longer tenable. Nevertheless, according to the FCC, with the concurrence of the courts, it is not the comparative number of print and broadcast outlets that is the most significant factor. The limitation on publishing is the result of the operation of the law of supply and demand. But the number of stations is limited by the space on the radio spectrum—there are many who would join the ranks of broadcasters if frequencies were available. Because those who do have stations are a privileged group, there must be regulation. The scarcity argument will lose its validity on the day that anyone who wants to broadcast and has enough money can find a frequency to use. Until that day regulation will be a fact of life for broadcasters and controversy will continue over both philosophy and details.

Free Speech

The regulation of scarce radio frequencies has been one factor altering free enterprise in broadcasting. Even more important has been our commitment to the concept of free speech stated in the First Amendment to the Constitution:

> *Congress shall make no law respecting an establishment of religion, or prohibiting the free exercise thereof; or abridging the freedom of speech, or of the press; or the right of the people peaceably to assemble, and to petition the government for a redress of grievances.*

While some feel we have taken too many liberties with free enterprise, free speech has suffered far less because there is general recognition that democracy can flourish only as citizens have unfettered access to information. Even in times of war we have gone to great lengths to avoid censorship. The significance of free speech in this book is that, in the final analysis, any governmental relationship to broadcasting can be interpreted as an infringement on it. In fact, when modern broadcaster regulation emerged in 1927, legislators were so concerned that freedom of speech had been inadequately protected that they added a section clarifying their intent:

> *Nothing in this Act shall . . . give the licensing authority the power of censorship over radio communications . . . and no regulation or condition shall be promulgated . . . by the licensing authority which shall interfere with the right of free speech by means of radio communication.*

In spite of general agreement on the importance of free speech, it is still the source of much controversy in the field of broadcast regulation because of conflicting views on the meaning, intent, and implications of the concept. Broadcasters and regulators tend to see it from the two different points of view of the "literalist" and the "functionalist."

Freedom to Speak   The literalist argues that free speech means just what it says—the absence of all government restrictions under ordinary circumstances. There is agreement that freedom is not guaranteed to the person who would falsely yell "Fire!" in a crowded theater, or to one whose remarks are certain to incite a mob to violence, or to one who would slander the good name of another. But, aside from a few exceptions such as these, the literalist maintains that free speech is an inherent right of citizens (including broadcasters) that will by itself accomplish the original goal of rendering government incapable of impeding the free expression of ideas it might consider improper. Absence of such governmental restrictions will ensure the free flow of information required in a democracy.

The broadcasters' concern goes far beyond censorship when government says something is forbidden. To the broadcasters free speech means that they can program their stations as they wish and that when they are required to use their facilities in a given way, their freedom has been unconstitutionally abridged or impaired. For example, broadcasters argue that when a station allots time to a political candidate and is then required to give equal exposure to a second, the time used by the opponent has been removed from the broadcaster's control, and freedom of speech is suspended until the second candidate has finished his remarks.

Some of the specific arguments about free speech boil down to acceptance of "broadcaster judgment." The theory of public regulation is based on the assumption that the FCC will select the best among the applicants for a frequency and then depend on the winners to use their best judgment on how to serve the public interest. On several occasions (especially related to Section 315 and the Fairness Doctrine) both Congress and the FCC have gone to great lengths to emphasize how heavily they rely on broadcaster judgment and how they will not question the outcome unless it is blatantly out of line. On other occasions the FCC has not hesitated to reverse a subjective judgment by broadcasters—thus insisting upon its own judgment, which happened to be different. As noted in Chapter 12, there is considerable room for discussion as to what constitutes "reasonable access" for candidates for federal elective office. When the Carter-Mondale Committee in December 1979 asked the networks for a prime-time half-hour to announce their candidacies for re-election, the broadcasters replied that it was too early for such a presentation. There were still eleven months before the general election and two months before the opening of the primary season. The FCC disagreed, ordered the networks to provide the time, and was upheld by a court of appeals. The broadcasters felt their judgment was far from being "blatantly out of line," and under the theory of public regulation they should have been upheld. As it was, literalists felt the FCC decision was an infringement of free speech.

Freedom to Hear   Functionalists argue that freedom of speech is only a means to the more important end of guaranteeing that ideas and information will be permitted to circulate and that in matters of controversy, people will be able to hear all points of view. Functionalists believe that this right of the people was the paramount concern of the founding fathers and that the First Amendment focused on government because only government had restricted the freedom of the colonists to hear different opinions. By extension, the people's right to hear would have to be protected in those media that are limited by scarce resources and where the few who obtain licenses tend to come from a limited and affluent portion of our society. More bluntly, the functionalist says the First Amendment not only prohibits government from interfering with the free flow of ideas, the amendment also denies that right to those who are licensed to broadcast. It is permissible for a newspaper to give only one point of view in its news and editorials because anyone is free to start another paper representing the other side. But, the private ownership of a transmitter can no more be permitted to stifle the free flow of information and ideas than the ownership of both riverbanks can justify impeding navigation between them.

In implementing the right of the people to hear all points of view the government has moved in two directions. First, it has sought to make individual stations independent of excessive outside control that might limit expression of ideas. In the free enterprise system there is a tendency for a few powerful participants to extend their ownership as widely as possible. We have already noted that no single licensee may own more than seven stations in one category (AM and FM radio and TV), thus making it difficult for one person or company to impose its ideas too widely. There are also cross-ownership rules forbidding a newspaper publisher in a small town from owning the only broadcast station or stations and prohibiting the creation or transfer of cross-ownerships regardless of community size. There is a series of chain regulations promulgated by the FCC to prevent a network from having undue influence upon its affiliates, although there are few restrictions on how much network programming a station can voluntarily carry.

Secondly, both Congress and the commission have enunciated a "fairness concept" that requires broadcasters to extend use of their facilities to political candidates and devote time to discussion of controversial issues. Once a station enters the field of controversy (however unwillingly), there must be additional material implementing the public's right to hear the opposing views.

While literalists and functionalists are not diametrically opposed to each other and while both have a paramount interest in making democracy work, their differences ensure that broadcast regulation will always be controversial.

The Use of Compromise to Resolve Differences

American politics has been defined as the "art of the possible," and regulation in all fields has consisted of seeking to steer a middle course between extremes. For example, this country is committed to free enterprise, but if the system were to be maintained without restrictions, there would be no child labor laws, no safety requirements for factories and mines, no municipal fire departments, no limit on rates charged for electricity and telephone services, no antitrust laws, no food and drug laws to ensure the quality of food and drink, and no social security system. In all these instances some citizens feel regulation has gone too far while others feel it has not gone far enough. Conflict exists between supporters of extremes, and compromise is the accepted method of conflict resolution.

There is the same conflict in broadcast regulation and the same resort to compromise that frequently fails to satisfy anyone fully. There is an inevitable conflict between our desire to serve the largest number of potential homes and our concern that minorities have the right to hear programs that will meet some of their needs. There is a conflict between requiring that broadcasters be fair when entering the field of controversy and ensuring that they have the necessary freedom to seek out and report the news some government officials would like to keep secret. There is a conflict between the belief that licensees should be permitted to control their own operations within the free enterprise system and the concept that those who are privileged to use scarce natural resources must have somewhat less freedom than those who engage in other kinds of business.

The history of broadcast regulation is the story of conflicts that have emerged between important priorities. In some instances two significant priorities come into direct conflict. In a free enterprise system one should be able to hire as one pleases. Yet how does this affect the rights of minorities to employment in scarce publicly licensed frequencies? In other instances two very different interpretations of a commonly accepted concept may exist. Is freedom of speech primarily freedom to speak or freedom to hear? Sometimes the philosophical differences are subordinated to pragmatic interests—for example, in trying to plan for cable television and satellite usage we have to consider the American commitment to using advanced technology at the same time that we are concerned for the rights of viewers to continue receiving what they have come to expect.

By seeking to resolve these conflicts through compromise, government must at one time or another displease everyone. The losers will never be convinced that their priorities were less important than those that were chosen in a given instance. If the time ever comes when some people feel that our system is perfect, we can be assured that it has failed and that compromise has been abandoned in favor of some other method of resolving conflicting ideas and concepts.

1.3 AIDS TO UNDERSTANDING BROADCASTING

American broadcasting dates back to 1920 and has evolved into a fairly complicated structure. Discussion of national traditions gives insight into the philosophy underlying our system but still leaves unanswered many specific questions about practices and problems. Why are six out of seven commercial television stations owned by or affiliated with networks and how does the nonnetwork station survive? Why have program syndication and national spot business become so important? Why have the advertising agencies that once dominated radio programming become so much less important in television scheduling today? Why are stations so greatly concerned about license renewal? Why have ratings become so important and how can we evaluate them? Why was it necessary to add more than 250 noncommercial stations to our system? Why have Section 315 and the Fairness Doctrine generated so much controversy? The answers to these and other questions will come more easily as one notes the following circumstances.

Seeing Historical Evolution

Today's broadcasting has evolved from the past. At first, in the early 1920s, it was simpler, with people exploring something that was new and that grew with a minimum of government intervention. Networks came into existence in response to the needs of certain advertisers and broadcasters for a medium that was, from their points of view, more efficient. Modern regulation, which began in 1927, was the result of certain concerns that were inherent in our society. Succeeding steps in business practices and in regulation were seen as simple extensions of what had been done earlier. Most topics in this book will be treated historically by going back far enough to find the simple and logical practices that form the basis for the evolution that can be traced to the present.

Finding Interrelationships

Broadcasting today is largely a matter of complex interrelationships, and learning about it is like learning about an automobile. The description of a single unit like the spark plug of a car or the station representative selling broadcast time on a distant station becomes meaningful when one sees how it interacts with other components to make the whole an operable unit. The description of either the station or the network is complete only with an understanding of how they affect each other.

The Reality of Perception

The advantage of hindsight sometimes makes it difficult to understand why people acted as they did. There may be little logic in the events of history until one is reminded that everyone reacts to reality as he or she perceives it and sometimes perception is inaccurate. For example, Chapter 7 contains a fairly detailed description of the WHDH-TV case which, in retrospect, was quite unimportant. However, it assumed significance at the time because of the way broadcasters perceived it—even to the extent of almost persuading Congress to change the Communications Act.

Coping with the Tendency to Exaggerate

Controversy about broadcasting is characterized by rhetorical hyperbole. It is to be expected that people will overstate their opinions when seeking to make a point. The more they are personally involved, the greater the overstatement or rhetorical hyperbole is apt to be. When the opposition seems to be more strongly entrenched and immune to criticism, the pitch is raised.

Those who feel broadcasting is shortchanging the public and who see little response to public demands raise the intensity of their criticism to the point where it bears little resemblance to reality. They would have us believe that broadcasters are evil and appreciate nothing but profits and that the broadcast schedules contain nothing but pap at the best and deliberate attempts to destroy society at the worst.

Broadcasters respond by implying that radio and television are the greatest contributors to our society since the writing of the Constitution. Obviously the truth lies somewhere in between and those who would understand must learn enough facts to have confidence in their own judgment.

1.4 THE STEPS IN UNDERSTANDING BROADCASTING

This book seeks to aid in the understanding of broadcasting by approaching the subject from several points of view. Chapter 2 provides the basic technical information needed to understand how the media work and how they are limited by physical characteristics. A historical perspective of the growth of broadcasting and of cable is presented in Chapters 3 through 6 to enable the reader to see better the cross-currents between different electronic media. Chapters 7 through 11 are primarily descriptive of the way the industry is regulated and works. Chapter 12 is devoted to two topics where the free-speech controversy has been greatest—Section 315 of the Communications Act and the Fairness Doctrine. Public broadcasting is covered in Chapter 13, and Chapter 14 discusses from an American perspective radio and television around the world. Finally, the Epilogue reports on the controversies arising from criticism of the media and looks ahead to the possibilities for better broadcasting in light of the understanding at which this book is aimed.

GLOSSARY ITEMS

The following words and phrases used in Chapter 1 are defined in the Glossary:

Amplitude Modulation (AM)	**Cross-Ownership**
Ascertainment	**Demographics**
Barter	**Fairness Doctrine**
Cable Television	**Frequency Modulation (FM)**
Chain Regulations	**Group Owner**

Independent Station

National Spot Business

Network

Network Affiliate

Off-Network Syndication

Original Syndication

Program Packager

Program Syndication

Rating

Station Representative (Rep)

PREVIEW

Understanding broadcasting requires familiarity with a few engineering concepts that both make possible and limit our use of the airwaves. Visualizing the individual radio wave and its characteristics helps one grasp the concept of the radio spectrum, small portions of which are used for broadcasting. Radio and television programs are "transported" from studio into home receiver by imposing patterns on electrical and radio energy. Modern recording techniques involve the imposition of magnetic impressions on plastic tape or discs. Broadcasting is divided into four categories—AM, short wave, and FM radio and television—that have many similarities and a few significant differences. Creating the program involves integrating patterns of energy from several sources. There are several methods of distributing programs around the country and the world. All are variations on the same basic theme of working with energy patterns.

CHAPTER 2

BASIC TECHNICAL INFORMATION

2.1 WAVES AND THE RADIO SPECTRUM

There are around us many forms of energy that have the power to affect or change that with which they come in contact. There is the energy in gravity that pulls all objects toward the center of the earth. There is the energy we exert when we push or pull against something. There is the energy created when powder in a firecracker explodes and there is the energy in sound waves that can affect our eardrums. There is also a panoply of what we call electromagnetic energy, including electrical current that can run machines, light waves that can affect our eyes, and waves with which we can make X-ray photographs of the body. Radio and television programs are conveyed by radio energy which constitutes a portion of the electromagnetic spectrum.

Designation of Waves by Length and Frequency

Radio energy exists in waves that travel at a constant speed of 186,000 miles per second and that are characterized by length and frequency. While it is difficult to envision radio waves, it might be helpful to imagine a distance

of one mile over which all passage is at the speed of twelve miles per hour—
it takes five minutes to travel the mile. If a very tall person whose stride
(distance covered in one step) is ten feet long, that person will move his
or her feet at a certain frequency (approximately two strides every second).
The next person is much shorter and can cover only five feet with each
stride so, if that person is to run the mile in the same five minutes, his or
her feet must move twice as fast or at twice the frequency. A child whose
legs will span only two-and-a-half feet must move his or her feet four times
as fast as the very tall person we first described. Finally, if we consider a
centipede that can cover only a tenth of an inch with each stride, the
centipede's legs must be going so incredibly fast we can't distinguish their
individual movements.

So it is with radio waves. For our purposes a single wave, as shown
in Fig. 2.1, has the same two important characteristics. The *length* of the
wave (corresponding to the stride above) is the distance (in inches, meters,
miles, or any other unit) between the crests as measured from A to B or
B to C. The *frequency* of the wave is the number of cycles (strides) in a
given period of time, usually one second. (A cycle occurs when the entire
wave from crest to crest passes a given point.)

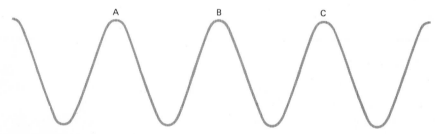

Fig. 2.1
A single radio wave.

Now consider two imaginary waves (Fig. 2.2) that are travelling at a
speed of four inches per second. We can compare these waves in two ways:

1. Wave A has a length of one inch, while Wave B is one-half inch long.

2. Wave A has a frequency of four cycles per second, while Wave B will
pass a given point eight times per second.

(Note the inverse relationship of the two characteristics. As the wave length
increases, the frequency decreases, and vice versa.)

Radio waves are designated in precisely the same manner, although the
lengths will vary from several miles to a fraction of a centimeter, and the

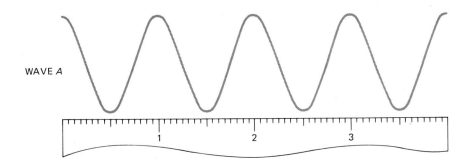

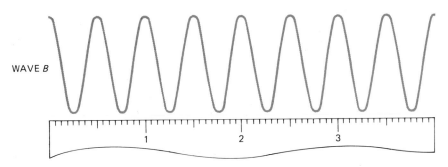

Fig. 2.2
Two radio waves.

frequencies will be in the order of thousands, millions, and billions of cycles per second. A visualization or chart of all the radio waves is called the "radio spectrum" (Fig. 2.3).

For many years radio waves were described in "kilocycles" (kcs), or thousands of cycles per second. As an honor to Heinrich Rudolph Hertz, a nineteenth-century German physicist who laid the theoretical framework for the development of radio, the "cycle per second" is now called a "Hertz" and the basic unit for designating lower radio frequencies is the "kiloHertz" (kHz). (The change in nomenclature is fairly recent and one still encounters the "kilocycle" on occasion.)

To give a number of kiloHertz is to describe a position on the spectrum. A radio station at 880 on the dial is located at 880 kHz on the spectrum. Saying a television station is on Channel 4 means it occupies the space between 66,000 kHz and 72,000 kHz.

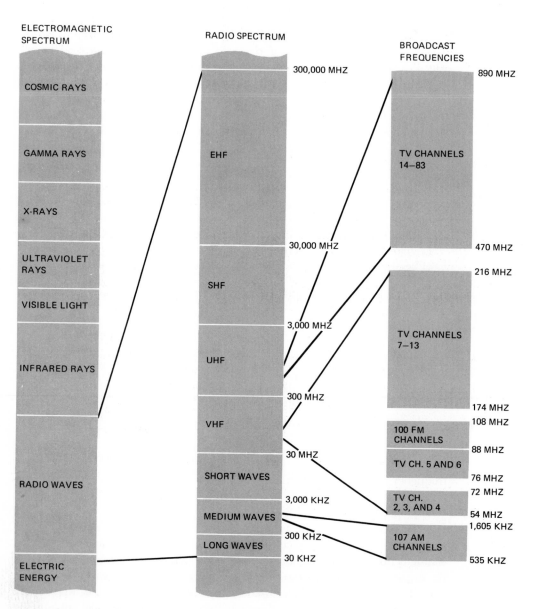

Fig. 2.3
Diagram of the spectrum.

When the number of kiloHertz gets too large for easy manipulation, we change from thousands of Hertz to millions. One thousand thousand Hertz (1,000 kHz) is the same as one million Hertz or one megaHertz (mHz). The use of megaHertz is illustrated by noting that Channel 4 is the space on the spectrum between 66,000 kHz and 72,000 kHz, or between 66 mHz and 72 mHz.

Divisions of the Radio Spectrum

For purposes of description and discussion the radio pioneers divided the spectrum as they knew it into three parts: "long waves," "medium waves," and "short waves." As later scientists learned about more of the spectrum beyond the short waves, it was necessary to continue dividing it and labelling the portions. At first they tried using adjectives like "shorter," "shortest," and "super short." Since that designation was awkward they described the newer portions in terms of "frequency" (Hertz) and then renamed the first three portions in the same manner. Thus, the spectrum today is divided as follows:

30 to 300 kHz	Low Frequencies (LF) (Long Waves)
300 to 3,000 kHz	Medium Frequencies (MF) (Medium Waves)
3,000 to 30,000 kHz	High Frequencies (HF) (Short Waves)
30 to 300 mHz	Very High Frequencies (VHF)
300 to 3,000 mHz	Ultra High Frequencies (UHF)
3,000 to 30,000 mHz	Super High Frequencies (SHF)
30,000 to 300,000 mHz	Extremely High Frequencies (EHF)

This represents the end of the radio spectrum for all practical purposes. Note that each portion is ten times as extensive as the portion that precedes it. Thus, the extent of the entire spectrum is almost unimaginable.

Broadcasting

Broadcasting, by definition, is the transmission of radio and television signals to the public wherever people may be—e.g., in homes, in offices, in automobiles, on picnics. Nonbroadcast transmissions are called "point-to-point" and are intended for a limited number of specific receivers. Broadcast stations in the United States are authorized to use less than one-fifth of one percent of the 300,000 mHz in the spectrum. (See Fig. 2.3.)

1.07 mHz are assigned to standard AM radio broadcasting
20.00 mHz are assigned to FM radio broadcasting
492.00 mHz are assigned to television broadcasting

The rest of the spectrum is used for point-to-point communications and for medical, industrial, and experimental purposes. Among the point-to-point communications assignments are bands for police and fire departments, for taxis and ambulances, for airplanes and space satellites, for forest rangers and amateur operators, for citizens' band and the military and the like.

Broadcasting Channels

A "channel" is the segment of the spectrum assigned to a station. Channels are of different widths. The wider channels can convey more complicated signals than the narrow ones.

Consider an analogy in which sand is to be moved by conveyor belt from a beach to a field a short distance away. If the belt is one inch wide, it can move a small amount of sand in a given time. If it is twenty inches wide, more sand can be moved. Finally, if the belt is 600 inches (fifty feet) wide, it can transport a vastly increased amount. The three illustrative widths of the belts were selected because they represent the ratio between the three channel widths used for broadcasting.

10 kHz channels are assigned for AM radio
200 kHz channels are assigned for FM radio
6,000 kHz (6mHz) channels are assigned for television

Modulation of Carrier Waves

Within its channel the station transmits a "carrier wave" on which program material is "imposed." Pioneer transmissions in radio-telegraphy were simply a matter of turning the carrier wave on and off for short (dot) and long (dash) durations. Later it was learned that carrier waves had several characteristics and a program might be imposed on them by altering or "modulating" one of the features. Early transmissions of voice and music involved modulating the "amplitude" or strength of the carrier wave and were called "amplitude modulation" (AM). For example, if a station is transmitting with a power of 5,000 watts, that figure represents the average around which the actual power varies. The strength of the carrier wave changes almost instantaneously from zero and intermediate points up to more than 10,000 watts. In the receiver the variations in carrier-wave power are translated into variations in electrical energy that can cause a speaker to reproduce sound or a screen to reproduce sight.

Many radio stations now modulate the "frequency" of the carrier wave and are called "frequency modulation" (FM). In FM the power of the carrier wave remains constant while its frequency ranges up and down within the confines of the assigned channel. The variation in frequency is then used, as is the variation in AM power, to vary electrical energy that will in turn cause reproduction of studio sound.

The latest and most sophisticated treatment of carrier waves is called pulse code modulation (PCM), which uses computers and microprocessors to speed up the primitive "on-off" system of the earliest radio communications. Where a human operator could turn a signal on and off a few times (ten to fifteen) a second, it is possible now to program equipment to do the same thing millions of times faster. This new technology makes possible "digital" audio and television in which sound and light waves are encoded into series of "zeros" and "ones." It may never be used for broadcasting since it would require a complete replacement of existing receivers, but its other current applications, especially in recording both sound and video, promise great advances in the field. Some high-fidelity records now sold in stores are made directly from digital audio, which provides better quality than those records made conventionally from tape. Digital pictures are returned from hundreds of millions of miles in deep space with amazing clarity; some of the satellite transmissions are by PCM.

Ground, Sky, and Direct Waves

Transmitters send out "ground waves," "sky waves," and "direct waves." All three are present in all transmissions but there are major differences in the efficiency of each in various portions of the spectrum.

The *ground wave* travels along the contours of the earth—over and around mountains and other terrain features. It is most efficient in the medium-wave portion of the spectrum.

The *sky wave* goes upward from the transmitter and will either go out into space or strike against a portion of the ionosphere called the Kennelly-Heaviside layer and bounce back to earth at a distant point that may be several hundreds or thousands of miles away. The sky wave is most efficient in the short-wave portion of the spectrum all the time and in the medium waves at night.

The *direct wave* travels by line of sight from the transmitting antenna to the receiving antenna. Its distance is limited by antenna heights, by the curvature of the earth, and by mountains or other terrain features. It is most efficient in the higher portions of the spectrum starting with the VHF, where FM radio and television broadcasting are located.

2.2 USE OF ENERGY PATTERNS IN BROADCASTING
"Transportation" of Programs from Studio to Receiver

Before sound can be heard on the radio or television receiver or a television picture seen on the home screen there must be modulation of various kinds of energy. Patterns existing in sound waves and light waves are imposed on electrical and radio waves. An analogous situation would be an archaeologist in the field who finds a ceramic artifact of unusual shape that she cannot remove from the country but which she wants her colleagues at home to study in exact similarity. She could make a plaster cast and send it on its way by messenger. The messenger arrives at a border between countries and is told he can take the plaster no further, so he makes a wax impression that is identical with the shape of the original artifact. At a further point he knows the wax will melt, so a plaster impression is made from it. The second plaster cast reaches the home museum where a ceramic copy is made. The transportation of the pattern has involved the original ceramic, then plaster, wax, and plaster with a final reconversion to ceramic. If care has been taken along the way, the ceramic copy will be a faithful replica of the original.

The "transportation" of sound waves from the studio to the home also involves imposing patterns on different media. The pattern in the sound waves in the studio is imposed on electrical energy, then on radio energy, back to electrical energy, and, finally, the pattern emerges in sound waves nearly identical to those in the studio.

As a singer performs in the studio her song consists of sound waves that strike against a microphone which serves as a miniature generator. The vibrations of the sound wave cause fluctuation (modulation) of the resulting electrical energy. The fluctuation in electrical energy then causes modulation in the carrier wave from the transmitter. As the modulated carrier wave strikes the antenna of a receiver, it imposes its pattern upon electrical energy in the receiver which will then cause a speaker to emit sound waves similar to those in the studio. (See Fig. 2.4.)

Similarly, as the singer performs in the studio, light waves are reflected from her face, hair, costume, and the background. The function of a television camera is to create fluctuations in (modulation of) electrical energy that correspond to the pattern of light waves reflected in the studio. (See Fig. 2.5.)

When the light waves enter the television camera they fall upon thousands of light-sensitive elements, each of which reacts to the amount of light it "perceives." As each element is the target of a stream of electrons from an electron gun, a greater or lesser quantity of electrons will be

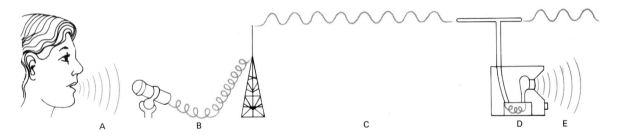

Fig. 2.4
A. Sound waves travel from the singer to the microphone.
B. Varying electrical current comes from the microphone and goes to the transmitter.
C. The fluctuations of the electrical current are imposed on the transmitted radio carrier wave.
D. The modulated carrier wave causes fluctuations in electrical current in the receiver.
E. The fluctuations in electrical energy cause sound waves to come from the speaker.

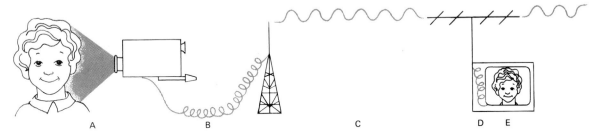

Fig. 2.5
A. Light waves reflected in the studio enter the television camera.
B. Fluctuating electrical energy emerging from the camera and sent to the transmitter.
C. Radio energy on which the fluctuations have been imposed leave the transmitter and enter the receiver through the antenna.
D. Electrical energy in the receiver fluctuates in the same pattern as the electricity coming from the camera.
E. Light waves coming from the picture tube have the same pattern as those that entered the camera in the studio.

reflected depending on the amount of light hitting the element. The quantity of the reflected electrons from an element will in turn determine the flow of electrical energy from the camera.

An electron gun is a scanning device that focuses on each element in a row before going to the elements in the next row. There are 525 lines or rows of elements in one television picture and the electron gun scans each of the rows thirty times each second. The result is a flow of electrical energy from the camera that is fluctuating precisely as the flow of electrons fluctuated when they were reflected from the scanned individual elements.

In color television the elements in the camera are composed of three cells each. Each of the three is sensitive to light waves in one of the three primary colors—red, green, and blue. As electron guns scan the elements, one is focused on the red cells, the second on the green cells, and the third on the blue cells. Again, the critical result is that from each of the cells there is a reflection of differing amounts of electrons that will, in turn, cause fluctuations in the flow of electrical energy from the camera.

The fluctuating (modulated) electrical energy from the camera is amplified and sent to a transmitter where the carrier wave is modulated by imposing on it the patterns in the fluctuating electricity. As the modulated radio waves strike the antenna and are led to the receiver in the home, they impose on the set's electrical energy the patterns of the electrical energy that came from the camera. As the fluctuating electrical energy reaches a "kinescope," or picture tube, electrons sweep back and forth across the face causing phosphorescent material to glow and reproduce the light waves reflected from the singer in the studio.

It should be noted there was never a picture taken in the studio in the conventional sense of the word. There was only the transportation of patterns (fluctuations) through various media.

From a semitechnical point of view, radio and television can be defined as transporting modulation patterns through several energy media.

Recording of Programs

Until the late 1940s radio programs could be recorded only on "electrical transcriptions" (ET's). This involved sending the fluctuating electrical energy from a microphone to a stylus that would cut a groove in a sixteen-inch disk. When a playback needle was placed in the groove, the irregularities made by the recording stylus caused the needle to vibrate and recreate the fluctuations in the electrical current.

During World War II wire recorders were developed that could make an indestructible record of voices in combat flight and other situations that might be subject to disaster. As fine wire went from one reel to another through a recording head, a magnetic impression was imposed. When the wire with the magnetic impression was subsequently passed through a playing head (or a recording head with a playback capacity) the machine would reproduce the fluctuating electrical current caused by sound waves striking a microphone. By 1950 recording devices had progressed from wire through paper to the current plastic tape familiar in portable recorders.

Video Kinescope Recording

Until 1956 TV recordings could be made only by the "kinescope" method. The fluctuating electrical energy from the camera went directly to a kinescope (picture) tube where light waves were created corresponding to those in the studio. Directly in front of the picture tube was a 16mm camera that simply made a movie of the picture on the screen. (It was necessary to take into account the fact that the television picture consisted of thirty frames per second while the motion-picture film had twenty-four frames per second.)

After the 16mm film was developed, it could be run through a projector focused on a television camera that would emit fluctuating electrical current similar to that which originally came from the studio camera. (See Fig. 2.6.)

Unfortunately, there are many inherent limitations in the quality of kinescope recordings as the modulation pattern is transported among so

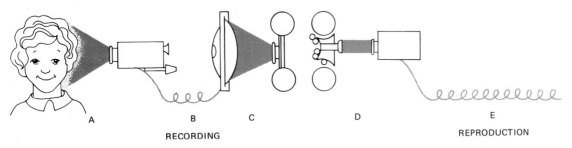

A   B   C   D   E
RECORDING   REPRODUCTION

Fig. 2.6
A. Light waves in studio enter television camera.
B. Fluctuating electrical energy is carried from camera to kinescope tube.
C. Light waves from kinescope tube enter motion-picture camera.
D. Light waves from motion-picture projector enter television-film camera.
E. Fluctuating electrical energy from television-film camera is carried to transmitter or other destination.

many media. Viewers at home immediately knew they were seeing a kinescope recording because the picture quality was so much poorer than that
of the live program and the sound was frequently distorted to the point of
being annoying.

Videotape Recording

In 1956 the Ampex Company demonstrated a videotape recorder (VTR) at
the annual convention of the National Association of Broadcasters. The
networks and largest stations immediately placed their orders and in a few
short years the VTR had replaced the kinescope recorder and had revolu-
tionized station and network operations. (See Fig. 2.7.)

Not only can the VTR provide a playback instantaneously (as contrasted
with kinescope film which has to be developed), it can also reproduce
perfectly the electrical modulation from the camera. It is impossible for
the average viewer to tell if a program is live or on videotape. In some
communities the evening news on any of the networks is usually a videotape
recording of the newscast that was sent across the country earlier. Most
"specials" and some series are also prerecorded on videotape.

Most viewers are also familiar with the "instant replays" of sporting
events. Instead of working with tape, the magnetic impression is laid on
a disk; the electrical modulation can be recreated by moving the "stylus"
back to the starting point.

VTRs that can tape programs of broadcast quality are quite expensive—
about $75,000 to $100,000 each.

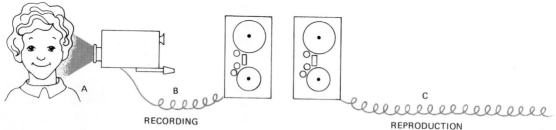

RECORDING   REPRODUCTION

Fig. 2.7

A. Light waves from the studio enter the television camera.
B. Fluctuating electrical current goes to VTR where magnetic impression is made
   on the tape.
C. During the playback the magnetic impression on the tape recreates the fluctuations in electrical energy that came from the camera.

Less expensive are three-quarter-inch machines which are used in electronic news gathering (ENG). For about $20,000 a network or station can buy equipment to record events outside the studio that can then be integrated into news programs.

2.3 TYPES OF BROADCASTING

AM Radio

The radio stations found on the dial between 540 kHz and 1600 kHz (some receivers drop the final zero and show only 54 to 160) are known by three names. *AM* (amplitude modulation—referring to the method used to impose the program on the carrier wave), *Medium wave* (referring to the portion of the spectrum where it is found), and *Standard* (referring to the fact that it was for many years the only radio broadcasting known).

AM stations are assigned to 10-kHz channels. The carrier wave is 5 kHz in width, leaving 2.5 kHz on either side unused to minimize interference between stations. The human ear can normally detect sounds up to a pitch of about 20,000 cycles per second. Since AM radio can carry only 5,000 cycles per second, it is lacking in fidelity or faithfulness in bringing all the sound from the studio. It might be called "low fidelity" in contrast to the "high fidelity" of FM that can accommodate all the pitches the ear can discern.

In 1980 the FCC approved a system of stereophonic AM for broadcasting. It will be comparable to FM stereo, described shortly, in that one will hear two versions of a program picked up by microphones at different points, giving the listener the impression of being present in an auditorium. However, the quality will still be low fidelity and its greatest use is anticipated in automobiles. It is assumed that those who want the best listening in their homes will continue to rely most heavily on FM.

Most AM reception is accomplished by picking up the ground waves transmitted by the stations. During the hours of sunlight the sky waves go into space because the Kennelly-Heaviside layer reflective power is weakened by the sun's rays. After nightfall the layer, in the absence of the sun, will cause the AM sky waves to bounce back, sometimes so efficiently that a receiver several hundred miles away can pick up the signal as well as one within ten or fifteen miles of the transmitter. It was reception of the AM sky wave that was so exciting in the 1920s as people "dial-twisted" at night to see how many signals they might pull in from distant points.

It has been possible to authorize approximately 4,600 AM stations on 107 medium-wave channels in the United States by creating a very intricate pattern of channels accommodating transmitters varying in three respects: power, directionalized antennae, and hours of operation.

The channels are divided into three major categories: clear, regional, and local. The early clear-channel stations had power of 50,000 watts and were intended to serve large rural areas. The regional stations were authorized to use power of 1,000 to 5,000 watts in serving metropolitan areas. The local stations were the least powerful—250 watts—and were licensed to smaller communities.

As pressure for additional stations mounted in the 1940s and 1950s, more transmitters were placed on each channel. The clear channel today normally has one 50,000-watt station plus from two to a couple dozen more medium- and low-power outlets located in distant areas where they will not interfere with the dominant station. The regional channel accommodates thirty to fifty stations with power allocations from 1,000 to 5,000 watts, while the local channel may have well over a hundred of the 250-watt stations. Thus, the designation of channels today is important primarily as an indication of the maximum power permitted on each.

If a broadcast station (AM, FM, or TV) uses a simple antenna arrangement with a single tower, its signal will radiate in a circle with equal strength in all directions. To minimize interference among AM stations, most are required to directionalize their antennae so signal power is concentrated in some directions and diminished in others.

To further lessen night-time interference some AM stations are authorized to operate only during the hours of sunlight when the sky waves will not bounce back from the Kennelly-Heaviside layer of the ionosphere. Others are required to use less power at night or to directionalize their antennae differently.

It is generally true throughout the radio spectrum that the lower frequencies are more efficient than the higher ones. This is especially important in the medium waves, and the stations at the lower end of the dial cover substantially more area than they would with the same power on a higher frequency. At one time the 50,000-watt station on the lower frequencies commanded far more audience than did the regional and local stations that might have higher assignments. The difference in coverage is now less significant as the number of stations has become so great that most listeners tune in to local broadcasts which are available almost everywhere.

Short-Wave Radio

About 3,000 kHz have been set aside in nine bands of the short-wave portion of the spectrum (between 3 mHz and 30 mHz) for long-distance broadcasting. Neither the ground wave nor the direct wave is very efficient for short-wave stations, but the sky wave is particularly strong during both day and night hours. There is no standard channel width that all countries are required to use, but the accepted figure for most nations is 5 kHz. Throughout most of the world short-wave stations are used for international transmissions. Through selecting the proper short-wave bands and directionalizing the antennae, it is possible to aim programs at given distant areas.

Aside from a few stations with religious affiliations, all short-wave transmitters in this country are operated by the Voice of America (VOA) to relay programs to other United States short-wave transmitters overseas. Many countries beam programs to the United States, but because Americans have never been accustomed to tuning in foreign stations their impact is negligible.

FM Radio and Multiplexing

FM was developed in the 1930s by Major Edwin Armstrong, who pioneered its growth to the point where it was authorized for broadcast purposes in 1940.

FM held great promise of technical superiority over AM since the United States was committed to the 10-kHz AM channels with no prospects of change. It was assumed from the beginning that FM would be placed in a portion of the spectrum that was then comparatively uncrowded and that much wider channels would be provided. The greater channel width would make possible high-fidelity broadcasting of all the pitches the ear could perceive. Since FM reception is primarily from the direct waves (the sky waves go out into space and the ground waves are comparatively inefficient) there would be much less danger of interference among stations. The signal of each would go only to the line-of-sight horizon. If a listener were between two distant stations, the stronger signal would override the weaker and there would not be the "jamming" that occurs in a similar situation with AM stations.

When the FCC authorized FM broadcasting in 1940, space was allocated in the VHF between 42 and 50 mHz. There were forty channels, each 200 kHz in width. In 1945 the FM band was moved on the spectrum to provide one hundred channels between 88 mHz and 108 mHz that, it will be noted, are between television Channels 6 and 7.

A significant difference between our AM and FM systems is that in the latter there are no great discrepancies among facilities. There are no important differences among the FM frequencies and practically all commercial FM stations are permitted sufficient power to reach the horizon. Some educational FM stations operate with only ten watts of power but are still able to enjoy significant coverage of their areas.

As the frequency of the FM carrier wave varies, it has the capacity to carry far more than the approximately 20,000 cycles per second of sound that are audible to the human ear. It is possible to add a second program on the carrier by transposing it from audible sound to the inaudible range. In the receiver the second program is transposed back to audible sound and fed to a separate speaker or speakers from those reproducing the sound of the first program. This is called "multiplexing."

A multiplexed service familiar to many is stereophonic broadcasting, which is the simultaneous transmission and reception of two aspects of a single program. If it is a live orchestra pickup, one program would consist of the music as captured by microphones on one side of the hall while the second program would carry the music as heard on the other side. When the multiplexed stereophonic programs are received, one is fed to one set of speakers while the second is heard through another set usually located in another part of the room. The sound thus reaches the ears of the listener much as it would if he or she were in the hall listening to the live orchestra. The broadcasting of a stereo record also separates the recording into two parts that are then sent by the receiver to different speakers.

Quadraphonic FM is multiplexing so that four signals are being transmitted on a channel. Each is a different version of the program—for example, music picked up by microphones in four different locations. When the four programs are received in the home, each is sent to a different speaker and the effect of the sound from four locations gives an even greater sense of reality than does stereo broadcasting.

Other multiplexed programs cannot be picked up by receivers purchased in the stores, thus providing a "private" service available only to those who have the proper sets. There is functional music for doctors' and dentists' offices. There is "storecasting," which consists of background music and commercials intended for shoppers, in the supermarkets. For a while there was "transitcasting"—a special program service for people riding in public transportation. In Philadelphia there is a multiplexed service available only to blind persons who have been provided with receivers by the Radio Information Center for the Blind.

Television

When television broadcasting was authorized in 1941, the FCC set aside eighteen VHF channels, each of which had a width of 6,000 kHz, or 6 mHz. Thus one television channel had space equivalent to 600 AM channels or thirty FM channels. The great width is required to transmit both the picture (AM) and the sound (FM) of the television program.

During the Second World War five of the original eighteen channels (14 through 18) were taken by the government for military purposes. Later, in 1948, the FCC decided it was necessary to use Channel 1 for purposes other than television. There are twelve remaining VHF television channels.

Channels 2, 3, and 4	54 mHz to 72 mHz
Channels 5 and 6	76 mHz to 88 mHz
Channels 7 through 13	174 mHz to 216 mHz

When channels were being assigned to specific communities the FCC had to make allowance for co-channel and adjacent-channel separation. There must be a minimum distance between two stations on the same channel and a lesser separation between stations on adjacent channels. It should be noted that two channels may have consecutive numbers without being adjacent. There is a 4-mHz space between Channels 4 and 5, and an 86-mHz gap between Channels 6 and 7. As a consequence, a community can be assigned Channels 4 and 5 or 6 and 7 simultaneously.

In 1952 the FCC added seventy more 6-mHz television channels, numbered 14 through 83, between 470 mHz and 890 mHz in the UHF. As there was a failure to make full use of the UHF channels, the FCC is withdrawing Channels 71 through 83 from general broadcast use on a selective basis.

There is the same variation in the efficiency of television channels that one finds in AM radio. The lower-numbered channels are more effective than the higher ones. However, the FCC authorizes more power for those in the higher channels so that all are theoretically able to send strong signals to the horizon.

Comparison of Broadcast Services:

	TYPE OF MODULATION	SPECTRUM LOCATION	CHANNEL WIDTH	EFFECTIVE WAVES
AM	AM	MF	10 kHZ	GROUND (SKY, AT NIGHT)
SHORT WAVE	AM	HF	5 kHZ	SKY
FM	FM	VHF	200 kHZ	DIRECT
TV	AM - VIDEO FM - AUDIO	VHF UHF	6 mHZ	DIRECT

Since the direct waves of television transmission (like FM) are the most effective, reception is best when there is a line of sight between the receiver and the transmitter. For this reason the television transmitting antennae are placed in the highest possible spots, and it is not unusual to find all the stations in a community sending out their signals from the same location. In New York City, for example, all VHF television transmitters were once in the Empire State Building but have been moved to the World Trade Center which is higher.

"Creating" the Television Program

The program seen on the home screen is usually a succession of segments taken from different sources: from cameras in the studio, from cameras on a "remote" (out-of-studio) location, from "film" cameras, and from videotape recorders.

The camera used in the studio can also serve on remote locations. The TV camera used for slides and motion pictures is smaller and less expensive than the others because its source of light waves can be so closely controlled and is so intense. It is called the film-chain camera. Focused into the film-chain cameras are motion-picture and slide projectors that are only a few inches away. The function of the film camera (as with the others) is to emit electrical energy fluctuating with reference to light waves from the film or slides.

In the average program there may be three studio cameras that are placed in different positions (see Fig. 2.8) and that can adjust their lenses to different focal lengths, thus making possible "closeup" shots in which a person's face may fill the whole screen or "long" shots in which a person may be a part of a larger picture. As each camera picks up the scene from different angles and with different focal lengths, the director in the control room chooses the one that will make up the program at a given moment. He or she can add variety to what the viewer sees, and direct the viewer's attention to the more important parts of the action.

The setup for network coverage of a football game would be far more complicated, but would be designed for the same flexibility. If six cameras were to be used, they might be located as follows: one high up above the stands at the fifty-yard line, one in each end zone, two half-way up in the stands at the thirty-yard lines, and one a few feet above field level that could move with the plays.

In either a simple studio program or a complicated remote from a football game, the director is positioned in a control room where he or she can see a monitor for each picture source and select the one that will make up the program at the moment. (See Fig. 2.9.)

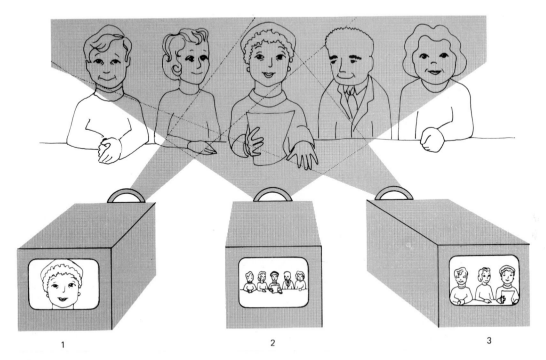

Fig. 2.8
A typical studio setup for televising a panel discussion. Camera 1 has a "closeup" of the moderator's face only. Camera 2 has a "long" shot that includes the whole panel. Camera 3 is covering the moderator and the two participants on her right. The setup is designed to give the director maximum flexibility in telling the camera operators how to move and change their focal lengths to cover all the possible shots they might want to use.

As the director decides which particular scene should be sent over the air, a member of the production staff pushes a button so the desired picture is sent to the transmitter or VTR. The selected image shows up on the "line" monitor also. Thus, the line monitor shows the succession of pictures going to the home receivers.

There is almost no end to the technical capacity of a television program to use material from different sources. A network might do a program that would involve instantaneously switching between pictures taken by cameras in a studio in Chicago, at a football game in Los Angeles, at a political convention in St. Louis, at a gathering in St. Peter's Square in Rome, and in a spacecraft circling the earth.

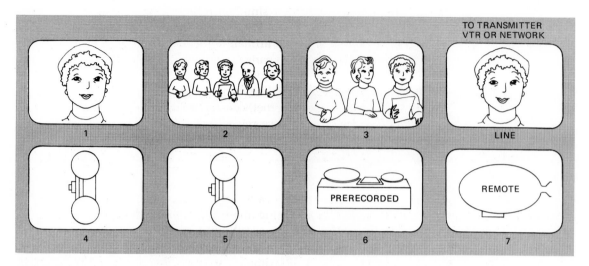

Fig. 2.9
A typical set of monitors in front of the director in the control room. Monitors 1, 2, and 3 show what is being televised by the studio cameras bearing the same numbers. Monitors 4 and 5 are for two film cameras with motion-picture film and slides. Monitor 6 is for prerecorded material on the VTR. Monitor 7 is for a remote camera in another location. The "line" monitor shows which picture from one of the other seven has been selected to constitute the program at any moment.

2.4 DISTRIBUTION OF TELEVISION PROGRAMS

To this point the discussion has assumed that a program is either sent directly from the control room to the transmitter or that it is tape recorded for later broadcast. However, most television programs (aside from local news) are carried by more than one station so they must be distributed from the point of origin to distant station transmitters from which they are delivered to home receivers. If a program is on film or on videotape, it may be circulated to stations on a "bicycle-network" basis. The film or tape is sent to a station that airs it and then mails the copy to another station for use at a later time. This is appropriate only for the comparatively "timeless" program that loses none of its value if it is seen several months apart at different stations.

Since the bicycle network is extremely cumbersome, involving much duplication of film or tape, bookkeeping, and remailing, most national network programs are carried simultaneously by stations in at least two time zones and later by stations in the rest of the country. When a network wishes to feed a program to its affiliates, it will contract with the American Telephone and Telegraph Company for the distribution. AT&T will use its own facilities and handle all the details so the network has no concern once the program has been fed to a line going to the telephone company center. Technically, AT&T uses two methods for sending programs around the country: co-axial and microwave relay.

Co-axial Cable

The program is imposed on a radio carrier wave that is then sent out by cable instead of to a transmitting antenna that would broadcast it through the air. The co-axial cable is a combination of wires within a shield that makes possible transmission of more signals for much greater distances than would be possible with ordinary wire connections. The cable is buried ("installed") underground with amplifiers (two or more per mile) to strengthen the signal. Simple co-axial cable may be built comparatively inexpensively to carry signals a few feet—for example, it is used in some apartments to connect TV receivers to a master antenna. AT&T cable, which may be two or more inches in diameter, has a capacity for carrying several television programs, plus radio programs, plus telephone conversations, plus computer data.

Microwave Relays

In mountains and other terrain where it is difficult to install co-axial cable, AT&T uses microwave relays, which have a capacity comparable to co-axial cables. The relays use radio waves in the UHF and SHF portions of the spectrum and focus the signals as one concentrates the narrow ray from a flashlight on a target. One relay will consist of a transmitter located on a mountain or tall building or tower focused on a receiver on another high point as far distant as possible within the line of sight. When there is a series of relays, each location on a high spot will be occupied by a receiver that picks up the incoming signal and a transmitter that sends it on to the next receiver. Under normal circumstances a relay will cover about thirty miles. A program from New York City to the West Coast once went part of the way by co-axial cable and part of the way by microwave relay. The methods are interchangeable. Now microwave relays are used exclusively for long distances and co-axial cable is used within cities.

Fiber Optics

The most important innovation since the transistor and solid-state technology has been the use of fiber optics to distribute television programming. The fluctuating electrical energy from the television camera is sent to a light-emitting diode that imposes the modulation pattern on light beams that are then sent through an optic strand less than a hundredth of an inch in diameter. The strand is a glass core surrounded by a material called "cladding" that prevents the light beams from leaving the core. Around the cladding is a polyester jacket for protection. At the other end of the core a photo diode transforms the modulation of light energy back into modulation of electrical energy.

The importance of fiber optics lies in its low cost, the flexibility of the cable, the decreased need for amplifiers or repeaters, and the increased resistance to electromagnetic interference. While co-axial cable is made of copper and other shielding materials that may some day be in short supply, the fibers are made of glass, whose primary component is sand, one of the most abundant materials on earth. While co-axial cable may be up to several inches in diameter and comparatively inflexible, the fibers can be laid in almost any pattern to accommodate the conduit in which it travels. The light rays are not affected by electrical interference from machinery or static and require only about half as many repeater units in a given distance as does co-axial cable. As the new technology progresses, it is anticipated that six optic strands in a quarter-inch plastic tube will, by use of a laser, be able to carry up to a thousand television programs simultaneously.

In the summer of 1976 Teleprompter started using fiber optics to carry its pay cable programs from a receiving point on the roof of a building in Manhattan some 800 feet to headend equipment on the lower floors. From its first use Teleprompter reported "the picture is coming in razor sharp." ABC used many miles of optical fiber to cover the 1980 Winter Olympic Games in Lake Placid, New York. The only problem was keeping the fibers warm until installed, since they became brittle in extreme cold.

Satellite Relays

Until the early 1960s there was no way of sending live television programs between continents. It was not practical to lay co-axial cable on the ocean floors and there were not enough islands for line-of-sight microwave relays. When there was an event of special interest such as the Coronation of Queen Elizabeth in London, motion-picture film would be shot and then sped by jet plane across the Atlantic to a point where the program could be delivered to AT&T facilities.

The first satellites to carry transponders (*trans*mitter and res*ponder*) that could receive and retransmit television programs were orbiting the earth approximately every hour and a half. A satellite would be in line-of-sight position with both Europe and North America for only a few minutes at a time. A program could be relayed for about fifteen minutes and then it was necessary to wait a little more than an hour for another short transmission.

In 1962 Congress enacted the Communications Satellite Act under which COMSAT, a privately-owned corporation, was authorized to launch and operate a satellite system that would serve the world. In 1965 the first satellite was placed in "synchronous" orbit about 22,300 miles above the equator. At that altitude it circled the center of the earth at the same rate that the earth was rotating—once in twenty-four hours. This synchronicity meant that the satellite was "parked" in space and would remain above a single spot on the equator and could be used for communications between given spots all the time.

There are three primary satellite positions (all at the equator) above the Atlantic, the Indian, and the Pacific Oceans. In those positions three satellites can receive from and transmit to almost all points on the globe. (See Fig. 2.10.)

Satellites are powered by solar energy captured from the sun and transmit with comparatively little power—less than 100 watts as compared with 100,000 for a low-channel VHF broadcasting station. Consequently it is necessary that the signals be received by "Earth stations" that have very large receiving antennae focused on the satellite and especially sensitive equipment. They have had to be located at a distance from large cities and other areas where there would be electrical interference. The first two Earth stations in the continental United States were at Andover, Maine, and Etam, West Virginia. From each of those locations, programs from the Atlantic Ocean satellite are delivered to AT&T for distribution. The major Earth Stations also operate transmitting equipment beamed at the satellites. Since 1980 improved technology has made it possible to receive satellite transmissions with "dishes" only two feet in diameter. (See discussion of DBS later in this chapter.)

The most common television use of satellites has been the transmission of news coverage from overseas correspondents to the three national networks. The first COMSAT satellite in 1965 linked only those countries around the Atlantic Ocean position. In 1967 two satellites were launched—one over the Atlantic and the other over the Pacific—which made it possible for American networks to get material from two-thirds of the world. From that point on satellite segments have become more common in newscasts.

The satellite use with which Americans are most familiar is the coverage of the Olympic Games every four years. These sports events are covered

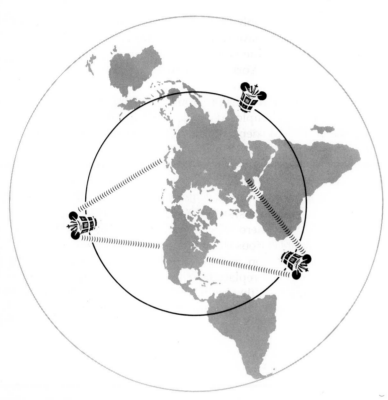

Fig. 2.10
Map of world shows three satellite positions over Atlantic, Pacific, and Indian Oceans. Signals from Tokyo and Beirut are coming to the United States via the Pacific satellite to the West Coast and via Atlantic satellite to the East Coast.
Courtesy: COMSAT

with many cameras and the programs of the events and other materials are sent by microwave relay to the nearest Earth station, which beams it to the satellite system for transmission to Earth stations in the United States and in many other countries.

In the mid-1970s satellite use was initiated for circulation of television material throughout the United States, thus reducing the need for AT&T's microwave relays. In 1976 Home Box Office started distribution of pay cable programs to systems by satellite. Receiving Earth stations were built in key locations where they could not only feed the nearest cable system but could also send it to others by microwave relay. The commercial networks began using satellites to deliver a remote event like a football game in Texas back to their home studio in New York from which the program is sent to affiliated stations by AT&T facilities. The Public Broadcasting Service is using a satellite for distribution of its programs to affiliated stations. Three channels on the satellite are employed so the stations will have three programs from which to choose, depending on the stations' time zones and the interest they have in different kinds of material.

Each satellite contains twenty-four transponders and thus has the capacity to relay twenty-four television programs simultaneously. Among the biggest users to date have been broadcasters sending programs to studios from remote locations and cable systems distributing program services.

At the end of the 1970s there were nine domestic satellites "parked" over South America to serve various United States needs. In December, 1980 the FCC authorized construction and launching of twenty new domestic satellites. While some will be replacements for current satellites as they become obsolete, it is estimated that by the middle of the 1980s the number of transponders will have more than doubled, from 156 to 340.

Simultaneous Transmission and Recovery of Alternating Pictures (STRAP)

In the summer of 1980 the American Forces Radio and Television Service (AFRTS) announced long-range plans to increase programming for military personnel in overseas camps and on naval ships by using satellite relay to send two television programs at the same time on one channel. This is to be accomplished by "Simultaneous Transmission and Recovery of Alternating Pictures" (STRAP), which involves using alternating fields or "frames" of conventional television for different programs. The frames are encoded prior to transmission and then decoded for either recording or delivery to receivers from conventional transmitters.

2.5 NONBROADCAST DELIVERY OF TELEVISION PROGRAMS

In 1950 the only anticipated use for a television receiver was to pick up conventional broadcasts intended for anyone with a set wherever it might be located in range of the transmitter. By 1980 more than a half-dozen other communications delivery channels were in wide usage with an equal number on the horizon for development in the 1980s.

Closed-Circuit Television (CCTV)

In the 1950s "closed-circuit" was used as a phrase to contrast with "open-circuit" broadcasting available to anyone in the area who had a receiver. CCTV was primarily wired television most commonly used to deliver programs to classrooms in a college or school system. As the potential of CCTV became more evident there were other educational and industrial uses. For example, CCTV could carry signals from cameras focused on dials in high-risk nuclear areas. Police departments use it to monitor high-crime areas or prison cell blocks; apartment houses to provide surveillance over entrances, elevators, and corridors; hospitals to permit students and doctors to observe operations at close range; and stores to monitor shoppers.

CCTV might also involve a nationwide "sales meeting" such as an automobile company might provide for its dealers when introducing a new model. The "program" showing the new car and talking about its sales features might be produced in a studio or in space at corporate headquarters and delivered to AT&T for distribution around the country. In each city it would be seen on monitors in various convenient places where dealers and their salespersons were gathered.

In some respects, any transmission of point-to-point television signals not intended for off-the-air reception might be considered closed circuit. The microwave relays and satellite transmissions fall into this category. Various combinations of radio and wire transmission are used—for example, in theatervision. It is possible to televise a prizefight in Africa, send the signal by microwave to a nearby Earth station and then up to a satellite. An Earth station in the United States can receive the signal and deliver it to AT&T for distribution to theaters around the country where it is viewed on large screens by those who have paid for tickets.

Instructional Television Fixed Services (ITFS)

Another variation on the closed-circuit concepts is the Instructional Television Fixed Services (ITFS) category established by the FCC for use in schools and colleges. Frequencies were set aside for distributing programs from a central point on a campus or in a school system. From rooftop receivers the signals are delivered by cable to individual classrooms in the buildings.

Subscription Television (STV)

In subscription television (STV), which is also called Pay TV, a conventional television station delivers a scrambled signal into the home. The signal is unscrambled or decoded by a device that must be rented from the station.

It is the rental fee of the unscrambling device from which the station makes its profit. STV is differentiated from "broadcasting" in that the signal is not intended for everyone with a set—only for those who have paid to rent the device.

Community Antenna Television (CATV)

The earliest cable systems were called community antenna television because an antenna was placed on top of a mountain or high hill to serve an entire community. (See Fig. 2.11) This step was required because the direct waves of a television signal would not follow the horizon to the homes behind the mountain.

COMMUNITY ANTENNA TELEVISON

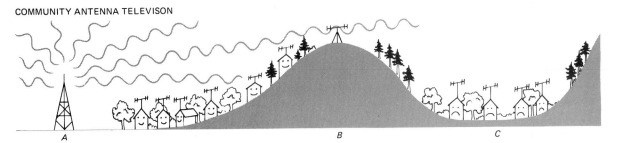

A   B   C

Fig. 2.11

Community Antenna Television. At Point *A* is a television station whose signals go in straight lines as indicated. All homes between the station and Point *B* on the mountain can get a good signal. However, people in the community at Point *C* can get no reception because the signals going beyond the mountain are several hundred feet above their homes. By receiving the signals on top of the mountain at Point *B*, amplifying them, and sending them through the community by cable, the CATV operator can provide homes with good reception.

Cable Television

CATV became "cable television" at the point where an operator started delivery of signals in addition to those that could be received locally directly off the air. The operator would place a receiver near a distant city to pick up regular broadcast signals and then send them to the primary antenna by microwave relay (see Fig. 2.12). This service was called "importation" and was the original distinguishing factor between CATV and cable. As

CABLE IMPORTATION

Fig. 2.12

Cable Importation. In the television market at point *A* there is only one station that is being received and fed by CATV to the community at Point *C*. In a major city at Point *E* many miles beyond the community there are three stations whose signals go past the mountain-top at point *D*. An antenna is placed on that mountain to receive the signals that are then amplified and sent by microwave relays to the headend of the system at Point *B*. They are then distributed along with the CATV signals from the station at Point *A*. The subscriber can now tune in to four stations without being in any of their coverage areas.

noted in Chapter 12, the services of cable have grown tremendously in recent years.

"Superstations"

In the mid-1970s importation reached a new level of sophistication when the signals of a conventional television station in Atlanta, Georgia were sent up to a satellite and relayed back over the whole country. By installing an earth receiving station, a cable operator could pick up the Atlanta station that might be thousands of miles away and deliver the signal to subscribing homes. The half-dozen stations thus available to cable in the early 1980s are called "superstations" although their program offerings differed little from those of other nonnetwork schedules.

Pay Cable

For cable homes that want more than CATV and importation, many operators provide a pay cable service. This consists of recently released movies and other nonbroadcast programs without commercials for which the subscriber pays an additional fee. The method of payment is rental of a device similar to that used in subscription television. Since the mid-1970s Home

Box Office (HBO), the first major pay cable service, has been distributing its signals to cable systems by satellite.

Multipoint Distribution Service (MDS)

In 1970 the FCC authorized an extension of the ITFS concept for use by private companies wishing to communicate with several offices or plants in an area. The new category was called Multipoint Distribution Service (MDS). In 1975 its potential was utilized for quite different purposes by HBO. In areas where there were demands for pay cable service in homes that had not been wired for cable, HBO set up MDS transmitters and then offered to install a special receiver on the roof of any apartment house in which enough tenants would sign up to make it profitable. The signals were then delivered from the rooftop antenna to the individual apartments by wire. For a substantial installation fee the same service was made available to individual homes.

Interactive Cable

When the FCC passed extensive cable regulations in 1972 it required that new systems in major markets must have an "upstream capacity"—the ability to send a nonvoice (computer) signal from a home to the cable system's studio. This is called "Interactive Cable." In Columbus, Ohio, since December 1977 Warner Communications has been operating "Qube," a two-way service in which cable subscribers can send back signals indicating their preferences in programs or their votes on issues, or they can participate in video games. Eventually, the two-way capacity may lead to cable homes where subscribers have computers with which to transact their banking, marketing, and other business.

Satellite-to-Home Transmission (DBS)

It was assumed from the beginning that the day would come when "direct broadcast satellite" (DBS) signals might be picked up in homes without any intervening delivery system. By the mid-1970s some individuals with the technical knowhow and $10,000 were building their own Earth stations and bringing in a wide variety of sporting events and the "Johnny Carson" feed from the West Coast to NBC studios in New York City where such programs were to be edited for broadcast.

In 1979 Satellite Television Corporation (STC), a subsidiary of COMSAT, filed a formal petition with the FCC seeking permission to start planning for a DBS system that in 1985 would deliver three pay channels to homes around the country. The transponders would have much more power than those currently in use, so that reception would require antenna dishes only some thirty inches in diameter.

Home Videotape Recorders (VTRs)

By the mid-1970s videotape recording technology reached the point where equipment was produced for home use. Since then the recorders have improved greatly and prices have come down. Home VTRs are used to record programs off the air, to play cassettes of movies and other programs sold in the stores, and to record and play back original material comparable to home movies.

Video Discs

The technology of the 1970s also made possible the recording of television material on discs similar in appearance to audio records. Now, at the beginning of the 1980s it is anticipated that discs and disc players will be on the market shortly. The biggest question is which of two systems will eventually be the more successful and dominate the market. One uses a stylus in a grooved record similar to audio recording while the other uses a laser beam that is modulated as it is reflected from a rotating disc. A major difference between video discs and home VTRs is that disc owners cannot make their own programs but are limited to what can be bought.

Teletext and Viewdata

At the end of the 1970s American stations were looking into a system for using television sets as receivers for printed material. Two methods have been pioneered and are being used commercially in Europe: Teletext is a method of using digital technology to transmit a printed page over the air to be received by an adapter to the television set simultaneously with regular programming. Viewdata does the same thing but the information is delivered into the home by means of a telephone circuit.

Three-Dimensional Television

A novelty in the early 1980s is three-dimensional television, which has been primarily developed in other countries. Again, it is computer technology that enables the camera in the studio to produce a signal that gives the illusion of depth when viewed with special glasses. A distinguishing feature from early three-dimensional movies is that if one watches without glasses there is still a clear two-dimensional picture.

Closed Captioning (CC)

As a service to the deaf and hard-of-hearing the networks in 1980 are presenting some of their programs with "closed captioning" (CC). By using elements of the television channel that are not normally utilized in broadcasting, written subtitles can be received on the screens of those who have special adapters.

SUMMARY

Advances in technology have been a source of wonder to every generation since the first broadcasts of 1920. By 1940 radio had become worldwide and part of everyday life; television was new. By 1960 there was nationwide television in color and videotaped programs that were faithful to the originals. By 1970 people took satellites for granted and their use to distribute pictures and sounds of men on the moon. Still, people were unprepared for the explosion of the late 1970s with the sophistication of cable allowing satellite-fed pay services, superstations, and interactive aspects. The 1980s will see rapid progress into the age of home video recorders, video discs, home computers, and other advances associated with cable.

Through all these developments radio and television programs and other information reach homes via waves from very limited and crowded portions of the radio spectrum and from cable. Between sounds and pictures in the studio and their reproduction in the home flow patterns of modulation in different energy media. It is broadcasting's expanding ability to create and transmit these modulations of energy that has made possible its present capacity and future promise.

GLOSSARY ITEMS

The following words and phrases used in Chapter 2 are defined in the Glossary:

Adjacent Channels	**Cable Television**
Amplitude Modulation (AM)	**Carrier Wave**
Bicycle Network	**Channel Separation Factor**
Broadcast Channel	**Closed Captioning (CC)**
Broadcasting	**Closed-Circuit Television (CCTV)**

Co-axial Cable

Community Antenna Television (CATV)

Digital Television

Direct Broadcast Satellite (DBS)

Direct Wave

Directionalized Antenna

Earth Station

Electromagnetic Spectrum

Electron Gun

Electronic News Gathering (ENG)

Fiber Optics

FM Multiplexing

Frequency Modulation (FM)

Ground Wave

Hertz

High Fidelity

Importation

Instructional Television Fixed Services (ITFS)

Interactive Cable

Jamming

Kennelly-Heaviside Layer

Kinescope

Magnetic Impression

MegaHertz (mHz)

Microwave Relay

Modulation

Monitor

Multipoint Distribution Service (MDS)

Pay Cable

Pulse Code Modulation (PCM)

Quadraphonic Broadcasting

Radio Spectrum

Radio Wave Frequency

Radio Wave Length

Satellite Relay

Satellite Subscription Television (SSTV)

Sky Wave

Stereophonic Broadcasting

Subscription Television (STV)

Superstation

Teletext

Transponder

Upstream Capacity

Video Disc

Videotape Recording

Viewdata

PREVIEW

By 1945 radio had achieved a dominant role in American society it would never again enjoy. Its history to that date falls into four fairly discrete periods. In the years until 1920 radio was discovered and the foundations were laid for radio broadcasting. In the early 1920s radio quickly passed through its infancy and established its claim on the attention of Americans. In the ten years ending in 1937 radio emerged in a form very similar to that of television in the 1970s with dominance of the networks and advertising and a reputation for giving people what they wanted. Throughout World War II radio was the primary source of the latest news. As the war came to an end the trials and tribulations of FM began.

CHAPTER 3

HISTORICAL PERSPECTIVES I
1890–1945 with Emphasis on Radio

In the closing years of the 1880s Heinrich Rudolph Hertz demonstrated that energy could be sent between two points without the use of connecting wires. The transmission was by "Hertzian waves," which are now known as radio or electromagnetic energy. The trail from the Hertz laboratory in Germany to modern broadcasting is long and replete with details. For our purposes, however, the main steps can be rapidly traced.

AN OUTLINE HISTORY OF BROADCASTING

I. Radio

1890–1920	Prebroadcasting radio
1920–1927	Radio's infancy
1927–1937	Radio's adolescence
1937–1945	Radio's maturity
1945–1960	Changing patterns of radio
1960–1970	Steady growth of FM
1970–1980	Dominance of format programming

II. Television

3.1 1890–1920 PREBROADCASTING RADIO

Marconi and the Beginnings

Of all those who were intrigued by Hertz's experiments, none was more enthusiastic or more successful in advancing the knowledge of radio than the Italian youth, Guglielmo Marconi. He saw radio as a potential means

GUGLIELMO MARCONI 1874–1937

Guglielmo Marconi (right) and David Sarnoff at RCA transmitting center in 1933
Courtesy: NBC

"Few great inventors have lived to see such great results from their first modest efforts and fewer yet have been honored in life and death as Marconi was honored."*

Born in 1874, Marconi was a thoughtful and shy lad who grew up on his father's estate in Italy. He was very close to his Irish-born mother who was sympathetic to his scientific interests, but he felt rather distant from his father who could be dictatorial and who discouraged all his efforts until after his experiments had succeeded. When Marconi was twenty he read about Hertz and developed an interest in wireless that lasted the rest of his life. In the third-floor space of his home he first sent radio energy across the room and then gradually increased the distance until his signals were being received some two miles away. Two years later as a resident of England he was the cofounder of the Marconi Wireless and Signal Company which was to dominate worldwide radio communication for several decades.

His daughter has suggested it was un-

* *Broadcasting*, August 1, 1937, p. 14.

fortunate that by his twenty-third birthday in 1897 he had completed his basic experimentation, had been accepted by the world as a great inventor, and was being inundated with honors that would continue to flow until after his death. At a time when most men were just getting started, he had achieved a pinnacle of success and found it increasingly difficult to lead a normal happy life.

In 1905 he married the daughter of an Irish peer. His home was in England but he was constantly traveling around the world overseeing his companies and interests. After the births of his children his wife was unable to continue traveling with him and they gradually lost rapport with each other. In 1924 they were divorced, and three years later he married a much younger woman from Italy. Most of his last ten years were spent in that country where he was honored and encouraged in his work by Mussolini, who was especially interested in Marconi's pioneering efforts in radar.

Marconi's death in 1937 followed a succession of heart attacks.

One of his great strengths was his ability to recruit and supervise the work of an excellent staff. Some engineers contend that he made no significant inventions after 1902, although there is no attempt to denigrate the importance of what he did in the years before. He is distinguished as one of the few inventors in history who from the beginning thought primarily of the practical applications of his work. While experimenting in his father's home, he was thinking about the use of wireless to send messages. He had a knack of finding dramatic demonstrations of his equipment and in 1899 received great attention when he reported by radio on an international ship race between the *Columbia* and the *Shamrock* near New York City. It was a combination of inventiveness, utilitarianism, business acumen, and good public relations that made him a giant of his time.

of supplementing telegraphy, the most important long-distance communications medium of the late nineteenth century. He worked on the transmission of long and short bursts of energy which in various combinations might serve as substitutes for letters of the alphabet when sending messages.

When the Italian government showed no interest in his experiments, he and his Irish mother traveled to London where the English, because of their world-wide colonial system and maritime tradition, were greatly interested in new developments in communications. In 1897 he demonstrated his equipment, secured basic patents, and joined with wealthy and powerful Englishmen in forming the Marconi Wireless and Signal Company. Two years later they formed the subsidiary Marconi Wireless Company of America. By insisting on contracts to lease equipment rather than making outright sales the Marconi companies dominated the early development of radio throughout the world.

The Marconi Company first used radio to replace the telegraph in areas where it was impossible to lay wires: from islands to the coast, from ships at sea, and over mountainous terrain. Success and worldwide enthusiasm were almost instantaneous. Other nations signed contracts to lease from Marconi the equipment that would fill an obvious void in their communications capacity.

International Radio Conferences

In less than five years it became evident that if all countries were to enjoy the potential benefits of radio, they would have to engage in a new and unprecedented era of cooperation. Radio signals were "universal" in that, once emitted, they paid no heed to manmade boundaries but would cross lines between countries to the extent of their power. Radio signals also demanded "exclusivity" in that the use of a frequency by two persons in the same area at the same time would result in jamming or mixing the signals so no one would benefit.

The first international radio conference was held among European countries in Berlin, Germany in 1903. Its principal outcome was agreement that a problem existed and future conferences should be held for the signing of formal treaties. A subsequent Berlin conference in 1906 laid the foundation for the international cooperation that extends to this day.

The third international radio conference, held in London in 1912, was the first at which representatives of the United States were present. This country agreed with other signatories to abide by the basic principle that each nation should regulate use of radio within its jurisdiction. To implement that agreement, Congress passed the Radio Act of 1912 requiring that anyone wishing to use radio must obtain a license from the Secretary of Commerce and Labor. This constituted the first radio regulation in the United States since the only preceding legislation to mention radio had been the Wireless Ship Act of 1910, a maritime safety measure. It provided that passenger ships carrying fifty or more persons might not leave a port in this country unless it had "efficient apparatus for radio-communication in good working order."

Subsequent radio conferences through 1959 were models of international amity since only a few countries were in a position to make extensive use of the radio spectrum and there was plenty of space for them. After a twenty-year interval the major nations approached the World Administrative Radio Conference (WARC) of 1979 with some trepidation because they would be outnumbered by less-developed countries of the Third World who were in a position to demand that their future radio needs be considered. Especially troublesome was assignment of satellite positions and frequencies. The United States had already nearly saturated the positions available to the Western Hemisphere, and Latin American countries were fearful that when they were ready to use such facilities, they might not be available. The African nations had the same fear that Europeans would tie up the capacity the African countries would need in future years.

As a result, this conference adjourned not for the normal twenty-year interval but for only five years. At the end of that time there would be another conference to work out the details of satellite usage that would assure the Third World an opportunity to participate.

The Sinking of the *Titanic*

One of the most dramatic tragedies of all times occurred in 1912; it made many people aware for the first time of the new communications device called radio. The *Titanic*, safest and most modern ship ever constructed, was on its maiden voyage from Europe to New York City carrying many of the world's famous people. It was built with a system of water-tight compartments on the theory that if the hull were pierced at one point, the ship would remain afloat. As the captain was racing through the night trying to establish a new speed record, the ship struck a giant iceberg that ripped the hull from bow to stern. The water-tight compartments, built with such care to make the *Titanic* unsinkable, were nullified in a matter of seconds.

What impressed the world, aside from the magnitude of the disaster in which over a thousand lives were lost, was the subsequent knowledge that the ship had received radio signals from others in the area telling of the unusual number of icebergs. The radio operator of the *Titanic* refused to make note of the warnings and finally told the other operators to "clear the air" so he could get caught up on all the messages he was supposed to transmit from the passengers to friends in Europe and America. Had the captain received and heeded the warnings, he could have proceeded at a speed that would have enabled him to avoid the collison.

It was also later learned there were other ships almost in sight of the *Titanic* that could have arrived in ample time to save many more than the 700 who were rescued. However, their radio operators had "signed off" for the night and gone to bed. They never received the SOS signals the *Titanic* operator was sending so feverishly shortly after midnight. As it was, those who were saved owed their lives to the fact that more-distant ships heard the distress calls and steamed many miles to pick up the survivors.

This was the first time in history that people learned about a distant tragedy of this magnitude almost as it was taking place. The distress messages were picked up in London and New York by the Marconi operators who had been decoding the messages from the passengers. Receiving the signals in New York was a young man named David Sarnoff who was to play a most important role in the development of American broadcasting. As the messages came from the *Titanic*, he was one of the first to know (even before some who would go down with the ship a few hours later) that it had struck an iceberg. He followed the transmission of distress signals and the responses of other ships speeding to the rescue. Sarnoff passed the word to bystanders and to the newspapers. During that fateful April night and the following days people suddenly realized that radio existed and could dramatically serve as a lifesaving device and as an information medium to speed news to the public through the newspapers.

From David Sarnoff's 1915 Memorandum to the General Manager of the Marconi Wireless Telegraph Company of America:

I have in mind a plan of development which would make a radio a "household utility" in the same sense as the piano or phonograph. The idea is to bring music into the home by wireless.

While this has been tried in the past by wires, it has been a failure because wires do not lend themselves to this scheme. With radio, however, it would seem to be entirely feasible. For example, a radio telephone transmitter having a range of say 25 to 50 miles can be installed at a fixed point where instrumental or vocal music or both are produced. The problem of transmitting music has already been solved in principle and therefore all the receivers attuned to the transmitting wave length should be capable of receiving such music. The receivers can be designed in the form of a simple "Radio Music Box" and arranged for several different wave lengths, which should be changeable with the throwing of a single switch or pressing of a single button.

BRIGADIER GENERAL DAVID SARNOFF 1891–1971

Courtesy: NBC

David Sarnoff was a man of vision as well as accomplishment. His 1915 memorandum

foreseeing a "radio music box" is famous. Less known is his 1923 statement to the RCA Board of Directors:

I believe that television, which is the technical name for seeing as well as hearing by radio, will come to pass in due course. . . . It may be that every broadcast receiver for home use in the future will also be equipped with a television adjunct by which the instrument will make it possible for those at home to see as well as hear what is going on at the broadcast station.

Born near Minsk, Russia in 1891, he was brought to the United States at the age of nine. After the death of his father he became the main support of his family. Selling newspapers, working as a delivery boy and a messenger, he saved money to study Morse code and wireless telegraphy. Starting as an office boy with the American Marconi Company, he became an operator a year later at the age of seventeen. After serving on ships and in shore stations, he was on duty in New York City in 1912 when he received word of the *Titanic* disaster. He remained at his post for seventy-two hours, receiving and passing on messages to relatives of the passengers and relaying news of the rescue operations to the world.

As Assistant Traffic Manager of the American Marconi Company, he worked very closely with the American military forces in World War I on their communications capabilities. By 1917 he was Commercial Manager, and kept the same title with RCA when, in 1919, it bought out Marconi's American operations. He became General Manager in 1921, and it was his decision that RCA should buy WEAF and form the National Broadcasting Company in 1926. In 1930 he became the President of RCA, and in 1947 he became Chairman of the Board, a title he held until his retirement in 1969.

Throughout the 1930s he had a consuming interest in the development of television and its introduction to the American people. In 1944 the Television Broadcasters Association honored him as the "Father of American Television."

He was appointed a Lieutenant Colonel in the United States Army in 1924 and then promoted to Colonel. In World War II he became a major leader in the field of military communications. He was appointed special consultant to General Eisenhower and was promoted to Brigadier General in 1944.

In the postwar years he was not as close to broadcasting as he had been in the earlier days when he personally arranged for Dr. Walter Damrosch to conduct the "Music Appreciation Hour" and brought the Metropolitan Opera to the nationwide network he had founded. He did, however, make the overall decision that NBC should subsidize its color programming for some ten years before the other networks joined in a full-color service. Without his vision it is likely that color television and many other developments in the field would have been delayed for many years.

The Development of Radiotelephony

For the first twenty years the most practical use of radio was in wireless telegraphy—using the new medium to send messages in dot-dash code where it was impractical to have telegraph wire connections. The essential intermediate step to broadcasting was radiotelephony in which the sounds of voice (and music) could be transmitted and received. By 1910 the pioneers Lee DeForest and Reginald Fessenden had completed the first steps, and by 1920 many were focusing their attention on development of radio to the point where it would have practical uses far beyond supplementing the telegraph. The period of point-to-point radio was about to give way to a new era in which the public would become most intimately involved.

Formation of the Radio Corporation of America (RCA)

The earliest radio experimentation in America was carried on by individuals who later became associated with large companies like General Electric (GE), Westinghouse Electric, and Western Electric, a subsidiary of American

Telephone and Telegraph Company (AT&T). No American company could compete with American Marconi, which was virtually the only source of most radio equipment in this country. During World War I (1914–1918) radio became indispensable to military communications, particularly for units at sea. The United States Navy considered it unthinkable that our vital communications in the future should depend on equipment leased from a company whose home was in a foreign country.

During the War, the Navy Secretary had persuaded American companies to pool their patents for military use. In 1919 the American Marconi Company was negotiating with GE for exclusive worldwide rights to the Alexanderson alternator, which was expected to revolutionize long-distance radio communications. Under urging from the United States Government, GE Board Chairman Owen D. Young proposed the formation of a new corporation that would hold all American patents and be a service organization for American companies. GE set up a $2.5 million fund to buy out shareholders of American Marconi and shortly joined with AT&T and Westinghouse Electric in ownership of the new Radio Corporation of America (RCA). RCA continued under joint ownership until the government forced its separation from the parent companies in the 1930s. There was a division of labor whereby GE and Westinghouse would use pooled patents to manufacture receivers that RCA would sell. Western Electric was to specialize in making transmitters.

PREBROADCASTING CHRONOLOG TO 1920

1844	Morse telegraph circuit operating between Washington, D.C., and Baltimore, Md.
1864	James Clerk-Maxwell published "Dynamical Theory of the Electro-Magnetic Field."
1875	Alexander Graham Bell invented the telephone.
1877	Thomas A. Edison succeeded in audible reproduction of recorded sound.
1888	Heinrich Hertz published "Electro-Magnetic Waves and Their Reflection."
1895	Marconi's experimentation in Italy.
1897	Marconi made first official demonstration of ship-to-shore wireless in England.
	Formation of Marconi Wireless Telegraph and Signal Company in England.
1898	First commercial wireless message.

1899   Marconi sent wireless signals across the English Channel.

Formation of Marconi Wireless Company in America.

1900   Oliver Heaviside and Arthur Kennelly suggested mirror theory whereby radio waves would be reflected from a layer in ionosphere later called "Kennelly-Heaviside Layer."

1901   Marconi succeeded in first transatlantic signals.

1903   First international radio conference in Berlin.

1904   Lee DeForest received patent on "Phonofilm" to make movies with sound.

1905   Ernest F. W. Alexanderson built alternator for use in radio-telephony experimentation by Reginald Fessenden.

1906   Lee DeForest invented three-element (triode) tube called the "audion."

Second international radio conference in Berlin.

Fessenden broadcast Christmas Eve program of speech and music received by ships at sea.

1908   DeForest broadcast music from Eiffel Tower in Paris.

1910   Passage of the Wireless Ship Act of 1910.

1912   Sinking of the *Titanic*.

United States represented at international radio conference in London.

Passage of the Radio Act of 1912.

1913   Edwin H. Armstrong invented the regenerative "feedback" circuit.

1915   David Sarnoff wrote memorandum proposing a "Radio Music Box."

Marconi visited General Electric to see latest Alexanderson alternators. War delayed negotiations to secure exclusive use.

1917   Alexanderson designed 200 kilowatt high-frequency alternator that would revolutionize long-distance radio.

1918   End of World War I found technology ready for radiotelephony.

1919   Formation of Radio Corporation of America.

Note: The Alexanderson alternator, the Armstrong regenerative circuit, and the DeForest audion tube were all important in the development of radiotelephony and broadcasting.

3.2 1920–1927 RADIO'S INFANCY

Frank Conrad and Station KDKA

In 1920 Frank Conrad, a Westinghouse engineer, was experimenting with radiotelephony. He had a transmitter in the garage of his home in a Pittsburgh suburb and an assistant had a receiver in his home a few miles away. Because it was both tiring and inconvenient to talk all the time during the experiments, Mr. Conrad brought out his phonograph and connected it to the transmitter so music was being sent by radio.

Amateur radio operators ("hams") had been growing in great numbers since 1912 when radio had been so prominent in the news of the *Titanic* disaster. Those living in the Pittsburgh area quickly learned that if they built their sets to receive the proper frequency, they could pick up Mr. Conrad's music. The word circulated, and in September the Joseph Horne Department Store advertised kits (from $10 up) that people could use to make their own sets to hear this new phenomenon.

Mr. Conrad received cards and calls—some wanting to hear favorite records and others protesting that some of the disks were getting too "scratchy" from overuse. He began putting his transmitter on the air for a couple hours in the evening to meet the demand. When Westinghouse saw what was happening, the decision was made to build a special transmitter for the listeners as a means of stimulating demand for the receivers it was preparing to produce.

On November 2, 1920 Westinghouse inaugurated station KDKA by giving the results of the Harding-Cox presidential election as provided by a newspaper from its telegraphed reports. There is controversy as to whether KDKA was clearly the first broadcasting station in the country. WHA in Madison, Wisconsin, and WWJ in Detroit, Michigan, also lay claim to the honor. However, it is the consensus that KDKA has an extremely strong case. We do know it was the first station to receive a license specifically for broadcasting. Thus, America entered a new age in which radio signals were broadcast—transmitted for the purpose of reaching as many listeners as possible. There were and are many applications of point-to-point radio where signals are sent to a few specific receivers but, for our purposes, the word "radio" will be used to designate broadcasting only.

Hoover's Regulatory Philosophy

The man most clearly associated with the beginning of broadcast regulation is Herbert Hoover, who was to be elected president of the United States in 1928. *Broadcasting*, in its obituary story about Mr. Hoover, said, "He was, more than anyone else, the father of the American system of broadcasting."

Foresighted advertising. This famous advertisement, placed by the Joseph Horne Company in the Pittsburgh *Sun*, stimulated public interest in Dr. Conrad's early radio broadcasts. To Horne's, radios meant a new item for sale. To H. P. Davis, Westinghouse Vice President, the ad was an inspiration. He reasoned that the real radio industry lay in manufacturing home receivers and broadcasting programs.
Courtesy: Westinghouse Broadcasting Company

HERBERT CLARK HOOVER 1874–1964

Courtesy: NBC

At the time of his death, Herbert Hoover was honored as a highly successful mining engineer who had worked all over the world, as a great humanitarian who had organized massive efforts to relieve the suffering of war, and as the thirty-first President of the United States. To *Broadcasting* he was "more than anyone else the father of the American system of broadcasting."*

He was born in Iowa in 1874. Before he was ten years old both of his parents died and he was raised by relatives in Oregon. In 1895 he was a member of the first graduating class of Stanford University in Palo Alto, California. After spending a year as a mine laborer ($5 for a ten-hour day, seven days a week) he became a mining engineer in Australia and China. As a Quaker (Society of Friends) he was deeply affected by suffering

and in 1900 directed a food relief program for destitute victims of the Boxer rebellion in China. He later set up his own engineering consulting firm and was in demand in many nations.

In 1914 he established relief committees in Europe and was probably the only American who had free access to the capitals of the nations on both sides of the lines throughout World War I. After the war he was appointed by President Wilson as director general of a program for the relief and reconstruction of Europe. His organization was responsible for distributing nearly fifty million tons of food to famine-threatened populations in thirty countries.

From 1920 to 1928 he was Secretary of Commerce under Presidents Harding and Coolidge, charged (among other duties) with licensing radio operators. Until the Zenith decision of 1926 he was successful in persuading operators to share the limited available frequencies and to engage in self-regulation that would lessen the possibility of government control of programming. His most successful medium of leadership was the series of four annual broadcasting conferences starting in 1922. In them he gave to the broadcasters his own vision of the medium and his own concepts of future directions. His one notable failure to understand the role of the medium was his conviction that "direct advertising would be the surest way of killing radio." Thirty years later he admitted he had been wrong. In 1928 he was elected President of the United States. It was his misfortune to be in the White House when the Depression came and for many years he was maligned for failing to prevent the inevitable and for doing too little once economic collapse oc-

---

* *Broadcasting*, October 26, 1964, p. 80.

curred. In the closing years of his life he was accorded the honors due him. After World War II President Truman asked him to be coordinator of a Food Supply for Famine operation that again alleviated the suffering of war victims.

Congress established the "Hoover Commission" to make recommendations on reorganization of the Executive branch of government. When he died he had been for two decades a respected elder statesman of his country.

As Secretary of Commerce (the Labor Department had been separately established since the Radio Act of 1912) Mr. Hoover was charged with issuing licenses to those who wished to use radio. He later recalled that when he took office in 1921 there were 2 stations on the air and about 400,000 receivers; a year later there were 300 stations and over two million receivers.

Had a lesser man been in Hoover's position, it is likely that total confusion might have emerged as our system of broadcasting grew under a law that had been written only for point-to-point radio. As it was, the system developed during four to five critical years with a sense of order. When a court finally ruled the Radio Act of 1912 did not provide a sufficient basis for effective regulation, Congress had a starting point for corrective legislation. In 1927 it wrote into law many of the principles by which Hoover had been proceeding.

Hoover's regulatory philosophy was a direct outgrowth of the four elements of the American tradition described in Chapter 1:

1. He conceived of broadcasting as free enterprise and at no time suggested that government should be involved in it.

2. He recognized the scarcity of freqencies and had no hesitation in allocating their restricted use in the public interest.

3. He was dedicated to free speech for broadcasters and thought the most effective way of avoiding government control was self-regulation whereby the broadcasters themselves would agree on their responsibilities. The National Association of Broadcasters (NAB) was formed in 1923 to speak for all radio operators in a confrontation with the American Society of Composers, Authors, and Publishers (ASCAP) over permission to broadcast copyrighted music. The NAB expanded its concern to other broadcast problems and was instrumental in working out "standards of good practice" as a vital part of self-regulation.

4. He was adept at compromising when the demand for frequencies far exceeded the supply. In fact, it will be noted that it was his attempt to compromise supply and demand that eventually led to the demise of the Radio Act of 1912 under which he operated.

In 1922 Hoover called the first of four annual national radio conferences to discuss the problems of broadcasting and other uses of the radio spectrum. Through the conferences he was successful in persuading operators to share the limited frequencies and to pursue his concepts of how the new medium should evolve.

It is impossible to give accurate statistics on the numbers of stations existing in the early 1920s. We do know there were 2 stations on the air in 1921 and more than 500 in 1925. However, these figures and all others should be considered minimal because there were many people who built their own five- and ten-watt stations and operated them sporadically and without authorization from the government. There have been estimates that the actual numbers were three or four times as large as the official figures.

Mr. Hoover first assigned one frequency (830 kHz) for broadcasting. A year later he added another—750 kHz. In 1925 the spectrum between 550 kHz and 1350 kHz was reserved for this new use of radio.

Because there were so many operators and so few frequencies, it was necessary for Mr. Hoover to issue licenses whereby a place on the dial would be shared by several stations in a community throughout the week. This was reasonably satisfactory, but it was inevitable there would be an occasional conflict. In New York City the broadcaster who used a frequency for the early part of the evening liked opera; the one who followed preferred jazz. The opera fan went to great trouble and expense to get some artists to do a live broadcast that was not accurately timed in advance. Just as the company reached the finale, the other operator started airing the jazz program. When the opera listeners called to protest, they were told to call the person who put on the jazz. The number of complaints was so great that the second operator agreed to postpone programming when there was live opera on the air until the earlier performance had been completed.

Listening to Many "Firsts"

Much of the listening in the early 1920s was "dial-twisting" to see what distant stations might be picked up. This was such a popular pastime that it became customary for all the stations in each city to observe a "Silent Night" one evening a week. On that night all local stations would refrain from broadcasting so listeners might concentrate on bringing in the sky waves of distant stations.

In the first half of the 1920s many kinds of programs began that were to become commonplace in broadcast radio. There were, for example, the first coverage of sporting events, the first live orchestras, the first opera, the first church service, and the first drama.

Finding a Financial Base

There was little consensus in the early years about how radio should be financed. Some thought stations, like libraries, should be endowed by wealthy philanthropists. Others felt subscribers should pay "dues" to cover the expenses of the programs they enjoyed. Some manufacturers, like Westinghouse and GE, operated stations to stimulate demand for the receivers they made. A large number of colleges and universities tried to justify operating radio stations as a way to provide continuing education to the public.

Probably the most influential broadcaster in the early 1920s was AT&T. Drawing on its telephone experience, it built WEAF in New York City as a "toll" station to sell time to those who wanted to communicate with the public. (Other stations saw this as a logical move for AT&T but did not see advertising as a concept they also might adopt.) The first true commercial was probably a ten-minute talk by a real estate dealer in Queens who purchased the time for $50 on WEAF on August 28, 1922. There had been from the beginning pseudo-commercials in the "swap deals" whereby station operators received products or services in return for mentioning a manufacturer or dealer on the air. (When Mr. Conrad put his transmitter on the air in the evenings as a service to listeners, he used phonograph records donated by a local music store in return for telling who had provided them.)

It was not until the mid-1920s that there was general agreement on advertising as the best way to finance stations. Even then, the practice was far different from the advertising with which we are familiar today. It was expected that companies would pay for time and programs and only their names would be mentioned at the beginning and end of the presentations. The hope was that people would patronize their stores or buy their products out of gratitude for the programs they had provided. In many ways the institutional advertising of those days resembled the "patron plan" of public television today in which a company donates money to make a program available and is mentioned only by name before and after the telecast. Technically, this is not now considered advertising.

The early advertisers on WEAF were pleased with the results of their program sponsorship and wanted to extend the effort. Because AT&T had telephone lines connecting various cities, it was feasible to make arrangements for other stations to carry some WEAF programs and advertising. The first commercial network of "two or more stations carrying the same program simultaneously" consisted of WEAF and WNAC in Boston. As other stations joined from other cities, the AT&T network soon extended from coast to coast for certain special events.

RCA also operated a station in New York City and was interested in building a network. However, AT&T refused to lease its lines to RCA so the latter was forced to use telegraph lines, which were much less satisfactory. The RCA network remained smaller and less effective than the AT&T network. Because AT&T had a clear commitment to accept advertising and because it had the only satisfactory network connections, it dominated the growth of broadcasting in the mid-1920s.

Regulatory Breakdown

There had been an initial erosion of Hoover's regulatory authority in the 1923 *Intercity* case.* The Intercity Radio Company had engaged in wireless telegraphy, but Hoover refused to renew its license in 1921 because of anticipated interference with other operators. A court ruled that he might not refuse a license to qualified applicants but must assign to them a frequency on which they might transmit. In 1926 Hoover's authority was almost completely eliminated. He had been able to arrange a reasonably satisfactory use of the limited broadcast frequencies by licensing each operator to use limited power during certain specified hours of the week. In the *Zenith*† case it was ruled that once a person met the qualifications of the Act of 1912, that person must be licensed and might broadcast full time on any frequency designated for such use. This amounted to a full elimination of discretionary power to issue the restricted broadcast permissions that had been the basis of the whole system.

3.3 1927–1937 RADIO'S ADOLESCENCE

The next year Congress passed the Radio Act of 1927. Seven years later it acted to bring regulation to all electronic communications under one agency, and the Radio Act of 1927 became Title III of the Communications Act of 1934. There were slight differences in language between the two but there was no substantive alteration in the regulatory pattern established in 1927. Both provided that broadcasting should be conducted "in the public interest, convenience, and necessity."

During the next ten years radio passed through its adolescence by improvising and then formalizing many of the practices that still characterize television.

Development of the Networks

The networks that dominated radio in the early 1940s as networks now dominate television started to assume familiar form just as the new law was being drawn up. AT&T had earlier decided it would give up station

---

* *Hoover v. Intercity Radio Co.,* Inc., 286 F. 1003 (D.C. Cir.) February 5, 1923.

† *United States v. Zenith Radio Corporation et al.,* 12 F. 2d. 614 (N.D. Ill.) April 16, 1926.

operation and concentrate on the telephone industry and long-distance interconnection of radio stations. RCA purchased WEAF for $1 million (an astounding price in those days) and took over the AT&T network to be operated by the National Broadcasting Company (NBC), a wholly-owned subsidiary formed for that purpose in 1926. Because RCA already had its own minor network, it identified the old and the new by colors. The AT&T network became NBC Red and the RCA network became NBC Blue. The latter never did achieve the stature of the Red. In the late 1930s NBC was accused of keeping the Blue network in operation only to prevent competitive new networks from getting started.

The third network (if we count NBC Red and Blue as the first and second chronologically) grew from a shaky beginning. In 1927 a program service put together a network with sixteen affiliates to be called United Independent Broadcasters. The network agreed to buy ten hours of time a week from each affiliate at a price of $50 per station per hour. When it became difficult to sell the time, the Columbia Phonograph Company took over the ten hours. It used some of them to advertise its own records and sold some to other advertisers. The name of the network was changed to the Columbia Phonograph Broadcasting System and then to the Columbia Broadcasting System (CBS).

One of the few early advertisers on CBS was the Congress Cigar Company of Philadelphia. In one year sales of its "La Palina Smoker" rose from 400,000 per day to over a million. This intrigued the advertising manager of the Congress Company, William Paley, son of the owner. When he learned the phonograph company's contract for ten hours a week on the network was for sale, he persuaded his relatives to help him buy it. On September 2, 1928, the sale was consummated and he took a three-month leave of absence from the cigar company to get the new enterprise started. He very quickly decided the job was more than he could handle part-time and too interesting to leave. He devoted all his energies to broadcasting and the story of CBS from that day on is the story of Mr. Paley who five decades later was still Chairman of the Board.

The fourth network came into being in 1934. There were four stations in New York City, Chicago, Detroit, and Cincinnati that wanted to give advertisers more exposure on the most popular programs that had been developed in each city. The key program was "The Lone Ranger" on WXYZ in Detroit. Because the four stations were banding together for their mutual benefit, they called the network the Mutual Broadcasting System (MBS). They saw it only as a sales organization. Unlike NBC and CBS, MBS owned no stations. Each affiliated station was to be paid according to its published list of charges after the network kept 15 percent to cover its expenses. By the end of 1936 there were 39 affiliated stations and five years later there were 160, making it the largest network in the country in number of outlets.

Its coverage was less than may be expected since many of its stations were comparatively weak in power.

WILLIAM S. PALEY b. 1901

Courtesy: CBS

CBS Board Chairman William S. Paley has placed his stamp on CBS to a degree that few founders of other large corporations can match. He saw his network grow from two or three hundred employees in the late 1920s to a giant whose four groups employ some 30,000 persons. Through most of the intervening years it was decisions that he made personally that shaped not only his own network but also much of the industry.

Born in 1901 in Chicago, Paley received his BS degree from the University of Pennsylvania in 1922. For the next six years he was Vice President, Secretary, and Advertising Manager of the Congress Cigar Company, a family-owned business in Philadelphia which was one of the early successful sponsors on radio. Upon purchasing the CBS network contracts, he assumed the Presidency and has been the leader of the company ever since.

In the 1930s his program decisions affected the style of the networks for years to come. Because CBS was smaller and more flexible than the established NBC networks, Paley was able to move more quickly and to exploit his conviction that it was stars who made successful programs. While on an ocean liner going to Europe, he heard a recording of Bing Crosby, radioed instructions to sign him up, and gave him his first national showcase on CBS. He missed a luncheon date one day to hear the Mills Brothers in their first major audition, then hired them and saw them rise to become among America's top entertainers on his network. His interest in news dates back to the early 1930s when he thought CBS should start its own news organization because the press associations resisted selling their services to radio. It was he who decided that CBS should buy Columbia Records at a time when most thought radio had ruined the record business.

During World War II Paley was Deputy Chief of Psychological Warfare for the European Theater under General Eisenhower. Subsequent to the war his service to the nation included the Chairmanship of President Truman's Materials Policy Commission studying the long-range problems of our natural resources. The Commission's report has been called a landmark in the field.

In the immediate postwar years Paley moved to acquire for his network first a parity in radio with NBC and then to move ahead to number one in television in the 1950s. He took personal charge of the talent raids that saw Jack Benny and other stars move to CBS under capital-gains arrangements. It was also his decision that CBS should invest many millions of deficit radio dollars getting started in television.

President Franklin D. Roosevelt delivering "fireside chat" during the Depression
Courtesy: NBC

The importance of the networks became evident in the 1932 presidential election in which Franklin D. Roosevelt owed much to radio. He was overwhelmingly opposed by publishers who controlled the news and editorial comments of the press. Before radio, newspapers had been the only windows through which citizens could see and get to know their candidates. Publishers tended to come from the "establishment." Most were at least fairly wealthy and primarily concerned with preserving the status quo. Radio owners differed little from publishers in that respect. But it was not editorial support from licensees that FDR needed in the election—he needed the use of their facilities to talk directly to the poeple. Those facilities would have done little good if they had not been tied into networks and into millions of homes. Roosevelt could no more go around giving speeches on individual stations than he could argue with individual editors throughout the country trying to enlist their support. By going directly to the people with his message, FDR was elected.

Four months after the 1932 election, there was more evidence of the impact radio could have on society. It is impossible to describe adequately the hopelessness and despair that prevailed in this nation in 1932 and 1933. There was a psychological depression fully as deep as the financial decline— both hit a low this country had not known before. It is quite likely that only those who lived through the period can fully appreciate the lift that came on March 4, 1933, when in his inaugural address broadcast coast to coast, President Roosevelt ringingly declared, "The only thing we have to fear is fear itself." This speech was followed by "fireside chats," a series of radio talks in which FDR took America into his confidence in discussing the situation and explaining the solutions. While his policies were subjects of great controversy, there is little doubt that the people rallied behind him and were lifted from their despair by his speeches. Without his ability to speak to them in their homes through network radio, the history of our country might have been quite different.

Mutual was a pioneer in "cooperative programming" whereby the network would distribute a program with open times for commercials but with no national sponsors. The individual stations could sell the open time in the network program to local sponsors who were thus able to insert their advertising in programs of high quality.

As MBS got larger, it started providing more of the functions (public service sustain programs, for example) that the other networks had undertaken.

Development of Advertising

During the early 1930s radio developed many of the commercial practices that are characteristic of television today. It was not coincidental that this happened as the Depression deepened and radio stations found it necessary to concentrate on maintaining their revenues.

In 1930 all companies were beginning to feel the Depression and thought they should be more cautious in allocating their advertising dollars. For years newspapers had been able to give advertisers certified figures on how many copies were sold. There was additional research to estimate the number of people who would read an advertisement in each copy and the number who would remember it at a later point. It was natural that advertisers should seek comparable data concerning the effectiveness of radio.

The national advertisers sought to answer the questions about radio by setting up the Cooperative Analysis of Broadcasting under the direction of researcher Archibald Crossley to ascertain the listenership to programs on which advertising was placed. He hired interviewers across the country who called homes inquiring about listening for the past several hours (telephone-recall method). This was the beginning of the ratings that today play such an important role in television and advertising.

The early 1930s also saw a movement from institutional advertising into the era of "hard sell." At first advertisers mentioned specific prices of their products in a tentative way, not certain that people would accept the commercials. When there were no objections from listeners, the practice spread. In subsequent years many listeners and viewers have said they like the way products are advertised on broadcasting because it gives them an opportunity to learn about new items and to do comparative shopping in the comfort of their homes.

Development of News

It was not until the approach of World War II that radio became an important news medium. In its earliest days it had been customary for stations to buy the morning and evening papers and to summarize them in newscasts. Then they started purchasing news directly from two of the three principle news agencies—United Press (UP) and International News Service (INS). The Associated Press (AP) was owned by the newspapers it served and refused to sell its services to radio stations.

As the Depression deepened, newspapers were concerned about losses of advertising dollars to radio. Publishers were especially upset to see sponsorship of network newscasts and commentators. Because newspapers were still the biggest customers of UP and INS, the publishers brought pressure on them to discontinue selling news to broadcasters. CBS started its own news service and NBC made plans to enter the field also.

In December 1933 a meeting was held in the Biltmore Hotel in New York City to hammer out the "Biltmore Agreement" between publishers, networks, and press associations. It was agreed that the networks would receive from the press associations enough news items to present two five-minute summaries a day. The morning news was not to be given before 9:30 A.M. and the evening news had to come after 9:00 P.M. Thus, there was to be no competition to the newspapers during the hours when they were "hitting the streets." There could be no advertising on the newscasts. CBS agreed to give up its news organization and NBC agreed not to enter the field.

The Biltmore Agreement lasted only a few months. A new organization, Trans Radio Press, began selling news to stations that gave newscasts whenever they wished and with sponsorship. The publishers reached the point where their first concern was to drive Trans Radio Press out of business. The most effective means was for the established organizations to sell news to the stations, and they proceeded to do just that. The networks also were soon back in the scheduling of news.

Through the mid-1930s the network news consisted mostly of commentators who gave the background of stories and interpreted the news. Some, like Lowell Thomas and H. V. Kaltenborn, were household names with large followings. As the situation in Europe moved closer to open hostilities, networks started gathering their own news and by 1941 radio became the first source to which people turned for the latest developments in the war.

Development of Programming

Following the beginnings in the early 1920s, the first "major" radio program was the "Eveready Hour," sponsored by the National Carbon Company on the WEAF network starting in 1924. As the networks grew, the most popular programs were the "Hours" presented by different products—Eveready, Palmolive, and Atwater Kent. Aside from sports and the coverage of special events such as the 1927 Lindbergh ticker-tape parade in New York City, the one program that dominated America's attention in the late 1920s was "Amos 'n Andy," which was so popular that President Coolidge would not miss an episode for any reason. Theaters delayed their evening openings so people could hear "Amos 'n Andy" before going to the movies.

By the late 1930s radio had developed a wide spectrum of entertainment programming comparable with television thirty and forty years later. Most spectacular were the big bands with the singers and comedians who rounded out the variety hours. Some became as well known to postwar generations as they were to the listeners of the thirties—Kate Smith, Jack Benny, Burns and Allen, Edgar Bergen and Charlie McCarthy, Eddie Cantor, and Ed Wynn. For the children there were programs like "Little Orphan Annie" and "Jack Armstrong, the all-American boy." For drama and suspense America tuned to "Inner Sanctum," "The Shadow," "Gangbusters," and "Mr. District Attorney."

One of the most important developments of the early 1930s was the birth of the daytime serial. Advertisers were searching for inexpensive programming to put in the daytime hours. They devised serials in which the stories of people in trouble moved slowly from one crisis to another. Because so many of the serials were sponsored by makers of soap products, they became known as "soap operas." The serials probably evoked more loyalty among their listeners than any other program form. The heroines of "Portia Faces Life," "Our Gal Sunday," "The Romance of Helen Trent," "Stella Dallas," and others were very much members of a listener's family. When a baby was to be born in one of the series, gifts were sent in by the thousands. If there were an accident, there would be messages of sympathy. Many listeners wrote to say they had been better able to solve their own problems after seeing how similar situations were worked out in a serial. In many ways the soap operas were among the most significant programs presented by American radio.

Regulating the Traffic

When the Federal Radio Commission was created in 1927, it faced a monumental task of creating order out of the chaos that had ensued after Hoover gave up issuing limited licenses. Congress had thought it would take about a year and provided that at the end of that time the commission would be disbanded and licensing would be handled again by the secretary of commerce. It took much longer than anticipated. Time-consuming hearings were required to determine who should have the privilege of using the scarce frequencies. The commission's licensing authority was extended until it was replaced by the Federal Communications Commission in 1934.

Throughout the ten years from 1927 to 1937 both commissions devoted most of their attention to allocating facilities to applicants. On only a few occasions did they get into other areas of defining the public interest.

An especially interesting action of the Federal Radio Commission concerned one of the famous broadcasters of that time, Dr. John Brinkley. Dr. Brinkley was largely self-taught and was licensed to practice medicine only in the state of Kansas in which he had received an honorary medical degree (upon payment of a large sum of money to an unaccredited medical school). His specialty was a goat-gland operation designed to renew sexual vigor in elderly men. Observers said he was an extremely competent surgeon.

Men came from all over the country for Brinkley's operation. In 1923 he built a station primarily to entertain his patients while they were in the postoperative stage of recovery. In the late 1920s, somewhat to his surprise, he found people in the area were listening and were writing in for medical advice. When his first station burned down he built another with greater power and used it to tell about his services and to answer questions he had received in the mail.

He had an arrangement with druggists throughout the Midwest. When a person came in and asked for a Dr. Brinkley prescription by number, the druggist would fill it and send part of the money to the doctor.

In a typical broadcast he advised:

You are listening to Dr. Brinkley speaking from his office over KFKB. . . . She states her case briefly, which I appreciate. She had an operation, with her appendix, ovary, and tubes removed a couple years ago; she is very nervous and has dizzy spells. She says the salt solution and constipation and liver medicine has already benefited her. In reply to your question, No. 1, I am more or less of the opinion that while the symptoms are to a great extent those of a premature menopause, I think they are not, but they are due to the fact that you have a very small amount of ovarian substance remaining. In my practice in such cases as this, I have for many years used Prescription No. 61 for women. I think you should, as well as Special Prescription No. 50, and I think if you would go on a vegetable diet, a salt-free diet, for a while and use Prescriptions No. 64, 50 and 61, you would be surprised at the benefit you would obtain . . .

Responding to pressure from the American Medical Association, the Federal Radio Commission refused to renew Dr. Brinkley's license. It ruled that giving medical advice by radio without having examined the questioners was contrary to the public interest. Not only might the prescriptions be the wrong ones for those who had written in, it was also feared others who heard the broadcasts would diagnose themselves and undertake harmful remedies. The commission further noted that responding to letters was using a broadcast frequency for point-to-point communication.

It should be noted that the passage of the Communications Act of 1934 is not considered important enough to mark the division between two periods in this outline history of broadcasting. It made no change in the regulatory patterns of broadcasting.

By 1937 radio had passed through its adolescence and most of the characteristics of modern television had been adopted by the older medium. (1) The networks were established at the heart of radio programming and had essentially the same relationships with their affiliates that the television networks have today. (2) Listening had passed from the period of "dial-twisting" into a time when people turned on their sets for specific popular programs. (3) The ratings were the basis on which many programming decisions were being made. (4) Radio news was ready to assume a position of leadership.

3.4 1937—1945 RADIO'S MATURITY

When World War II ended in 1945 radio had achieved the stature television was to reach three decades later—it was the dominant entertainment and news medium of the country.

Radio and World War II

Radio schedules were nearly sold out during the war years, partly because a shortage of newsprint made it impossible for newspapers to add enough pages to include all the advertising they might have sold, and partly because manufacturers were unable to get materials for expanding their plants, thus freeing more dollars for advertising. Radio at the network level was never again to be as healthy as in 1945. It was to be another ten years before radio found its current niche in new formats and the unexpected strength of local advertising.

Radio made important contributions to the war effort by participating in drives to sell war bonds and urging people to conserve scarce materials and to cooperate in various rationing plans. Incidentally, there was no censorship during the war years. The government indicated certain information that would be helpful to the enemy and stations voluntarily eliminated those items from the news. For example, it was known that weather tends to flow from west to east and if an enemy submarine off the North Atlantic coast were able to get weather reports from Chicago, Buffalo, and Boston, it would have good clues as to what might be expected in its area of operations for the next few days. Thus, stations did not give weather reports and they never mentioned if there were large troop movements within their coverage areas or if there were developments in war plants, such as the hiring of a thousand new workers.

As World War II approached, radio threw off the last remnants of the Biltmore Agreement shackles and became a vital news source with its ability to broadcast events of the day within minutes or hours of the time they occurred. CBS had been fortunate in having Edward R. Murrow in Europe on an assignment to line up cultural programming during the hectic days when Hitler started his military conquests. Murrow was able to enlist a cadre of news persons who reported from various capitals on fast-breaking developments. NBC followed very shortly, and throughout the war it was customary to tune in for the latest news on radio and then to read the papers for more details.

Drawn for BROADCASTING by Sid Hix
"I thought you preferred radio—where your imagination could paint the scene more vividly than reality!"

Reprinted, with permission, from Broadcasting

Radio as an Art Form

In the late 1930s and early 1940s radio achieved great heights as an art form. When conveying concepts radio was able to take advantage of an incredibly effective ally—the human imagination. For example, a singer on television may appear to be attractive to some and quite ordinary to others. But when a singer performed on radio in those days, listeners created in their minds an image to match the voice and imagination might be better than the real thing.

When television attempts to communicate suspense in a graveyard at midnight, someone has to create for the screen what the creator personally conceives as frightening. The scene created may make little impression on some viewers. Radio needed only to suggest the suspense with a few subtle sounds and listeners took it from there. They mentally filled the graveyard with whatever was most frightening to them.

Many of today's viewers can never appreciate how listeners once gleefully anticipated the weekly opening of the closet on "Fibber McGee and Molly." It was loaded with far more than could be shown on television and when the door was opened, the cascade of items had to be imagined—in truth they could never exist. There was a pleasure, an excitement, and a satisfaction in listening to radio that the television viewer can never hope to experience.

The person who listens to the radio of the 1970s and wonders how sound alone can be as effective as television should read a study of the Orson Welles broadcast, "The War of the Worlds," on the night before Halloween 1938. Welles thought the script had little credibility and did not look forward to doing it. But as people heard the descriptions of the alien creatures coming out of space capsules and taking over the New Jersey countryside, they fled their homes and prepared for a battle none of them thought could be won. A television program could never have such an impact because the creator's visualization of the vehicle and the creatures from space could never be as convincing as the imagination of the average listener who was terrified.

In 1941 radio was a powerful vehicle used to turn a nation around. People had been told the war in Europe was none of this country's business and that the United States would never get involved. After Pearl Harbor (December 7, 1941) the fact that stations were organized into networks made it easier for the administration to persuade a whole nation to change its posture and support participation in two wars—in Europe and in the Pacific.

In retrospect, it is difficult to know how much of radio's impact was due to skillful use of the medium and how much was due to a lack of public sophistication in that earlier day. Regardless of the reasons, it is safe to say that radio between the early 1930s and 1945 achieved an almost unbelievable hold over America and Americans.

Regulatory Activism

Outside of determining who could use the airwaves, the commissions were relatively passive between 1927 and 1937. During the 1937–1945 period the FCC became extremely active in an investigation into network practices resulting in passage of the "Chain Regulations." (See Chapter 9.) The investigation grew out of a concern with possible network control of affiliated stations and a determination that stations be able to make their own judgments.

The Birth of Frequency Modulation (FM)

Frequency modulation became a reality in 1933 when it was unveiled by Major Edwin Armstrong. He had worked for ten years on the concept and it promised to revolutionize the technical transmission of radio programs.

FM had a high-fidelity capacity to convey all the 20,000 cycles of sound that the ear could perceive. It was resistant to static from lightning and other interference. If a receiver were between two stations, the stronger signal would override the weaker and prevent interference. The FM signal did not fade in and out as AM signals did at a distance. Of even more importance was the fact that the sky waves were not reflected back at a distance and the ground wave was inefficient. Since only the direct waves were significant, there could be many more FM stations on a channel than was possible with AM.

MAJOR EDWIN H. ARMSTRONG 1890–1954

Photo courtesy of Broadcasting

The "father of FM" was a suicide at the age of 64, despondent over years of patent litigation and the resulting deterioration of his home life. A brilliant inventor had been de-feated by those who would use the fruits of his labor and force him into the courts to seek remuneration and the recognition that he had been the one responsible for a new medium.

Born in New York City in 1890, Armstrong acquired an early interest in radio by reading about Hertz, Marconi, and other pioneers. By the time he was graduated from Columbia University in 1913, he had already invented the regenerative circuit that was to make possible many future developments in the field. While a major in the United States Signal Corps in France in World War I he made a second important contribution—the super-heterodyne principle.

Through the 1920s his attention was divided among patent litigation that was, perhaps, inevitable in such a new field; his development of frequency modulation; and his marriage to the secretary of RCA's David Sarnoff. Sarnoff had given strong early support and encouragement to Armstrong's FM research but they later became bitter enemies.

In 1933 he received a patent on FM and amazed both engineers and the general public with his demonstrations of static-free high-fidelity radio. As a professor at Columbia University, he continued his research. His last patent, issued within a year of his death, was for multiplexing on the FM channel that made possible stereo broadcasting and other services.

In 1940 the FCC acknowledged his advances in FM and authorized its use for broadcasting. Although there were only some fifty stations on the air during World War II, he and other engineers looked forward to great expansion when the war was ended. In 1945 he fought bitterly against the FCC's decision to move FM to a higher range in the VHF. The arguments and protests of the man who had invented the medium were, however, ignored.

As FM grew in the immediate postwar years, Armstrong saw more and more companies manufacturing FM receivers without acknowledging his patents or paying him royalties. They developed new tubes to combine functions of his principles and claimed they had a completely new invention. In 1949 he embarked on a five-year battle over patent infringement in the manufacture of FM receivers by RCA. The legal process seemed interminable, but he refused to settle out of court. The fight not only cost the personal fortune he had received from other patents, it also destroyed his relationship with his wife. When he realized what had happened, he wrote her a letter saying he could not understand how he could have let it come about. Then—fully dressed—he stepped out of a window of his thirteenth-floor apartment in Manhattan and plunged to his death.

He did not live to see the rebirth of FM in the 1960s. RCA settled with his widow for a million dollars shortly after his death and in subsequent years many more millions were paid to his estate by other manufacturers. Today his peers consider him one of the most productive of all the radio pioneers.

In 1940 the FCC approved FM for broadcasting (effective January 1, 1941) and about fifty stations went on the air before the World War II shortage of materials froze further growth. In 1945 the FCC, in a highly controversial decision, moved FM from the 42–50 mHz band where it had been operating to the 88–108 mHz band where it is today. The reason given at the time was the fear that sunspot activity would interfere with the FM signals at the lower band. The need for such fear was refuted by Major Armstrong and other engineers. There were charges that the FCC was only interested in protecting AM radio and television by deliberately weakening FM just as it reached a point of high promise with the end of the war and the easing of wartime restrictions. Whether or not the FCC reasoning was correct, the movement of the FM band at the end of World War II laid the foundation for the remarkable growth of FM in the 1970s to its present status as a strong competitor to AM.

3.5 LOOKING AHEAD

In its first quarter-century since Mr. Conrad's experiments radio broadcasting grew rapidly and became a vital part of life. At no point was there serious question about radio's health and its bright future. Although the optimism was justified, few could have predicted the course of events over the next few years. It was only after another quarter-century that one could look back and see that 1945 climaxed growth of one kind and that a restructuring of the medium would be required before it would rise to even greater size and strength.

GLOSSARY ITEMS

The following words and phrases used in Chapter 3 are defined in the Glossary.

Broadcasting

Frequency Modulation (FM)

Institutional Advertising

Network

Network Affiliate

Network Cooperative Programming

Patron Plan

Public Interest, Convenience, and Necessity

Public Service Programming

Radiotelephony

Sustaining Program

Wireless Telegraphy

RADIO BROADCASTING CHRONOLOG 1920–1945

1920   Frank Conrad's experimental broadcasts.
KDKA began broadcasting service with results of the Harding-Cox election.

1921   KDKA broadcast first religious service, first boxing match, first theatrical program, first tennis match, first baseball game.

1922   AT&T put WEAF on the air in New York City; first commercial was a real estate advertisement.
The secretary of commerce convened first of four annual radio conferences.
First experimental network broadcast—WJZ in Newark, New Jersey, and WGY in Schenectady, New York—does World Series.

1923   First regular network programming—WEAF in New York City and WNAC in Boston, Massachusetts.

1924   First major sponsored network program—"The Eveready Hour" presented by the National Carbon Company.

1926   The *Zenith* case ended effective regulation under the Radio Act of 1912.

AT&T sold WEAF in New York City to RCA.

RCA formed subsidiary National Broadcasting Company which operated the Red network (formerly AT&T network) and the Blue network (formerly the RCA network).

1927   Passage of the Radio Act of 1927.

Formation of the United Independent Broadcasting network (UIB) which became CBS.

1928   William S. Paley bought CBS.

1930   Brinkley's license not renewed.

1933   President Franklin D. Roosevelt's Inaugural Address followed by "fireside chats."

Biltmore Agreement signalling end of one phase of press-radio war.

Edwin Armstrong demonstrated FM.

1934   Passage of the Federal Communications Act.

Mutual Broadcasting System started as a four-station cooperative network.

1938   Orson Welles broadcast "War of the Worlds."

Edward R. Murrow started building overseas CBS news in Munich crisis.

1941   Beginning of FM commercial broadcasting.

1945   FM moved to VHF band between 88 mHz and 108 mHz.

PREVIEW

In the postwar years networks fell so far below their 1945 peak that many gave up on the future of radio generally. FM development was especially disappointing. The 1950s were a period of continued confusion and pessimism; a network affiliation no longer assured success. Yet by the end of the 1960s the future of both AM and FM radio was assured in format programming. Now, in the early 1980s, radio is healthier than ever before. Although it has accepted a role secondary to television in appealing to Americans' full-attention entertainment needs, its financial prospects are stronger than ever before.

CHAPTER 4

HISTORICAL PERSPECTIVES II
1945–1980 with Emphasis on Radio

On its sixtieth birthday in 1980 commercial radio was "alive and well." The number of AM stations had more than quadrupled from under 1,000 in 1945 to over 4,550. The number of FM stations had grown from 50 in 1945 to nearly 3,300. Radio billings had increased every year but two (1954 and 1961) and reached a level of nearly $3 billion with every indication of continued growth. The majority of AM stations and AM-FM combinations were reporting profits. Radio listening was rising as more people found that specialized stations offered services they wanted. Broadcaster confidence in both AM and FM was reflected in the rising prices of buying stations and the steady increase in the number of FM stations on the air.

Radio has undergone vast changes since the mid-1940s when it was in its traditional prime. Of the following generalizations one might have made about radio then, not one is true today.

1. It was the most popular entertainment and news medium. To a degree, the radio receiver was the center of the home and family activities frequently revolved around the broadcast schedule.

2. It attempted to be "all things to all people." The average station schedule

had something for everyone from news and commentary through variety and comedy to religion, discussion, sports, and children's programs.

3. The most popular programs came from the networks. Most of the more powerful stations were either network-owned or affiliates.

4. The most prevalent form of advertising was "sponsorship" in which the advertiser bought a segment of time and provided the program and all the commercial messages.

5. Most radio music was live. There was no convenient way to make program recordings, and it was generally agreed that playing recorded music (aside from sound effects, mood music, and special seasonal tunes) was not quite respectable.

Of radio today we can make the following generalizations, none of which was true in 1945.

1. Radio is higly popular but secondary to television, especially as a home-centered "full-attention" medium.

2. Radio's emphasis is primarily on serving the music and informational needs of its audiences. The key to programming is format.

3. The regularly scheduled programs attracting the most listeners are originated by the stations or by schedule syndication companies with which the stations have contracted. A network affiliation no longer has the great value it once possessed.

4. Most advertising is participatory with commercial messages inserted into programming provided by the stations.

5. Programming consists primarily of recorded music, dialogue, and newscasts with a bow to nostalgia in the old radio comedy and drama programs being revived.

The history of radio from the days of its traditional prime in 1945 can be divided into three periods.

1945–1960   Changing Patterns
1960–1970   Steady Growth of FM
1970–1980   Dominance of Format Programming

4.1 1945–1960 CHANGING PATTERNS

Changing Patterns in AM Radio

When World War II ended in 1945 there were fewer than 1,000 AM stations on the air. There was no reason to expect the number to change significantly, but by the end of 1950 there had been an increase of 135 percent to 2,231.

The increase was motivated by the financial success of radio in the early 1940s and facilitated by two changes in FCC criteria for new stations.

First, in the *Sanders* case (1940) the Supreme Court ruled negatively on one of the key factors that had held down the number of new stations in the 1930s—economic injury.

For some years it had been the responsibility of an applicant for a new station to argue that there was enough potential advertising in the community to support its proposed operation along with the existing stations. Until the approach of war brought the nation out of the Depression, it was almost impossible to show an abundance of advertising anywhere.

The Sanders brothers operated a station in East Dubuque, Iowa, and had opposed the application of a new station on the grounds that the current station would suffer when the advertising was divided between it and the newcomer. The FCC disagreed with the Sanders brothers and granted the new application. The case was appealed to the courts. The Supreme Court rejected the Sanders brothers' appeal on the narrow grounds that they had attempted to show only that they would suffer economic injury if the new station were approved—they had not taken the next step of showing that both stations might have so much difficulty in securing advertising that the *public* would suffer from reduced services. In reviewing the background the Court pointed out that the airwaves were the property of the public and the FCC was charged with regulation in the public interest. The economic welfare of the individual station should be of no concern to the commission. But if the addition of a new station could be shown to place all stations in a community in financial jeopardy, the commission was free to inquire whether that potential jeopardy would hurt the public by lessening the service available to it.*

The Court was thus careful to specify that its decision was limited to one particular aspect of economic injury, but the FCC proceeded as though the whole matter had been placed outside its area of responsibility. When a vastly increased number of new applications began coming to the FCC in 1945 and 1946, the commission simply ignored the economic-injury question.

Secondly, the FCC itself decided to provide less protection for existing stations against "electrical interference" (jamming) than it had given in the past. In the 1930s new applicants were expected to demonstrate that their signals would cause very little or no interference with either ground or sky waves of stations already on the air. In the late 1940s they had to demonstrate only that their signals would not interfere with the primary ground-wave coverage of existing stations.

---

* *Federal Communications Commission v. Sanders Brothers Radio Station*, 309 U.S. 470, March 25, 1940.

We will never know all the reasons behind the change in policy (some guessed the FCC felt limiting the efficiency of AM stations was a way of helping FM), but there is no question about the mushrooming of stations in contrast to very slow growth in earlier years.

Growth of AM Stations—1945–1960

```
1945 —   950
1948 — 1,911
1950 — 2,231
1955 — 2,808
1960 — 3,526
```

Changing Finances

1. *Average Station Revenue:* During the war years virtually every radio station made substantial profits. However, as the number of stations grew by 150 percent from 1945 to 1952, total radio revenues increased by only 50 percent.

YEAR	APPROXIMATE NUMBER OF STATIONS	APPROXIMATE RADIO REVENUES ($ MILLION)	APPROXIMATE AVERAGE STATION REVENUES ($ THOUSANDS)
1945	950	310	326
1952	2,375	473	203

A factor that lessened the impact of the decline in average station revenues was that expenses were also being cut sharply. In 1945 the average station was located in the heart of its community's high-rent downtown district. Expensive studios were built for programming by live orchestras and to impress the public and advertisers.

By 1952 many stations had moved their business offices and studios into their transmitter buildings on the outskirts of town and were using records extensively. The number of employees at each station was drastically cut. The decreased average revenues still permitted profits for more stations than one would expect by looking only at the revenue figures.

2. *Network Billings:* Offsetting the apparent health of individual radio stations was an obvious decline in network business. Table 4.1 shows comparative figures for the different categories of radio billing at five-year intervals. Television total billings are also given to show the contrast in trends.

Table 4.1
Comparison of Network, National Spot, and Local Radio Billings,
1945–1960: All dollar figures in millions; %'s in parentheses.

	1945		1950		1955		1960	
	($)	(%)	($)	(%)	($)	(%)	($)	(%)
Network*	134	(43.2)	131	(28.8)	64	(14.0)	35	(5.6)
National Spot	77	(24.8)	119	(26.2)	120	(26.3)	202	(32.4)
Local	100	(32.2)	203	(44.7)	272	(59.6)	385	(61.8)
Radio Totals	310		454		456		622	
Television Totals	—		90		681		1,147	

* Broadcast billings and business are traditionally divided into these three categories: "local" refers to the local business interests buying time through the local salesperson; "network" refers to the national advertiser buying time through the network salesperson; "national spot" (also called "national nonnetwork") refers to the national advertiser buying time on the local station without involving the network either as salesperson or program distributor.

Source: *Broadcasting Yearbook*, 1975.

The radio figures are put on a chart in Fig. 4.1.

The failure of network radio billings to grow in the first postwar years cannot be attributed primarily to television. (By 1948 total television network billings were only $2.5 million.) Rather, it was a reflection of the fact that network radio revenues had been artificially inflated by wartime circum-

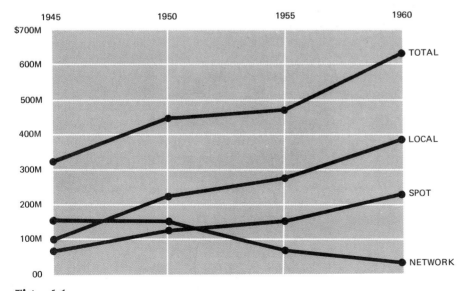

Fig. 4.1

stances. As soon as newspapers could expand to handle all the national print advertising demands and as soon as materials were available for plant expansion, the extra dollars that had been forced into radio went back to the purposes for which they would have earlier been spent.

In the late 1940s, sponsorship was still the most prevalent form of advertising. As sponsors withdrew funds from the networks, the network schedules became less attractive. People were thus encouraged to spend more time listening to independent stations, which were beginning to specialize in popular recorded music. The networks themselves were not in a position to invest heavily in radio programming since they were using radio income to support their entry into television. This combination of factors hastened the decline in network-radio listenership until the advent of network television made the trend irreversible.

That the trend away from network dominance in radio was to continue is illustrated by comparative figures for station revenues from different sources in 1945 and 1975 (see Table 4.2).

Table 4.2
Comparison of Station Revenues from Different Sources

	1945	1979
Network	25%	0.7%
National Spot	33	20.9
Local	42	78.2

Impact of Changing Financial Pattern

The first five postwar years (1945–1950) were a period of great optimism as reflected by the increasing numbers of stations. The slight declines in network revenues failed to register importantly since they were always published a year or more after the fact and it was thought that the trend would be reversed. But from 1950 to 1955 radio was pervaded by a strong pessimism. The chief reason was the sharp drop in finances of the networks, which had been considered as much the heart of radio as they were later to be the heart of television. Many people equated the networks with the whole industry. They assumed that if networks were in trouble, then all of radio must be. The decrease in average station revenues was also noted, but insufficient attention was paid to decreased costs. The increase in local revenues was not dramatic because it amounted to small gains in each community and lacked the impact of the large network decreases.

By 1955 it became clear that the increase in local revenues would continue. During the war years many small companies had been unable to advertise on radio because prices were high and the national advertisers dominated the best spots. As the network business declined and as many new local stations came on the air with low time charges, those retailers who had thought radio was out of reach now found they were welcome and could afford the prices. Some of the new local business came from retailers in small communities that were getting their own stations for the first time. In the late 1950s there was a renewed confidence in radio that led to the strong surge of the 1960s.

Changing Patterns in FM Radio

In the immediate postwar months the optimism about radio extended to FM. Applications for new stations poured into the FCC. The number of commercial FM stations grew very rapidly in the late 1940s but declined in the early 1950s.

Year	Number of FM Stations
1945	50
1946	100
1947	596
1948	698
1949	743
1950	676
1951	650
1952	626
1953	561

By 1952 television had moved to center stage and many observers had written off FM as an idea whose time was still several years in the future. By the end of 1959 the number of FM stations was still only 664.

How did it happen? In retrospect, it resembles a "comedy of errors" in which most of those involved either did the wrong thing or failed to do anything when vigorous action was indicated. Those who would be hurt by the development of FM were able to retard its growth by simply sitting still.

Participants in the FM Story   Movement of the FM assignments upstairs on the spectrum was probably justified as a matter of long-range planning. But as Major Armstrong and others had feared, it proved disastrous in the short run.

The FCC   Those who had become faithful FM listeners during the war found their sets had become obsolete and were often too discouraged to buy new receivers. Satisfied FM listeners would have been the best advocates for the new medium but instead were alienated.

Set manufacturers   Even if the earlier set owners had wanted to replace their receivers, they would have found it difficult to do so. Assembly lines were busy catching up with the demand that had accumulated during the war for radios. The greatest demand was for AM sets. Since there was little call for FM, production never reached the large numbers that would have brought the prices down.

The AM operators   A disproportionate number of the first FM stations were licensed to the
of FM   more successful AM stations that wanted a hedge against the future. Others who wanted to enter broadcasting for the first time applied for AM rather than FM because standard radio was a proven medium and offered more promise of quick returns.

This left FM largely in the hands of those who would lose the most if it were successful in replacing AM. The most profitable AM stations were on the better frequencies near the lower end of the dial and had power authorizations of from 5,000 to 50,000 watts. But there were to be no favored positions on the FM dial and each station was to be authorized enough power to reach the horizon. The only advantage AM operators would have in FM would be their experience and contacts. There is no evidence that AM operators of FM stations tried to sabotage the new medium, but it would appear they could have done more to make it successful.

The American   The AFM ruled that a musician being heard live on both AM and FM must
Federation of   receive double pay. This effectively ruled out putting the most popular AM
Musicians (AFM)   programs on FM, and the economics of the new medium would not permit hiring live musicians for the extremely small audience then available. Since recorded music at that time did not have high fidelity, it meant there were no programs on the air that could exploit the high-fidelity capacity of FM. The only reason to buy FM was to hear AM program quality without interference. Many stations did go to a classical-musical schedule in the hopes that it would attract audiences but there were too few fans among the potential listeners to make the effort worthwhile.

After three years the AFM decided FM did not pose a serious threat to musicians and the rules were changed to permit duplication of AM programs. At that point station salespeople were asked by their managements if they could sell FM as a separate medium. Since there had been few sales in the past at 10 percent of the AM rates, the salespeople recommended that FM simply duplicate the AM schedule and that the FM listeners be given to advertisers as a bonus. Until the mid-1960s there were only feeble attempts at offering popular program services on FM aside from duplicated AM programs.

The American people The most disappointing factor in the initial failure of FM was the lack of interest most people had in hearing programs with greater fidelity. Even when records were available that carried the full range of sounds, few cared enough to purchase sets. So long as they could hear radio reasonably clearly and without too much interference they were satisfied. One sees the same effect in the lack of attention to audio in television programs and the lack of high-fidelity speakers in the sets. In the mid-1950s the growth and popularity of television sealed the temporary demise of FM.

Whether any one of the various factors was more significant than the rest is unimportant at this late date. FM, which had started with such promise, languished until the mid-1960s when a combination of circumstances gave it the impetus it needed.

Changing Program Patterns

The increase in AM radio stations in the late 1940s saw no comparable increase in the number of network affiliates. There was some shifting among networks in individual markets as ABC and Mutual signed contracts with more powerful stations than those with which they had been affiliated. But each new station on the air normally meant one more local programmer independent of any network.

The general pattern was for nonnetwork stations to turn to recorded music. They acquired large record libraries that were necessary because there was a general feeling one should not repeat songs too frequently. At first they emulated traditional radio schedules by trying to provide something for everyone. Different parts of the day were devoted to different types of music. They soon found, however, that some types appealed more than others and started specializing. Among the most successful from the beginning was the country-and-western (C&W) category, which approached folk music status.

Format Radio By the early 1950s some stations had made significant moves toward the current "format" or demographic radio in which a single segment of the audience is selected and all programming is designed for it. Rather than seeking to move from one audience to another throughout the day, there was an emphasis on those who would be attracted by a single type of service. Obviously, an all-C&W schedule could work on only a limited number of stations. The next step was the "Top-40" format in which the most popular tunes were chosen either by consulting the trade press or talking with record stores or checking fan mail requesting favorite numbers. The most popular forty tunes would be presented by the disk jockey (DJ) interspersed with comment, commercials, and news summaries. When they had all been played, it would start all over again. Thus the same tunes might be played ten or twelve times during a day.

The Top-40 stations were anathema to the more traditional broadcasters (especially those at the networks) who thought that program materials should rarely be repeated and that the audience of every station was entitled to a well-rounded service. The networks even repeated some series episodes during the summer, almost as a "throwaway" that was expected to fill time but not get much audience. People indicated their disagreement with this traditional philosophy by turning on their radios in increasing numbers to format stations—especially a growing number of younger people who controlled the expenditure of many dollars and were thus attractive to advertisers.

Changing Patterns in Listening

With the growing popularity of television in the early and mid-1950s, a new pattern of radio listening emerged. No longer did people gather in the living

Drawn for BROADCASTING by Sid Hix

"Don't forget our thousands of car radio listeners who never leave the room when the commercial comes on!"

Reprinted, with permission, from Broadcasting

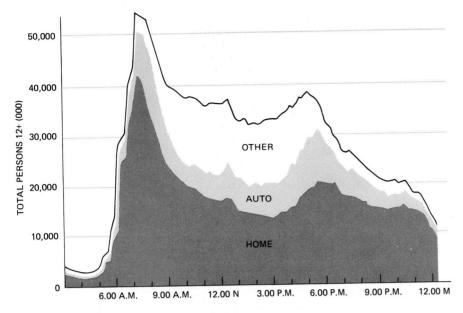

Fig. 4.2

The RADAR chart shows the growing importance of radio listening outside the home. Especially significant during the morning and afternoon drive-time periods are the auto listeners who as part of the working population constitute an important target audience for many advertisers.

Used by permission of Statistical Research, Inc.

room to hear their favorite radio program—they gathered for television. But, while television was dominating the living room, the radio receiver had become smaller and less expensive and was available in the other rooms of the home and wherever people went. The transistor radio was in its early stages of development and for the first time there was a truly portable radio small enough to be carried easily and requiring so little power that flashlight batteries might be used. While some members of the family were viewing television in the living room, the rest were elsewhere, frequently listening to radio. (See Fig. 4.2.)

At the same time there was development of better techniques for measuring radio audiences. No longer were surveys focused only on the living room. There was an increase in the use of diaries and personal interviews that reported listening habits in other places and throughout the day and night. C. E. Hooper experimented with measuring automobile listening by sending interviewers out to busy intersections throughout a city. When a traffic light turned red, the interviewer would walk along the stopped line of cars tabulating the number who were using their radios and the stations to which they were tuned. With each new development in measurement of radio listening, it became apparent there was still a significant audience that advertisers wanted to reach.

The Independent Operation

Midway in the 1950s there was an excellent illustration of the fact that stations might do better as independents than as network affiliates. It was also the forerunner of a new format that is still common today. In the summer of 1956 Westinghouse Broadcasting Company (WBC then—Group W today), a wholly-owned subsidiary of the Westinghouse Company that had started KDKA in 1920, "disaffiliated" four of its stations from NBC. Later in the year it withdrew a station from ABC.

The independents of ten years earlier had been stations that could not acquire network affiliations. The WBC move was unique in that several strong and well-established stations were deliberately choosing to go their own nonnetwork ways. The following year Donald McGannon, President of WBC, reviewed what had happened and looked at the prospects. At the end of the first six months the WBC independents were billing 30 percent more than for the same period a year earlier when they were network affiliates. Because networks compensated the stations at such a low rate, McGannon estimated the prospects for profits were up by about 50 percent. This was an eyeopener to the traditional licensees who had thought they were fated to rise or fall with the networks. Many looked at the facts very carefully and the trend away from networks was accelerated.

WBC researchers had come to a revolutionary conclusion, "people don't tune to radio programs—they tune to stations." This represented an important change from the days when the broadcaster went over each program in the schedule, compared it with the competition, and tried to win each time slot individually. WBC said the more important fact was to establish a "character" for the station that would attract people whenever they wanted to listen to the radio. Frequent tuning from program to program had become a television phenomenon only. Establishing "character" was another way of saying the station should choose a format. McGannon also reported that the WBC experience proved advertisers were less interested in purchasing commercial time within specific programs than they were in "saturation buying" throughout the day in order to reach the largest possible audience.

There were three program elements to which he attributed the WBC success. First was a very aggressive local news policy in which the regular news staff of each station was doubled. "Stringers" (who reported news from a community and were paid by the story rather than being carried on the regular payroll) were added throughout the listening areas. Extensive use was made of new devices like the "beeper phone" (which made possible incorporating telephone reports from stringers into newcasts) and tape recorders that could be easily carried around.

News was repeated frequently, but there was a constant rewrite so the listener who heard a news item at ten o'clock and again an hour later would get different perspectives on it. WBC also built a Washington news bureau that concentrated on national news as it related to the communities in which its stations were located.

Secondly, the stations invested large amounts of money to hire strong personalities to host the music programs that were the backbone of the schedule. WBC was adamant that its stations should be more than a series of "jukeboxes" in which records were simply played without any station "character." As each host attracted a following, the stations benefited from the increased ratings and the resulting higher rate cards.

Thirdly, every attempt was made to put a strong emphasis on public service to the local community, even in the sponsored material. Where possible, programs were geared to local needs. The weather reports on Mondays would comment on whether it would be a good washday. Weekend reports related the forecasts to sporting events and picnics. Economic news was interpreted in terms of the impact on the individual pocketbook when the consumer went to the supermarket.

Twenty-five years later the WBC move seemed too simple for much attention, but in 1956 it was a pioneering effort. In retrospect, the WBC stations were breaking ground in the "middle of the road" (MOR) format that is one of the most prevalent modern types.

By 1960 radio stations were using more and more music, but there was not the degree of specialization that was to come later. There was a general concern among broadcasters tht the FCC would frown upon a station that programmed the same all day long.

"Payola"

As stations turned more and more to the Top-40 format, there was the rise of a new phenomenon called "payola," the payment of unreported remuneration to DJs for including certain records in programs. Many stations were using recorded music 60–70 percent of the time. The number of record companies increased from half a dozen in 1945 to somewhere between 1,500 and 2,000 fifteen years later. Some of them were marginal concerns that might last only a few weeks or months, but when any went out of business, others were ready to take their places. There were up to 250 new single releases each week, exclusive of albums.

As one might have expected, the records that were played the most on radio stations were the ones that sold best in the stores. Since record companies made money by selling records, they were willing to do whatever was necessary to get their products broadcast as frequently as possible.

In 1959 *Broadcasting* did a special report on the many rumors and few facts that were being widely discussed.* The average DJ of a strong music station would get as many as 150 new releases in the mail each week and would be visited by representatives of record companies and distributors who wanted their releases included in the programming. It was rumored that some DJs were offered as an incentive "a piece of the action" whereby they might get a penny for every record sold in their markets after it was used on the air. Some were said to have received new roofs on their homes or new landscaping. From DJ conventions came one of the idioms of the day—"Booze, Broads, and Bribes"—describing the entertainment lavished on them by the record companies.

The one indisputable fact was that if a DJ were prominent enough and wanted to make extra money, there was ample opportunity. One man familiar with the trade thought it quite possible for top DJs in a major market to add from $50,000 to $150,000 to their annual salary. As noted in Chapter 7, a law was passed making "payola" a crime.

Responsible broadcasters were perturbed by the possibility they were being "used" by the record companies. They had no objections to advertising records but wanted the pay to go into the station's bank account rather than the DJ's pocket. More important, they realized that payola constituted a violation of Section 317 of the Communications Act which requires an announcement to be made when program materials are broadcast because someone pays to have them aired.

In the early 1950s most DJ's had been permitted to choose their own tunes, but then the stations formed juries or committees that would evaluate the sales reports, the mail, and other polls and make the choices of records for programs. Some sort of similar procedure is now standard with many stations.

4.2 1960–1970 STEADY GROWTH OF FM

The 1960s were characterized by continued growth of format programming. Financially, radio did very well.

1. Network radio failed to make a comeback. It showed only slight growth from $35 million in 1960 to $51 million in 1970.

2. National spot billings increased from $204 million to $349 million.

3. Local advertising showed a ten-year increase from $385 million to over $800 million.

---

* *Broadcasting*, August 31, 1959, p. 34.

The medium as a whole had grown to become an over a billion-dollar-a-year business. The increases were attributable to a number of factors. There was the increased attractiveness of format radio. Transistor radios were improved to make it easier to listen anywhere. Ratings companies improved the measurement of radio audiences so that advertisers were convinced they could communicate by radio to people beyond the reach of television.

Formats

In the early 1960s there was continued experimentation with formats, which were becoming more specialized year by year. Stations came to the conclusion that the FCC would not require each of them to offer a variety of services. The attempt of a station to reach its own particular segment of the audience was evident during nearly all hours of the broadcast day—although marginal hours were occasionally still used to insert a little variety into the schedule. Perhaps the most important break with tradition came with the all-talk stations that threw away their music libraries except for the very late night hours.

Emergence of FM

The most dramatic story within the industry itself was the breakthrough of FM in the 1960s. As the decade started, FM was receiving little attention. By 1970 there was a rush for FM licenses and optimism was the order of the day. Consider the following growth figures for AM and FM stations over a thirty-five-year period:

Commercial Radio
Number of Stations at Year's End

	AM	FM
1945	950	50
1950	2,231	676
1955	2,808	536
1960	3,526	785
1965	4,042	1,323
1970	4,319	2,184
1975	4,459	2,752
1980	4,572	3,265

It is obvious that important changes were taking place. From 1960 to 1965 AM stations continued to grow at a rapid pace, but for the next five years the gain was much slower. At the same time, growth of FM had increased remarkably. The changes can be traced in part to three actions of the FCC.

FM Stereo

In 1961 the FCC approved stereophonic broadcasting on FM. This action stimulated receiver sales to those who wanted finer quality in listening.

AM Freeze

In 1962 there was a partial freeze on new AM stations. The FCC had become concerned that AM was reaching the saturation point and that interference among stations would be intolerable. After 1962 the commission proposed stricter technical standards for new AM stations so it became easier to request and to receive FM authorizations. This proposal did not have a dramatic effect at the moment but provided a clue as to what was to come. In 1968 the FCC realized its 1962 partial freeze on AM stations had not sufficiently slowed their growth. A more severe freeze was imposed with indications that it would not be relaxed or lifted in the near future. People who wanted to enter broadcasting had to apply for FM licenses.

Nonduplication of AM and FM

In 1965 the FCC ruled that when a single licensee had both AM and FM stations (called AM-FM combination) in a city of more than 100,000 population, it might not duplicate the AM schedule on the FM transmitter for more than 50 percent of the time. (At this point about 75 percent of all FM stations on the air were owned by AM operators.) When the nonduplication rule finally took effect in 1967, it meant that owners of combinations either had to provide separate programming for their transmitters or give up the FM.

By the mid-1960s it had become apparent to all that the most successful stations were those with format programming. Owners of joint facilities adopted separate formats for their FM outlets and, to their surprise, began to get audiences. The transistor trend had reached the point where many of the smaller portable receivers could pick up FM. The development of high-fidelity records meant that FM was delivering a signal superior to the AM transmission. Finally, the FM operators discarded the notion that their stations were appropriate only for classical music and began to experiment with other kinds. It is probable that the appearance of rock music on FM stations did much to encourage its general acceptability.

The growth of FM and the change in broadcaster attitudes toward it are reflected in the headlines of three *Broadcasting* special reports:

"FM Sniffs Sweet Smell of Success"   (July 31, 1967, p. 55)
"FM, at Long Last, Is Making Its Move"   (February 23, 1970, p. 47)
"The Rites of Passage Are All Over for FM Radio:
  It's Out On Its Own"   (September 24, 1973, p. 31)

4.3 1970–1980 DOMINANCE OF FORMAT PROGRAMMING

Radio today occupies a unique role in our society. While our attention at one level is focused on television, we lean more heavily on sound during those hours not reserved for full-attention entertainment with video. Although the traditional radio stations sought to be "all things to all people," today's radio comes closer to meeting the basic needs for companionship so prevalent in an impersonal and computerized world. Although it is the television newscasts that people list as a major source of news, it is radio's constant repetition of news capsules that makes people feel they know what is going on in a community. While the individual radio station specializes to a high degree, the medium offers so much diversity through its collective stations that most people in our society find what they seek to make listening pleasant.

The radio receiver has become truly ubiquitous. It may be found in every room of the home, in cars, on bicycles, on the sidewalk, in places of work and business, on picnics and outings, at vacation spots, and wherever and whenever else one wants radio's many sounds. It is a boon to the teenager and the elderly and those in between. It is the twentieth-century "town crier" with local news and the source of whatever type of music meets an individual's needs.

The FM Breakthrough

With each succeeding year of the 1970s the differences between AM and FM listenership have diminished. FM penetration (percentage of sets able to receive it) has steadily increased each year both in and out of the home. In 1976 studies showed that in six years the FM share of the radio audience had doubled from 20 to 40 percent in the top ten markets. By 1980 the FM audience had edged over 50 percent and the only significant factor that seems to keep FM from competing with AM on even grounds for advertising dollars is the lower percentage of car radios that can receive the signals. Since radio's "prime time" is morning-and-afternoon "drive time" and many advertisers want to communicate with auto commuters during those hours, FM has a built-in disadvantage that will disappear only when car manufacturers make FM standard equipment. There have been efforts to persuade Congress that car radios should be required to have an FM capacity. Until such a legislative move occurs or demands by car buyers increase the FM automobile penetration, FM will operate under a handicap.

In the meantime, advertising agencies have started buying FM audiences that are large enough to be measured by the rating services. The long-standing refusal to even consider FM has disappeared. There are fewer FM stations in the red each year, and in the 1980s FM stations may become more desirable and expensive to purchase than their AM cousins.

Dominant Formats

Radio today is format broadcasting in which each station chooses a particular segment of the population as its target audience and seeks to reach only that segment throughout the entire schedule. Although they may use different descriptive titles for their formats, most commercial station schedules fit into the following categories:

Classification of Radio Formats

1. Middle-of-the-Road (MOR)
2. Talk
3. All-News
4. Music Specialization
   a. Classical and Semiclassical
   b. "Easy Listening" or "Beautiful Music"
   c. Country-and-Western (C&W)
   d. "Oldies"
   e. Top-40 or Contemporary
   f. Rock
5. Ethnic
   a. Black, Puerto Rican, Mexican-American, etc.
   b. Foreign Language
6. Religious

Middle of the Road   The MOR station comes closest to the traditional programming of "something for everyone" since it has targeted for itself the largest audience segment and provides for it a variety of material. It concentrates on adults from twenty to fifty years of age in the center of the socioeconomic and educational scales. More stations claim it than any other format.

The MOR station is characterized during drive time by a personable host who is heard not only on radio, but also appears at various community functions to become better known. The program includes a lot of information and advertising and a little music. There are frequent newscasts with promises to interrupt anything else for important bulletins. There are frequent weather reports and lists of closed schools in inclement weather. If stations in the larger cities can afford it, there are helicopters giving reports on traffic.

Throughout the rest of the day there are interview programs, telephone dialogues, coverage of sports, and music that falls near the center of the spectrum and will likely be popular with the target audience.

Drawn for BROADCASTING by Jack Stelling, WMMS Bath, Me.

"And now it's Candlelight and Wine, *a quarter-hour of sophisticated music for dining."*

Reprinted, with permission, from Broadcasting

Talk   Few in the 1950s would have suspected how popular talk radio would become. It is an element in the MOR formats and some stations program nothing but talk all day long. The most common talk programs involve telephone dialogues between hosts and listeners on a "topic of the day" that may or may not be accompanied by a studio panel discussion. Topics cover the whole range of subjects in which people are interested, including politics, religion, psychology, sports, and sex. It would appear that the talk programs have tapped a deep-seated need of people as the daytime serials did in the 1930s. They provide companionship for the lonely plus an opportunity to hear what others are thinking about various subjects. There is a circulation of ideas and information that can be significant. For many, listening to the radio telephone dialogues has become a major contact with the world.

News   Related to talk radio is the all-news station that carries news, features, and commentary all day. No news station expects listeners to tune in for long periods of time. The aim is to establish a reputation for being the place to get the latest headlines at all hours in the hope that listeners will tune in for an update before turning to other formats with which they may stay for longer periods. To date, all-news stations have been successful only in the largest markets.

Music Specializations

The all-music stations are alike in two respects: each seeks to attract a small segment of the audience with its type of music and each carries its specialization all day long. The "sound" of the station is much the same whenever one tunes in. These stations appeal to advertisers because they tend to attract a much more homogeneous audience than the MOR radio station or the television stations. While there will be exceptions, the advertiser knows that the audience for various music formats will be reasonably consistent:

1. Rock stations are most popular among teenagers and younger adults.
2. Top-40 and Contemporary stations appeal to young adults—twenty to thirty years of age.
3. "Oldies" (popular tunes of fifteen to twenty years earlier) will draw adults from thirty to forty-five.
4. Country-and-Western has a broader appeal that makes it difficult to characterize listeners by age.
5. "Easy Listening" or "Beautiful Music" will appeal primarily to those over fifty years of age.
6. Classical music appeals to those who have come to appreciate it through exposure. Their age will tend to be higher than the "Oldies" audience, but the more important characteristic is the higher socioeconomic group attracted.

Ethnic

There have been radio stations for blacks since the late 1940s, but the "sound" has changed over the years as broadcasters and advertisers have realized black audiences are neither monolithic nor unsophisticated in their listening tastes. With the civil rights movement of the 1960s, black stations focused more on the problems of blacks and news of their communities. At the same time, advertisers began to realize that ethnic groups represent important purchasing power.

Religious

Owners of religious stations tend to be from the conservative fundamentalist Protestant sects. Most programming is evangelical, seeking to make converts and to confirm the faith of adherents. Much of the programming is sponsored to the extent that other religious groups buy time, prepare programs, and make pleas for money to help in their work.

Format Radio and Advertisers

That format radio stations are valuable to advertisers is indicated by the increasing amounts of dollars spent in the medium each year. Through radio the advertising agencies can pinpoint target audiences, pay for less "waste circulation," and achieve a lower cost per thousand of specific potential customers. A major deterrent to even greater expenditures by national advertisers is the difficulty of buying radio compared with television. There are up to twenty station representatives through whom an agency can buy time on most of the powerful television stations in the country and achieve coverage of most of the potential viewers. Each contract may involve large amounts of money and sponsors are guaranteed a "proof of performance" affidavit from each station to indicate the advertising was actually aired.

While an agency can deal with fewer than 500 stations and still feel it has considered most of the important television coverage in the nation, it must make its selections of radio stations from some 8,000 commercial operations. Even if it rules out half of them as being marginal, there are still 4,000 from which to choose. The number of station representatives is much larger than in television and it is necessary to write far more contracts to spend as much money as is allocated to television. Since agencies receive their revenues primarily from retaining 15 percent of their media expenditures, it is natural they should want to make larger commitments to a few television buys as compared with almost innumerable smaller radio contracts required to make the same amount.

Radio Networks

The traditional radio networks that formed the backbone of American broadcasting in 1945 had lost their dominance by 1960. After experimentation by several of them in the 1950s and 1960s, the primary network service now is in the area of news, information, and commentaries. A move by ABC illustrates the trend.

In 1968 ABC Radio, after receiving an FCC waiver, changed its organization to provide services to 1,750 stations in four distinct networks serving four kinds of stations. In 1975 ABC described its four networks as follows:

1. *American Contemporary Network:* Contemporary-formatted news, sports, and features are fed to stations that program the latest sounds to appeal to tastes of young adults and teens. The network's listeners generally use radio as their primary medium.

2. *American Informational Network:* News, sports, and features are fed to affiliated stations that program news, information, talk, and adult

music. Adult listeners use the medium as their primary source of news and information.

3. *American Entertainment Network:* Affiliated stations are fed news, sports, and features that are consistent with their MOR, "good-music," and country-music formats. The network's listeners generally use the medium as a primary source of entertainment and diversion.

4. *American FM Network:* A news service is sent to affiliates with emphasis on stereo music and programming for the tastes of young adults and teens.

As shown in Fig. 4.3, the typical hour is split so that there are separate newscasts of four to five minutes in duration for each of the four networks. The rest of the time is used to send out to the stations sports, features,

ABC FOUR NETWORK SERVICES DAILY FEED PATTERN

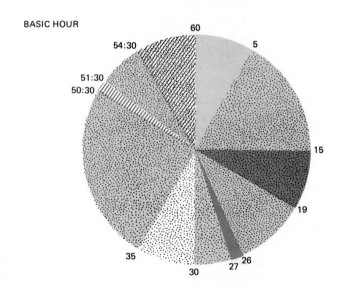

Fig. 4.3
Division of ABC's basic hour among its four radio network services.
Courtesy: ABC

TIME USED FOR (CLOSED CIRCUIT) SPORTS, FEATURES, COMMENTARIES, AND NEWS CALLS

CONTEMPORARY RADIO NEWS

ENTERTAINMENT RADIO NEWS

INFORMATION RADIO NEWS

CONTEMPORARY NEWS IN BRIEF

ENTERTAINMENT NEWS IN BRIEF

commentaries, and other material that can be taped and used at the station's discretion. A major difference between the ABC network services and the traditional network is that while some of the major stations are compensated for carrying the news and commercials, the majority pay the network.

For several years in the mid-1970s NBC experimented with a News and Information Service (NIS) that made it possible for stations in small markets to adopt an all-news format. As with the ABC services, affiliates generally paid the network rather than receive compensation. NIS was dropped in 1977 when the number of affiliates failed to meet expectations. MBS also departed from traditional practice by offering a special black network with news and other programming designed for black audiences.

By the end of the 1970s there was a resurgence of interest and activity in radio networks spurred by the availability and economy of satellite distribution, the success of format (demographic) radio, and the desire of advertisers to spend more money in radio if they could do so easily. ABC was considering adding a fifth to its four networks which were over a decade old. NBC was starting a new network, "The Source," a service designed for stations concentrating on album-oriented rock (AOR). RKO, an important group owner, started its own network primarily for the eighteen- to forty-nine-year olds. The National Black Network and the Sheridan Broadcasting Network were aimed at ethnic audiences. CBS Radio had not started a demographic emphasis but was continuing its concentration on news, comment, and sports with million-dollar contracts for major attractions like NFL football. Mutual was considering addition of a new service. AP Radio and UPI Audio were servicing nearly two thousand stations between them with news and information.

The big factor was the abundance of satellite facilities that made possible distribution of high-fidelity programming at increasingly reasonable costs. Perhaps the forerunner in satellite development was National Public Radio (NPR), discussed in Chapter 13, which had plans for four satellite channels adding more choice and diversity to individual stations.

There seems little reason to expect that radio networks will ever again be as dominant as they were in the mid-1940s, but they have passed beyond the disappointing 1960s when most thought these networks were relics of the past.

Syndicated Radio Scheduling

For stations with specialized-music formats there have for years been syndication companies providing tapes appropriate to all tastes, from Contemporary to Country-and-Western to "Beautiful Music." This situation eliminates the need for maintaining a music library and personnel to choose the selections each day. Further, the choice of tunes is far more sophisticated, with subtle changes possible according to the hour of the day and activities of listeners.

Currently, in the early 1980s, there has been an "explosion" in the radio syndication business as the increased popularity of FM has forced AM stations to seek more quality in talk shows and other nonmusic programming. The number of syndicators has proliferated and the most successful ones are adding new offerings to the formats that gave them their initial success. Services available range from short commentaries to special theme programs that will fill a weekend.

Prices to the stations range from $600 to over $6,000 per month, depending on the size of the markets. Because so many stations use the tapes of a syndicator, it is possible for the syndicator to pay more attention to technical quality and to the careful selection of music and other material. In effect, the job of the station's radio announcer is reduced to reading a few commercials (most commercials will be on tape) and the brief news summaries each hour.

Regulation of Formats

The dominance of specialized-format radio stations has led to two regulatory problems that are unique to radio.

Section 326 of the Communications Act forbids the FCC to interfere in any way with freedom of speech by broadcasters. Both commissioners and broadcasters have interpreted this to mean that a station may control its own programming without government supervision unless there is some serious infringement upon the public interest. The commission felt its program responsibility was at an end once it had selected the best of the applicants as the licensee of a facility. It was then up to that individual to interpret the public interest and to program to meet the needs and interests of the community.

In spite of this, the commission was forced by the courts to consider programming in sales of format stations that provided a unique service to their communities. In 1968 the only classical-music station in Atlanta, Georgia, applied for permission to sell its facilities and transfer its license to a new operator who announced his intention to change the format. The FCC approved the transfer but a citizens' group protested to a court of appeals which ordered the FCC to further consider the case. Eventually there was a settlement that did not require any further FCC action, but the precedent was established that if a format is unique in a community, the FCC must be more concerned with the transfer than if a station is one of a number providing essentially similar services.

Shortly thereafter the commission approved without a hearing the transfer of WEFM in Chicago to a company that proposed to do away with the classical format that had been on the station since 1940. Again, a citizens' group appealed to the court even though there were two other classical stations in Chicago. The court ruled that the FCC had erred in approving the transfer without a hearing. Since the commission was ordered to hold a hearing on the transfer, the implication was that a transfer cannot be automatic when citizens object to the loss of a format in a community.

The commission was greatly concerned about the broad implications of the court's order and held an inquiry to determine whether it should be involved in consideration of program services at the time of station transfer. In 1976 the FCC issued a policy statement indicating that regulation of entertainment formats would not be compatible with its statutory authority to regulate broadcasting in the free enterprise system. As anticipated, the policy statement was taken to a court of appeals which rejected the commission's view of the law and ordered that the court's interpretation in the WEFM case be implemented. In the Spring of 1981 the Supreme Court reversed the court of appeals, thus permitting the FCC to implement its policy of noninterference with licensee programming judgment, even at the time of station transfer and even if the public had come to depend on a certain format and protested vigorously. This decision had several important implications.

First, it served as a brake on the expansion of the functionalist free speech point of view that the Supreme Court had consistently upheld with regard to ensuring the public's right to hear all sides of controversial issues. The court of appeals decision would have extended that concept to giving the public a right to hear a variety of program formats. The Supreme Court in this case was limiting free speech consideration to discussion of issues. Had it done otherwise, the FCC might have found itself eventually in the untenable position of deciding not only what formats were in the public interest, but also whether a particular "unique" program might be dropped if enough people protested their right to continue hearing it.

Second, the Supreme Court decision was an affirmation of the FCC's supremacy in matters of judgment. As will be noted in Chapter 7, all FCC decisions may be appealed to the courts, but only on the limited grounds that the commission has exceeded its authority or followed improper procedure. Since the commission had not exceeded its authority nor proceeded improperly, the Supreme Court found no basis for reversing its judgment.

Third, the Supreme Court decision was an encouragement to the FCC's desire to deregulate broadcasting as discussed in the following pages. Through the late 1970s the FCC sought to drop specific requirements for radio stations on the ground that "marketplace forces" would better insure broadcasting in the public interest than would regulation. Had the appeals court decision been upheld, the FCC might have had difficulty in maintaining its deregulation posture. The Supreme Court in its affirmation of FCC policy seemed to be giving the green light to the concept of less regulation if that was compatible with the commission's judgment.

Questions About Indecency

In the original Radio and Communication Acts broadcasters were specifically forbidden to air obscene and indecent material. Subsequently, the prohibition was removed from the Communications Act but penalties for airing such material were added to the Criminal Code. Obscenity and indecency were never a serious problem with television or with radio as long as stations were trying to reach large mass audiences. But when radio stations began to specialize in format broadcasting and the competition for audience became more intense, problems arose.

In the early months of 1973 commissioners and broadcast leaders were upset about some of the popular talk programs, which were nicknamed "topless radio" or "sex radio." Although fewer than a hundred stations were involved, it was feared that the trend might grow to the point where all would get a bad name and that regulation might be forced on radio by Congress. In choosing their "topic of the day" many hosts included sex but the majority had handled it in good taste. Some, however, who were seeking the quick gain of sensationalism, not only selected sex topics but made the dialogues highly specific. Women were told to give only their first names and to avoid any possible identification. There were no other restrictions. Some typical topics were "The first time I had sex" and "How I get my husband in the mood." The hosts encouraged highly explicit details.

Irate listeners wrote to the FCC complaining that their children were hearing the programs. Equally important, listeners also wrote their congressional representatives asking what might be done about such programs. The legislators brought pressure on the FCC. The commission did not feel it should get involved, since Section 326 of the Communications Act forbade its entering into program decisions. Furthermore, the FCC had watched the Supreme Court unsuccessfully wrestle with a definition of obscenity.

As the pressure mounted, the FCC was forced to take action. A sample tape was made from some of the most blatant programs around the country and the commissioners took the unprecedented step of gathering to hear the tape. The broadcasters, who in the earlier years had objected to any consideration of schedules by the commission, raised no outcry. Ironically, the only commissioner who refused to listen to the tape was the one whom the broadcasters had criticized the most—Nicholas Johnson, who felt it was a constitutional infringement of licensee freedom to monitor tapes.

The FCC selected the one station that seemed to have been the worst offender, WGLD-FM in Oak Park, Illinois, a suburb of Chicago, and fined it $2,000 for broadcasting obscene and indecent material. At the same time, it almost begged the station to refuse to pay the fine and to pursue a court case that would clarify the responsibility of the FCC for such regulatory action. WGLD-FM had already dropped the offending dialogue programs since they were not necessary to the financial success of the station. The station weighed the alternatives of paying the $2,000 fine or investing many times that amount in paying lawyers for a court test. The practical solution was to pay the fine. When an Illinois citizens' group appealed, the court of appeals upheld the FCC fine.

In the meantime, the NAB, at its 1973 convention, brought all its persuasive powers to bear on operators who had used the dialogue format to get into sex radio. As a result of the efforts of the NAB, an exhortatory speech by the FCC Chairman, and the fine by the FCC, sex radio disappeared from the American scene.

In 1974 the commission received a letter from a listener in New York City objecting to an afternoon program on WBAI-FM discussing the use of language. As part of the program, the host played a record made by comedian George Carlin, "The Seven Dirty Words You Never Say on Television." The words were the familiar "four-letter" words or variations thereof. The program did not meet the definition of "obscene," which hinges on appeal to a prurient interest or stimulation of sexual impulses. Rather, the FCC found WBAI-FM to be guilty of broadcasting indecent material, which it interpreted to be "patently offensive" references to sexual and excretory activities and organs, without any socially redeeming value. The commission, in effect, was defining "indecency" without using the prurient concept; indecent material was that which was not acceptable in the average American home. In its *WBAI-FM* decision and others the commission emphasized its concern with material aired during the hours when children have the most access to radio and implied that what might be indecent at some hours of the day would be acceptable at other times.

In March 1977 the Court of Appeals in Washington, D.C., overturned the commission action of the grounds that the ruling was too broad and vague and infringed on freedom of speech by broadcasting.

A year later the Supreme Court surprised many students of the First Amendment by upholding the FCC's original decision that the material was "indecent" and might therefore be barred from broadcasting. Especially important in the decision was the court's reasoning that radio was so pervasive and so "uniquely accessible to children" that special applications of the First Amendment were appropriate. Indecency was in this instance classified as a nuisance—something patently offensive to some people who might be listening. At the same time, the Supreme Court was careful to note that its decision was a narrow one—applicable only to the specific instance at hand and that it was not making wide generalizations about all uses of particular words.

The commission, whose composition had changed in the intervening years, immediately sought to reassure broadcasters that it would not go around looking for material that might be called indecent. Subsequently, there was scarcely a ripple at the airing of "Scared Straight," a program showing teenagers visiting a prison in New Jersey and hearing from the convicts what life was like behind bars. The language was far stronger than Carlin's but there were mitigating factors: the purpose to be accomplished was important (redeeming social value); the program was aired late in the evening and it was preceded by warnings to those who might be disturbed. It appears that changes in our society will year by year reduce materially the language that some people may find "patently offensive."

Deregulation of Radio

Radio broadcasters began seeking fewer restrictions as soon as the first modern regulation was imposed under the Radio Act of 1927. The standard argument for regulation was the "scarcity of the frequencies" and the evidence usually cited was the far greater number of newspapers than stations in those early days. By the 1960s there were more radio stations than newspapers. The Supreme Court in the *Red Lion* case* then redefined "scarcity" as the existence of more would-be broadcasters than there were frequencies to accommodate them, thus justifying continued regulation.

In 1977 the Carter administration embarked on a general deregulation policy that included not only broadcasting, but also airlines, railroads, and trucking. In line with that policy the FCC in 1980, following hearings and much public comments, moved to eliminate four of its specific requirements on the grounds that marketplace pressures would be sufficient regulation in light of the large number of operating stations. It proposed dropping:

■ The requirement for "ascertainment," the formal process by which a station satisfies the FCC that it has adequately surveyed the interests and needs of its community and has aired programs to meet the conditions found.

■ The keeping of detailed logs (records of material aired).

■ The limit on the number of commercials in an hour, since very few stations were carrying the maximum eighteen already permitted.

---

* Red Lion Broadcasting Co., Inc., et al. v. Federal Communications Commission et al., 395 U.S. at 390, June 9, 1969.

■ The guidelines on a minimum of nonentertainment programming (news and public affairs), since most stations were exceeding them anyway.

Although there have been negative comments submitted by consumer groups, it appears that radio will have fewer specific regulations in the near future.

Minority Ownership of Stations

As will be noted in the discussions of television in Chapter 5 and Chapter 7, there was great pressure in the early 1970s for more minority employment and more minority-oriented programming in both radio and television. In the latter half of the decade advocates shifted their primary emphasis to more minority ownership of broadcast facilities. Under the Carter administration several new policies were initiated that helped minorities become licensees of both radio and television stations. The following are described in more detail in the part of Chapter 5 concerning television in the 1970s:

■ An FCC policy of granting "tax certificates."

■ An FCC policy of "distress sales."

■ A Small Business Administration (SBA) change in policy to permit loans for the purchase of broadcast properties.

Under these changes in policy the number of minority-owned radio stations doubled in five years to about 150.

Of special significance to radio had been the policy of giving considerable weight to the participation by minorities when awarding licenses. The effectiveness of that policy depended on the availability of new stations and in 1980 the FCC was working on several steps to increase the number of radio outlets:

■ Reducing the width of AM channels from 10 kHz to 9 kHz, thus increasing the number of frequencies on which stations could be assigned.

■ Reducing the protected-coverage areas of clear-channel AM stations (with the most powerful 50,000-watt transmitters) from 1,500 miles to 750 miles; this change permits adding new stations on those frequencies.

■ Changing FM allocation standards to permit more FM stations than had been provided.

As any or all of these proposals are implemented, there may be up to a thousand new radio stations for which minority applicants will be favored. There are also proposals that will be discussed in Chapter 5 to increase the number of television stations.

SUMMARY

It would have amazed broadcasters in the 1950s to think the day might come when the future of radio looked brighter than the future of television. Radio has met unique needs that seem to be beyond the capacity of any other medium. While there is great concern about cable's impact on television in the short range and the assumption that television stations as we know them today may disappear in a few decades, there seems to be no prospect of a decline in radio.

GLOSSARY ITEMS

The following words and phrases used in Chapter 4 are defined in the Glossary:

AM-FM Combination	Participating Advertiser
AM-FM Duplication	Payola
Billings	Penetration
Cost Per Thousand (CPM)	Prime Time
Demographics	Radio Schedule Syndication
Distress Sale	Rating
Drive Time	Satellite Relay
Economic Injury	Sponsorship
Format Radio	Station Representative (Rep)
Independent Station	Syndication
National Spot Business	Tax Certificate
Network	"Topless Radio"
Network Affiliate	Waste Circulation

RADIOBROADCASTING CHRONOLOG 1945–1980

1946	FCC changed criteria for licensing new AM stations.
	1. Stopped consideration of economic injury to existing stations (*Sanders* case of 1940).
	2. Lessened degree of protection against interference with existing stations.
	Numbers of AM and FM stations started dramatic growth.
ca. 1950	Radio networks continued noticeable decline.
	FM optimism faded.

	AM stations were turning to recorded music and format scheduling.
ca. **1955**	"Payola" started to become a problem.
1962	FCC imposed partial freeze on new AM stations.
1965	FCC limited duplication of AM programming on FM.
1968	FCC imposed more severe freeze on new AM stations.
	ABC inaugurated four-network news services.
ca. **1968**	FM was growing rapidly.
ca. **1970**	Growth of radio-syndicated scheduling.
1973	Brief period of "sex radio."
1974	Appeals court ordered FCC to hold hearing on license transfer if demanded by the public.
1975	FCC held WBAI-FM guilty of broadcasting indecent material.
1976	FCC policy statement on format consideration in transfer cases.
1977	Appeals court overturned FCC action on indecency in WBAI-FM case.
1978	Supreme Court upheld FCC on indecency in WBAI-FM case.
	FCC announced policy on tax certificates and distress sales.
	Small Business Administration changed policy to give loans for purchase of stations.
	WEFM sale approved by FCC.
1979	FCC proposed 9-kHz channel width for AM.
	Appeals court reversed FCC policy on format consideration in transfer cases.
1980	FM achieved 50 percent of radio listenership.
	FCC approved AM stereo.
	Supreme Court heard case on FCC policy on format consideration in transfer cases.
	FCC started deregulating radio.
	FCC proposed increase in FM allocations.
	FCC reduced protection of clear-channel stations.

PREVIEW *Until 1948 the growth of television was sporadic and uncertain. The Television Freeze from 1948 to 1952 was, perhaps, the most important single action ever taken by the FCC. It was a period of long-range planning from which emerged television as we know it today. The 1950s were in many respects the "good old days" when television boomed even beyond the expectations of its enthusiasts. Continued economic health brought commercial television to full maturity by 1970 when it had achieved most of its expected stature. While the 1970s brought continued growth, the decade was also marked by important confrontations between television and government, consumer, and minority factions.*

CHAPTER 5

HISTORICAL PERSPECTIVES III
1920–1980 with Emphasis on Television

5.1 1920–1945 EXPERIMENTAL BEGINNINGS AND WARTIME HIATUS

By the early 1920s engineers knew that pictures as well as sound might be conveyed by radio waves. By the mid-1920s they were transmitting video experimentally and had relayed it by cable between New York City and Washington, D.C. The picture was seen on a screen measuring only a few inches on each side and was created by *mechanical* television which involved a physically moving part, a rotating disk with a spiral of holes through which the picture passed. At the end of the 1920s engineers came to the conclusion that mechanical television had too many inherent limitations and shifted their efforts to *electronic* television, which did not contain moving parts. This shift was largely due to the final development in 1928 of the iconoscope tube by Vladimir Zworykin, a Russian émigré.

By 1935 electronic television was being demonstrated to the trade press and other insiders by RCA and other companies. In 1939 RCA presented television publicly at the New York World's Fair. Two years later the FCC authorized television as a broadcast service. During World War II (1941–1945) only six stations were on the air broadcasting limited schedules to fewer than 10,000 sets. For all practical purposes, the story of television broadcasting in America starts after the end of the war in 1945.

5.2 1945–1952 SLOW GROWTH AND THE FREEZE
Color Confusion

Enthusiasm had run high when the FCC authorized commercial television broadcasting in 1941. At the end of the war there was every reason to expect a mushrooming growth, especially since there were more than 150 applications for new stations in the hands of the commission. Then confusion set in, followed by a period of general pessimism.

When the FCC decided in 1941 that television was ready for public reception, it considered the question of whether the system should be monochrome (black and white) or color. It was the general consensus that color was not sufficiently developed at that time and the commission authorized only monochrome TV on 6-mHz channels.

During the war, engineers for CBS Labs (a division of CBS) went ahead with color experimentation and reached the point where they could transmit a picture of far better quality than that which had been rejected in 1941. In 1946 CBS asked the FCC to replace the monochrome system with its new color system that had three important drawbacks:

1. It was mechanical.

2. It was incompatible with the monochrome system. The color receiver could not pick up the black-and-white signals and the monochrome receiver could not pick up the color transmission even in black and white.

3. Each channel required three times as much spectrum space (eighteen mHz) as did monochrome.

When CBS asked that its color television supplant monochrome, there was great confusion. Changing to color at that time would have required moving all television to another portion of the spectrum and every receiver and transmitter already built would become obsolete. Many CBS radio affiliates had faith in their network's proposal and delayed filing applications for existing television channels. Others also found the CBS arguments persuasive. In the first few months of 1946 nearly half of the pending applications for new television stations were withdrawn. In 1947 the commission refused to grant CBS's request to change the system. Although there was no longer confusion stemming from the CBS color petition, few expected TV to become a mass medium that could compete with radio. Television receivers were far more expensive than radio sets. There was no network service, so any station going on the air had to plan to do practically all its own programming. The equipment was still primitive and difficult to operate. Cartoons of the time featured the oppressive heat in the studios from the powerful lighting required for production.

The Freeze

As noted in Chapter 2, spectrum space had been allocated for eighteen television channels at first and then was cut back to twelve. By the summer of 1948 the commission had authorized 124 stations of which about 50 were already on the air. Even at that early stage, it became obvious that the twelve VHF channels were too few to support a national system of television with adequate service to the public.

The situation resembled that of a motorist driving in the country who realizes he or she is on the wrong road. Rather than continuing on to the end, the motorist stops, gets out a road map, asks questions, and decides what to do next. The FCC, when it realized the twelve channels were a "wrong road," simply stopped processing new applications and announced a "Freeze" during which it would try to map out the long-range future. Stations already approved, but not yet built, were permitted to go ahead with construction of the 124 Pre-Freeze authorizations. Eventually 108 appeared on the air. Applications that had not been approved were held in abeyance.

When it announced the Freeze in September 1948, the FCC thought it would need about six months in which to allocate more channels for television. A few months after the Freeze began, the commission decided it must also select a system of color. It was not until June 1952 that the Freeze was finally lifted. The expected six months had stretched to nearly four years.

Four Problems to Be Solved

The Freeze was one of the most significant actions ever taken by the FCC. It was a major attempt to look ahead and make long-range plans. The commissioners hoped that when the Freeze was lifted the nation would have a blueprint for a system that would last for decades. Designing that blueprint involved consideration of four problem areas:

1. Utilization of the UHF range.
2. City-by-city channel assignments.
3. Selection of a color system.
4. Assignment of educational reservations.

Utilization of the UHF

The first problem was purely technical. The twelve VHF channels were inadequate, and the FCC felt there was not enough additional VHF space available. It was necessary to decide how many channels to allocate in which portion of the UHF and then to make decisions on how much power must be assigned to stations on different channels and how far apart they had to be spaced. The details were worked out by engineers using their slide rules and data from an experimental UHF transmitter built by RCA in Bridgeport, Connecticut.

City-by-City Channel Assignments

When the commission moved FM to a new portion of the radio spectrum in 1946, it took note of a major criticism that had been leveled at how licenses for AM stations had been granted in earlier years—assignments had been on a first-come, first-served basis. Since radio operations first appeared to be more profitable in the larger cities, the best assignments were first made in heavily populated areas and in later years it had been very difficult or impossible to find room on the dial for stations in small communities. The commission proposed but did not implement a system of "fixed assignments" for FM in which space would have been reserved for small markets where operation of stations might not be economically attractive for several years.

In the Freeze the FCC decided to draw up and adhere to a table of fixed assignments that would indicate how many television stations on which specific channels should eventually be operating in each city and community in the country. Licenses were to be granted only when an applicant requested a facility that appeared in the overall table. Thus, channels would be available where needed at the times they could be operated on a practical basis. In preparation for making the city-by-city assignments, the FCC laid down three guidelines that would govern its decisions.

Population density guidelines

The commission believed that every part of the country was entitled to service from at least one station and that the great majority of homes should be able to receive two signals or more. Larger cities should have more stations than smaller ones.

COMMUNITY SIZE	DESIRED ASSIGNMENTS TO EACH
up to 50,000	1 or 2
50,000 to 250,000	2 to 4
250,000 to 1,000,000	4 to 6
1,000,000 or more	6 to 10

Technical guidelines

To minimize the possibilities of interference among stations it was necessary to require a minimum distance between stations on the same channel (co-channel separation) and a lesser distance between two stations on adjacent channels (adjacent-channel separation, e.g., Channels 2 and 3). The co-channel separation figures varied between the VHF and UHF stations and among various "zones" of the country.

Maximum permissible power varied with channel position:

Channels 2–6	100 kilowatts
Channels 7–13	316 kilowatts
Channels 14–83	1,000 kilowatts

Protection of the status quo

The Pre-Freeze authorizations were to be left undisturbed. Prior to the Freeze, television authorizations, like AM licenses, had been granted on a "first-come, first-served" basis. Since some stations were already on the air and others were in various stages of construction, the FCC decided to permit their operation under their existing plans.

Having established its three guidelines, the FCC was ready to start working on a "three-dimensional jigsaw puzzle" without the aid of today's sophisticated computers that would have made the task easier.

The first step was to consider a single channel such as Channel 9. On a map of the United States and adjoining areas in Canada and Mexico, the commission would indicate all of the Channel 9 authorizations already made. Then a circle would be drawn around each representing the co-channel separation as an indication of where other Channel 9 stations might be assigned. In this manner the whole country could be covered showing the Channel 9 communities as separated by the minimum co-channel mileage.

A smaller circle would have to be drawn around every Channel 9 assignment to show the necessary adjacent-channel separations for stations on Channels 8 and 10. Then, one could start plotting the Channel 8 stations already authorized and making provision for new assignments while observing the separation factors. (See Fig. 5.1.)

It very quickly became apparent that when people of this nation had settled in towns and cities, they had not been motivated by future television-channel-separation figures. Rather, people had tended to locate in large numbers where there were ports for ships; rivers for commerce and inexpensive power; railroad junctions; or where there would be abundant trading, as in the centers of farming and ranching areas. Some cities were conveniently located with regard to possible television channels in neighboring cities, but in other parts of the country the spacing made it impossible to permit a neat assignment of television channels.

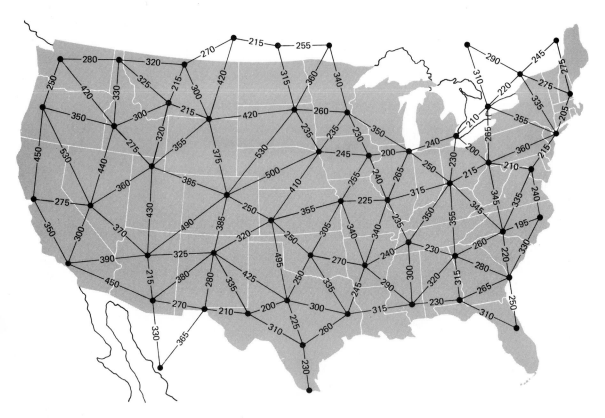

Fig. 5.1
FCC map showing locations of Channel 9 assignments in the commission's *Sixth
Report and Order* ending the Freeze.
Reprinted from *Broadcasting* April 4, 1952, Part II, p. 184.

The "jigsaw puzzle" was especially complicated by the desire to protect
the status quo—the continuation of 108 stations that had been authorized
before the Freeze started in 1948. For example, there were seven Pre-Freeze
VHF stations in the New York City area—six assigned to New York City
itself and one to Newark, New Jersey. All had their transmitters in the
Empire State Building. This situation made it impossible to assign sufficient
VHF stations to serve other east-coast cities like New Haven, Connecticut,
and Philadelphia, Pennsylvania. Similar situations existed throughout much
of the country where there were cities entitled to four or more stations but
located in close proximity to larger markets where Pre-Freeze applications
had been granted.

The only solution was the creation of "mixed markets" in which there were assignments on both the VHF and the UHF. To take five communities at random, the table of assignments looked as follows (asterisk indicates a channel reserved for educational use):

New York City—2, 4, 5, 7, 9, 11, *25, 31 (13 was assigned to Newark)

Columbus, Ohio—4, 6, 10, *34, 40

Des Moines, Iowa—8, *11, 13, 17, 23

Albuquerque, New Mexico—4, *5, 7, 13

Fresno, California—12, *18, 24, 47, 53

Selection of a Color System

In the summer of 1949, the FCC added selection of a color system to the problems to be solved in planning for the long-range future of television. For the next twelve months the Commission conducted hearings and watched demonstrations of various systems.

Although there were several color systems in contention, the two leading competitors were CBS Labs and RCA. Both could transmit color in the six-mHz channel width used by the existing monochrome stations as opposed to the earlier need for up to eighteen mHz. There were still two important differences between them, however:

1. CBS was *Mechanical* and *Incompatible*.

2. RCA was *Electronic* and *Compatible*.

The CBS color system still used the spinning disk that, according to some people, meant there was one more opportunity for things to go wrong. The RCA system was electronic, so on looking into the back of an operating receiver one could see nothing except the glow of the tubes.

The incompatibility of the CBS system meant that a CBS color set could not pick up the existing black-and-white pictures and the existing monochrome receivers could not pick up CBS color, even in black and white. But RCA color sets could pick up monochrome signals and monochrome sets could pick up the electronic color in black and white.

CBS and RCA were competing for a very lucrative prize. Obviously, only one system could be approved for the whole country. It would have made no sense to require a home to have two sets if two stations in the community chose different color systems. Whichever company had its system chosen by the FCC would make large amounts of money, not only by manufacturing sets, but also by making licensing arrangements that would permit others to use its basic patents. The winner would receive royalties from every set made by another manufacturer. Literally hundreds of millions of dollars were at stake.

By the summer of 1950 pressure was mounting on the FCC to end the Freeze, which was then nearly two years old. People in the many cities without television were reading about programs on the air elsewhere and wanted the opportunity to see them. Congress began complaining to the commission that broadcasters and other constituents were impatient. For a year the FCC had been mired in the color controversy. (At the same time it had to continue its regulation of radio and the other electronic media—telephone, telegraph, and so on.) Although it was clear that all systems needed more improvement, the FCC bowed to the pressure and announced it would hold one more set of hearings and demonstrations and then make its decision.

In September the long-awaited announcement was made—the CBS color system had been selected for American television. The first reaction was shock and disbelief. It had been assumed the FCC would choose a compatible system that would permit the continued use, during a changeover transition period, of the nearly ten million sets already in American homes. Few had dreamed that a totally incompatible system would be chosen. The FCC said the CBS quality was better at that time and asked manufacturers to investigate the possibility of making adapters to sets to create a compatibility. However, it stayed with its decision favoring CBS even when the engineers reported adapters were impractical.

RCA immediately went to the United States Court of Appeals in Chicago seeking an order that would force the FCC to delay implementation of its color decision and to reopen the hearings. The basis of the suit was that RCA had made new discoveries that vastly improved its electronic color to the point where RCA claimed its picture quality was at least as good as that of the CBS system.

The Chicago court refused to order the FCC to reopen the hearings but, noting each side was prepared to appeal, did order that further implementation of color television be halted until the case had been heard by the Supreme Court.

The Supreme Court heard the case in the spring of 1951.* RCA repeated its arguments that the FCC had not followed the proper procedure, that it had made an "arbitrary and capricious" ruling before all the evidence was in. It said the FCC should have waited until RCA had completed its studies and further refined its system.

The Supreme Court studied the record and found that the FCC had made a reasonable effort to get all the pertinent data available at the time. Courts realize that regulatory agencies reach points where decisions must be made and that it is sometimes impossible to wait for the time when everything is clear beyond question. The Supreme Court was primarily

---

* *Radio Corporation of America* v. *United States*, 341 U.S. 412, May 28, 1951.

concerned with whether RCA had been given an equal opportunity with CBS and whether the evidence reasonably indicated the CBS system was better at the time the FCC made its decision.

As noted in Chapter 7, the courts are limited in what they may consider when hearing an appeal from an FCC decision. The Supreme Court, in this instance, explained it was in no position to judge the "wisdom" of the FCC in making its decision. It had no authority to substitute its own "public interest judgment" for that of the commission that was charged by Congress with making all its decisions on the basis of the public welfare. Therefore, after concluding that the FCC had given both sides full and equal opportunity and that the FCC had reasonably found the CBS system to be better at the time of decision, the Court's responsibility was at an end. Its ruling in the spring of 1951 upheld the FCC. CBS was the winner, and there was no opportunity for further appeals.

CBS then announced the beginning of limited colorcasting and sent sales representatives to take station orders for color equipment. The response was negative. Stations had already built large audiences with monochrome signals. Since one cannot operate two transmitters simultaneously on a channel, during any time devoted to colorcasting there would have been no service to all existing sets. To pick up the color signals each home would have had to make an investment of up to $1,000 for a second set which would then be of no use while the station was programming in black and white. In effect, operators were being asked to install a system that would mean ruinous competition to their already successful broadcasting, an action they refused to take.

A few months later the Office of Defense Mobilization said there was so much military need for certain metals (for the Korean "police action") that none could be spared for color television. CBS color production and sales efforts came to a halt.

Into this hiatus came the National Television Systems Committee (NTSC), which had been formed by equipment manufacturers before the war to advise the FCC on the original technical standards for television. Made up of engineers from all the major companies, the NTSC was highly prestigious and had rendered important services for the commission. It had never been disbanded, and in 1951 it considered what its role might be in the color situation.

Its chairman, Dr. W.R.G. Baker, vice president of General Electric, approached the FCC and asked whether the whole issue might be reopened if the NTSC could devise a better system of color that would utilize whatever patents were needed, regardless of their ownership. Since CBS Labs was represented on the NTSC and entered no objection to the NTSC request, the FCC indicated it would reopen the hearings if the NTSC came in with its own system.

The NTSC did come to the FCC later with a proposed color system that was electronic and compatible—basically the RCA system, but an improvement because it involved some patents of other companies. The FCC reopened the hearings and in December 1953 approved the NTSC color system that is used by American television at the present time.

Assignment of Educational Reservations

Midway through the Freeze the FCC announced that hearings would be held near the end of 1950 concerning setting aside some of the fixed assignments for exclusive use of educational institutions. It was not expected that the hearings would be especially significant or that the commission would be any more moved by arguments of educators than it had been in 1934 when Congress directed it to hold hearings into setting aside radio frequencies for education. (The FCC had then recommended against such reservations.) The hearings were much more dramatic than expected because several educational organizations combined to form the Joint Committee for Educational Television (JCET), which secured funding from the Ford Foundation. At the end of the hearings, which are described in more detail in Chapter 13, the FCC set aside 242 assignments for use by educational institutions.

The End of the Freeze in 1952

In April 1952 the FCC issued its *Sixth Report and Order*, which ended the Freeze, effective July 1. Provision was made for over 2,000 station assignments in nearly 1,300 communities. The assignments were divided among VHF and UHF stations in the following way:

1. Commercial: 617 VHF and 1,436 UHF
2. Educational: 80 VHF and 162 UHF

When it was time to start processing applications, over 500 were in the commission's file.

Programming during the Freeze

Television at the end of the Freeze was vastly different from the bewildered medium of 1945 and 1946. There were 108 Pre-Freeze authorized stations on the air. AT&T had limited network facilities from coast to coast that were shared by the networks. Advertisers were convinced they should spend increasing amounts in television. There were seventeen million receivers in American homes, and viewers were talking about "really big shows," like Ed Sullivan's "Toast of the Town," NBC's "Saturday Night Review," "Arthur

Godfrey and His Friends," and the star of stars, "Uncle Miltie" Berle. "What's My Line?" was opening its long stand on the network and in syndication. Edward R. Murrow was presenting "See It Now," and there was the beginning of the live drama that some have identified as television's "golden age." Television had survived its infancy and was ready for a vigorous adolescence.

5.3 1952–1960 TELEVISION'S ADOLESCENCE

In retrospect, the 1950s were the "good old days" in which growth was rampant and enthusiasm unbounded, with only hints of the regulatory confusion that characterized the 1960s. The number of commercial stations on the air grew from 108 at the end of the Freeze to 522 by the end of the decade. Total television-time sales nearly quadrupled from an annual $283 million in 1952 to over a billion dollars in 1959. AT&T network facilities were expanded until they could accommodate all networks simultaneously in all parts of the country. CBS, which started as a distant second network to NBC, drew even in 1955, and by the end of the decade ABC was ready to move into a highly competitive position.

Blacklisting and the Murrow-McCarthy Confrontation

It was during the blacklisting and Murrow-McCarthy years of the early 1950s that television became prominent in areas other than entertainment. For the first time it not only appeared to reflect society but to have an influence on history as well.

Shortly after World War II the Russians showed they had no intention of living up to agreements and understandings that had been reached and acclaimed when they were our wartime allies. The Russians also made clear that their avowed purpose was to extend their ideology into as many countries as possible, including the United States. The "Communist menace" became a matter of overwhelming concern to many Americans. Fears deepened when the Russians exploded their first atomic bomb in 1949.

It was a time during which some felt there was nothing more important than weeding out Communist sympathizers. In 1947 a new magazine, *Counterattack*, was published listing the names of people who had in some way been identified, either recently or in the dim past, as associated with a "Communist-front" organization. There was no attempt to prove an individual was a Communist Party member or a Communist sympathizer or that he or she was then or ever had been dedicated to overthrowing the government of the United States. The mere appearance of one's name in a news item about an allegedly subversive group was sufficient. Since broadcasting was so visible, many announcers, newspeople, writers, producers, and other talent at whom the finger of suspicion might be pointed were listed.

In the summer of 1950 a new magazine, *Red Channels*, listed 151 people it claimed had a "Communist background" (using the *Counterattack* criteria) and who were then banned from work in television and radio without any specific charges ever having been made and without any opportunity to defend themselves. (Indeed, these people were even without specific information that their being listed was responsible for their loss of employment.) The primary pressure was brought on advertising agencies, which had much control over individual programs and talent. The simple refusal of the "super patriots" at *Counterattack* and *Red Channels* to "clear" a name was enough to make the listed individual unacceptable in broadcasting.

Had it been only the advertising agencies that engaged in "blacklisting," the networks would have been guilty only of passively standing by while the civil liberties of people in programming were being suspended. But the networks themselves subscribed to various blacklists and then started keeping their own lists. At no point did they declare, "This is wrong and we will have no part of it even if it does cost us money."

Senator Joseph McCarthy (R-Wis.) was the self-appointed spokesman of the "anti-Communists." The hearings of the Senate subcommittee of which he was a member were widely carried by the networks, which continued their practice of making sure no one ever appeared on their facilities who might in any way attract Senator McCarthy's displeasure. The only bright exception in television during the McCarthy era was Edward R. Murrow, who in one of his early "See It Now" programs fully discussed the case of a Lieutenant Milo Redulovitch who was forced out of uniform because his sister and father were accused of being Communist sympathizers.

In March 1954 Murrow made history by standing up to the senator in forthright fashion. Of all those in network broadcasting, he seemed to have seen most clearly the dangers of McCarthy's methods and where they were apt to lead. Certainly, he was the only figure of major stature who displayed the courage to speak out. Going through the CBS file films of McCarthy hearings, he selected instance after instance where McCarthy's sneer and sly innuendo were most pronounced.

Murrow opened his "See It Now" program with a statement of his conviction that McCarthy was a menace to the country and announced that he would let McCarthyism speak for itself. After showing the Senator's methods, he said that if McCarthy would like to "answer himself," time would be given to him on a subsequent "See It Now" program.

Edward R. Murrow's broadcast of McCarthy film footage may be one of the most important single programs ever aired. McCarthy did respond, but most ineffectively. Others began to speak out against him. His influence began to wane. Unfortunately, network and agency blacklisting continued for at least another two years. To many broadcast leaders it was more a "public relations" problem than a crisis in individual rights. Since there was never a public admission that blacklisting existed, there was never a specific moment when it could be said to have ended. It certainly lasted far longer than it should have, and some would say that its influence still lingered a quarter-century after it started.

EDWARD R. MURROW 1908–1965

Edward R. Murrow in the streets of London during World War II
Courtesy: CBS

Night after night in the early days of World War II Edward R. Murrow opened his broadcasts from bombed-out London with the simple "This—is London." His descriptions of the city under siege and of the reactions of its citizens were most influential in bringing Americans close to Londoners, in encouraging American support for early lend-lease aid to England, and eventually for this country's entry into the war. His dedication to reporting was shown by his disregard of danger when he spoke from the roof of Broadcast House in London with the bombs falling and when he hitched rides on allied bombers raiding deep into Europe.

Upon his death from cancer in 1965 he was universally hailed as the man who did most to establish—and elevate—the standards of broadcast journalism. As one who won nearly every journalism award given and as the recipient of honors from many nations and universities, Ed Murrow, more than any other individual, dignified the stature of journalism in broadcasting.

It was a mark of his prestige to have been invited for dinner at the White House; ironically, however, on December 7, 1941, the day of the Japanese attack on Pearl Harbor. Although President Roosevelt did not come to the dinner table, he kept sending word that

Murrow should not leave. Late that night he found time to talk with America's most famous radio correspondent. Murrow's death a quarter-century later left a void in American journalism that many feel will never be filled.

Murrow was born in North Carolina and moved with his family to the state of Washington when he was still a child. He was a Phi Beta Kappa graduate of Washington State College in 1930. For two years he was president of the National Student Federation and for the next three years he was the assistant director of the Institute of International Education. In both capacities he made many friends throughout the country and the world. In 1935 he joined CBS as director of talks and education and in 1937 became European director. As World War II intensified, Murrow quickly moved to line up the staff of foreign correspondents who were to become responsible for CBS's dominance of the news in the early days of the war.

For two years after the war he was a vice-president of CBS and director of public affairs, but he never found satisfaction in desk work. Returning to the air with his "See It Now" program, he did a number of telecasts that are remembered as classics. Most famous was his 1954 confrontation with Senator Joseph McCarthy which was important in terminating the period of witch-hunting for Communists. One of Murrow's last programs was "Harvest of Shame" about the plight of migrant farm workers, which was a fitting conclusion to an illustrious broadcasting career.

In 1961 he joined the Kennedy administration as director of the United States Information Agency but had to resign for reasons of health. After an unsuccessful operation for lung cancer, he retired to his farm in Pawling, New York, where he died at the age of fifty-seven.

The "Quiz Scandals"

Television's adolescence ended with the "quiz scandals." The first of the big-money quiz programs, "The $64,000 Question," appeared in the mid-1950s. A contestant selected a specialized field (e.g., baseball, the Bible, English history, classical composers) and tried to answer questions that grew progressively harder each week as the money prizes were doubled until they reached the top, $64,000. This program was followed by the "$64,000 Challenge," "Twenty-One," and others using somewhat similar formats except that they pitted contestants against each other.

Some educators assumed the quizzes were "rigged," especially those that involved competition between two contestants. Usually one was more interesting than the other and it would make for a better "show" if this contestant were able to win and return the following week. It was assumed, however, that the "rigging" was honest to the extent that it consisted of getting to know the strengths and weaknesses of the players and choosing questions that would probably be answered correctly by the more appealing contestant.

The producers either did not know it might be done that easily or preferred to take no chances. In their desire to create suspense as well as retain the desired contestant, they not only gave the correct answers in advance to some contestants, they also rehearsed them in facial expressions to give the impression of agony as they appeared to struggle for the answers. After much expressive visual contortion, the correct answers would usually be blurted out just as the gong was about to sound.

Eventually, one of the losing contestants complained to the District Attorney in Manhattan. Hearings were scheduled by the FCC and by congressional committees. In retrospect, the significance of the situation lay in the embarrassment of upper-level network management who had to confess they had no idea of what was going on. The quiz programs were among their biggest audience attractions and it never occurred to them to regard them as anything more than "show business" attempts to earn high ratings. It appeared that the public took television programs more seriously than those who were responsible for them. As network executives had once regarded blacklisting as only a public-relations problem, so they now saw their schedules as only a vehicle for advertisers.

The congressional response was to amend the Communications Act by adding Section 509, which made it unlawful to employ deceptive practices in a "purportedly *bona fide* contest of intellectual knowledge or intellectual skill." The TV industry's response was to cancel all the big-money quiz programs.

The UHF Problem

Without doubt, the greatest disappointment to the FCC in the 1950s was the inability of UHF stations to attract significant audiences that would have led to economic viability. They were unable to compete in mixed markets against VHF licensees and they had great difficulty in new television areas where CATV had been established. The UHF problem and attempts to solve it reveal a great deal about television "facts of life" in the 1950s and about the FCC.

By the end of 1952 there were 3 UHF stations on the air and many were encouraged that within six months of the lifting of the Freeze, three applicants could get through all the red tape at the FCC, order and accept delivery on their equipment, and begin broadcasting. A year later the number had risen to 115 and there was reason for optimism. However, in the summer of 1953 there had been stories in the trade press about UHF stations that were encountering serious audience and financial problems. By the end of the year some had given up. The year-end figures for UHF stations on the air in the 1950s were as follows:

YEAR	NUMBER OF UHF STATIONS
1952	3
1953	115
1954	116
1955	102
1956	91
1957	84
1958	77
1959	76

By mid-1954 the viability of UHF was in serious doubt and investigations were initiated by the FCC and Congress. The commission was especially concerned because its whole concept of a national system of television depended on the ability of UHF stations to round out the VHF coverage. It was to that end that a four-year Freeze had been imposed in 1948.

The first inclination of many in Washington (as with radio in the late 1930s) was to blame the networks. It was noted that very few of the popular network programs ever appeared on UHF stations and some felt there must be a conspiracy against the newer-type stations. If there were three VHF stations and a fourth UHF in a market it would be normal to expect to find the major networks on the three VHF stations and for the UHF station to be independent. But even when the number of VHF's was smaller, the network affiliations were similar. Three hypothetical markets would exhibit this pattern of network affiliation:

Market *A* VHF—NBC
            VHF—CBS
            VHF—ABC
            UHF—Independent

Market *B* VHF—NBC + ABC
            VHF—CBS + ABC
            UHF—Independent

Market *C* VHF—NBC + CBS + ABC
            UHF—Independent

As members of Congress and commissioners looked into the situation closely, however, they found the networks had comparatively little to say about it because the decisions were made by the advertisers who ordered the network lineup. For example, in 1954 ABC added a Walt Disney program to its schedule on Wednesday evenings. It was the first time Disney had done television and there was great enthusiasm about it among both stations and viewers. As ABC was lining up the coverage for the Disney program throughout the country, the advertiser would have to choose between stations in typical Market *C* above. There were two alternatives: the program could be live on the UHF station on Wednesday evening or it could be delayed on the VHF station—perhaps at noon the following Sunday. A look at the ratings would quickly reveal that the program on the VHF Sunday at noon (or at any other time) would draw far more viewers than it would on the UHF station. Since audience size was the only factor of interest to the advertiser, the UHF station would fail to get the Disney program from ABC.

If the Freeze had ended in 1948 rather than 1952, the UHF problem might not have developed to any significant degree. There were, at the earlier date, only fifty stations on the air and fewer than a million receivers in the country. When families bought television sets for the first time, it would have been much easier to persuade them to pay extra for a built-in UHF tuner and to put up antennas that were appropriate to the UHF signals as well as to the VHF. In many markets the UHF stations would have arrived as early as the VHFs and the difference between them would have been minimal.

But by the time the Freeze ended in 1952, there were 108 VHF stations on the air broadcasting to more than seventeen million VHF homes with antennas purchased for VHF only. To receive UHF in those homes would have required the purchase of a converter (a small box usually placed on top of the VHF television set and costing from $25 up) and an addition to the antenna. Even then it was more difficult to get the UHF station because one had to carefully "tune it in" rather than simply click it to a pre-set position as with the VHF.

The UHF station trying to get started in a mixed market found itself caught in a vicious circle. People would buy converters when some of the popular programs they wanted to see were on the UHF stations. The top programs came to a station when an advertiser was willing to buy the station's circulation. The circulation became attractive to an advertiser only when people had bought converters to see the programs.

In seeking to solve the problems of the UHF stations, the FCC took three approaches in the 1950s:

1. Changing the multiple-ownership rules.

2. Deintermixture.

3. Requesting five VHF channels from the military.

Changing the Multiple-Ownership Rules

When the FCC decided there was no network conspiracy against the UHF stations, it made a move that would automatically place some of the most popular programming on UHF stations—it changed the multiple-ownership rules. In 1954 the maximum number of television stations that might be owned by one licensee was five. The FCC changed the limit from five to seven, with the provision that no more than five of the seven might be in the VHF. This was an open invitation to each of the networks to acquire two UHF stations, and both NBC and CBS did so.* This meant that those UHF stations would become network property and carry the full network schedules.

The NBC experience in Buffalo, New York, characterized the difficulty of solving the UHF problem. There were three stations in the community—two VHFs and a UHF. The two VHF stations had had primary affiliations with NBC and CBS and each carried some ABC programming. The UHF station had been independent. There was only about a 20 percent UHF penetration (percentage of television homes that could receive the UHF). Advertisers would not buy time on the station and it was ready to give up.

NBC bought the UHF station, leaving the two VHFs to the other networks. In 1954 NBC was still the number-one network—CBS would achieve a parity and then move ahead only after another year or so. ABC was a distant third. For the first time there was a UHF station in a highly competitive market carrying the full NBC schedule, and this should have broken the vicious circle. People should have bought converters to see those programs.

Unfortunately, that failed to happen. The UHF-set penetration failed to increase significantly. Within three years NBC wrote off the experiment as a bad investment. It gave the studio and transmitter to an educational television council in Buffalo which then operated it as the first noncommercial station in New York State. The other NBC UHF station and the two purchased by CBS were also dropped. In the markets where they had been temporary UHF owners, both networks reaffiliated with the VHF stations with which they had formerly been associated.

Deintermixture While the FCC was waiting to see if putting full-network schedules on some UHFs would work, it moved to the next stage of trying to "deintermix" some of the mixed markets by making them all-UHF or all-VHF. It was thought that if all stations in a market were on the UHF, the public would have no choice but to buy the appropriate receivers. The theory was fine, but when the commission tried out the plan in areas where VHF was well established it proved unworkable.

In March 1957 the commission proposed to deintermix several markets, including three in which the VHF assignments were already in use. The

---

* CBS acquired UHF stations in Hartford, Connecticut, and Milwaukee, Wisconsin, while NBC bought stations in New Britain, Connecticut, and Buffalo, New York. ABC did not buy any UHF stations.

experience in the capital-cities area of New York State (Albany-Schenectady-Troy) is illustrative. There was one VHF station, WRGB (named after Dr. W. R. G. Baker of General Electric and NTSC) operated by General Electric, and two UHFs. WRGB was primarily NBC but also carried some CBS and ABC programming. The two UHFs were independent except for the few network programs that could not be placed on the WRGB schedule.

The FCC announced it would move WRGB from Channel 6 into the UHF, thus creating an all-UHF market. The chairman of the FCC thought he had cleared the move with the chairman of the board of General Electric in a telephone conversation. When the announcement was made, there was no immediate response from WRGB until it could find out about the telephone call. After acquainting the chairman of GE with some of the television "facts of life" concerning UHF, the station announced it would fight the move all the way to the Supreme Court, if necessary.

It soon appeared that the FCC had picked a poor location to start its deintermixture. WRGB was one of the first experimental TV stations and had been among the first licensed for commercial broadcasting. More important was the fact that the area was surrounded on three sides by mountainous regions where VHF sets had been purchased and antennas put up to receive WRGB. Most were unable to receive the UHF stations even if they used converters and special antennas. If the area were deintermixed, those remote places would have no service at all and the FCC would be violating the first guideline it had established in the Freeze—making sure everyone had access to at least one television station. The commission did deintermix the capital-cities area—by finding two more VHF channels for the two UHF operators. (One of the UHFs gave its studio and transmitter to a local educational television council which then became the second educational station in the state.) Thus, although the commission had devoted a great deal of time to deintermixture, it was no nearer a solution than when it started consideration of the possibilities in 1955.

Requesting Channels from the Military

When engineers came to the conclusion that part of the UHF trouble might be attributed to the inherent limitations of the UHF for broadcasting, the FCC asked the Office of Defense Mobilization (ODM) if there might not be space released by the military in the VHF for broadcasting. (It would still have taken several years for manufacturers to put on the market receivers that could pick up such channels.) There was special interest in the five channels (14 through 18) that the military had taken in World War II after they had been assigned by the FCC for commercial television. However, the ODM said it could not spare the channels. In fact, there were rumors from time to time that the ODM might even have to take over Channels 2 through 6 for military purposes.

Programming in the 1950s

Until the advent of the videotape recorder in the latter half of the 1950s, the most exciting programs were the live dramatic series—"Studio One," "General Electric Theater," and "Producers Showcase," among others. As costs rose and the VTR made possible a more polished performance and repeat showings, live drama largely disappeared. Other distinguished programs included the NBC innovations of "The Today Show," "Tonight," "Home," "Wide Wide World," and specials.

Television also entered its period of "trends" in which one especially successful program was copied until there was a plethora of them and a new type emerged. The 1950s were the era of the western and the beginning of the situation comedies (sitcoms). Westerns declined quickly in the 1960s but sitcoms have continued to the present time.

5.4 1960–1980 TELEVISION'S MATURITY

In the 1960s television achieved much of its current stature. All major markets were served by at least three stations and each of the three commercial networks had a lineup of primary affiliates that made it competitive with the others. Advertisers gave television a resounding vote of approval by increasing their annual expenditures on it to over $3 billion. The increased competition of the networks led to the color breakthrough that had been pending for nearly ten years.

The UHF "Solution"

In April 1960 the FCC finally deintermixed a market in which a VHF station had been on the air—as opposed to markets in which no VHF grant had been made or the grant had not been activated by station construction. Channel 12 was deleted from the assignments in Fresno, California, and the community became all-UHF. Significantly, the move was not opposed by the VHF operator. (The rumor was that he welcomed it since he already had four other VHF stations and changing his Fresno station to UHF would free him to seek another VHF outlet in a larger market.)

In the summer of 1961 the FCC proposed deintermixing eight markets, each of which had one VHF assignment. Most of the VHFs had been activated and the broadcasters brought increasing pressure on Congress to turn the commission away from its deintermixture course. When members of Congress talked with commissioners, the FCC response was that it would drop deintermixture if Congress would take action by passing an all-channel receiver bill. In 1962 the Communications Act was amended to give the

FCC the power to require that all television sets sold in interstate commerce include the UHF tuner. Since 1964 receivers have had to comply with the all-channel requirements.

Deintermixture was abandoned as a way of solving the UHF problem. Only one active VHF station had been deleted. There were a handful of other markets that were deintermixed but none of them had included VHF assignments in use. How successful were deintermixture and the all-channel receiver bill? Returning to the assignments at the end of the Freeze and comparing them with stations on the air almost thirty years later reveals the following:

	1952 ASSIGNMENTS	1980 STATIONS
Commercial VHF	617	517
Commercial UHF	1,436	229

Color Breakthrough

The spread of color had been disappointingly slow in the ten years after the NTSC system was approved. In the early 1960s only NBC offered substantial programming in color. The breakthrough came as a number of seemingly unrelated events coincided.

In the fall of 1964 ABC became fully competitive with the other two networks. Its programs were attractive, it gained a publicity advantage by starting its fall season a week ahead of the other two networks, and it delayed acceptance of political programming in the presidential campaign until the last two or three weeks before the election. As a consequence, for the first time, less than one average rating point separated the three networks.

Early in 1965 there was a little-noted announcement of the results of a study of color-television homes. It revealed that color homes preferred color programs to a significant degree. For example, "The average rating of all NBC color programs in the 7:30–11:00 P.M. period was given as 39.3 in color homes against 22.2 in black-and-white homes . . ."* NBC estimated that the advantage had accounted for one full average rating point in the current season and would give a yet more sizeable advantage in the coming year if the other two networks stayed with black-and-white programs.

Very shortly CBS announced its plans for color in the coming fall season and ABC announced it would program primarily in color a year later. When

---

* *Broadcasting*, March 1, 1965, p. 32.

the 1965–1966 season was underway the schedules of all three networks were predominantly in color. In another year or two the black-and-white network show had almost disappeared.

Almost simultaneously the price of color receivers fell into the $500 range and a new picture tube was developed so that receivers required far less adjustment between programs and between stations than in the past. From the mid-1960s on, color grew rapidly and steadily to its current near-universality.

Programming in the 1960s

Television entertainment programming continued to follow the "trends" in which the success of one program generated others very nearly the same. As the westerns died down, the medical and lawyer programs came into their own. Sitcoms multiplied from year to year. Sports programming grew by leaps and bounds. It was also in the 1960s that the networks began to carry feature movies and for a while there were eight prime-time movies a week split among the three networks. As the audience began to take entertainment programming for granted, it was the "reality" programming that tended to be remembered after a decade or more. Most viewers forgot individual entertainment programs but could easily recall the weekend of the Kennedy assassination, the Olympics brought from around the world by satellite, the space shots climaxed by pictures of men walking on the moon, and the nightly horrors from Vietnam.

As the 1960s ended, television had achieved the greater part of the commercial stature that had been promised at the end of the Freeze. Service was truly nationwide; three networks were profitably affiliated with stations in over 200 markets, and advertisers were using most of the available commercial time. In subsequent years there would be the addition of marginal stations but no significant increase in the size of the system.

The 1970s can best be characterized as a decade of confrontations for American broadcasting due primarily to the fact that television had become so rich and powerful that it was a tempting target. The most notable protagonists were the Nixon administration, parents concerned about the effect television advertising might be having on their children, and minority groups that wanted a piece of the action.

Confrontation with the Nixon Administration

A major concern of broadcasters in the early 1970s was countering a concerted attack upon them by the Nixon administration. It stemmed from the fact that television news had "grown up" in the 1960s and achieved a new importance in American life. In 1963 the network evening newscasts expanded from fifteen minutes to half an hour in length. A year or so later the placement of a satellite over the Pacific Ocean permitted the networks to show news from Vietnam on the day it happened. These two factors served to make television the primary "agenda setter" for the American people. They felt that items covered by television were important and tended to consider insignificant those not making the newscasts.

Through the mid and late 1960s there was extensive coverage of the antiwar demonstrations and an increasing number of reports from Vietnam that refuted some of the claims made in Washington. By the spring of 1968 the attitude of the American people had reached the point where President Lyndon Johnson felt free to travel to only a few spots around the country where security could be extremely tight, and he announced he would not be a candidate for reelection.

President Nixon felt he had never received fair coverage from the American press—newspapers, magazines, radio, and television—and he had a great distrust for reporters. When he had assumed office, however, he had less antipathy toward television because when he had last run for office in 1962 television had not been as significant; he also felt that his televised "Checkers" speech of 1952 had kept him on the Republican ballot.

One of Nixon's major campaign promises had been to end the war in Southeast Asia, and upon his inauguration in January 1969 war opponents took the position, "Let's wait and see what happens." There was a cessation of demonstrations, and comparative peace prevailed between Nixon and the protesters and between Nixon and television. During the summer the militant youth began to lose patience, and television newscasts reported on stepped-up antiwar activity. In "instant analyses" after presidential speeches, commentators pointed out the differences between Nixon's campaign promises and what he had just finished saying. ("Instant analysis" is not a completely accurate description, since copies of the speeches were frequently circulated in advance and there was an opportunity for the commentators to think about what they would say at the conclusion.)

On November 3, 1969 President Nixon made a major televised speech in which he told of his determination to "hold firm" in Vietnam while seeking a negotiated peace. Commentators had expected the speech would be about disengagement from the war and expressed their surprise which the White House interpreted as disapproval. A Vietnam protest march on Washington was scheduled later in the month and billed as the largest ever to take place. In response to the instant analysis treatment of Nixon's speech and out of concern that television would give extensive coverage to the upcoming march on Washington, Vice President Spiro Agnew accepted an invitation to address a Republican fundraising dinner in Des Moines, Iowa. The networks were informed it would be a major speech so they carried it nationwide. In his remarks Agnew made a major attack on network television news. His specific complaints are found in two excerpts:

The audience of 70 million Americans gathered to hear the President of the United States was inherited by a small band of network commentators and self-appointed analysts, the majority of whom expressed in one way or another their hostility to what he had to say. It was obvious that their minds were made up in advance. . . .

How many marches and demonstrations would we have if the marchers did not know that the ever-faithful TV cameras would be there to record their antics for the next news show?

For the next four years network television news appeared to be under an orchestrated attack from various branches of the government. Dean Burch, the recently appointed chairman of the FCC, said he found the Agnew speech "thoughtful, provocative," and deserving of "careful consideration by the industry and the public." Although Burch went on to point out that Agnew had not called for censorship, Burch's stamp of approval on the general content of the speech was startling. It was also pointed out that Burch had two weeks earlier called the heads of the three networks and asked each to provide him with transcripts of what commentators had said at the conclusion of the November 3 Nixon speech.

Following the Agnew speech, Clay T. Whitehead, Director of the Office of Telecommunications Policy (OTP) in the White House, attacked the networks as engaging in "elitist gossip" and "ideological plugola." In September 1970 presidential counsel Charles Colson wrote a memo telling of his calls to the network presidents to ensure Nixon's easy access to network time. In November 1971 Whitehead made a speech to the National Association of Educational Broadcasters warning them that any attempt to create a "fourth network" of educational television stations would be resisted by the administration. He was obviously concerned that the educational interconnection was carrying news and analysis that closely paralleled what the commercial networks were carrying. Throughout the debate on the extent to which cable television should be free to compete with over-the-air television, Whitehead consistently favored cable as a way of cutting back on the strength of commercial television. When a group of actors and other Hollywood workers protested to the FCC about the number of network reruns of entertainment series episodes, Whitehead and Nixon supported their petition and used it as another way to keep the networks off balance.

In January 1972 petitions were filed by Nixon supporters challenging the renewal of licenses for television stations owned by the *Washington Post–Newsweek* group, which had been a leader in liberal news reporting.

In April 1972 an antitrust suit was filed by the Department of Justice seeking to bar networks from producing any of their own entertainment programming or from leasing their facilities to other entertainment producers.

Pressure from OTP Director Whitehead centered around "localism," the removal of news and programming decisions from the networks to the local stations. There was undoubtedly a realization that radio had been insignificant in the political arena before the development of networks in the 1930s and the knowledge that diminishing the strength of the television networks in the 1970s would lessen television's power to influence public opinion. In December 1972 Whitehead made a "carrot-and-stick" speech in which he said his office was proposing legislation to make license renewal easier for the stations to get and for longer periods but that would require that news judgment be centered at the station level.

For two or three years the administration succeeded in enlisting support from its "silent majority" of conservative Americans who supported the war in Vietnam and were disgusted with the methods of the opposition and with the networks that reported them. The confrontation between Nixon and the television networks seemed to fade in the fall of 1973. As the President's Watergate cover-up fell apart and more Americans became convinced he had badly erred, so the influence of his administration waned. Agnew resigned in disgrace, and Whitehead lost his clout in Washington. Television emerged a stronger force than when it had entered the fray in 1969 but with the realization it had traveled through a troubled time and run great risks.

Confrontation with Concerned Parents

A second major confrontation with the broadcasters moved onto the front pages as the conflict with the Nixon administration was coming to a close. It was initiated by parents who were concerned about the effects of advertising during the "kidvid" hours and who quickly received the support of other public interest groups.

Since the early 1950s, psychologists, sociologists, and others had been greatly concerned about the effects of televised violence on children. There was fear that it might lead to overly aggressive behavior among children who viewed literally thousands of hours of mayhem not only in the cartoons but also in adult programming. Hundreds of studies were conducted but the total results were inconclusive. Because there were so many factors in a child's environment, none could be isolated. It could be statistically demonstrated only that some television programs might have an adverse effect on some children some of the time.

In February 1970 a group of concerned parents from the Boston area opened a new front in the war over children's television. Action for Children's Television (ACT) petitioned the FCC to make rules with regard to aspects other than violence. There was a request that broadcasters be required to provide specific amounts of weekly programming for children in three age categories (2–5, 6–9, and 10–12), but the major emphasis was on advertising directed at children.

ACT claimed that most advertising exploited children by use of sophisticated techniques before the youngsters had developed the normal adult defenses. ACT was especially critical of those who were trying to sell cereals, vitamins, candy, and other products that would affect children's health. The concerned parents thought it was bad enough to make children want cereals loaded with sugar and vitamin pills that tasted good, but it was unconscionable to turn children into salespersons who would badger and tease parents for some things that the parents might feel were inferior in nutritional and health values. ACT asked that no advertising be permitted on programs designed for children. Then, on the assumption that the first request would be turned down, ACT further demanded a strict limitation on the number of commercials in a program and a clear separation of advertising from program content. The group pointed out that children considered a program host or cartoon character a member of the family and an object of great devotion. It was inexcusable for the entertainment figure to change roles and tell children to ask their parents for specific brands of products.

As news of the ACT petition spread, there was a tremendous outpouring of mail from other parents and groups complaining to the commission about the television fare being provided for children. Pressure was also brought on members of Congress to push the FCC into taking some positive action. Although the commission had serious doubts about its ability to do anything without violating the First Amendment and Section 326 of the Communications Act, the petition was received and placed on the agenda and comments were invited.

The commissioners' focus was on commercial practices. The members expressed their concern at broadcasters' conventions and urged industry leaders to accede voluntarily to some of ACT's demands so further regulation would be unnecessary. The National Association of Broadcasters amended its Code of Good Practices for television to reduce the number of commercials to be included in children's programs and to eliminate the use of program hosts as salespersons.

In the fall of 1974 the commission issued a report on its findings regarding the ACT petition. No affirmative action was taken, but the commission did call on broadcasters to be more sensitive to the needs of children and to the dangers of their being exploited by advertisers. Specifically, the FCC recommended that broadcasters:

1. Observe the new NAB code standards limiting the time permitted for advertising in children's programming.
2. Provide a reasonable amount of programming for children, a significant amount of it educational.
3. Air programs oriented to children throughout the week and not just on weekends.
4. Observe the code recommendation that there be no host selling.
5. Provide a clear separation between programming and sales messages.

ACT was bitterly disappointed that the FCC felt it could be no more responsive to the petition. Realizing that the First Amendment and Section 326 of the Communications Act probably precluded the FCC from being more helpful, the members of ACT transferred their attention to the Federal Trade Commission (FTC), which had been created to weed out "deceptive" advertising in all media. The FTC had made a clear distinction between deceptive advertising and "puffery" that largely depended on general claims: "_____ is best," "_____ will make you feel good," "_____ will make you more popular," and "_____ will get your day off to a good start." Such claims were considered legitimate advertising devices and thus beyond the concern of the FTC.

Deceptive advertising, on the other hand, was advertising that made specific claims that had the ring of scientific truth and implied that the claims could be (or had been) corroborated by experiments or testing. One of the best-known examples involved a mouthwash company that said use of its product would lower the chance a person might catch a cold. When it could produce no scientific evidence to support the claim, the FTC required the company not only to discontinue the commercial but also to add in subsequent advertising that no such benefit was implied. Similarly, if a company making automobiles, drugs, cereals, or any other product made specific claims, it must be prepared to back them up or face action by the FTC.

In 1977 Act went to the FTC asking it to rule that all advertising aimed at children up to age eight be ruled deceptive on the grounds that the youngsters had not yet developed the adult understanding of puffery, hence did not have adult defenses against it. As ACT president Peggy Charren explained to the *New York Times:*

> *What we're saying is that advertising to young children is*
> *inherently deceptive because of the nature of children, their lack*

of cognitive ability, their lack of experience in dealing with the marketplace and their inability to make rational choices based on information.

She added, "Deceptive commercial speech has never been protected by the First Amendment."

In February 1978 the FTC staff made three rule-making proposals for consideration by the commission:

1. To ban all advertising on television directed to children under the age of eight.

2. To ban from television all advertising of those products that pose the most serious dental risks to children under the age of twelve.

3. To require that advertisers of sugared products pay for commercial spots designed to promote good nutrition and health.

Following FTC acceptance of the staff report and an announcement that hearings would be held, advertisers and their trade associations moved in opposition on two fronts. The first step was to remove the FTC chairman from the proceedings. It was common knowledge that Chairman Michael Pertschuk had been supportive of the ACT position and that he had encouraged the staff work on the report suggesting the FTC proceed as though advertising to children were inherently deceptive. The advertising interests petitioned Mr. Pertschuk to disqualify himself from participating in the hearings and voting on the issue. When he refused to do so, a request was made to the District Court in Washington that Pertschuk be barred because he had already made up his mind. In November 1978 the judge concurred in the advertisers' assertion and ordered that Pertschuk not participate further. The judge termed the situation unique because the chairman's public speeches had gone so far in showing his partiality.

A year later the court of appeals reversed the decision on the grounds there was no evidence Mr. Pertschuk had made an irrevocable decision and might not have been persuaded to change his mind if the evidence were overwhelmingly in support of such a change. The appeals court panel pointed out that commissioners and others involved in decisions frequently exercised the right to express their own opinions. The key issue was whether their opinions unreasonably precluded them from making a final decision based on evidence received.

Two weeks later Chairman Pertschuk voluntarily withdrew from the hearings saying that his presence had become controversial in itself and he did not want attention diverted from the main issue of whether advertising to children was inherently deceptive.

The second front opened by the advertisers was in the halls of Congress where they tried to persuade the legislators to force the FTC to discontinue the hearings and any possible actions on children's advertising on television. There was an honest difference of opinion as to whether the authority of the FTC should be limited to individual deceptive commercials or extended to wide-sweeping regulations aimed at a whole industry. The advertisers of children's products were joined in their lobbying by representatives of the funeral directors' industry that had also felt the sting of FTC scrutiny. Congressional subcommittees made it clear to the FTC that there should be delays until Congress had had a chance to consider the matter but the commission voted to go ahead. There were attempts to cut off all FTC funding unless the hearings were dropped, but interim funding kept the commission alive. President Carter indicated he would veto any action that would cripple the FTC.

In the Spring of 1981 the FTC staff bowed to the political realities of the Reagan administration's *laissez-faire* philosophy. The 1981 elections had placed in the administration and in the halls of Congress persons who would have little sympathy with increased regulatory activism. The staff reiterated its belief that young people are not able to cope with sophisticated advertising. However, since the only remedy appeared to be banning television advertising directed at children, and since that was impractical, staff members felt there was no point in further consideration of proposed rules and recommended dropping the whole matter.

In late 1979 the FCC received a staff report on the effectiveness of its 1974 actions on children's television. The staff concluded that the report had made a difference only with regards to the very specific points related to advertising—the lessening of commercial time and the clear separation of program and advertising. In other respects—specifically the provision of more children's programming throughout the week—the staff reported there had been no significant progress and that the commission should consider further mandatory regulations. Although the commission voted to accept the report and asked for further recommendations, it was clear that the question of First Amendment and Section 326 infringement was extremely important and would probably work against any decisive action being taken.

Confrontation with Minority Groups

The third arena of confrontation for broadcasters involved minority employment. The first major efforts were by black and women's groups but later others such as Hispanics began demanding "a piece of the action."

When the civil rights drives started in the 1960s minority representation in broadcasting was probably comparable to that in banking, publishing, and other areas—practically zero. There were no black executives in networks, stations, or other broadcast organizations. There were no black writers or producers. Seldom was a black seen on screen except as dramatic talent. Women were employed only as secretaries.

The FCC promulgated guidelines for equal employment opportunities under Title VII of the Civil Rights Act and brought pressure on broadcasters to increase minority employment, but a far greater impact was made by a 1966 decision of the U.S. Court of Appeals in Washington, D.C.—the WLBT(TV) license renewal case that is discussed in some detail in Chapter 7. In that case the FCC was told that it was not by itself an adequate representative of the public and that it must permit members of the affected community to be heard in renewal cases. Three years later when the commission had observed the letter of the ruling but ignored the spirit, the court not only reprimanded the FCC, it also revoked the license that had been renewed and ordered the FCC to start all over again and to proceed more properly.

From that day in 1969 minority groups have had a clear entry into the regulatory process and have used their status to great advantage. It is probably safe to say that while a few broadcasters would have integrated their operations of their own volition, perhaps 90 percent of the progress in minority employment has been the result of the WLBT(TV) case. Minorities are now the rule rather than the exception in newsrooms and have been slowly finding their ways into better office jobs although the industry is still primarily dominated by white males.

In the second half of the 1970s the FCC, with the vigorous support of the Carter administration, moved actively on at least four fronts to increase the representation of minorities among broadcast owners. Although the statistics do not appear to have changed significantly at the beginning of the 1980s, the trends have been clearly established.

In 1978 the FCC announced a policy of granting "tax certificates" when a station was sold to a group with substantial minority representation and where "there is a substantial liklihood that diversity of programming would be increased as a result." The tax certificate made it possible for the seller to defer the capital gains taxes on the profit made from the sale and was a strong incentive for some.

At the same time the FCC also announced it would permit "distress sales" by owners whose licenses were in danger of either revocation or nonrenewal. Such an owner would be permitted to sell the station to an applicant with minority representation at a price of up to 75 percent of fair market value. If the proposed new owner met all other qualifications for licensing, the transfer would be approved and the former owner would avoid possible hearings before the FCC and the risk of losing the license entirely.

By the end of the 1970s only a handful of stations had been transferred to minority groups by the tax-certificate and distress-sale routes. However, for the first time minorities were owners of VHF network affiliates in substantial markets, and the FCC's program was considered successful, with more promise for the 1980s.

Another government agency, the Small Business Administration (SBA), has also changed policy in such a way that minority ownership of broadcasting stations will be encouraged. For many years the SBA refused to make low-interest loans for purchase of broadcast stations on the ground that a government agency should not be that closely involved in communications. In the 1970s loans were approved for the purchase of stations, and while minority individuals have not been the only ones to receive them, some have been aided by the SBA to get into broadcasting. To increase the effectiveness of the above actions, the FCC further moved in 1980 to substantially increase the number of stations for which minorities might apply.

For nearly twenty years there had been requests for "VHF dropins," the addition of new stations with lower power than those approved in the 1952 allocations at the end of the Freeze. As the commission drew its original table of allocations, it had been concerned only with full-service stations, operating with full power and broadcasting to large areas. This policy meant there were many locations that lay between coverage areas where stations with lesser power might be assigned. The major objection stemmed from the need to protect UHF stations that had been assigned to those markets and that might not be able to succeed against new VHF competition.

By 1980 the FCC had completed studies that concluded that UHF stations had received enough protection and should be able to stand on their own feet. In September there was initial approval of four dropins that would operate with less than half of full power and with directionalized antennae where necessary to protect existing stations on the same or adjacent channels. There was also an indication that other dropins would be approved as applicants if they could demonstrate they would not interfere with stations already on the air.

At the same time the FCC approved the concept of "low-power television" for stations operating with 10 watts on the VHF and up to 1,000 watts on the UHF. These would have coverage areas of up to fifteen miles and it was hypothesized that thousands might be licensed throughout the country. Licensing would be on a first-come, first-served basis with priority given to minorities and with fewer programming requirements than are imposed on more powerful stations.

There have also been several moves in the private sector to increase minority ownership of stations. Probably the most notable has been the

Minority Assistance Investment Fund set up by the National Association of Broadcasters (NAB). As a consequence of these moves by both government and private groups, banks have looked upon loans to minority groups with a great deal more favor. As already indicated, such efforts came too late for dramatic results in the 1970s, but most people anticipate significant increases in minority ownership in the 1980s.

Programming in the 1970s

The 1970s were marked by intense competition among the three television networks with ABC assuming first place for the first time. As the competition grew greater, there was less and less innovative programming and more emphasis on tried-and-true sitcoms and programs about crime. The single most important development was the mini-series, of which ABC's "Roots" was the most successful example. It completely dominated the ratings for a week and was followed by similar efforts on the other networks. Otherwise, there was little that was outstanding.

SUMMARY

The story of television until 1952 involved experimentation, a shaky start, a holding pattern during World War II, and uncertainty until the end of the Freeze. Since 1952 television has prospered, increasing its influence more than any other medium, although the UHF stations are only beginning to realize profits. In the 1970s there were confrontations with the Nixon administration, with concerned parents, and with minorities. In the 1980s the greatest challenge to conventional television comes from cable. As new communications technology develops, there may be important changes in the dominant position television has enjoyed.

GLOSSARY ITEMS

The following words and phrases used in Chapter 5 are defined in the Glossary:

All-Channel Receiver	**Distress Sale**
Blacklisting	**Educational Television**
Channel Assignments	**Electronic Television**
Channel Separation Factor	**Fairness Doctrine**
Deintermixture	**Fixed Assignments**

Mechanical Television   Penetration
Mixed Markets   Pre-Freeze Station
Multiple-Ownership Rules   Tax Certificate
Pay Television   Television Freeze

TELEVISION CHRONOLOG

1862   Abbe Caselli (Italy) invented crude system of sending photos by telegraph.

1884   Paul Nipkow (Germany) invented scanning disc later used in mechanical television.

1905   Julius Elster and Hans Geitel (Germany) developed the photo-electric cell.

1917   Vladimir Zworykin started research on television in Russian laboratory.

1923   Herbert Ives of Bell Laboratories started experimentation on telephoto process that led to further work in mechanical television.

Z David Sarnoff predicted home television to RCA's board of directors.

Zworykin (now located in United States) made application for first patent on iconoscope tube that was key to electronic television.

1927   Ives sent mechanical television pictures by wire between New York City and Washington, D.C.

Philo Farnsworth got first of many patents in television.

1928   Zworykin perfected iconoscope tube.

1930   Research emphasis shifted from mechanical to electronic television. RCA made heaviest commitment to development of new form.

NBC put experimental television station on air in New York City.

1936   British Broadcasting Corporation started television service.

1939   RCA introduced Orthicon tube—improvement over iconoscope.

1939 NBC demonstrated television at World's Fair in New York City.

1940 CBS announced mechanical color television system.

1941 FCC authorized commercial telecasting.

1945 RCA demonstrated Image-Orthicon tube.

1946 CBS petitioned FCC for immediate approval of mechanical color television in the UHF.

1947 FCC denied CBS petition for approval of color television.

1948 First transistor demonstrated by Bell Labs.

FCC deleted Channel 1 from television.

FCC imposed "Freeze" during which no new TV station applications would be received or considered.

1950 FCC approved CBS color-television system.

1951 Supreme Court refused to overturn FCC decision on CBS color.

CBS agreed to halt color development due to shortage of materials; NTSC started tests on compatible system.

AT&T completed television network connections from coast to coast.

1952 The Freeze was lifted.

1953 FCC approved NTSC electronic and compatible color system.

1954 FCC changed multiple-ownership rules to permit addition of two UHF stations to five VHFs.

Edward R. Murrow program on Senator Joseph McCarthy.

1955 NBC bought UHF station in Buffalo, N.Y.

In first move on deintermixture, FCC requested comments on deleting VHF assignments in four mixed markets.

FCC asked Office of Defense Mobilization to release military VHF channels for television.

1956 AMPEX demonstrated videotape recorder at NAB convention.

ODM denied FCC request for VHF channels.

1958 NBC gave Buffalo UHF station to educational group.

1959 The quiz scandals.

1960 FCC deintermixed Fresno, California. Deleted VHF channel.

The "Great Debates" between presidential candidates Kennedy and Nixon.

1961 FCC Chairman Newton Minow delivered "vast wasteland" speech to NAB convention.

1962   AT&T launched Telstar as first step in global satellite service. COMSAT founded.

FCC ruled that all TV sets sold after April 1964 be equipped to receive all television channels.

1963   Networks moved to thirty-minute evening newscasts.

Coverage of President Kennedy's assassination and funeral.

1964   Coverage of civil rights demonstrations and confrontations.

1965   Breakthrough for color television as ABC and CBS joined NBC in presenting majority of schedule in color.

1969   Television coverage of the first man to walk on the moon.

Agnew speech against the networks in Des Moines, Iowa.

1970   Establishment of Office of Telecommunications Policy. First director was Dr. Clay T. Whitehead.

Action for Children's Television petitioned FCC on commercial practices in children's programming.

1972   Report of Surgeon General's committee on television violence.

1974   FCC refused to respond to ACT petition on commercials in children's programming.

1977   "Roots" broadcast by ABC.

Jury rejected "TV insanity" plea and found Zamorra guilty.

ACT petitioned FTC on finding children's advertising deceptive.

1978   FCC announced policies on distress sales and tax certificates.

NBC cleared in "Born Innocent" case.

FTC proposed rules for television advertising to children.

Small Business Administration changed policy to make loans to purchase broadcast stations.

1979   FTC held hearings on television advertising to children.

FCC staff reported children's television still deficient.

1980   FCC approved VHF dropins.

FCC approved low-power television.

PREVIEW

In the 1980s cable television and subscription television (STV) pose threats to the audience domination of conventional, television-supported "free television." For twenty years the stories of cable and STV were quite dissimilar. CATV (community-antenna television) and cable started in small communities and thrived under a minimum of regulation. The greatest potential of STV was seen in the major markets; it was unable to prove itself because the FCC refused to permit its operation. When STV was finally approved in 1968 it seemed to be an idea whose time had passed; cable was the big story. Cable lagged behind expectations in the early 1970s, but during the latter half of the decade it soared. A principal aspect of cable's success was its pay service which, in turn, opened the way for a rebirth of optimism in STV.

CHAPTER 6

HISTORICAL PERSPECTIVES IV 1950-1980 WITH EMPHASIS ON CABLE TELEVISION AND SUBSCRIPTION TELEVISION

By mid-1950 television was beginning to make an impression on America. There were 107 stations on the air in 63 markets. More than nine million homes had receivers. The "Saturday Night Review" was dominating its time period. Milton Berle, Arthur Godfrey, and Ed Sullivan were starring in comedy and variety programs and the golden age of video drama was about to begin. The television Freeze was ending its second year and people beyond the reach of stations were getting impatient to receive the new medium about which they were reading and hearing so much.

6.1 1950–1960 CATV AND EARLY CABLE

Most of the areas without television had to wait for the end of the Freeze before they might have service. Some homes, however, were just beyond the range of stations and found a way to receive signals without waiting for FCC action. A few had a master antenna that served several families. It might be located on top of a tall apartment house, or several homes might get together to place the antenna high enough to receive pictures and sound that they could share. The breakthrough from these highly informal and noncommercial master antennas came in 1950 in Lansford, Pennsylvania.

CATV

Lansford was seventy miles from Philadelphia, a city that had three stations. The signals from those stations passed directly over Lansford but were beyond the reach of either rooftop or master antennas. An enterprising individual placed an antenna on an eighty-five-foot tower at the top of a mountain where he picked up the Philadelphia stations, then amplified the signals and relayed them by wires through the streets of the town. The result was perfect reception for connected homes. Because one antenna was serving a whole community, it was called community-antenna television (CATV). The "headend" was the point from which the signals arriving from the mountain-top antenna were sent through the community by cables attached to electric and telephone poles. Connections were made from the main cable into homes so the signals traveled from the community antenna to the receivers without the use of the airwaves. (See Fig. 2.11 in Chapter 2.)

There were three factors that differentiated CATV systems from the earlier master-antenna setups.

1. They served more homes in larger areas necessitating amplification of the incoming signals.

2. They used the community rights of way to a degree that required a franchise or official permission to run cables through the town.

3. They were planned as profit-making operations in which installation fees and monthly subscription payments would more than cover all expenses.

In its earliest stages CATV was one of those rare developments that seemed ideal for everyone. The stations, networks, and advertisers were glad to get extended coverage at no expense. The subscribers enjoyed the service that would not otherwise have been available. The CATV operator was making a profit.

CATV Becomes Cable

The transition from CATV to cable television occurred first in those communities where only one station could be picked up directly off the air at the headend. From that one station came some of the most popular programs, but there were other shows that were getting national publicity and that subscribers wanted to see. The system operators knew that if there were more stations on the cable, the service would be in greater demand, so they looked for chances to expand. Expansion involved "importation" whereby a receiving antenna was installed in an appropriate location to get programs directly off the air from stations in another city. The signals were then sent back to the headend by microwave relay and distributed along with the original station to subscribers. (See Fig. 2.12 in Chapter 2.)

Cable Services   At this point the operator had moved from pure CATV into "cable television." The modern system may offer as many as five distinct services to its subscribers.

1. *CATV:* Distribution of "local" broadcast signals received directly off the air at the headend.

2. *Importation:* Distribution of "distant" broadcast signals taken off the air many miles away and relayed to the headend by microwave or by satellite from a "superstation."

3. *Origination:* Distribution of material not received from a broadcast station. Material may be produced in the system's own studio or elsewhere and received by satellite.

4. *Access Channels:* Distribution of signals prescribed by the FCC or by local franchise agreement.

5. *Pay Cable:* Distribution of material for which the subscriber must pay in addition to the basic monthly charge that covers the first four services.

Lack of Early Regulation

Since there were no complaints about it, the FCC paid little attention to CATV for nearly two years. Systems operated under franchises granted by local communities. They had no reason to communicate with the commission or any other central agency, so for about twenty years there were only estimates of the numbers of installations and subscribers around the country.

In the fall of 1951 the FCC began to consider the implications of cable. J. E. Belknap & Associates of Poplar Bluff, Missouri, filed an application for a microwave license to import signals to local CATV systems. When Mr. Belknap made inquiries at the FCC, he learned the commission was afraid "that community antenna TV systems may mean the doom of small-market TV stations," especially those on the UHF.* The commission delayed a decision on the technicality that microwave was intended as a common carrier providing more services than just importation. The authorization

---

* *Broadcasting*, November 19, 1951, p. 76.

was finally granted in May 1954 after minor changes were made in the application and after showing there was no ownership connection between Belknap and the cable systems the company proposed to serve. In granting the application the FCC "specifically stated, however, that it is making no determination at this time on whether or not it has jurisdiction over community television operations."*

Aside from its natural inclination to avoid new involvements as long as possible, there were logical reasons why the FCC felt it could not regulate CATV. CATV did not use the airwaves that were clearly within commission jurisdiction. Neither was CATV a common carrier or interstate communication by wire which designations would have also brought it within the FCC's area of responsibility. Finally, the chief argument of the first complaining broadcasters was that CATV posed a threat of economic injury to television stations. Since the *Sanders* case in 1940 the commission had interpreted the court's decision as a mandate not to consider the economic welfare of stations. In 1954 Commissioner John Doerfer responded, to broadcaster complaints, "Jurisdiction over CATV not only is doubtful, but, in my opinion is undesirable."† He was speaking for many who felt the laws of supply and demand should be paramount in determining cable growth and development.

In 1956 the FCC received the first formal request from stations that some CATV systems be regulated because they threatened the existence of stations. The petition was dismissed two years later on the ground that the Communications Act did not give the FCC authority to intervene. In 1958 "Bonus Baby Is Problem Child" was the headline of a *Broadcasting Magazine* story pointing up the difficulty new stations were encountering in communities where CATV was well established.‡ By 1959 the FCC acknowledged that a problem existed and informed Congress that legislation was necessary if the commission were to exert any regulatory control. It suggested a law to provide that CATV systems must get permission from broadcasters to use their signals and that they also be required to carry all local signals if the local stations so requested. In the following year the Senate failed by one vote to take any action on the commission's request.

The Regulatory Dilemma

The role of the FCC in regulating cable has from the beginning been subject to great criticism from both broadcast and cable interests. Each has called favorable decisions wise and justified and criticized adverse rulings on self-

* Ibid., May 10, 1954, p. 67.

† Ibid., November 15, 1954, p. 80.

‡ Ibid., May 12, 1958, p. 33.

serving grounds. The development of cable regulation in the 1960s should be assessed in light of the philosophical commitment the commission made during the Freeze to a nationwide system of television with emphasis on local service.

When the commission had published its table of assignments in 1952, it based the system on a number of priorities. The first two were that every home should have television service from at least one station and that the majority should have access to a minimum of two signals. Under the free enterprise system stations could be expected to operate where there was a reasonable hope of making a profit from advertising revenues. The commission's concern was that new broadcasters in one-station markets might find it impossible to compete profitably with a cable system that was providing three or four signals from outside. Advertisers would soon learn that most of their potential audience was tuned to distant stations on cable, so the advertisers would refuse to buy time on the local station. In the mid-1970s an operator in Salisbury, Maryland told the FCC that "a national advertiser had reduced by 40 percent the money spent on his television station because of the 'spill over' of other television signals imported by the cable systems in his area."

This situation might force some stations off the air and prevent others from even trying to operate. (By the mid-1970s only about 700 of 1,750 commercial assignments had been activated.) For two reasons this impact on local stations would be intolerable in light the commission's desire for a nationwide system of local television.

First, was the fact that the residents of cable communities without broadcast stations would receive no local television service—no local news, no discussion of local issues, no programs attempting to communicate a community identity.

Second, and of greater significance, was the fact that a substantial portion of the population in cable areas without stations would be totally deprived of any service. It is in the nature of cable operation that money can be made only when there is a relatively high density of population per mile of installed lines. For example, if it cost $3,000 to install a mile of cable on existing poles (a reasonable figure in 1960) and if there are 100 homes along that mile, the installation cost per home is only $30. Since the subscriber normally pays an installation fee plus a monthly subscription of, say, up to $5, the per-home cable investment could be fairly easily amortized. But, if there were only fifty homes in the mile, the installation cost per home would be $60 and it would take that much longer to pay off the initial expense before starting to make a profit. When the population density was substantially below fifty homes per mile, the cost per unit for installing cable would be prohibitive and the cable company would make no plans to serve such homes either immediately or in the long run.

This would mean the commission's first priority of minimal service for everyone had been violated. If there is only cable in an area, there will be some homes denied access to television indefinitely. Even if all channels in the table of assignments came on the air, there would be perhaps 1–2 percent of homes beyond the range of good signals. If many areas had only cable there might be another 10–20 percent without hope of service because systems would not find it economically feasible to run lines past their homes. Should cable be permitted to grow without restriction to the point where it might destroy station viability in small markets and thus make television service totally unavailable to a portion of the population? That was the philosophical question facing the commission. At the same time, it was clear that cable was providing a valuable service to many people and that it did represent a technological advance. Simply resisting such a development was counter to American philosophy.

6.2 1950–1960 SUBSCRIPTION TELEVISION EXPERIMENTATION

As early as June 1946, E. F. McDonald, Jr., president of Zenith Radio Corporation, predicted that advertiser dollars would never be sufficient to pay the costs of television programming. He recommended exploration of several systems whereby people would pay directly for each program. Over the years the concept was variously known as "subscription television" (STV), "pay television," and "toll television."

Early Tests

In 1950 the FCC warily approved a ninety-day test in Chicago of Zenith's Phonevision system. The experiment started in January 1951 with transmission each day of popular movies. A viewer wishing to see one of the movies would call the telephone operator to request transmission over the telephone line of a signal to clear the jumbled TV transmission. The viewer would then be billed one dollar at the end of the month for each movie seen. Zenith termed the experiment successful beyond expectation and petitioned the FCC to make rules that would permit general use of any transmitter for STV purposes.

Reluctance of the FCC

Throughout the 1950s subscription television was a major issue. Zenith's petition to approve STV remained on the commission agenda without resolution. Adherents of STV claimed that the "pay to see" system would make available programming that advertisers could not afford to support, primarily in the fields of education and culture. Conventional broadcasters argued that the STV promoters were only interested in making money and that once a system was approved, the emphasis would be not on education and culture but on outbidding the networks for their most popular entertainment features. Congress was drawn into the debate and the House Committee on Interstate and Foreign Commerce asked the FCC to delay any final decision.

6.3 1960–1970 INTERMEDIATE CABLE REGULATION
Cable Optimism

The early 1960s were heady years for cable operators. Between 700 and 800 systems were in operation. About 50 were importing and providing more signals to their subscribers than could have been expected off the air under the FCC's table of assignments. Cable operators at the National Cable Television Association (NCTA) conventions were discussing origination financed by advertising sold in competition with over-the-air television. Cable had been so successful in small communities that some operators were looking forward to moving into the major cities.

Part of the optimism was due to the FCC's apparent lack of ability to control growth. Microwave relay authorizations were being granted for importation, and Congress had refused to amend the Communications Act to give the commission a clear-cut mandate to regulate cable. It was apparent some changes would take place but no one knew what to expect. The confusion and the optimism began to dissipate with the *Carter Mountain* case.

Carter Mountain Case

The Carter Mountain Transmission Corporation operated microwave relays that imported television signals to cable systems in the Rocky Mountains. It applied for permission to increase its facilities so it might provide an importation service to CATV in the Riverton, Wyoming, area, which was served by a single station, KWRB-TV. This was a typical small-market situation where the station was in the red. In 1959 the commission staff granted Carter Mountain's request on a routine basis without a hearing. KWRB-TV protested the award, saying addition of the importation service would force the station off the air, thus depriving TV service to all homes outside the cable area. In 1962, after a hearing, the FCC reversed the microwave grant.

A principal basis for the reversal was the 1958 appeals court decision in the *Carroll* case. Carroll Broadcasting Company operated a station in Carrollton, Georgia, which served a population of about 11,000 persons. When the FCC granted a construction permit to a new radio station, the owner of the existing station protested to the court that there was not enough advertising revenue in the area to enable two stations to serve the public well. The court took note of the *Sanders* case, which the commission had felt ruled out economic injury as an issue in authorizing new stations. It went on to emphasize the Supreme Court's comment that if economic injury meant impaired service to the public, then it should be considered. After quoting the appropriate passages from the *Sanders* case, the appeals court said:

> *Thus, it seems to us, the question whether a station makes $5,000 or $10,000 or $50,000 is a matter in which the public has no interest so long as service is not adversely affected; service may well be improved by competition. But, if the situation in a given area is such that available revenue will not support good service in more than one station, the public interest may well be in the licensing of one rather than two stations. To license two stations where there is revenue for only one may result in no good service at all. So economic injury to an existing station, while not in and of itself a matter of moment, becomes important when on the facts it spells diminution or destruction of service. At that point the element of injury ceases to be a matter of purely private concern.**

In the *Carter Mountain* decision the FCC applied the *Carroll* case reasoning to the granting of microwave licenses for importation. Accepting the statements of KWRB-TV that the proposed importation of signals into its community would force it to go off the air, the commission adhered to its basic policy of providing television service for everyone and denied the Carter Mountain application.

> *We will not shut our eyes to the impact upon the public service which is our ultimate concern, when it appears that the (microwave) grant may serve to deprive a substantially large number of the public of a service. . . . We will not permit a subsequent grant to be issued if it be demonstrated that the same would vitiate a prior grant, without weighing the public-interest considerations involved.†*

---

* *Carroll Broadcasting Company v. Federal Communications Commission*, 258 F.2d. 440 (D.C. Cir.). July 10, 1958.

† In re: *Carter Mountain Transmission Corp.*, 32 FCC 459, February 14, 1962.

On the matter of economic injury the FCC added:

> *Hence, when the impact of economic injury is such as to*
> *adversely affect the public interest, it is not only within our*
> *power, but it is our duty to determine the ultimate effect, study*
> *the fact, and act in a manner most advantageous to the public.*

The commission denied the Carter Mountain application but said another request might be filed if there were assurances that the cable system
would agree to carry the KWRB-TV signal and avoid importing programs
scheduled to be aired by the station. Carter Mountain disputed the FCC's
authority to limit the use of microwave, but in May 1963 the court of
appeals upheld the commission. This was clear authorization for the FCC
to move ahead in one aspect of cable regulation without congressional
action. The FCC had the responsibility for overseeing development of a
national system of television and if that system were threatened by importation, then the FCC had authority to regulate microwave relays to control
importation.

Cable Regulations of 1965 and 1966

Following the court's affirmation of the *Carter Mountain* decision the FCC
started working on minimal cable regulations. In 1965 it announced rules
for cable systems that were importing distant signals and in the following
year extended them with slight variations to all systems.

1. All cable systems were required to carry all local broadcast signals if
   the stations so requested. This guaranteed the local stations the same
   access to cable carriage as those being imported and local UHF signals
   were given equal cable status with VHF.

2. All systems had to protect local station programming by "blacking out"
   or not importing a program on the same day it was being aired locally.

3. No new microwave license would be routinely granted for importation
   into a top-one-hundred market if any local station objected. Since it
   was inevitable that a local station would object, this meant that an
   application would be bogged down in hearings and other lengthy procedures for so long that it was not worth the effort. This third regulation
   was, in effect, a "pseudofreeze" on cable in the big cities.

4. There was a "grandfather clause" that permitted existing systems to
   continue practices that were prohibited to new systems.

The pseudofreeze was particularly frustrating to cable interests since
by 1965 the most promising of the smaller markets were already wired and
the greatest remaining potential was in the cities. The lure of the large

markets was increased by the breakthrough of color, which required better reception conditions than did black and white. Considering their success in outlying areas, cable operators were looking to the major markets as an almost unlimited source of revenues. But they realized they would probably have to provide imported signals to make their service attractive to potential subscribers in markets already well served by network-affiliated stations.

From 1965 to 1972 cable was in a state of suspended animation with growth limited to extension of systems in small communities or into large markets like New York City where the concentration of highrise buildings in Manhattan resulted in poor off-air reception and where there were so many independent stations there was no need for importation. In June 1968 there were two important Supreme Court decisions—one gave comfort to the broadcasters, the other to the cable operators.

The *Southwestern* Case

The *Southwestern* case was a challenge to the right of the FCC to promulgate and enforce importation rules on cable systems. Southwestern Cable Company operated a system in San Diego, one of the top-one-hundred markets, and had been importing signals from Los Angeles, a little over a hundred miles to the north. Midwest Television, which operated one of the San Diego stations, requested from the Commission an order that would prohibit Southwestern from offering its imported programs to any new customers although it could, under the grandfather clause, continue providing them to former subscribers. The FCC ordered Southwestern to restrict its services to new subscribers until a hearing could be held. Southwestern asked the U.S. Court of Appeals for the Ninth Circuit to rule that the commission was exceeding its authority under the Communications Act and the court did so. The FCC appealed the ruling to the Supreme Court.

The Supreme Court in June 1968 reversed the lower court's ruling and in two ways affirmed the authority of the FCC to regulate cable television.

1. The Court rejected the argument that cable was not interstate and therefore not subject to federal regulations:

> *Nor can we doubt that CATV systems are engaged in interstate communication, even where, as here, the intercepted signals emanate from stations located within the same State in which the CATV system operates. We may take notice that television broadcasting consists in very large part of programming devised for, and distributed to, national audiences; respondents thus are ordinarily employed in the simultaneous transmission of communications that have very often originated in other States.*

The stream of communication is essentially uninterrupted and properly indivisible. To categorize respondents' activities as intrastate would disregard the character of the television industry. . . .*

2. More significantly, the Court held that FCC regulation of cable was essential to fulfill the congressional mandate for development of broadcasting:

Moreover, the Commission has reasonably concluded that regulatory authority over CATV is imperative if it is to perform with appropriate effectiveness certain of its other responsibilities. . . . The Commission has reasonably found that the achievement of each of its purposes is "placed in jeopardy by the unregulated explosive growth of CATV." . . . There is no need to determine in detail the limits of the Commission's authority to regulate CATV. It is enough to emphasize that the authority which we recognize today . . . is restricted to that reasonably ancillary to the effective performance of the Commission's various responsibilities for the regulation of television broadcasting.†

Thus, the Court was agreeing with the FCC posture in *Carter Mountain* that it had the responsibility for planning nationwide television based on the concept of local service. Within the "reasonably ancillary" restriction given above, the commission might regulate anything that threatened the overall design. From that point on there was no question about the FCC's authority to regulate cable.

The *Fortnightly* Case

A week after the *Southwestern* decision that pleased the broadcasters, the Supreme Court handed down a decision in the *Fortnightly* case that was equally pleasing to the cable interests. It concerned obligations of cable operators under the copyright law of 1909, which generally provides that the creator of a book or play or other work is entitled to compensation if someone else makes money using it.

In the early CATV days, stations wondered whether they might be entitled to some compensation because cable systems were making money distributing their programs. For the most part, however, they were so pleased with the extension of their audiences that they did not make copyright payments an issue. Thus CATV systems were obtaining for free the

---

* *United States et al. v. Southwestern Cable Co., et al.*, 392 U.S. at 168, June 10, 1968.

† Ibid., at 173.

product they were selling subscribers. When a few broadcasters did try to prevent cable from carrying their programs, they were rebuffed by the state courts.

In 1960 United Artists Television, Inc., which held copyrights on some movies being used on television, sued Fortnightly Corporation asking copyright payments for broadcast movies being delivered by CATV to homes in West Virginia. When the case reached the Supreme Court eight years later, the decision handed down was based on application of a key word found in the Copyright Act—"perform." In ruling against United Artists, the Court said:

> CATV systems do not in fact broadcast or rebroadcast. Broadcasters select the programs to be viewed; CATV systems simply carry, without editing, whatever programs they receive. Broadcasters procure programs and propagate them to the public; CATV systems receive programs that have been released to the public and carry them by private channels to additional viewers. We hold that CATV operators, like viewers and unlike broadcasters, do not perform the programs that they receive and carry. . . . We take the Copyright Act of 1909 as we find it. With due regard to changing technology, we hold that the petitioner did not under that law "perform" the respondent's copyrighted works.*

The Supreme Court emphasized it was ruling on only one specific instance and avoiding broader implications. Some took this to mean that the Court might find differently in another case where there had been importation. In March 1974 the Supreme Court heard another copyright case in which CBS sued Teleprompter for importing some of its programs. The Court reaffirmed its original stance:

> The reception and rechanneling of these signals for simultaneous viewing is essentially a viewer function, irrespective of the distance between the broadcasting station and the ultimate viewer.†

This broadened the 1968 decision so that cable was free of copyright liability whenever it carried broadcast signals although a system would have to pay for permission to use copyright material originating in its studio or "performed" on its own film chains or videotape playbacks.

---

* *Fortnightly Corp.* v. *United Artists Television, Inc.*, 392 U.S. at 400, June 17, 1968.

† *Teleprompter Corporation et al.* v. *Columbia Broadcasting System, Inc.*, 415 U.S. at 408, March 4, 1974.

The NCTA was delighted with the 1968 copyright decision and the NAB was dismayed. The FCC realized it must take a fresh look at the problem. According to *Broadcasting:*

> *Chairman Rosel H. Hyde and other members of the Commission had long counted on copyright to lighten the Commission's regulatory burden in CATV. They felt that, if CATV systems were held liable for copyright payments, the systems would be forced to compete on more equal terms with stations and that, as a result, the Commission's need to afford broadcasters economic protection against CATV competition would be reduced.**

Had cable been liable for copyright payments to broadcasters, the relationships between cable and television might have evolved naturally in the marketplace without the need for further regulation. Such was not to be the case.

6.4 1960–1970 FCC APPROVAL OF SUBSCRIPTION TELEVISION (STV)

As the decade started, the commission felt it needed more information about STV and in June 1960 approved the sale of WHCT(TV), Channel 18 in Hartford, Connecticut, to RKO General, Inc., for a three-year test of Zenith's Phonevision. The trial lasted for six years and apparently answered the commission's questions. In 1968 it approved the concept of STV and issued rules to cover it. STV would be authorized for only one station in a community and only where there were four or more commerical stations in operation. Such a station could not be full-time STV, but had to carry a minimum amount of regular broadcasting.

The Antisiphoning Rules

There were a number of antisiphoning rules that prohibited STV from buying those programs that had been most important to networks and stations. The presentation of movies was limited to those that were less than two years old except that there could be one movie a month that was over ten years old. Since most stations used one or more films every day and the majority had been released between two and ten years before airing, this protected the supply on which broadcasters were dependent.

---

* *Broadcasting,* June 24, 1968, p. 19.

No sports event could be shown on STV if it had been on regular television during the preceding two years. Promoters of professional sports were very anxious to tap the larger amounts of money they thought STV could provide but the new ruling meant that promoters would have to keep their events off conventional television for two full years before any such arrangements could be made. STV was not permitted to present a series where individual episodes had either an interconnected plot or substantially the same cast of principal characters. There was to be no sale of time for advertising in STV programming.

STV proponents contended the new regulations were to protect conventional television operators and were an unfair impediment to development of the new medium. They charged that the commission was the captive of those it was supposed to regulate. Broadcasters responded that the public would now have to pay for programs it had been getting free. They failed to emphasize sufficiently that for many people STV was more than a matter of having to pay for popular programming—they would otherwise have no opportunity to see it even if they were willing to pay.

When advertisers pay for televising sporting events, they justify the costs by the size of the audience. When all revenues for commercials in an event like a 1960s World Series game were added together and divided by the number of sets tuned in, it was apparent that all advertisers combined had been paying approximately ten cents per viewing home. That figure could not be materially increased in light of existing cost-per-thousand limits the advertisers had imposed upon themselves. The limit for STV, on the other hand, was determined by how much each viewing home would be willing to pay. If, for example, each home were willing to pay fifty cents per World Series game, STV could outbid conventional television for the rights even if the number of viewing homes were substantially lower. Since professional sports is a business, one must assume the rights would go to the highest bidder.

However, STV would be present only in the largest markets where there were good prospects of its economic success. There might be justifiable debate about whether a person living in a community served by STV should be required to pay for seeing a game, but there was no question about the unfairness to an individual in a community without STV who would be deprived of the opportunity to see the game even if he or she were willing to pay for it. Thus the FCC saw its apparent protection of conventional television as a more important protection for the public.

Subscription television turned out to be a concept whose time had passed during the years of controversy. When STV was finally approved, pay cable seemed to have a far brighter future. Promoters who wanted to sell sports and other programming for greater amounts than conventional television could afford were beginning to consider pay cable. Development of STV was dormant for the next ten years.

6.5 1970–1975 THE END OF THE PSEUDO-FREEZE
The FCC Search for Accord

Following the *Southwestern* decision in June 1968 the responsibility for regulating cable fell squarely on the shoulders of the FCC. Its earlier pseudofreeze on importation into the top-one-hundred markets remained in effect and everyone waited for indications of what was to come. The commission realized its regulation would have to find a middle ground between protecting broadcasters so they might continue serving audiences beyond the reach of cable while at the same time giving cable a chance to realize its eventual potential.

The FCC became the focal point for intense pressures by both broadcasters and cable operators. There were charges that the commission was the "captive" of the broadcast industry and intent only on protecting its interests. Indeed, there was evidence for that suspicion but the motivation was quite different from that attributed by the NCTA, speaking for cable operators. The commission was being consistent with its stance dating back to the *Carter Mountain* case—the development of a nationwide system of television where most people would have access to at least two television signals even if they did not live in a cable area. There was a tacit suspicion that cable, with its technological capacity to provide every home with twenty or forty or more channels, might some day replace over-the-air transmissions. But if broadcasting lost its economic viability before cable was ready to serve the whole nation, there would be many people without any television reception at all.

The FCC had little difficulty formulating the broad outline of cable regulations, but it felt the specific details of regulating competition between the two media ought to result from negotiations by both sides. It had been assumed for some years by both broadcasters and cable operators that there should be some payment for use of programs but there was no consensus on how much it should be. The FCC was essentially saying to both sides, "Come up with reasonable proposals on which you can agree and we will formulate regulations to implement them." Meetings were held between the NAB and NCTA with little progress. Commission Chairman Rosel Hyde and OTP Director Clay Whitehead were unable to bring them together.

In August 1971 FCC Chairman Dean Burch (Mr. Hyde's successor) wrote a letter to Congress spelling out a commission position on cable regulation generally but reported he was unable to get the NAB and NCTA to subscribe to details. The frustration with the uncertainty and the delay began to mount as it had toward the end of the 1948–1952 television Freeze. Finally, in November OTP Director Whitehead called the parties to the White House and handed them what seemed to him to be an acceptable compromise with the ultimatum: take it or leave it.

The Whitehead compromise, which was filed with the FCC as the "OTP Consensus Agreement," was largely a matter of affirming or making slight changes in various aspects of the Burch letter of August 1971. The most significant portion dealt with copyrights. It called for "compulsory" licenses for all local signals that would require that they be carried as specified by the FCC. On the matter of payment, the agreement said:

> *Unless a schedule of fees covering the compulsory licenses or some other payment mechanism can be agreed upon between the copyright owners and the CATV owners in time for inclusion in the new copyright statute, the legislation would simply provide for compulsory arbitration failing private agreement on copyright fees.*

Thus, the major issue of copyright payment was postponed for later consideration in order that cable might be free to start its expansion.

Each side felt great pressure to accept the proposal. The Supreme Court had ruled that broadcasters were not entitled to copyright payments from cable. Only FCC regulations or congressional passage of a new copyright act could protect broadcasters from competition they felt would be detrimental to them. The Court had told the cable operators they were subject to FCC regulations. For more than six years there had been a pseudofreeze that had kept cable from expanding into the major markets where operators felt their most promising future lay. With a sigh of relief, the two parties (plus copyright holders in Hollywood) agreed to the compromise even though it failed to solve the basic problem.

The 1972 Regulations

In February 1972 the FCC issued cable regulations that for the most part conformed to the Burch letter of the preceding August with minor changes reflecting the Whitehead compromise. By the beginning of the 1980s these regulations had been all but totally abandoned. However, they are important to the understanding of cable: they mark the beginning of the modern era and were an important prelude to the explosive growth of the late 1970s. Furthermore, some of the dropped or voided FCC regulations were incorporated into local franchises, thus shaping the medium for the indefinite future.

Three of the 1972 regulations were comparatively noncontroversial at the time but worthy of note:

1. Certificate of Compliance.
2. Carriage of Local Signals.
3. Minimum Capacity.

Certificate of Compliance All cable systems were eventually required to hold a "certificate of compliance" from the FCC. The certificate was intended to be largely *pro forma* and given to the holder of a valid local franchise and, indeed, this requirement was dropped by the end of the 1970s. However, it provides useful insight into the "three-tiered" cable regulation of the mid-1970s in which responsibility was divided among the traditional three levels of government:

1. The local community gave the franchise.
2. Some states established cable commissions that set standards to govern community actions.
3. The FCC granted the certificate of compliance and laid down regulations.

Local regulation A certificate of compliance was comparable to a station license in that it is a required document issued by the FCC. In most respects, however, the cable equivalent of the broadcaster's license is the franchise granted by the local community giving permission to install cable above or beneath city streets and to sell broadcast services to residents.

When a community is considering cable television it will normally make a public announcement, invite proposals, and hold public hearings. The authorities determine the size of the fee to be paid by the cable company, the specific geographic areas for which franchises are to be issued, and the timetable for installing the cable. They will look into the character and financial capacity of the applicants and their promises to operate in the best interests of the community. They will also consider plans for studios to be used by the community and its residents and the ways in which cable will be useful as well as entertaining to citizens. When local communities were writing franchises after 1972, it was natural that they should include some of the FCC requirements such as the access channels.

State regulation As cable operations became more attractive in communities of all sizes, an obvious problem was that in some smaller towns there were no officials with expertise to make sure the franchises were beneficial to local citizens. To protect the communities many states set up commissions to consult with local governments and to lay down minimum requirements for franchisees.

Federal regulation   At the federal level, as noted, the FCC required a cable system to have a certificate of compliance. Its primary value was in enforcing the other regulations. For example, the FCC required all systems to carry all local signals. If a system failed to do so, the FCC could cancel its certificate and thus force it to stop operating.

Carriage of Local Signals   The second noncontroversial regulation of 1972 was the first to be written by the FCC in 1965. All systems were required to carry all local-station signals. This presented no serious problem since in 1972 the channel capacity usually exceeded the number of local stations and, as time passed, technology increased the number of channels available. The primary significance of this regulation lay in the increased coverage of UHF stations—both commercial and public.

Minimum Capacity   The third regulation called for a minimum technical capacity of new systems in the major markets. Each had to provide at least twenty channels although few could then see the possible usage of that many. More significant to later development was the requirement that the system have an "upstream capacity" or the ability to carry a signal from the subscribing home back to the studio. It was not necessary to return a television picture or even the spoken word—only a computer signal. From this requirement came the concept of "interactive cable" illustrated by Qube, which is described shortly.

The three regulations that became highly controversial and critical in the development of cable were:

1. Access Channels.
2. Importation.
3. Pay Cable.

Access Channels   To provide for the local public interest, the commission ruled that systems in the top-one-hundred markets must provide one other-purpose channel for each used to carry broadcast programs. Among the nonbroadcast channels must be four "access" facilities.

a) *Public Access:* One channel must be available to the public on a first-come, first-served basis so individuals can communicate whatever they wish on the system. There can be no charge for use of the channel, and production facilities must be maintained for use at a minimal cost. The cable operator can exercise no control over the program content other than to prohibit advertising and presentation of obscene or indecent material.

b) *Educational Access:* One channel must be assigned for full-time use by educational authorities and institutions. Since few schools are equipped to use cable, those channels have been comparatively unused.

c) *Local Government Access:* One channel must be reserved for local government. Since few municipalities are organized to use mass media and since the connection of homes is still far from universal, there has been little use of these channels either.

d) *Leased-Access Channels:* Cable systems are required to offer their unused channels for lease to individuals and organizations. There are no advertising restrictions, so producers who experiment on public access and think they have a salable commodity can lease time on another channel and try to sell advertising. For example, a group that produced "soft porn" on public access in New York City at a cost of $50 per hour went to a leased channel, raised its budget to $1,500 per program, and offered spots to advertisers.

Importation The regulation on importation was one that lifted the pseudofreeze on cable in major markets. Cable systems were given the right to import signals under certain conditions that varied according to the size of the market. Every system could import to the extent necessary to provide three "full-network" stations that in prime time carried 85 percent of the programs offered by their networks. All might also import independent stations within the following general limits:

- three into the top fifty markets
- two into the next fifty markets
- one into television markets below the top one hundred
- without restriction into nontelevision areas

Importation was subject to "leapfrogging" rules, which required that systems bring in outside stations from among the nearest sources. The imported full-network station must be the closest available. Independent stations could be imported only from the two closest of the top-twenty-five markets. For example, if a cable system in central Missouri were going to import independent stations, it must do so from St. Louis or Kansas City and not go all the way to Chicago or San Francisco or New York City for such signals.

Importation was also subject to program-exclusivity rules which protected local stations that had purchased syndicated programs. For example, if a local station broadcast the syndicated "Perry Mason" series and the local cable system was importing a station that showed the same series, the system must delete it from the imported signal. Thus the local station was protected against duplication of the shows that it had purchased for exclusive airing in the area.

Pay Cable Pay cable is by definition the delivery to homes of cable material for which the viewer must pay something in addition to the monthly subscription fee. It is significant to note that as the 1972 regulations were written, most people thought "per-program pay cable" would emerge whereby homes would pay for each individual program, in contrast with the "pay cable service" that later became dominant. The commission wanted to be sure that pay cable would not siphon off some of the most popular programs from conventional television and so its rules repeated almost verbatim the subscription television antisiphoning regulations it had promulgated in 1968. Pay cable was prevented from purchasing a sporting event that had been on television recently or from showing movies between the ages of two and ten years or programs with continuing story lines or characters. Pay cable also could not include any advertising except for upcoming attractions.

Disappointing Growth of Cable

When the rules were announced in February 1972 there was great enthusiasm for the future of cable. It had been unable to move into most of the major markets since 1965. With the lifting of the pseudofreeze and the establishment of ground rules, cable companies planned to proceed rapidly and their stocks soared on the exchanges.

Fifteen months later, in June 1973, there were the first hints that cable still had major problems. Cable penetration (percentage of connected homes in areas where cable was installed) in the major markets was growing more slowly than anticipated. In New York and other cities it appeared to be leveling off at about 30 percent. Further examination revealed it was the CATV aspect of cable that had persuaded homeowners to become subscribers. They signed up for the service when they had difficulty getting good off-the-air signals because of high buildings and terrain features. When a home had good reception, the origination and importation services were not enough to attract large numbers of subscribers. It should also be noted that many of the major markets had one or more independent stations. Since any imported stations would also be independent, there would be many programs that the nonduplication rules would have forced the operator to eliminate. This would have caused serious operational problems.

At the June 1973 NCTA convention, pay cable attracted major attention as an essential service for success in the major markets. Pay TV, they were told and they believed, is the only extra CATV service now available that has been proved to bring in cash—and wiring the big cities is going to take a heavy capital investment. The cost of cable installation in big cities, where cables had to be buried under the streets, ranged from $75,000 to $90,000 per mile. At this time there was also a shortage of investment capital and interest rates were rising to unprecedented heights. The annual prime interest rate for banks' most favored customers was 11–12 percent. Cable companies were being charged 15–20 percent. There were dim prospects of being able to pay such charges on a penetration of substantially less than half the homes passed by cable.

In September 1973 there was a bombshell involving Teleprompter which served approximately 10 percent of all cable homes in the country. Trading of its stock was suspended on the exchange amid rumors it had overextended its borrowing for new systems and would have trouble paying its debts. Teleprompter announced it was releasing 20 percent of its employees and retrenching its development plans.

In October leaders of the NCTA and representatives of a stock-brokerage house met with the FCC pleading for fewer restrictions and especially asking for an easing of the antisiphoning rules on pay cable. In December cable was "banned in Boston." The city had conducted a study and concluded the potential income to the city from cable was too small to justify having the streets ripped up for installation of the lines. It further noted that in other large cities subscriber homes appeared to be limited to those that needed the CATV service, while most homes in Boston were getting reasonably good off-the-air reception. After considering all the aspects, Boston decided it neither needed nor wanted a cable system and that it would grant no franchise.

In February 1974, *Broadcasting* reported on a survey taken among the major cable companies and found them much less optimistic about major market cable. "But one of the most significant developments of cable (during 1973) was the growing realization by major cable concerns that the concept of the wired city must, for the time being, remain just a concept."*

6.6 1975–1980 SATELLITES AND DEREGULATION

The five years following the disappointing growth of cable in 1973 and 1974 were marked by an amazing turnaround stimulated by the growth of satellite usage and deregulation brought about as some rules were dropped by the FCC and others were voided by the courts. The latter years of the 1970s are discussed here in terms of each of the five traditional services provided by a cable system (CATV, Importation, Origination, Access Channels, Pay Cable) plus a sixth service, Interactive Cable.

CATV

CATV, or the carrying of all local stations, continues to be the heart of cable's appeal to subscribers. However, while CATV's importance has not been diminished, the growing appeal of the other services has changed the sales emphasis of cable systems.

---

* *Broadcasting*, February 4, 1974, p. 48.

Importation

Importation of distant broadcast signals entered a new era in December 1976 when WTCG(TV) in Atlanta, Georgia became the first "superstation." WTCG(TV) is licensed to Ted Turner who also owns professional sports teams in Atlanta and skippers American entries in international sailing races. It is a comparatively undistinguished UHF independent station showing the usual reruns and as many sports events as it can acquire. Turner incorporated Southern Satellite System (SSS), which picked up the Atlanta signal for transmission to a satellite and then back to earth over the entire country. Individual cable systems were invited to pick up the signals for delivery to homes on payment of ten cents per subscriber per month for full-time service and two cents per subscriber per month for the period from midnight to morning. (The latter arrangement was valuable for those systems that were already importing all the signals permitted by the 1972 regulation but could replace programming of one of the imported stations if it went off the air for part of the day.) By repeating sports events in the early mornings, Turner was making these events available to homes that had until then been limited to the Monday-evening and weekend-afternoon sports shows of the networks. The service proved highly successful in attracting new subscribers to cable systems and three years later WTCG(TV) was carried on over a thousand systems with five million subscriber homes.

In the fall of 1978 the FCC took a significant step in shifting the burden of proof in requests for importation waivers. Until then if a cable system wanted to import more stations than specified in the 1972 regulations, it had to prove the added importation would not impede the ability of the local stations to serve the public interest. The FCC received great criticism for this policy because it had only a hunch that such might be the case—there was no hard evidence. Subsequently, the burden of proof was shifted to the local stations. When a cable system wanted an importation waiver, it made application and received permission if the station could not prove economic injury that would impair service to the public.

This move was an open invitation to increased superstation service and two years later at the start of the 1980s there were four superstations available to cable systems WTBS(TV) (formerly WTCG(TV), WOR-TV in New York City, WGN-TV in Chicago, and KTVU(TV) in San Francisco. Arrangements for all are approximately the same—payment of ten cents per month per subscriber to the transmission company. The stations themselves receive no direct payment although they are theoretically able to raise their advertising rates if they can demonstrate significant additions to their audience.

At the same time, conventional importation by microwave relay has also grown. For example, WPIX-TV in New York City is carried by cable systems with one-and-a-half million subscribing homes outside the metropolitan New York area.

In 1980 the FCC dropped two of its major importation regulations: (1) it no longer limited the number of stations a cable system might import, and (2) it no longer required that an imported syndicated program be blacked out if it was also contracted to one of the local broadcast stations. The dropping of these limitations was appealed to the courts, but even a reversal would have had little impact. Cable systems could already import freely unless local stations could prove damage to their local service capacity, and only about 20 percent of stations had requested blacking out the imported syndication they were carrying.

ROBERT E. (TED) TURNER b. 1938

Courtesy: Turner Broadcasting System, Inc.

On a June night in 1980 Ted Turner officially opened his Cable News Network (CNN), a twenty-four-hour news service beamed to a satellite for relay to cable systems all over the country. The scoffers were muted in their predictions of failure because Turner was also the man who in 1976 had turned an undistinguished and money-losing Atlanta UHF independent station into the first "superstation," precursor of a new era in cable.

Born in Cincinatti, Ohio in 1938, Turner was an inveterate playboy. He attended Brown University where he was famous for a number of escapades, including the burning of his fraternity's homecoming parade float. When Turner was twenty-four his father had a nervous breakdown and committed suicide. Ignoring advice to give up a faltering family billboard business in the South, Turner was able with hard work and ingenuity not only to return the business to health, but also to make it a base on which to build a small empire. He began to take seriously the advice of a slogan he now has on his desk, "Either Lead, Follow, or Get Out of the Way." This reflects his competitive spirit. In 1979 he skippered the winning yacht in the America's Cup Challenge races and two years later won the Fastnet race in which an unexpectedly severe storm capsized many boats and lives were lost.

Against the conventional wisdom of the early 1970s he purchased a UHF station losing about a half-million dollars a year and with no possibility of network affiliation. Cable was growing rapidly throughout the country and Turner sensed the hunger of people for more sports events than the networks were providing on weekends. He put into the station's schedule all the sports events he could find and even bought the Atlanta franchises in major-league baseball and basketball. He also built a film library comparable to that of any other independent station in the country.

His next step was formation of Southern Satellite System (SSS), which sent his station's signals to a satellite from which they could be picked up everywhere. Cable systems were invited to use the signals as an importation service for ten cents per month per subscriber.

To start CNN Turner sold a second station he owned and pledged to spend $30 million a year running it. He made heavy use of people who were well-established in broadcasting, including a former president of CBS-TV whom he made head of CNN and Daniel Schorr, the widely respected former CBS correspondent whom he made chief of CNN's Washington bureau.

Origination

It was in the area of origination (delivery of programs that were not also being broadcast) that cable made its greatest advances in the late 1970s. For several years after passage of the 1972 regulations, origination consisted primarily of programming from the studios of individual systems. Some material was produced as simply as focusing a camera on a large clock and other instruments, allowing a viewer to check easily the precise time and outside weather conditions at all times. Other origination programming was as extensive as the contracts the two New York City systems had with Madison Square Garden for practically all Garden events that were not conventionally broadcast.

In January 1979 there was no available origination programming beyond what the systems themselves produced. However, the success of superstation importation had made it apparent that cable systems were interested in additional material and that domestic satellites made national distribution economical. By the end of 1979 there were three services available, offering sports events, coverage of Congress, and children's programs. Another dozen systems were making their plans to begin satellite transmission before the end of 1980. Among the most ambitious and promising of the early entries were the following:

Cable Satellite Public Affairs Network (C-SPAN). This service evolved after the House of Representatives installed video facilities to cover all its sessions. C-SPAN feeds those House sessions plus discussions of current events to cable systems around the country.

Entertainment and Sports Programming Network (ESPN). A Connecticut entrepreneur was looking for ways of distributing sports programming to cable systems in his part of the country and discovered that it was no more costly to use a satellite and cover the entire nation. Noting the success of WTCG(TV)'s sports programming, he persuaded the Getty Oil Company to become a partner (it purchased 85 percent) and he set about acquiring rights to sports on a national basis. For a year or so after the initial transmissions in June 1979, ESPN was operative only on weekends but in a year went to a twenty-four-hour service seven days a week.

Warner Cable's *Nickelodeon* presents fourteen hours a day of children's programs.

on June 1, 1980 Ted Turner started his twenty-four-hour Cable News Network (CNN) which provides continuous news for cable systems. This is a major effort that started with a staff of some 300 persons and an initial annual budget of $25 million.

Looking at some of the other proposals supports the assumption that cable systems may become national magazine stands with more programming aimed at selected minority audiences. Among the additional services competing for a share of the marketplace are those aimed at blacks, the over-fifty age group, the Spanish-speaking, the day-time audience, and the late-night crowd seeking "R-rated" films.

As origination programming from satellite increases, various patterns of payment are emerging. The cable systems themselves will pay for those services that impress franchise authorities and may increase subscribers— for example, C-SPAN and Nickelodeon. Some services such as religious networks will provide programming and distribution at their own expense for the privilege of being on the cable and being able to solicit funds. Most common will be barter service, similar in many ways to barter syndication on television stations. Both ESPN and CNN charge cable systems a small fee per subscriber per month, which is far short of covering expenses. But each receives money from national advertisers for inclusion of commercials in the service and each leaves vacant spots that can be sold by the local system which would then retain the additional revenue. As cable penetration reaches and surpasses the 30 percent level nationwide, it is anticipated that advertisers will increase their interest in the medium until they become a significant source of income.

Access Channels

In retrospect, it was the access channels that represented the FCC's desire that cable, like broadcasting, be required to serve the public interest, convenience, and necessity. The functional-free-speech point of view was clearly represented in the regulation that there be channels available for the public so anyone could express his or her ideas at a minimum cost. In the spring of 1978 a court of appeals struck down the access requirements on the ground they exceeded the authority of the FCC to regulate cable to the extent that such regulation was reasonably ancillary to the commission's primary responsibility of overseeing the development of television. When the court considered the FCC's explanation that the rules were designed to enhance First Amendment rights, it caustically noted, "We deal here with the Federal Communications Commission, not the Federal First Amendment Commission."

A year later the Supreme Court upheld the decision with the further comment that since in the Communications Act broadcasting was specifically exempted from common-carrier status, the FCC had no authority to impose it on cable. The access channels did impose it by specifying nondiscriminatory allotment of facilities on a first-come, first-served basis.

Elimination of the federal access channel requirements had no effect on cable operation since all franchises had either adopted the FCC access rules or expanded on them. These court decisions had no bearing on local jurisdiction and it is likely that most communities will continue to insist upon them. Indeed, the concept of service to the community has become the biggest single emphasis of companies competing for franchises in the large cities.

Again, in retrospect, the primary significance of the access-channel regulation is that it focused the attention of communities on what they might require from cable operators. This impact will continue in the field. At the same time, the court rulings were the final impetus in pushing the FCC out of cable regulation.

Pay Cable

When the 1972 antisiphoning rules were written, the FCC and the industry were thinking only of "per-program pay cable." This would have involved not only acquiring the rights to movies and sports events, but also installation of meters to sets in individual homes so subscribers could be billed for exactly what they viewed. The hardware for this purpose was not only complicated but also very expensive. So, few people saw pay cable as an immediate threat or possibility. By the spring of 1975 Home Box Office (HBO, a subsidiary of Time-Life) had completed experimentation with a "pay-cable service" whereby a monthly schedule (mostly recent movies) would be delivered into a home for a set fee. The only hardware was a simple device that fed programs into the individual receiver. Renting the device involved installing it and then adding the extra fee to the regular subscription bill each month.

In the spring of 1975 HBO announced it had committed $7.5 million over the next five years to rent satellite facilities so its programs could be received by any cable system willing to invest in its own Earth station or to arrange a microwave connection from a nearby satellite receiving point. Thus, any system could enter the pay-cable business by delivering HBO program materials through one of its existing channels. The standard arrangement for reimbursing HBO was to divide the first $6.00 from a home each month so HBO received $3.50 and the system kept $2.50. After the first $6.00 the income was divided equally. Satellite distribution of HBO started in September 1975 and two years later HBO was in the black with 800,000 customers in forty-six states.

In March 1977 the District of Columbia Court of Appeals overturned the FCC's 1972 antisiphoning rules because the commission had presented no evidence of pay cable's threat to conventional television, and therefore had not demonstrated the rules were reasonably ancillary to its mission of overseeing television development. The Supreme Court refused to review the decision. A few months later VIACOM and Teleprompter announced formation of a competitive pay-cable service, "Showtime." By the spring of 1980 "Showtime" was serving over a million customers on 600 cable systems and announcing significant increases in its program schedule. HBO, still the biggest pay-cable operation, announced a second supplementary schedule. Most impressive was the growth in the number of pay-cable subscribers in just one year. According to A. C. Nielsen estimates, the three-and-a-half million subscribers in February 1979 increased to five and three-quarters million in February 1980.

Interactive Cable

When the FCC required that cable systems in major markets have an "up-stream capacity," few had any notion of how it would be used. In December 1977 Warner Cable decided to find out and inaugurated its "Qube" system in Columbus, Ohio. (Neither the name nor the letters in it have any specific meaning—it was chosen for quick identification and because it would have no prior connotations.) Essentially, it is an experiment to find out how two-way cable can be used. Located in subscribers homes is a device about the size of a hardcover book with buttons that sends impulses back to the studio.

By using those buttons a viewer can participate by tuning in to games, town meetings, educational examinations, or a sales effort where an item is shown on the screen and can be ordered by the pushing of the appropriate response button. At the same time, the system can feed returning impulses from sets into a computer and tell the "rating" for every channel at any particular time. Qube also makes possible a return to the "per-program pay-cable" concept because it can automatically bill customers for any program that they view for more than two minutes.

Warner Cable spent between $15 million and $20 million to start up the project and had monthly expenses of up to a million dollars. There is no hope of returning a profit in the portion of Columbus served by Qube, but Warner is installing the system in other markets and it is certain that in the future all systems will have some kind of interactive mechanisms.

Among the most financially promising ways to use of the system is home security—sending alarm messages in case of fire and robbery.

"Tiered" Service

An indication of the scope a cable system may reach in the late 1980s as new systems are built and old ones are updated is found in the franchise awarded in 1980 to Warner-Amex by Dallas, Texas. The eighty channels there will be divided into "tiers" so homes will be able to select the level of subscription, just as some earlier systems offered pay cable at different levels.

The tiered service of Warner-Amex in Dallas includes the following: (1) For $2.95 per month the subscriber will get twenty-four channels carrying all local stations, the access channels, and local origination. There are also two pay services that can be added. (2) For $7.45 per month there are the twenty-four channels offered at the first level plus another twenty-four carrying importation and origination programming delivered by satellite. There are more pay services available at this level. (3) For $9.95 per month all eighty channels are available, including Qube with its interactive features such as per-program pay-cable and home fire and security alarms. It is estimated that if a subscriber took advantage of everything available, the monthly bill would be about $45.00.

NEW NAMES IN CABLE

Through the 1960s the three national networks and a few group owners led by Westinghouse (Group W) dominated broadcasting. As cable grew, new giants emerged and the interrelationships among them began to resemble the intermarriages of royal families in Europe a few centuries ago. Among the new entries were the following:

—in the 1960s *Teleprompter* emerged as the number one cable multisystem operator (MSO)

—shortly after 1970 national networks were barred by the FCC from program packaging with outside firms, from domestic syndication and from operating cable systems; since CBS was heavily committed in all three areas, its activities were taken over by a spinoff, *Viacom*, which prospered in these and other fields

    —from the Warner Brothers motion-picture empire came Warner Communications, Inc., which included Warner Cable, operator of many systems including Qube in Columbus, Ohio

    In the late 1970s several events illustrated the trend to large combinations: to compete with HBO pay cable, Teleprompter and Viacom joined forces to start "Showtime." Because Warner Cable needed cash for expansion, it merged with the American Express Company to form Warner-Amex. When Warner-Amex wanted to expand cable programming services, it joined with ABC to start the "Alpha network," an evening cultural schedule. In 1980 Group W, which had been involved in cable in a comparatively minor way, moved to acquire Teleprompter, a purchase that would make it immediately the largest cable operator in the country and a partner with Viacom in "Showtime."

Copyright Legislation

In the mid-1950s Congress started work on a copyright bill to replace the 1909 law. Though cable assumed it would have to make payments for carrying broadcast signals sooner or later, there was controversy over the size of the payments and the degree to which they would apply to small systems as well as the large ones. In 1971, when the Whitehead compromise was accepted, cable interests were so optimistic about the future they were willing to leave payment details to future negotiation. When cable growth after 1972 fell below expectations, the willingness to reimburse broadcasters was diluted. Some of the small systems felt they should pay no copyright fees at all. The larger systems talked about paying 1–2 percent of their gross income, while the broadcasters produced statistics showing cable could afford 15–25 percent.

    In the fall of 1976, after nearly twenty years of intermittent discussion, Congress passed a new copyright law to be effective in 1978. It gave the cable operators a compulsory license permitting them to pick up and distribute broadcast signals without negotiations with the copyright holders. However, the new license also provided that the systems would have to pay fees that depended both on the size of their gross revenues and the number of signals being imported from distant stations. The fees were to be paid to a tribunal that would then devise a formula for paying appropriate shares to the copyright holders. The fees were also subject to revision if the FCC changes its basic cable regulations.

The fees were to be paid to a Copyright Royalty Tribunal (CRT) that was charged with devising a formula for paying appropriate shares to various copyright holders. In 1978 cable systems made payments of $14 million to the CRT and in 1980 the money was distributed as follows:

75%	to Program Packagers
12	to Sports Organizations
5	to Public Broadcasting Service
4.5	to Music Performers
3.75	to Television Broadcasters
.25	to National Public Radio

Obviously, the broadcasters were most disappointed since they felt they should receive far more than the small share allotted to them.

6.7 1970–1980 EMERGENCE OF SUBSCRIPTION TELEVISION

For nine years after the 1968 FCC approval of STV there was no successful STV operation on the air. Although one or two entrepreneurs attempted it, the FCC hurdles were enough to foil them and to discourage the rest. Especially important were the antisiphoning rules prohibiting most sports events and movies between two and ten years after release. The limitation of STV to communities where there were at least four conventional stations also ruled out many markets from consideration. In addition, the technological problems of metering homes in order to charge for individual programs were beyond easy solution.

A change in climate was brought about by several factors in the mid 1970s. First was the HBO announcement that it was going to offer a pay-cable service that a customer would purchase by the month rather than by individual programs. Potential STV operators could see the leasing of decoding devices as simple and reasonably inexpensive. Second, in March 1977 the FCC's antisiphoning rules were voided by the courts and this ruling made available a much greater source of program supply. Third, as part of its overall deregulation pattern, the FCC in late 1979 proposed eliminating the provision that STV be permitted only in communities with four conventional stations on the air. Finally, there were many UHF stations that had been unable to make profits from conventional operation and they began to see STV operation as an alternative.

First Successful Stations

In 1977 Wometco Enterprises bought an STV station in the New York City area that had tried to operate three years earlier but failed. This became the first successful operation with a service called "Wometco Home Theater." Three years later there were eight stations—all on the UHF band—with over 400,000 subscribers. Each was offering an STV service with monthly charges of about $20. Typical scheduling included fifty hours a week composed of domestic and foreign movies (unedited and uninterrupted by commercials), sports events, and occasional specials.

Satellite Subscription Television (SSTV)

In 1979 COMSAT announced formation of a subsidiary, Satellite Television Corporation (STC) to plan for Satellite Subscription Television (SSTV). In December 1980 STC petitioned the FCC for approval of plans to have a three-transponder pay service in operation by 1985. The initial investment and first-year operating costs were estimated at $700 million. The transponder transmitters were planned to have enough power so that individual homes could receive a good signal with antenna dishes about thirty inches in diameter.

STC estimated that when the system was in place it would reach from five million to seven million homes or about seven per cent of the American total. Subscribers would pay about $100 for installation fees and $25 per month for the service.

The early successes of STV have been in areas where cable was slow in arriving. When homes have a choice between pay cable with its attendant other services and STV, it is difficult to see how the latter could enjoy much success. SSTV, on the other hand, seemed to be assuming that perhaps 20 percent of American homes would not have the opportunity to subscribe to cable and that if a third of them purchased the DBS service, a healthy profit could be made. The unknown factor was whether new technology—especially fiber optics—would some day make cable as ubiquitous as the telephone so that even remote homes would be provided service. If that comes to pass, the future of both STV and SSTV appears to be questionable.

6.8 FUTURE PROSPECTS

Cable television entered the 1980s with prospects brighter than ever before. Americans in all parts of the country and in all sizes of communities have indicated their willingness to pay for programming beyond that which they can receive over the air locally. Satellite technology has provided a plethora of such services. It seems reasonable to assume that at some point the United States will approach being a "wired nation" in which the majority of homes will be connected to cable. Homes without access to cable will be able to purchase program service from STV and SSTV. Although many of the ramifications are not yet clear, there seems to be little doubt that a communications revolution is approaching.

GLOSSARY ITEMS

The following words and phrases used in Chapter 6 are defined in the Glossary:

Access Channels

Antisiphoning Rules

Cable Franchise

Cable Penetration

Cable Pseudofreeze

Cable Television

Cable Three-Tiered Regulation

Certificate of Compliance

Community-Antenna Television (CATV)

Compulsory License

Cross-Ownership

Direct Broadcast Satellite (DBS)

Economic Injury

Full Network Station

Grandfather Clause

Headend

Importation

Interactive Cable

Leapfrogging

Local Carriage

Master Antenna

Microwave Relay

Minimum Channel Capacity

Origination

Pay Cable

Phonevision

Program Exclusivity Rules

Public Access Channel

Satellite Relay

Satellite Subscription Television
   (SSTV)

Superstation

Subscription Television (STV)

Syndication

Tiered Services

Upstream Capacity

CABLE CHRONOLOG

1950 Birth of CATV, probably in Lansford, Pennsylvania.

1951 FCC showed first concern about the effects of importation on stations planned for small markets.

1956 FCC received first formal request from stations to regulate some CATV.

1958 FCC refused to assume jurisdiction over CATV.

1959 FCC recommended congressional action to enable FCC regulation of cable.

1960 Senate failed by one vote to pass bill for cable regulation.

1962 *Carter Mountain* case—FCC denied microwave application for CATV that would have caused economic injury to a station and probably lessened the service the station could render to its public.

1965 FCC adopted rules for cable systems importing by microwave and imposed a "pseudofreeze" by restricting importation into major markets.

1966 FCC extended revised rules to all cable systems.

1968   Two Supreme Court decisions:
1. In *Southwestern* case, upheld FCC authority to regulate cable.
2. In *Fortnightly* case, ruled CATV need pay no copyright fees. FCC sought agreement between cable and broadcasting on new regulation.

1969   Cable-origination rule issued.

1971   FCC Chairman Burch outlined new regulations in letter to Congress.
OPT Director Whitehead persuaded cable operators and broadcasters to accept compromise.

1972   FCC announced cable regulations.

1973   Cable failed to reach growth goals.

    1. Teleprompter crises.

    2. Cable "banned in Boston."

    3. NCTA applied for relaxation of cable regulations.

1974   Supreme Court ruled no copyright liability for importation.

1975   HBO announced satellite network for pay cable.

1976   Congress passed new copyright law.
WTCG(TV) in Atlanta, Georgia became first cable superstation.

1977   Warner Cable started Qube in Columbus, Ohio.
HBO reported operation in the black.
Appeals court voided FCC's cable and STV antisiphoning rule.
Wometco reactivated STV in New York City area.

1978   Appeals court voided FCC's access-channel rules.
FCC eased policy on cable importation.
Viacom and Teleprompter joined in forming pay-cable "Showtime."
FCC approved satellite usage for more superstations.

1979   Beginning of C-SPAN and ESPN.
Supreme Court affirmed appeals court's voiding of access-channel rules.
Merger of Warner Cable and American Express into Warner-Amex approved.

1980   Group W purchase of Teleprompter announced.
Cable News Network started twenty-four-hour service.

FCC ended restrictions on importation of distant signals and exclusivity of syndicated programming.

Copyright Royalty Tribunal distributed first cable copyright fees.

COMSAT petitioned FCC for Satellite Subscription Television by 1985.

FCC approved doubling satellite transponders by 1985.

PREVIEW

The Federal Communications Commission has responsibility for regulating American broadcasting within limits laid down by Congress. The criterion for all FCC actions is "public interest, convenience, and necessity." The first business of the commission is issuing and renewing licenses. It also promulgates rules and regulations, issues policy statements, and seeks through negotiations to pressure broadcasters into changed practices. Some of the criticism of the FCC stems from its nearly impossible position combining legislative, executive, and judicial functions. At the same time it is subject to great pressures from Congress, other government agencies, the public, and the industries it regulates. The story of license renewals since 1945 illustrates many of the factors entering into the regulatory process.

CHAPTER 7

THE FEDERAL COMMUNICATIONS COMMISSION AND THE REGULATORY PROCESS

7.1 A DIAGRAMMATIC OVERVIEW

The day-to-day operation of the American commercial broadcasting system can be superficially and two-dimensionally charted as shown in Fig. 7.1.

The American public can be divided into two groups, as shown; the smaller group consists of those who vote in various elections, and the larger group consists of those who do not vote because they are too young, are not citizens, are not registered, or are not interested. Through the election process voters choose a president and members of Congress. From time to time the president, with the approval of the Senate, appoints members of the Federal Communications Commission (FCC). The FCC authorizes individuals and companies to operate stations that broadcast signals to homes, cars, places of business, or wherever else receivers are available. Rounding out the chart is the "business world" composed of all individuals and companies trying to make a profit through the sale of goods and services. There is a constant flow of dollars from people to the business world as they purchase goods and services. (Not shown is the return flow of dollars to people as the business world pays stock dividends, wages, and salaries.) Members of the business world then pay stations for inclusion of advertising in a broadcast schedule in the hope that the commercial messages will increase business and profits. Broadcasters have no significant source of income beyond the dollars they receive from advertisers.

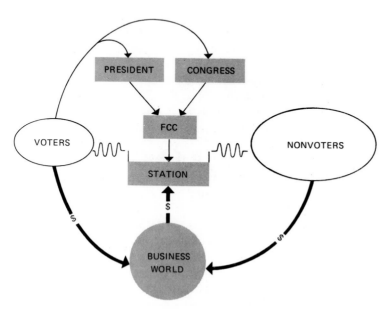

Fig. 7.1

A three-dimensional chart would show Congress enacting broadcast-related legislation signed by the president and the courts reviewing that legislation and FCC actions to ensure that regulation is consistent with the Constitution and specific laws. It would also include many auxiliary units such as networks, station representatives, and audience-measurement firms that provide services to broadcasters and advertisers.

A four-dimensional chart would show the informal but effective ways in which citizen groups, individual legislators, regulated industries, and others exert pressure upon various facets of the regulatory process. (See Fig. 7.2.)

The chief difference when educational or public stations are placed in the center of the chart is that the sources of income are more varied and there can be no advertising. Some dollars still come from the business world in the form of contributions, but the majority of funds are from local, state, and federal governments, from foundations, and from individual listeners and viewers.

7.2 THE END OF EARLY REGULATION

From its infancy in 1920, broadcasting was regulated under the Radio Act of 1912, which required users to obtain licenses issued by the Secretary of Commerce. (The Wireless Ship Act of 1910 and a 1912 amendment to it, reflecting an urgency generated by the *Titanic* disaster, were concerned only with maritime and other point-to-point radio.) In the 1923 *Intercity Radio**
case the regulatory authority of Commerce Secretary Hoover was diminished when a court ruled that he must issue a license to a qualified applicant for radio telegraphy even though the grant would probably lead to inter-ference with other users. In 1926 the *Zenith* case† brought to an end effective regulation under the law of 1912. The Zenith Radio Corporation of Chicago had been licensed by Hoover to use a frequency "only on Thursday nights from 10:00 P.M. to 12:00 P.M., Central Standard Time, and only when use of this frequency is not desired by the General Electric Company's Denver station." Zenith used not only its assigned frequency but also others beyond the designated hours. When Hoover sought to hold Zenith to the terms of its license, the U.S. District Court in Illinois held that "the Secretary has no power to impose restrictions as to frequency, power, and hours of opera-tion." The court ruled that "a station's use of a frequency not assigned to it was not a violation of the Radio Act of 1912."

In seeking to accommodate more operators than could normally use the limited frequencies, Hoover had assumed more authority than the Act had specifically delegated to him. After the 1926 court decision he was required to grant licenses to all who were qualified and all licensees were allowed to use the spectrum as they wished so long as they limited them-selves to the frequencies assigned to broadcasting. Many licensees took advantage of their new freedom and the ensuing chaos was so great that responsible broadcasters joined the public in demanding effective regulation. Congress responded by passing the Radio Act of 1927, modeled on Hoover's concept of government-licensed private enterprise under minimal regulation. Since the 1927 Act was almost totally embodied in Title III of the Com-munications Act of 1934, only the latter will be described here. Pertinent excerpts of the Communications Act are provided in Appendix A. Key amendments are in Appendix B.

---

* *Hoover* v. *Intercity Radio Co.*, Inc., 286 F. 1003 (D.C. Cir.) February 5, 1923.

† *United States* v. *Zenith Radio Corporation et al.*, 12 F. 2d. 614 (N.D. Ill.) April 16, 1926.

7.3 HIGHLIGHTS OF THE COMMUNICATIONS ACT
The Commission and Its Power

The Act establishes a commission of seven, each to be appointed by the president and confirmed by the Senate to a seven-year term. (Only on rare occasions has the Senate refused to confirm an appointee.) The president designates one as chairman. No more than four at any time may be from one political party. In theory, one commissioner should finish his or her term each year. In practice, it is not unusual for commissioners to resign before the ends of their terms, thus giving a president the opportunity to appoint more than one replacement in a year. Commissioners may also be reappointed at the expiration of their terms.

The Act sought to give the commission an extremely broad range, and the courts have generally confirmed not only the breadth of those powers but also the right of the FCC to extend them into areas not originally envisioned by Congress. Whenever the word "radio" appears in the Act, it is used generically and applies to television as well. Section 303(g) clearly empowered the commission to assume control of the experimental use of television and to authorize its general use when development of the new medium reached the point where it would be in the public interest.

Drawn for BROADCASTING by Jack Schmidt

"If you enjoy broadcasting, go into radio or television. If you don't, go to the FCC."

Reprinted, with permission, from Broadcasting

Establishing Public Ownership of the Airways

In Section 304 the FCC is forbidden to grant a license until the applicant signs a waiver of any claim to ownership of the frequency he or she wishes to use. This was especially important in 1927 because some of the early stations had been using frequencies for five or more years and were prepared to argue they had acquired "squatter's rights" by virtue of their tenure. Section 309(b)(1) reinforces public ownership of the frequency spectrum by specifying that a license shall not vest in the operator any rights beyond those that are clearly stated.

The "Public Interest" Criterion

Already noted was the major defect of the Act of 1912: its failure to give the regulatory authority (the Secretary of Commerce) any discretion in issuing and renewing licenses. The phrase "public interest, convenience, and necessity" that appears in Section 303 and is frequently repeated, provides the discretionary power that remedied the weakness of the earlier Act. For example, if a person with all necessary qualifications applied for permission to use a frequency already in use, the FCC would find that adding the new signal was not in "the public interest."

Very shortly after the passage of the Radio Act of 1927 it was established that the criterion's meaning lay in the whole phrase rather than in the individual words. It had been used in earlier railroad legislation and was interpreted to mean "for the welfare of the public," or "in the public interest." For example, a station is not licensed to program part of a day in the "public interest," another part of the day in the "public convenience," and the rest of the day in the "public necessity."

Licensing Broadcast Stations

The heart of broadcast regulation is the power of the commission to issue broadcast licenses and to renew them at three-year intervals. Essentially, the practice has been and still is to renew a license unless there is overwhelming evidence that an operator has failed to serve the public interest, convenience, and necessity. The power to license stations is supplemented by the further power to revoke licenses for making false statements or for anything else that would have precluded the original grant.

The Construction Permit (CP)

Section 319 (not excerpted in the Appendix because of its length and legally complicated wording) specifies that when one makes application for a new station, the FCC shall, if it is in the public interest, first issue a construction permit (CP). The CP authorizes the construction of the station and ensures the granting of the license if the completed station meets all the specifications set forth in the application. This procedure is necessary because the engineering data in the application are theoretically derived. Only after a station is broadcasting can all the details of the transmitted signal be provided. A CP is the equivalent of a license in that an applicant can go on the air and carry regular programming and advertising. The general public has no way of knowing if the station is operating under a CP or a license.

Equal Treatment of Candidates in Political Campaigns

Since the number of would-be broadcasters is greater than the availability of frequencies, Congress has passed legislation intended to prevent the privileged few from using their facilities to promote the chances of the political candidates they favored. Because of its importance and the amount of time both broadcasters and commissioners must devote to it, Section 315 is separately discussed in Chapter 12 of this book.

Sponsor Identification

Section 317 is an attempt to prevent deception of the public. For example, if a group buys time to argue against a certain kind of tax, it is important to the public to know who is paying the bills. When there are advertisers, it is assumed they are paying the costs and a subsequent amendment permitted the FCC to waive the identification requirement for such broadcasts.

Section 317 has an important bearing on the "patron plan" programming of public television stations. Many of these stations carry programs that have been purchased by funds provided by commercial companies. The station is required by this section to make an announcement to that effect at the beginning and end of each program. Some see such announcements as a form of advertising.

Freedom of Speech

It was Hoover's thesis that stations should be free of government regulation to the extent that such freedom was possible. To ensure a maximum of freedom, in Section 326 the commission was specifically denied the right to "interfere with the right of free speech by means of radio communication." Censorship, which means the right of government to demand that a script be submitted in advance and to force deletion of material, has never been a problem, even in wartime. Neither the FCC nor any other government agency suggests a desire to so infringe on broadcast freedom.

Nevertheless, Section 326 has generated more controversy than any other single portion of the Communications Act. Every extension of FCC authority has been opposed on the grounds that it interfered with or "abridged" freedom of speech. For example, if the FCC were to rule that every station had to take the time every day to read the Declaration of Independence, broadcasters could (and would) argue that during the time they were forced to devote to such reading they were being denied the freedom to present something else they might prefer. The illustration is extreme but in subsequent discussions of Section 315, the Fairness Doctrine, and other controversial issues, it will be seen that the broadcasters' principle is valid.

Appealing Commission Decisions

In conformity with the "checks and balances" philosophy of our government, persons may appeal FCC decisions and actions to the courts. The Communications Act provides that if an FCC decision has to do with a station license, the appeal must be directed to the U.S. Court of Appeals in Washington, D.C. To appeal an FCC rule or another action that does not pertain to a license, one may go to the court of appeals in Washington or in one of the other districts. If the FCC or someone else feels that an appeals court ruling is wrong, an appeal may be directed to the Supreme Court which may or may not agree to receive it. Occasionally, as in the trial on the Family Viewing Policy, the Commission may be required to defend itself in a district court.

Limitation on Court Review   When an FCC action or rule is appealed, a court's right of review is limited to two areas:

1. The court may find that the FCC exceeded or failed to use the powers specified in the Communications Act or implied in the Constitution. The principle was illustrated in the *Zenith* case when a court found that Secretary

Hoover had used discretionary power not designated in the Act of 1912. Broadcasters frequently cite the congressional limitation on FCC power to "interfere with the right of free speech. . . ." If an FCC action does indeed interfere with that right, a court may find that the commission exceeded its powers. For example, in the late 1940s the FCC ruled that quiz programs were contrary to the public interest. The courts ruled that the FCC had gone too far and voided the action it had taken.

2. A court may find that the FCC followed improper procedure and made an "arbitrary and capricious" decision. In effect, this guarantees to all who come before the commission "due process" and the right to adequate consideration of all pertinent data. It was noted in the discussion of the FCC color decision during the Freeze that RCA appealed the decision on the grounds the commission had acted too hastily. In the *WLBT* case, discussed later in this chapter, a citizens' group went to court complaining that the FCC had not provided an opportunity for it to appear in hearings to protest a license renewal. The court found the complaint reasonable and ordered the commission to hold hearings in the community. When, after the hearings, the FCC still voted to renew the protested license, the court found the action so inconsistent with the testimony that the FCC's grant was overturned.

Supreme Court recognition that the courts are limited in their power to review FCC decisions was most clearly stated in the 1943 Network case challenging the Chain Regulations.

> *The Regulations are assailed as "arbitrary and capricious." If this contention means that the Regulations are unwise, that they are not likely to succeed in accomplishing what the Commission intended, we can say only that the appellants have selected the wrong forum for such a plea. What was said in* Board of Trade v. United States, *is relevant here: "We certainly have neither technical competence nor legal authority to pronounce upon the wisdom of the course taken by the Commission." Our duty is at an end when we find that the action of the Commission was based upon findings supported by evidence, and was made pursuant to authority granted by Congress.* *

Since courts cannot rule on the wisdom of a commission action, this means the FCC is autonomous in matters of judgment unless Congress decides to amend the Communications Act in a way that restricts the freedom of the commission.

---

* *National Broadcasting Co., Inc., et al. v. United States et al.,* 319 U.S. at 224, May 10, 1943.

Emergency Powers of the President

The president is empowered to suspend actions of the commission in the event of an emergency. Aside from assigning five broadcast television channels to the military in World War II, this is a power that has not been used.

7.4 FCC IMPLEMENTATION OF THE COMMUNICATIONS ACT

Fig. 7.2 provides another overview of broadcast regulation. It starts with the four elements of American tradition discussed in Chapter 1. From those elements came Mr. Hoover's philosophy that played a major role in formulating the Radio Act of 1927. The Communications Act of 1934 simply repeated the provisions of the earlier act with addition of sections pertaining to other communications media. The FCC is then seen at the center of the figure, under pressure from many directions as it implements the Act in four ways. Three are official while the fourth is informal:

1. Issuing and renewing licenses.
2. Formulating and enforcing rules.
3. Issuing policy statements.
4. Regulating by negotiation.

Issuing and Renewing Licenses

Since 1927 the Radio and Communications Commissions have acted tens of thousands of times on licenses. Most decisions have been routine, but occasionally an action will provide a precedent for future action. As an example, the history of the Fairness Doctrine begins with the *Mayflower* case in which a station submitted a routine application for renewal of its license. The application was opposed by the Mayflower Company that wanted to use the frequency. In granting the renewal the commission took note of the station's having editorialized although the practice had been voluntarily stopped. Almost in passing and as though it were completely obvious, the FCC said, "the broadcaster cannot be an advocate." That statement became a general prohibition against editorializing by licensees. For the next decade it was a source of contention between broadcasters and the commission.

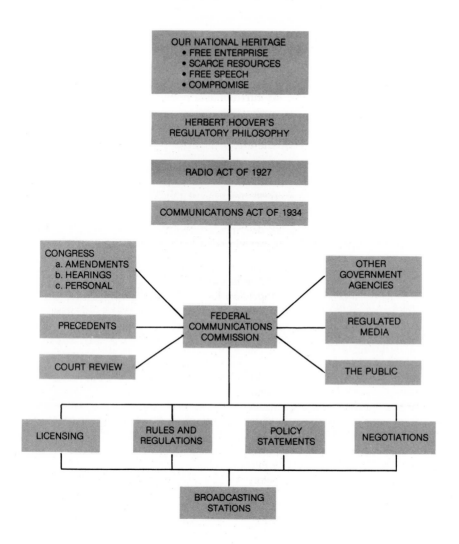

Fig. 7.2
An Overview of Broadcast Regulation

Formulating and Enforcing Rules

Section 4 of the Communications Act gives the FCC authority to ". . . make such rules and regulations . . . as may be necessary in the execution of its functions." Section 303(i) went further and authorized the FCC to make special rules that would be applicable only to those stations engaged in chain (network) broadcasting. Throughout its history the FCC has promulgated rules that have had the effect of "spelling out" its concept of the public interest.

APPLYING FOR A LICENSE

Once an individual or company determines it would like to operate a station, it will normally follow certain steps in seeking a construction permit (CP).

Employment of Legal Counsel There are attorneys in Washington who specialize in practice before the FCC. While in theory anyone can deal directly with the commission, the competition for available frequencies makes it important to be represented by counsel. An essential restriction on the choice of a lawyer is that one must find an individual who has time to handle the case and who is not already representing another client where there might be a conflict of interest.

Employment of an Engineering Consultant There are engineering firms that specialize in communications and that will complete all the technical data the FCC requires in the application. (The attorney will guide in selection of an engineer if necessary.) The engineer will provide an applicant with a complete design for the studios and transmitter with specifications down to brand name and part numbers. If the application for a CP is granted, the engineer will also oversee the construction and completion of the final data on the signal required before the license can be issues.

Filing the Application The lawyer will guide the applicant very carefully and very specifically while preparing the nonengineering data required by the FCC:

1. Proof of American citizenship.
2. Character of the individual or individuals making the application. They must demonstrate they can be expected to operate a station in the public interest. There should be not only a lack of negative factors in their background but also as many character references as possible from community leaders.
3. Proof of financial ability to put the station on the air and to operate it for the length of time it will take before revenues will equal or exceed expenses.

4. The proposed program schedule, based on evidence the applicant has made a diligent effort to ascertain the needs, interests, and desires of various segments of the community. The proposed schedule should be very specific with program titles and descriptions and an indication of plans for a network affiliation if such is contemplated.

Assuming there is no challenge from other applicants who would like the same facility or from current broadcasters who claim the new station would interfere with their signals, the FCC staff will evaluate the application. If everything is in order and it appears the new station would be in the public interest, the commission will issue a CP.

If there is opposition to the application, the procedure can be long and costly. An administrative law judge (ALJ) will be assigned by the FCC to hold hearings and to make a recommendation for commission action. Delays are frequently caused by the heavy workload of the commission and its staff, by bureaucratic inefficiency, and by the legal complexity of determining hearing issues.

Realizing that hearings can last for years and that appeals may take more years, the commission in the 1950s adopted the practice of authorizing "interim operations" while cases were being decided. All the applicants for a television channel would be invited to join in a new corporation that would build the facilities and operate them temporarily until the licensee had been finally selected. At that point, the successful applicant would buy out the interim operation (of which he or she had been a part) and continue operating the station alone.

Every three years a broadcaster must submit a routine application for renewal of the license. It will be reviewed by the FCC staff along with whatever materials may have been put in the licensee's file—letters complaining about the station and notices the FCC may have sent about a variety of matters. If the station's record is reasonably adequate, the license will be renewed by the staff on a routine basis. If there are major questions or petitions to deny renewal, it will be brought to the commissioners' attention and may be designated for hearings.

Among the most significant were the Chain Regulations in 1941 aimed at freeing stations from network domination. They were bitterly opposed by broadcasters on the grounds that the commission had exceeded the authority granted to it in the Communications Act. The significance of these regulations lies chiefly in the fact that the Supreme Court made a landmark decision affirming the FCC action and laying the basis for many of the other rules that have followed.

Rules have been written in many other areas of broadcasting. There are limits on the numbers of stations permitted to a single licensee. There are rules concerning employment rights for women and ethnic minorities. Portions of the Fairness Doctrine have been elevated to the status of rules.

Issuing Policy Statements

The Communications Act was worded very generally so it could remain applicable as times and circumstances changed. Much was and is left to the interpretation of the FCC. As regulatory policy has evolved, the commission has felt the need to articulate its thoughts so broadcasters would have guidelines by which to operate. Among the best-known examples that will be discussed in this book are the 1946 "Blue Book," a 1960 programming policy statement, and several statements on the Fairness Doctrine. Since these statements are usually made while the FCC is still forming policy, they are frequently confusing. Some, like the "Blue Book," are so strongly opposed that they never do become part of the regulatory process.

Regulating by Negotiation

Although there is no provision for it in the Communications Act, a significant activity of the FCC is the negotiating or jawboning it performs with the NAB, the networks, and some stations. This activity tends to occur when pressures from concerned citizens reach the point where something is advisable short of legislative action or regulatory rule-making. For example, in the summer of 1974 the ACT petition for FCC rule-making in the area of advertising on children's programming was attracting great attention. Concerned citizens were bringing pressure on both the Congress and the FCC. Seeking to avoid new legislation or regulation, the NAB changed its standards of children's advertising, but there was a consensus among members of Congress and the commission that further action should be taken. They were concerned that the early evening programming that was seen by many children contained too much sex and violence. By early 1975 the three networks announced their agreement to a family viewing hour. During the first hour of network entertainment-feed (8 to 9 P.M. Eastern and Pacific Times), only programs appropriate for viewing by the entire family were allowed to be shown. In April the NAB changed its code to preclude programming inappropriate to family viewing not only from the first hour of network feed but also from the preceeding hour. Although adherence to the NAB code is not a requirement for license renewal, the fact that a station has not programmed up to industry standards may be significant to the FCC at renewal time, especially is the performance of the station is marginal or deficient in other respects.

There were complaints at the time that the family viewing policy had been forced on the industry by government and thus constituted censorship. In the fall of 1975 the new policy went into effect while court action was initiated in the U.S. District Court in Los Angeles charging the FCC, the networks, and the NAB with abridgement of free speech. The suits were brought by writers', directors', and actors' organizations, claiming the policy would limit their freedom, and by Norman Lear's Tandem Productions and other packagers, who felt that the family viewing policy would make it impossible to sell many network series to stations after the network showings had been completed.

In his November 1976 decision, Judge Warren J. Ferguson detailed the meetings that had taken place between FCC Chairman Richard Wiley and the network and NAB leaders from the fall of 1974 through the April meeting at which the NAB code was changed. There was a day-to-day chronology of meetings and quoting of memoranda written by various participants summarizing developments. The judge concluded:

> *Based on the totality of the evidence accumulated in this case the court finds that Chairman Wiley, acting on behalf of the Commission (and with the approval of the Commissioners) in response to congressional committee pressure, launched a campaign primarily designed to alter the content of entertainment programming in the early evening hours.* *

The meetings between Wiley and industry leaders constituted a "jaw-boning" that resulted in a change in programming desired by government but which government could not constitutionally accomplish through regulation or legislation. In this particular instance, the pressure by the FCC had been so great that the judge ruled it an unconstitutional infringement on free speech. The reversal of the decision on technical grounds in 1979 in no way affected the conclusion about Chairman Wiley's regulation by negotiation.

A Final Complication

It must be noted that the FCC has been given an almost impossible combination of powers. To the extent that it issues rules, regulations, and policy statements, the FCC is a legislative body. It may be checked from time to time by the courts and by Congress, but for the most part it is free to interpret a vague piece of legislation as it sees fit. At the same time, the

---

* *Broadcasting,* November 15, 1976, p. 40.

FCC must be the judge of whether operators have abided by its rules, regulations, and policy statements. Finally, the commission carries a heavy administrative burden in implementing the basic law and interpretations thereof and in enforcing the judgments it has made.

Whether there should be some reassignments of responsibility is open to debate. In the meantime, the difficult position of the FCC has made it vulnerable to criticism for which it can plead extenuating circumstances.

7.5 PRESSURES AFFECTING IMPLEMENTATION OF THE COMMUNICATIONS ACT

Members of the FCC come to their task with certain personal inclinations based on their overall feelings about government and communications and their previous relationship, or lack of it, with the media. Some feel very deeply that broadcasters fall short of meeting their responsibilities. One FCC chairman in the early 1940s told the press that the NAB reminded him of "a dead mackerel in the moonlight—it both shines and stinks." Twenty years later Chairman Newton Minow challenged broadcasters to spend a full day watching their own stations and assured them they would find a "vast wasteland." Some commissioners feel that broadcasters have been very responsible in their stewardship and deserve the support of the regulatory agency, while others feel that "the least government is the best government" and that the FCC should do little more than make sure there is a minimum of technical interference among stations.

The first factor that may force commissioners to deviate from their personal inclinations in specific cases is the Communications Act itself. For example, a commissioner may feel it is ridiculous to require a station to give every minority candidate precisely the same treatment accorded the majority candidates. However, the Act very clearly specifies that equal opportunity must be accorded to all and commissioners cannot ignore the law.

Beyond the original law as amended, there are six factors that cannot be ignored by commissioners and that may impel them to act on occasion quite contrary to their best personal judgment:

1. Congressional pressure.
2. Precedents from earlier cases.
3. Expectation of court review.
4. Pressures from other government agencies.
5. Pressures from the regulated media.
6. Pressures from the public.

Examination of these pressures will help understand some FCC actions that may appear to be illogical from a common-sense point of view.

Congressional Pressure

Congress is ultimately responsible for the regulation of broadcasting. It enacted the basic legislation and can amend it. It approves the FCC budget each year and can call commissioners to account for their stewardship. The Senate must confirm all appointments to the commission. Congress brings pressure to bear on commissioners in three ways:

1. Power to amend the Communications Act.

2. Legislative hearings.

3. Personal leverage.

Power to Amend   Although Congress has not used its amending power with great frequency, it is always there and commissioners know that the media will immediately lobby to seek remedial legislation if the FCC departs too radically from what seems reasonable. In one instance Congress so responded to broadcast lobbying as to circumvent the very philosophy on which the Act was based.

The key to the American system of regulation is awarding licenses to those who can be expected to operate stations for the ultimate good of the public rather than for their own benefit. Since the mid-1930s the Commission was concerned with the propriety of approving the transfer of a license from one who had originally survived FCC scrutiny to a new individual who had, in effect, been selected by the licensee as the one to whom he or she wished to sell. In the 1940s the FCC tried to enforce its "AVCO Rule" that required that when licensees wished to dispose of a station, they must advertise for purchasers and give the FCC the right to choose among those who had made acceptable offers. Although the FCC dropped the AVCO rule, broadcasters were still concerned and persuaded Congress to amend Section 310(b) concerning the transfer of a license from one owner to a new one. The FCC was specifically forbidden even to consider whether the public interest would be better served by transferring the license "to a person other than the proposed transferee or assignee." (See Appendix B.) The effect of this amendment was to require the commission to transfer the license to a purchaser *selected by the original owner* unless it could be proven that the proposed licensee was not qualified to operate a station.

Perhaps the major reason such reversal by amendment has been rare is that commissioners have considered caution the better part of valor and have refrained from taking stands that they knew Congress would reject. At the same time, Congress has on many occasions been supportive of the

FCC and assisted in meeting problems as they arose. Certainly a very important tool of a successful commissioner is knowledge of how Congress will react in various situations.

Congressional Hearings   Congressional committees hold hearings ostensibly as a means of determining the need for legislation and of getting different points of view on what to put into proposed laws. A more subtle effect is to tell commissioners what members of Congress are thinking and to urge them to guide their actions accordingly. Since members of Congress represent ultimate authority to the FCC, it is natural that the views of members of Congress as expressed in hearings should be important. For example, the FCC's regulation by negotiation in pressuring the NAB to change its code on children's programming has just been noted. The FCC's own hearings and subsequent suggestions to broadcasters came after congressional hearings had made clear the views of legislators.

Personal Pressure from Congress   It is nowhere spelled out in print but it should be obvious that the mere expression of interest by a member of Congress is enough to put special importance on routine affairs. For example, if a station license is up for renewal and a call comes to the FCC indicating that a congressperson is interested in that situation, commissioners look at it with fresh perspective. Since members of Congress and their staffs have never been shy about making phone calls and writing letters, there is constant pressure on commissioners to look most carefully at those situations in which members of Congress have expressed interest.

Precedents Set by Earlier Commissions

If a nation is to have a government of laws there must be a large degree of consistency in regulation as in other areas. Citizens must have confidence that today's laws will be in effect tomorrow with comparatively few changes. Above all, there must not be regulation that is "arbitrary and capricious," dependent on the whim of the regulators. A complete reversal of policy must be justified by a dramatic change in circumstances that renders the earlier policy inadequate. Since the FCC is part of a government of laws, it must preserve a degree of consistency with earlier decisions whether or not the current members would have concurred in them had they been on the commission at an earlier time.

As an example, in 1967 the FCC ruled that cigarette commercials violated a Fairness Doctrine rule that when controversial issues are presented on a station, the other side must be heard. This resulted in the requirement for "countercommercials" to point out the hazards of cigarette smoking.

At the same time the FCC announced that because cigarettes were in a class by themselves, this ruling was not to be considered a precedent. Later, when the FCC refused to consider the Fairness Doctrine implications in commercials for high-powered automobiles and leaded gasolines, the appeals court ruled that the cigarette decision had indeed been a precedent, whether the commission wished to have it so considered or not. It had to be assumed that the commission had acted logically and legally in the earlier situation (it had been affirmed in court) and that the same logic and law would require a similar response in a similar situation in the future.

A precedent set by an earlier commission may be negated in either of two ways. First, the commission may be able to demonstrate that there has been a change that makes the precedent irrelevant. Secondly, the commission may plead *mea culpa*, arguing that it made an error in the earlier case, and trust that a court will agree, thus rendering the precedent invalid. This latter course was followed in the case of cigarette countercommercials and the application of the Fairness Doctrine to advertisements.

Court Review

The influences of statutory provisions and earlier precedents become especially strong when commissioners realize that every decision and ruling they make may be subjected to court review. It is assumed that every dissatisfied party in an FCC hearing will appeal his or her case to the courts. The result is an attempt to issue decisions and rulings that the courts will not overturn. This, in turn, results in regulatory conservatism on the part of the FCC and disinclination to "break new ground."

Pressures from Other Governmental Agencies

Although the FCC was established as an independent regulatory agency, commissioners can never forget that it is part of the total governmental machinery and must at least listen to other agencies. Perhaps the most significant in the early 1970s were the White House and its Office of Telecommunications Policy. Since it is the president who nominates members to the FCC, it is predictable that they would hold a regulatory philosophy fairly similar to the president's and that they would feel a sense of gratitude and responsibility to the individual who appointed them. After being in office for two or three years, a president will normally have appointed a majority of commissioners and certainly will have named the chairman.

That it is impossible to ignore White House pressure was illustrated in the fall of 1972 when President Nixon was running for reelection. The FCC had received several months earlier a letter from a film editor in

Hollywood protesting that the large number of prime-time reruns on the networks was hurting the film industry. The commission would have preferred to ignore the letter since it felt that any consideration of programming practices would be in violation of Section 326. In September, however, OTP Director Whitehead told the San Francisco chapter of the Academy of Television Arts and Sciences that Nixon was interested in helping the unions get more jobs. Later in the month Nixon assured Hollywood film workers that he was on their side and would do all he could to encourage the government to limit the permissible number of reruns. The FCC was forced to call for comments and to place the matter on its agenda where it remained for some four years in spite of a general consensus that it was not a proper item for commission action.

The OTP had been so politicized during the Nixon years that it was officially renamed the National Telecommunications and Information Administration (NTIA) and relocated in the Department of Commerce. It still makes recommendations and comments to which the FCC must be sensitive.

The Office of Management and Budget (OMB) is the White House mechanism for coordinating budget requests and legislative proposals to Congress. It is impossible for the FCC to submit suggestions to Congress that are incompatible with administration policy.

The Department of Justice occasionally asks the FCC to interpret the public interest in such a way that licenses will not be granted to those who the department feels are engaging in antitrust activities. For example, in the late 1960s the department selected several communities where jointly owned newspapers and stations accounted for some 80 percent of the advertising and asked that specific licenses not be renewed. Although the commission did not accede to this particular request, the pressure may have led to its later pronouncement that when a newspaper owned the only station in a community, the cross-ownership would have to be disolved.

The Federal Trade Commission (FTC) is charged with seeing that advertising avoids factual untruths in the permitted "puffery." It asked the commission to expand its Fairness Doctrine to the point where counter-commercials would be required whenever an advertisement based its claims on factual data that could be disputed. Although the FCC rejected this request, it had been forced to complicate its agenda and devote time to consideration of what it knew from the beginning was unreasonable.

Pressures from Regulated Media

The most intense pressure on the FCC comes from those it regulates, since they feel they have the most at stake—their investments and economic future. For many years it was broadcasters who were most concerned, and many critics charged the FCC was a captive of those it was supposed to regulate. Since the mid-1950s broadcaster pressure has been balanced by pressure from cable interests who want more freedom to grow to the marketplace potential. The commission is frequently caught in the middle and certain to make decisions that will displease one side or the other.

Pressures from industry groups become even more difficult to resist when one realizes that their lobbying efforts frequently are successful with the Congress and the administration. In the spring of 1976 the commission found itself in the unenviable position of trying to defend in court a series of revised regulations it had promulgated in the field of pay cable. Opposed to it in the case were the cable interests and the Department of Justice which felt the rules were still too restrictive on cable. Also opposed were broadcasters who felt the rules were too permissive. Waiting in the wings was Congress which has the power to change the law if either cable or broadcast interests persuade it to enter a controversy.

Pressures from the Public

There has been public disappointment with the FCC since the 1930s when advertising became the sole source of broadcast revenues, and when program schedules reflected sponsor decisions more than the choices of reviewers. The commission did not begin to feel public pressure as a major factor until after 1966 when a court of appeals ordered that the public be permitted to participate in the license-renewal process. Since 1969, when the same court of appeals reinforced its command that the public be heard, the commission has had to spend increasing amounts of time listening to various minority and special-interest groups. The court ruled that not only must the public be heard, the FCC must reasonably evaluate what the public says. As a consequence, the commission is subject to constant pressures from ethnic minorities, devotees of "unique" program formats, concerned parents, politically oriented groups, and others.

Criticism of the FCC

In their half-century of regulating broadcasting, the Radio and Communications Commissions have been as vigorously criticized and maligned as any other agency of government. There has probably never been a time in the last several decades when an action of the FCC has been universally applauded. There are always some who insist that the FCC has made serious errors, that its membership is unqualified to serve, and that its actions are unintelligently or illegally or immorally motivated.

The history of the commission does indeed contain apparent inconsistencies and points at which it seemed to have little commitment to logic. This is not, however, because presidents have appointed weak and unintelligent men and women or because commissioners lose all sense of public responsibility after being confirmed by the Senate. Rather, it is due to the fact that commissioners are subject to so many different kinds of restraints and pressures in addition to their own personal inclinations. Frequently, significant pressures are exerted in diametrically opposite dircetions. The wonder, in retrospect, is not that the commission should have had so many detractors but that it should have been able to accomplish so much in the face of its handicaps and problems.

7.6 A CASE IN POINT—LICENSE RENEWAL

Perhaps nothing more clearly illustrates the difficulties of regulation (especially when the FCC tries to raise standards) than a review of license renewal in the post–World War II years. It is a classic example of FCC confusion leading to industry confusion compounded by congressional intervention and unprecedented involvement by the courts.

The Status Quo in 1945

The early story of license renewal is summarized by a paragraph from a speech by FCC Chairman Paul Porter to the NAB convention in 1945.

> *The station is constructed and begins operation. Subsequently the licensee asks for a three-year renewal and the record clearly shows that he has not fulfilled the promises made to the Commission when he received the original grant. The Commission in the past has, for a variety of reasons, including limitations of staff, automatically renewed these licenses even in cases where there is a vast disparity between promises and performance.**

Chairman Porter was telling the NAB that a new era was dawning and the commission would begin to renew licenses on a less casual and routine basis. A month later the FCC demonstrated its seriousness by giving only temporary renewals to six stations while it took time to study further their services to the public.

---

* Public Service Responsibility of Broadcast Licensees, FCC Mimeograph No. 81575, March 7, 1946.

In 1946 the FCC issued an eighty-page document titled "Public Service Responsibility of Broadcast Licensees." This was a policy statement indicating that the commission would compare promise with performance in the renewing of licenses. It was so opposed by the broadcasters on the grounds of free speech that Congress pressured the FCC not to make substantial changes in its long-standing procedures.

In 1960 the FCC issued another policy statement that was notable because it used for the first time a phrase that has become the key to present applications for both initial licensing and renewal—"ascertainment." This required an applicant to report on the measures taken to determine the tastes, needs, and desires of the community and the manner in which the applicant proposed to meet those needs and desires. This policy statement, also, failed to make any significant impact at the time.

In 1969 two dissimilar cases reached their climaxes. One was considered a "renewal challenge" and the other a "petition to deny renewal." While the differences were not obvious at the time, they later became highly significant.

WHDH-TV

Throughout the 1960s the WHDH-TV case was among the most publicized and controversial news stories involving broadcasting. The situation was considered a renewal challenge and illustrates how perception can be more important than reality. It also illustrates the complexity and length to which regulatory proceedings may go.

In 1957 the FCC awarded VHF Channel 5 in Boston, Massachusetts to the Boston *Herald-Traveler*, a newspaper that already operated radio station WHDH. The case was sent back to the FCC by a court of appeals when there were rumors about irregularities in the commission's proceedings. The charges concerned *ex parte* (with only one side present) dealings where one applicant had met informally with a commissioner in the absence of other applicants. Specifically, it was alleged that there had been an *ex parte* meeting between President Robert Choate of the *Herald-Traveler* and Chairman George McConnaughey of the FCC.

The FCC found the charges warranted and vacated the grant to WHDH-TV while permitting it to continue broadcasting under temporary authority—not a license. While the matter was in litigation, a new element was introduced.

From time to time since 1935 the FCC had indicated its concern with "cross-ownership" in which a radio or television station was licensed to a publisher in the same community. But since there had been cross-ownership from the beginning, the commission had never done anything to force divestiture. In 1965 the FCC had issued guidelines for use in comparative hearings when there were several applicants for a *new* license. The guidelines stressed the importance of local ownership and said it would be even better if some of the proposed owners planned to work in the station. On the negative side, the commission said that cross-ownership with other media would be a distinct disadvantage for an applicant.

Four years later the FCC awarded Channel 5 to another applicant using the standard announced for new licenses. WHDH-TV was rejected on the grounds of cross-ownership.

However, broadcasters only saw that an operator who had been on the air for more than ten years was being replaced because of cross-ownership. Many other stations were also owned by newspapers and foresaw problems for themselves if the new policy were widely implemented. The FCC did little to dispel the confusion and the WHDH-TV case became an apparent prime example of a license renewal challenge in which one side opposes renewal because that party wants the license.

While the WHDH-TV case is not the longest on record, it does illustrate not only the way in which things can drag out but also the four points of decision in the regulatory process. Because of the complexity of this case, it helps to make a chronological diagram (Fig. 7.3) of the movement among these four points:

1. The hearing examiner makes a recommendation to the FCC.

2. The FCC makes a decision.

3. An appeals court reviews the FCC decision.

4. The Supreme Court reviews or refuses to hear an appeal from the lower court.

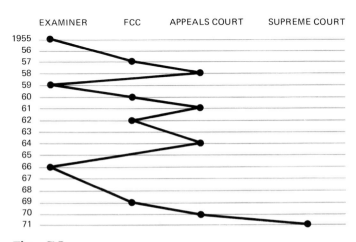

Fig. 7.3
Year-by-year chart of the WHDH-TV case.

Summary

1955	Comparative hearings ended.	
1957	FCC granted construction permit to WHDH-TV.	
1958	Appeals court affirmed grant but directed the FCC to consider the *ex parte* allegations.	
1959	Hearing examiner concluded WHDH-TV should be licensee since *ex parte* had not influenced the outcome.	
1960	FCC vacated WHDH-TV license but permitted continued operation.	
1961	Appeals court affirmed vacating of WHDH-TV license.	
1962	FCC found all applicants "flawed" and gave WHDH-TV four-month temporary license.	
1964	Appeals court noted death of Robert Choate and approved FCC's proceeding with new hearings for license.	
1966	Hearing examiner recommended WHDH-TV receive license.	
1969	FCC granted license to Boston Broadcasters, Inc.	
1970	Appeals court affirmed Channel 5 grant to Boston Broadcasters, Inc.	
1971	Supreme Court refused to review appeals court affirmation.	

WLBT (TV)

The broadcasters' fears aroused by WHDH-TV in January 1969 were greatly increased in June of that year when in a true renewal case a license was stripped from a television station in Jackson, Mississippi. WLBT(TV) had started operating in 1953. Its license had been renewed in 1958 only after "assuring the Commission that all points of view would be presented on local programs dealing with controversial issues." It had been one of eight stations studied by the FCC because of its biased coverage of the 1962 riots following the entrance of a black student into the University of Mississippi. In short, its record was not unsullied.

When WLBT applied for a renewal in 1964, it was opposed by local groups led by the Reverend Dr. Everett Parker, Director of the Division of Communication of the United Church of Christ (UCC). Blacks made up nearly half the population of the station's area, but news of local whites' attitude on segregation was thoroughly aired without any mention of blacks' point of view. There were no black employees at the station and there were no programs designed to meet blacks' needs and interests.

In 1965 the commission gave WLBT a one-year renewal, which was the equivalent of putting it on probation. (The normal renewal is for three years.) Dr. Parker was pleased with the short-term license, but expressed bitter disappointment that the FCC had not ordered renewal hearings as he had requested. He thought it important that the commissioners hear directly from community residents their dissatisfaction with the station. The FCC said it had feared hearings would inflame racial tension and do more harm than good. It adhered to its policy of limiting official consideration to those who claimed electrical interference or economic injury from the station seeking renewal. Ordinary citizens were denied such "standing" to participate in the renewal process.

The UCC appealed to court, pleading that community residents should have a chance to be heard in renewal cases. In 1966 the court of appeals agreed with the petition and ordered the FCC to hold hearings as requested.* In effect, the court pointed out that since stations are licensed in the public interest, there was no possible way to evaluate a station adequately if community residents were not permitted to speak. Hearings were scheduled by the FCC, and in 1967 a hearing examiner was sent to Jackson. At the hearings UCC and local black leaders asserted the station had failed to ascertain the needs of the community, to program for all the viewers, or to observe the Fairness Doctrine. After studying the evidence, the examiner concluded that the UCC had "failed woefully to support its allegations." He recommended that the station receive a full three-year renewal and the commissioners followed his recommendations by a 5–2 vote. The UCC again appealed to the court, while the membership of the commission engaged in vituperative disagreement among themselves about what they had done.

The procedure normally followed when a court feels the FCC has erred is to send the case back with directions that it be reopened and the procedure or basis for decision changed. This had happened in the earlier UCC appeal when the court ordered the FCC to hold hearings on the WLBT case. There are usually no instructions to the commission on what its final decision should be, only that it must use a different method of arriving at whatever decision the FCC feels is in the public interest.

The court's reaction to the second UCC appeal in the WLBT case is best summarized by the lead paragraph of the *Broadcasting* report:

An obviously angry U.S. Court of Appeals for the District of Columbia last week eviscerated the FCC, stripped the license from WLBT(TV) Jackson, Miss., a station accused of racism in

---

* *Office of Communication of the United Church of Christ v. Federal Communications Commission*, 359 F.2d 994 (D.C. Cir.) March 25, 1966.

> *its programming, and directed the Commission to invite new applicants for the Jackson Channel 3 facility involved.* *

The court found the commission's "administrative conduct" beyond repair, and ordered WLBT's license vacated. The decision was especially critical of the hearing examiner, who had treated the UCC and black leaders as "interlopers" and had placed on them the entire burden of proof.† It is unlikely that the commission throughout its history had ever been so soundly criticized by the court as in the WLBT case.

The remainder of the WLBT story is not pertinent to the renewal process. The commission was directed to start in *de novo* determining the best licensee for Channel 3 in Jackson. The court did not bar WLBT from applying, but it would have been sheer effrontery on the part of the FCC to grant the license to the same organization again. The station was turned over to an interim nonprofit group for operation until a new licensee had been selected. A black manager was hired and WLBT became highly integrated and quite successful financially. In 1980 a new company with 51 percent control held by blacks, finally emerged successful from lengthy FCC proceedings and took over operation from the interim group.

Summary of the 1969 Situation

Throughout the second half of 1969, license renewal was a major topic of conversation among broadcasters. The FCC itself appeared to have refused renewal to WHDH-TV on the ground of cross-ownership; many other valuable stations were owned by newspapers. The court of appeals had forced the FCC to admit community groups into the renewal of WLBT and then superseded the authority of the commission when it appeared that the examiner and commissioners had ignored the evidence in the hearings. Many other stations had within their communities minority groups ready to use the renewal process to express dissatisfaction with broadcasting. Because of broadcasters' fear that the WHDH-TV case would become a precedent, Senator John O. Pastore (D.-R.I.) prepared a bill aimed at "insulating broadcasters from irresponsible applications for their facilities at renewal time."‡ It would have required the FCC to find an incumbent licensee disqualified for continued operation of a station before accepting any competing applications or challenges. In the meantime, the FCC was

---

* *Broadcasting,* June 30, 1969, p. 42.

† Office of Communication of the United Church of Christ v. Federal Communications Commission, 425 F.2d 543 (D.C. Cir.) June 20, 1969.

‡ *Broadcasting,* May 5, 1969, p. 50.

unhappy that broadcasters would not believe commission assurances that WHDH-TV was not a precedent.

1970 Policy Statement on Renewal Procedure

By the end of 1969, it was apparent that the situation had deteriorated from the Commission's and stations' points of view; Congress was not ready to pass the Pastore bill, which was being attacked by minorities as racist. Renewal challenges were being filed in increasing numbers; nine were pending at the end of the year. In January 1970 the commission issued a policy statement on renewals that roughly paralleled the intent of the Pastore bill. The statement said the FCC "would favor an incumbent broadcaster over rival applicants if he can show in a comparative hearing that his programming has been substantially attuned to the needs and interests of his area." To speed up the process in challenged renewals, examiners were authorized to halt the proceedings once "the record established that the renewal applicant's service has been substantial on that determination."† (The policy statement also stressed that the WHDH-TV situation was unique and that future renewal applicants would not be endangered if the incumbent was owned by a newspaper in the same community.)

The 1970 policy statement was appealed to the courts by two companies challenging renewals in Hampton Roads, Virginia and in Boston, and by two Washington, D.C. citizen groups, the Citizens Communication Center (CCC) and Black Effort for Soul in Television (BEST). The basis for the appeal was that permitting an examiner to close hearings at an early point deprived the challenger of the right to a full hearing as specified by the Communications Act.

A year and a half later, in June 1971, the court of appeals ordered the FCC not to follow its policy of favoring the incumbent so long as service was "without serious deficiency." The immediate grounds for the order was the failure to guarantee a full hearing to the challenger, but the court went on to criticize the overall policy. The FCC had said it was seeking to bring stability into broadcasting; the court said it had, instead, induced *rigor mortis* because since the issuance of the statement not a single renewal challenge had been filed. The commission was told to reconsider any cases where this policy had been a factor in a decision. It was the court's view that an incumbent should be favored only after he or she had demonstrated superior service.*

---

† Ibid., January 19, 1970, p. 21.

* *Citizens Communications Center, et al.* v. *Federal Communications Commission and United States of America*, 447 F.2d (D.C. Cir.) June 11, 1971.

Petitions to Deny Renewal

By 1971 petitions to deny renewal had assumed greater importance than the challenges from those who would seek incumbents' licenses. When the UCC opposed the renewal of WLBT in 1964, Dr. Parker did not request that his or any other organization be given the license. He simply petitioned that the license not be renewed. The significance of the WLBT case is that it established the principle that members of a community have a right to participate in the renewal process. No longer could the FCC sit in isolated chambers and arbitrarily decide there was not enough evidence against an incumbent to justify failing to renew his or her license. Now the commission had to satisfy the courts that it had listened to the public and that its decisions were consistent with public testimony brought out in open hearings. The commissioners quailed at the prospect of having to hold hearings on all controversial renewals. Broadcasters realized that it would take hundreds of thousands of dollars to fight off petitions to deny renewal. Members of ethnic and other groups rejoiced that they were to be permitted to enter the proceedings and that sensitive pressure points of the stations had been exposed. Petitions to deny renewal poured into the commission.

**The Aim—
Negotiated
Settlements**

Community groups did not submit petitions to deny renewal in the hope that an incumbent would actually lose his or her license. Rather, they used petitions as a device to bring a station to the negotiating table and to agree to changes in programming and employment practices that had been resisted. The strategy was to submit a petition that would be withdrawn in return for concessions, thus saving the incumbent the costs of a contested renewal. Two examples illustrate the kinds of demands being made and granted.

**KTAL-TV
Texarkana, Texas**

One of the first petitions to be withdrawn in return for changes by the incumbent concerned KTAL-TV in Texarkana, Texas. The agreement was announced by Dr. Parker of UCC in June 1969, the same month in which the court of appeals vacated the WLBT license. It served as a model for future efforts.

The blacks in Texarkana had charged KTAL-TV with failing to provide programs for minority audiences, failing to consult black leaders about the needs of the community, and excluding blacks from newscasts and other programs using local talent. After negotiations the station agreed to meet certain demands in return for the dropping of the petition to deny. Among the items in the agreement were:

1. All sides were to be included in discussion of controversial issues.

2. Black leaders would be consulted in monthly meetings on programming.

3. Two black reporters would be hired and would appear on the air.

4. There would be no unnecessary reference to race of individuals.

5. Public service announcements would be aired for black organizations.

6. Programs would be prepared to publicize problems of the poverty-stricken.

7. There would be a better balance in religious programming.

8. There would be no preemption of network programs without consultation with black leaders.

Atlanta, Georgia   In April 1970 there was an announcement that twenty-two of twenty-eight Atlanta radio and television stations had agreed to terms advanced by the Community Coalition in Broadcasting composed of twenty black organizations. (The other stations were still negotiating.) There were differences in the agreements with various stations, but for the most part they said they would carry on a continuing consultation with black leaders about programming and provide on-the-job training and scholarships for blacks who would later be employed by the stations. Two of the stations agreed to put a black on the board of directors. There were to be more public service announcements for black organizations and no more preemption of network programs without consultation. In response, the Community Coalition withdrew its petitions to deny renewal.

The agreements in Texarkana and Atlanta typified the efforts community residents were making to participate in broadcasting. Their tool was the petition to deny renewal, although their aim was to improve cooperation from the present licensees rather than to force them out of business. Because there was an ulterior motivation in petitioning to deny renewal, the broadcasters felt petitions were comparable to blackmail. In the majority of cases there was no great fear that the FCC might actually deny renewal—few stations were as inadequately operated as WLBT had been. Rather, stations were faced with the expenditure of great sums in defending their applications if they did not negotiate with the groups of residents. For a while broadcasters thought the deck had been stacked against them and that every minority demand would have to be met.

WMAL-TV Washington, D.C.   The pendulum began to swing back with the disposition of the petition to deny renewal to WMAL-TV that was filed with the FCC in September 1969, three months after the WLBT case was decided for the second time by the court of appeals. The petitioners were sixteen blacks representing a variety of organizations in Washington, D.C., which was 70 percent black. They noted that only 15 (6 percent) of the station's 223 employees were black. They claimed the station had made misrepresentations when it filed its ascertainment reports and that the station claimed a much closer relationship with the black community than actually existed. They also pointed out that there was practically no programming designed specifically for blacks. A hearing on the renewal was requested.

The petition had been in its hands for sixteen months before the FCC announced by a 4–1 vote it was renewing the licnese for the full three-year period without a hearing. It said there had been some changes in station policy as the result of FCC clarification of its guidelines. It deemed some of the charges unfounded and concluded that renewal would be in the public interest. The petitioners said they had expected such a response from a commission that included no blacks and that they would appeal to the courts.

In the seventeen more months before the appeals court ruled in the case, petitions to deny renewal of a hundred more stations had been submitted to the FCC. Everyone was awaiting the outcome of the WMAL-TV case as an indication of what was to come. To the relief of the broadcasters, in 1972 the court affirmed the FCC's renewal of the license because the petition to deny was not sufficiently specific to warrant hearings. For example, the petition had indicated the low proportion of blacks employed by the station, but it did not give any instances where blacks had been discriminated against when they sought jobs. The petition complained about newspaper ownership, but it did not show how that cross-ownership had caused negative results. The court also rejected the argument that if 20 percent, or any other portion, of a community belonged to a particular group, it followed that the same portion of the station's programming should be aimed at the group.

The court made it clear that the decision was based on the specific facts of this one case and should not be interpreted to mean that the commission could in all cases dispense with hearings. Still, it was a great relief to broadcasters and commissioners that there had been no repetition of the WLBT decision, which would have thrown the renewal process into complete chaos.

1973 Renewal Statement

In March 1973 the commission issued a new policy and renewal forms on which it had been working during the nearly two years since the appeals court had overturned the 1970 statement. The FCC expressed its concern over the continuing rise in petitions to deny from community groups. There were 140 renewals that had been deferred because of such petitions and the commission could not possibly handle full hearings and other proceedings for all of them. At the same time, the WLBT case had made it clear that community residents could not ignored. The commission's problem was to work out a course that would permit community groups to participate in the renewal process and that would also eliminate some of the current chaos.

The commission gave as its intention provision of a local mechanism for resolving "such dissatisfaction as it arises and eliminating the need for the filing of a petition to deny license renewal." *Broadcasting* paraphrased the FCC aim: "Settle your problems with your communities before they erupt into petitions to deny at renewal time. At the same time the commission will make sure that the citizen groups have the information they need to keep a close check on their local stations' service."* The FCC announced that stations would be responsible for ascertainment of community problems throughout the license period. All members of the public were to be made aware that the licenses were up for renewal and that the stations would welcome suggestions from viewers. The date for filing applications was moved up to four months before the renewal date and community groups then had three months in which to submit petitions to deny.

The new policy was laying down ground rules for both parties. Community groups were not to have a voice in the renewal process unless they had over a reasonable period of time attempted to work with stations to negotiate whatever complaints they had. They could not go to the commission at the last minute and cause disruption of the process. Neither could community groups enter petitions to deny renewal with the expectation of being reimbursed by the station.

The stations were told that if they refused to bargain in good faith with the community groups, their renewals might be designated for hearings, which could be extremely costly. The commission was to be the final arbiter in the event that a petition to deny was filed. If a community petition seemed unreasonable, the FCC could refuse to act on it—but the commission must be prepared to convince a court that it had acted appropriately. If the petition appeared justified, the station would have to go through hearings. There has been a decided decline in the number of petitions actually filed with the FCC since the statement, although the number of agreements between stations and community groups has climbed. Many of the concessions to minority demands in the 1970s have been the result of community participation in the renewal process.

Limit on Licensee Concessions

As stations made more and more concessions to community groups to avoid costly hearings, the FCC became concerned that licensees might bargain away their freedom to serve the public interest. Reference to the danger

---

* *Broadcasting*, March 19, 1973, p. 35.

was made in speeches by commissioners and in the fall of 1974 expressed in a letter to the National Organization of Women (NOW). NOW had extracted major concessions from a group owner in return for dropping opposition to a transfer of station ownership. The letter to NOW warned that while the FCC was approving the transfer under the terms of the agreement, broadcasters must always retain freedom to change their policies if circumstances warranted. The concessions might not be binding in the future if the licensee felt the public could be better served in another way.

Alabama Educational Television Commission

That the new policy did not entirely rule out petitions to deny was illustrated by a completely unprecedented action taken by the FCC in January 1975. It refused to renew the licenses of eight public television stations (plus the construction permit of a ninth) operated by the Alabama Educational Television Commission (AETC). Complaints had been filed by the American Civil Liberties Union about racial discrimination in both employment and programming. The commission found both charges to be true, although it acted primarily on the issue of programming. The commission said there was substantial evidence that blacks, who constituted 30 percent of the state's population, rarely appeared on AETC programs; that no black instructors were employed in connection with locally produced in-school programs; and that unexplained decisions of discriminatorily applied policies caused the preemption of almost all black-oriented network programs. The FCC was unimpressed with the argument that AETC was a state-controlled organization like the Department of Education. The commission commented, "A licensee cannot with impunity ignore the problems of significant minorities in its service area."

The action was especially dramatic because it was the first time the FCC had taken such decisive nonrenewal action. The WHDH-TV case had not been a clear case of license renewal, and WLBT had been an action by a court rather than the commission. The FCC did give credit for improvement to AETC and indicated it might reapply for the licenses along with competing applicants, if there were any. Since public television stations have always received very lenient treatment from the FCC, the AETC decision was one that made commercial broadcasters more aware of the responsibilities to minorities.

Attempts at Renewal Legislation

In the 1970s there were two important attempts at amending the Communications Act so that license renewal would be easier. The first came out of President Nixon's confrontation with the television networks. Shortly after Nixon's reelection in 1972, Office of Telecommunications Policy (OTP) Director Whitehead entered the renewal picture. For three years since Vice President Agnew's Des Moines speech, there had been growing animosity between the White House and television stations over the coverage of the war in Vietnam and the demonstrations against it. The pressure was particularly intense on the networks. Whitehead had begun talking about "localism," or the centering of program and news responsibility at the station level instead of at the networks.

In December 1972 Whitehead spoke to the Indianapolis chapter of Sigma Delta Chi, an honorary journalism fraternity. He devoted most of his time to network bias in the news. His remarks were largely a repeat of the criticism voiced by Agnew and others until near the end he made a significant departure from the old charges:

> *Station managers and network officials who fail to act to correct imbalance or consistent bias from the networks—or those who acquiesce by silence— can only be considered willing participants, to be held fully accountable by the broadcaster's community at license-renewal time.*

Following this very direct implication that the Nixon administration was prepared to use the license-renewal process to punish stations that carried "biased network news," Whitehead announced his office was submitting to Congress proposed legislation changing the renewal process. He said he would recommend that licenses be increased in length from three to five years and that there be two primary criteria by which the Federal Communications Commission would assess a licensee's record:

1. That he or she has been attuned to, and made a good will effort to meet the needs of the community.

2. That he or she has afforded a reasonable opportunity for the discussion of conflicting views on controversial issues of public importance.

Taken by themselves, the proposals were acceptable to broadcasters. If licenses were to run for five years, there would be fewer occasions when they could be challenged. That would amount to a substantial saving of money and effort. Broadcasters were already charged by the FCC with the responsibility of being attuned to the needs of the community. The second point was simply a restatement of the Fairness Doctrine with which as broadcasters they were learning to live.

In the context of the speech, however, the proposals read quite differently. Being attuned to the community might imply that news programs should be geared to the interests of the local viewers, many of whom disapproved of the alleged liberal bias of the networks. Reasonable opportunity for discussion might imply that when a station aired liberal newscasts, it should then be prepared to balance them with a conservative approach to the news. Few stations felt capable of monitoring network news feeds and then balancing them to meet community attitudes. The other alternative would be for affiliates to tell the networks, "give us newscasts that will in no way rouse antipathy among our viewers so they would raise questions about our getting our licenses renewed. In short, make the newscasts so neutral that no one can possibly object to them."

The broadcasters were in a quandary about how they should respond to the Whitehead "carrot and stick" speech. The networks were obviously offended. Stations were torn between their desires for five-year licenses and their commitment to journalistic freedom. Most seemed to be saying, "let's see if we can get the five-year licenses and learn to live with the implications without surrendering too much."

In March 1973 the White House sent to Congress a bill based on the Whitehead ideas. Licenses were to be extended to five years. Licensees were to be judged on whether they were substantially attuned to the needs and interests of the public. They were also required to adhere to the Fairness Doctrine. A competitor might file for a frequency only after proving the incumbent had not met the two criteria mentioned above. The House of Representatives immediately started hearings. Senator Pastore, whose 1969 bill had never passed, decided the Senate should wait until the House had completed its action.

The renewal bill initiated by Whitehead failed for political reasons that were never fully apparent. Both houses of Congress passed similar bills but the chairman of the House of Representatives committee refused to appoint members to a joint committee that would report back a compromise that would have easily passed.

The second attempt at renewal legislation was initiated in the mid-1970s by Representative Lionel Van Deerlin (D.-Cal.), chairman of the House Subcommittee on Communications. He announced that his committee would rewrite the entire Communications Act with emphasis on taking away the difficulties of license renewal. Failure of the attempt could be traced back to the WLBT(TV) case of 1966 and 1969. Public-interest groups had become so well organized that Representative Van Deerlin was forced to introduce a tradeoff for easier license renewal—broadcasters would be asked to pay annual fees for use of the public spectrum. As soon as that notion was introduced, broadcaster support quickly melted. The reason was not that the fees suggested were so high. It was that once the concept of payment for use of the airwaves had been established, there was no guarantee that the fees might not later become far more onerous than the present problems of license renewal. In the summer of 1979 Representative Van Deerlin announced abandonment of his effort.

At the beginning of the 1980s broadcasters had received no legislative relief for their renewal problems and were focusing their attention on two aspects of FCC and court actions. Through much of the 1970s the renewal of WESH-TV in Daytona Beach, Florida had been in the headlines. The station was owned by Cowles publications and challenged by a local group. There was no important cross-ownership issue since Cowles had no local outlets, and the FCC voted to renew the license on the grounds that WESH-TV had provided "substantial" service well above the minimum level at which the commission would have considered nonrenewal if there had been no challenge. The FCC action was referred to an appeals court that in 1971 had said the incumbent should be favored at renewal time only if service had been "superior." As broadcasters awaited a final disposition of this case in the early 1980s, there was considerable doubt as to whether the FCC would be able to come up with a compromise that would enable it to make renewals more routine and still satisfy an appeals court that the provisions of the Communications Act were being met.

Although the commission voted to renew the WESH-TV license but was held back by the courts, the situation was quite different in WNAC-TV in Boston, owned by RKO—a subsidiary of General Tire and Rubber Company. Stations in Boston, New York City, and Los Angeles were challenged because of charges against RKO and its parent company. The Securities and Exchange Commission found that General Tire and Rubber had participated in illegal activities and obtained a consent order in which the company promised to refrain from such actions in the future. Then the commission found that the ties between RKO and its parent company were so close that they could not be separated and voted not to renew the licenses of RKO's television stations. The value of all the RKO broadcast properties was in excess of $400 million and the legal fight would probably continue for years before there was a final resolution.

SUMMARY

For the most part, honest and honorable people have served on the Federal Communications Commission and have sought to do what they considered best. They have had to work with a law that was intentionally vague while conforming to court decisions and FCC precedents. Commissioners have been subjected to formidable pressures from Congress, broadcasters, and the public. If they have not been properly qualified, it is the inevitable result of the presidential use of appointments to bestow political favors. Trying to determine which commissioners and which decisions have been best is largely a mater of the philosophy of the individual making the judgments.

GLOSSARY ITEMS

The following words and phrases used in Chapter 7 are defined in the Glossary:

Administrative Law Judge (ALJ)	Interim Operation
Ascertainment	Patron Plan
Blue Book	Payola
Chain Regulations	Petition to Deny Renewal
Community-Antenna Television (CATV)	Public Interest, Convenience, and Necessity
Construction Permit (CP)	Quiz Scandals
Countercommercials	Renewal Challenge
Cross-Ownership	Sustaining Program
Hearing Examiner	Television Freeze

LICENSE-RENEWAL CHRONOLOG

1945 FCC Chairman Paul Porter's speech to NAB about automatic renewals.

1946 FCC issued "Blue Book" (*Public Service Responsibility of Broadcast Licensees*) with emphasis on promise and performance.

1951 WBAL renewal marked end of Blue Book era.

1957 FCC awarded Boston Channel 5 license to WHDH. (For detailed Chronolog on WHDH, see text.)

1960 FCC issued "Program Policy Statement." Emphasized methods used to ascertain needs of audience and proposals to meet them. Listed fourteen program elements.

1964 UCC opposed renewal of two television stations in Jackson, Mississippi.

1965 FCC issued guidelines for comparative hearings when considering applicants for new stations.
FCC renewed WLBT in Jackson, Miss., for one year.
UCC protested lack of hearing in WLBT case to appeals court.

1966 Court ordered FCC to hold hearing on WLBT renewal.

1967 WLBT hearings held in Jackson, Miss.
Examiner recommended WLBT receive three-year renewal.

1968 FCC issued three-year renewal to WLBT.
UCC protested WLBT renewal to appeals court.

1969   FCC awarded Boston Channel 5 to BBI.

Appeals court said WLBT case so badly flawed, it was beyond repair. Vacated WLBT license.

Agreement between citizen groups and KTAL-TV in Texarkana. Station agreed to changes and petition to deny dropped.

Blacks submitted petition to deny license renewal of WMAL-TV in Washington, D.C.

1970   FCC renewal policy favored incumbent if programming was substantially attuned to needs and interests of area. WHDH case not to be precedent.

FCC ruled in Texarkana case that station cannot reimburse petitioner to deny for expenses incurred.

1970   Agreement between citizen groups and twenty-two stations in Atlanta, Gerogia.

1971   Appeals court ruled out FCC 1970 Renewal Policy.

FCC renewed license of WMAL-TV without hearing.

1972   Appeals court affirmed FCC renewal to WMAL-TV without hearing.

Whitehead "carrot-and-stick" speech on renewal.

1973   Whitehead submitted proposed renewal legislation to Congress.

FCC issued new renewal policy statement setting mechanism for resolving station-citizen disagreement.

1974   FCC warned station it cannot make too many concessions to NOW or other citizen groups.

House and Senate passed similar renewal bills, but legislation died because no conferees to joint committee were appointed by House committee chairman.

1975   FCC refused to renew licenses of Alabama Educational TV Commission stations because of racial bias in programming.

1979   WLBT assigned to permanent licensee.

Alabama Educational TV Commission received renewal of stations' licenses.

1980   FCC voted nonrenewal of RKO television stations.

PREVIEW

A broadcast station consists of (1) licensee, (2) equipment, (3) staff, and (4) contracts with outside companies. The licensee is the person or company to which the FCC grants permission to operate the station. The average television station and large radio stations are organized in a traditional fashion. Personnel are hired to manage the station, operate its equipment, coordinate the program schedule, provide news, and sell time to local advertisters. Comparatively little programming is done locally. Both entertainment and news come largely from outside organizations. There are also contracts with other outside companies to provide help in selling time to national advertisers and in measuring audience. For many stations the National Association of Broadcasters is a source of information about practices in other stations around the country.

CHAPTER 8

THE STATION AND LOCAL ADVERTISING

8.1 DEFINITION OF A STATION

The individual station is the heart of American broadcasting. Although network programs and personalities are the most familiar, it is the station that is the focal point of regulation and the primary link between broadcasting and the public. A station consists of:

1. A licensee (a person or company) authorized by the FCC to broadcast on a given channel in a given community.

2. The studio, transmitter, and other equipment that the licensee has purchased in order to operate the station.

3. The staff the licensee has organized to accomplish the various functions of the station.

4. The contracts the licensee has signed with other organizations to obtain ratings, programming, sales, and other services.

Today's television station is in most respects very similar to the radio station of the 1940s. This chapter will examine television stations and then note the differences between them and today's average radio station.

8.2 PRELIMINARY STATION ANALYSIS

There are three factors that differentiate the size and probable profitability of a commercial television station: (1) its channel number, (2) its network status, (3) the size of its market. If anyone wants to classify a station in his or her own community, the basic information is already known through observation. If one is interested in a station elsewhere, he or she can consult *Broadcasting Yearbook*, *Standard Rate and Data Service*, or similar publications.

The Channel-Number Factor

The most important characteristic of a station is whether it has a VHF of UHF channel. We have seen that UHF stations had great difficulty in getting started in the 1950s, especially when they were in competition with VHF outlets. While there are a few UHF stations making money today, they are generally by no means as profitable as those in the VHF. For example, FCC figures for 1975 show that while 492 VHF stations reported an average income (revenues less expenses before taxes) of more than $1 million each, the average UHF station reported only $56,000, up from an average loss in 1974.

The Network Status Factor

Commercial stations fall into three groups with regard to network status:

1. The network-owned-and-operated station (O&O).

2. The network affiliate.

3. The independent station.

A network O&O is licensed by the FCC to one of the three networks and is located in one of the largest markets.* The O&Os usually carry everything the network provides. These stations are both large and profitable.

A network affiliate has contracted with a network agreeing to carry most or all of the network programs in return for "compensation" or pay from the network to the station. Since the affiliate receives from the network

---

* The three national networks own television stations in the following cities: ABC—New York City, Chicago, San Francisco, Los Angeles, Detroit. CBS—New York City, Chicago, Philadelphia, Los Angeles, St. Louis. NBC—New York City, Chicago, Washington, D.C., Los Angeles, Cleveland.

the most popular programs that will attract large audiences, it will be among the largest and most profitable of the stations in its community.

An independent station has no contract with a network and includes no current network programs in its schedule except for the few occasions when it may carry a program has been rejected by the local affiliate. Of the approximately 750 commercial television stations in the country, over 125 are independents. A station is independent when it cannot get an affiliation, which usually is the case when there are more than three commercial stations in a market. If there are only three, each will usually have an affiliation. Since an independent does not have the popular current network programs, it will attract less audience and be less profitable than the affiliates in the same community. (For figures indicating the value of network affiliation, see Chapter 9.)

The Size-of-Market Factor

Stations are licensed to operate in specific communities but advertisers are more interested in the "markets" they serve. We think of a market as the area from which business tends to flow to a focal point. That point will usually be the largest city in an area. In it will be the largest banks, the major department stores, the wholesale centers from which food and other products are distributed to retailers, and the major airports.

For a consistent definition of individual markets, advertisers use the Arbitron "Area of Dominant Influence" (ADI) concept that divides the whole country into 209 markets. Each is made up of the counties that tend to cluster together in the flow of business to a central spot. For example, KCRA-TV on Channel 3 is licensed to operate in Sacramento, California. In Sacramento County there are 231,000 television homes. But the market area (ADI) served by KCRA-TV and its competitors contains 604,000 television homes, ranking it twenty-sixth in size among all markets in the country.

A. C. Nielsen uses a related concept of "Designated Market Area" (DMA) in which an ADI is divided into three parts: the Metro Area, the Local DMA, and the Adjacent DMA. Placement of a county in one of the categories depends on the consistency of viewing the stations in the center, or Metro Area.

When advertisers buy time on a station they are willing to pay a price commensurate with the size of the station's audience. The larger a market, the more a station can charge for its time if it has its fair share of homes tuned to it. Since station expenses tend to rise somewhat more slowly than revenues, this means the size and percentage of income (revenues less expenses) tend to be substantially greater as the size of the market increases.

To Summarize

If a station has a VHF channel in one of the larger markets and is a network affiliate or O&O, it is a highly valuable property. In the absence of one of the above factors, it will not do as well.

8.3 THE LICENSEE

The first of the four elements in a station is the licensee to whom the FCC gives authority to operate a station. Television stations are rarely licensed to individuals, partly because they have from the earliest days been very expensive. The average original cost of current television stations was estimated over $2,500,000, and purchase prices are now higher by many times. Secondly, for a number of years after World War II television was considered a high-risk investment and those individuals who could have afforded it would have been advised to put their money into something safer.

Group Ownership

As television has become more profitable and as large companies have sought either to increase their broadcast interests or to diversify into broadcasting, there are fewer licensees with stations in only one community. Nearly all today are "group owners" with properties in two or more markets. The most prominent of the group owners are the three national networks. Each owns the legal maximum of five VHF stations located in the largest markets. For many years the O&Os (network-owned-and-operated stations) were the largest source of network revenue. They are still highly profitable although not as dominant since other operations have become more remunerative.

The other group owners have little in common. Some, like GE and Westinghouse, first became interested in broadcasting because of their manufacturing activities. Others were started because radio seemed so closely related to newspaper and magazine publishing. Some started with one station many years ago and gradually added more radio and then television stations. Others entered the field after World War II because broadcasting was a profitable investment.

Aside from the network O&Os, it would be unusual for all the stations in any one group to be affiliated with a single network. Rather, one might find that in a group of five VHF stations, two would be affiliated with NBC, one each with ABC and CBS, and the fifth an independent station. Advantages of group ownership are that centralized management oversees all the stations at once and there can be great savings in bulk purchases of film and other program materials and in contracting with a station rep for national spot sales.

WESTINGHOUSE BROADCASTING COMPANY

The biggest names in broadcasting are the three networks—ABC, CBS, NBC. To people in the industry, Westinghouse Broadcasting Company (Group W) is the leader of all the rest. Since it started broadcasting with KDKA in 1920, Group W has been a pace-setter in the field. Today it consists of the following operations:

- The broadcast group with seven AM radio, four FM radio, and six television stations. While its television stations are mostly network affiliates, Group W pioneered independent-format radio in the 1950s.
- Its station-rep companies sell time for its own stations in the national spot market: RAR for radio time and TVAR for television time.
- Group W was a pioneer in original syndication production in the 1960s and is entering cable programming in addition to its broadcast production and syndication.
- Clearview Cable TV operates seven systems in the South and has partial ownership in several other cable systems. In 1980 Group W announced acquisition of Teleprompter, the largest MSO in the country. This acquisition also means taking over the half-ownership Teleprompter had in "Showtime," the principal competitor to HBO in pay cable.

Cross Ownership

Newspaper ownership is separated from the rest in both the individual and group categories because the FCC sees it differently. When an individual or company publishes a newspaper and operates a broadcast station in the same community, it is called cross-ownership. Since the mid-1930s the FCC has been concerned about such situations on the grounds that they were not conducive to the free flow of diverse ideas and opinions. Although commissioners expressed this concern with regularity, nothing was done for thirty years. Cross-ownership had existed since the 1920s and commissioners found themselves bound by decisions of their predecessors who had established and perpetuated the practice.

In 1965 the FCC took its first step in limiting the expansion of cross-ownership when it set new guidelines for comparative hearings in which a publisher was one of the applicants for a new station. In such an instance, if other things were equal, a nonpublisher applicant would be favored for the grant. In 1970 the commission announced a ban on the formation of new cross-ownerships pending a study of the problem. No publisher would be permitted to start a new station or purchase an existing one in a community where he or she owned a newspaper. In the event that a station involving cross-ownership was sold, the new owner would have to give up either the newspaper or the broadcasting station.

In 1975 the commission announced new rules that continued the ban on acquisition of new or existing stations by local publishers. It also announced that in sixteen small markets where the only broadcasting station or stations were owned by a local paper, the cross-ownership would have to be dissolved in five years. At the same time other existing cross-ownerships throughout the country were "grandfathered"—the commission said it would not force divestiture unless someone could demonstrate that a station involving cross-ownership was guilty of antitrust violations.

Within hours the National Citizens Committee for Broadcasting (NCCB) went to the Court of Appeals in Washington to protest the FCC's permission to continue all but a few cross-ownerships. In March 1977 the court, in effect, called the commission inconsistent for saying that cross-ownership inhibited the freedom of ideas to circulate while permitting most instances of it to continue. The court directed the FCC to adopt new rules that would lead to the dissolving of every cross-ownership unless a publisher could demonstrate that the public interest in his or her community demanded its continuation.

A year later the Supreme Court reversed the court of appeals and affirmed the commission's authority to order dissolution of the sixteen "egregious" or especially troublesome cases, while "grandfathering" the rest. In the early 1980s most of the sixteen egregious cases were resolved, either through sale or special waiver from the FCC; the current cross-ownership policy can be summarized as follows:

1. No new cross-ownerships may be established.

2. No purchaser of a cross-ownership may continue to operate both station and paper.

3. Existing cross-ownerships are "grandfathered" (permitted to continue).

It has also developed that cross-owned stations are especially vulnerable to challenges or petitions to deny at license renewal time. There have been instances of divestiture simply to avoid the anticipated legal tangles.

8.4 TELEVISION STATION EQUIPMENT

Licensees purchase the equipment needed to produce and transmit their own programs and to relay programs from the network or from tape and film that is mailed to them. In the studio are cameras, lighting, microphones, sets for newscasts and other local programs. In the control rooms are VTRs, TV film cameras, shading equipment (to insure consistency in brightness, and color contrast among all the cameras), and equipment to distribute signals from wherever they come to wherever they are to go (e.g., studio to VTR; network to transmitter; VTR to transmitter).

Located on a high hill or tall building is the transmitter that generates the broadcast signals and a tower on which the transmitting antenna is placed. Between the studio and the transmitter is a connection. It may be co-axial cable furnished by contract with the telephone company or a microwave "studio-transmitter link" (STL).

Various stations will have purchased additional equipment as it is needed and within budget limitations. There may be, for example, a remote unit—a truck fitted with a portable generator and cameras and VTRs that can tape programs outside the studio. Other equipment, especially for news gathering, may consist of portable film and tape equipment that can be carried around in a car.

8.5 THE TELEVISION STATION STAFF

A licensee hires the people needed to fulfill the functions of the station. The size of the staff will vary according to the size of the station. For example, the fifteen network O&O stations employ an average of 323 full-time people, the other VHF stations an average of 69, and the UHF stations an average of 36. Regardless of size, the functions to be performed are comparatively constant and the employees will be organized into the following departments: (1) management, (2) engineering (3) programming, (4) news, and (5) sales. (See Fig. 8.1.)

Management

In the early days of radio the licensee was frequently the general manager. (This same individual might also have been directly in charge of programming, the chief salesperson, and the one who swept out the station the first thing in the morning.) Today most television stations are owned by companies, and the first step of a licensee is to hire a management team.

The key individual is the station manager who reports to a vice-president of the parent company. The manager hires a staff to fulfill the administrative functions required in any kind of business—personnel, budgeting, accounting, legal, custodial.

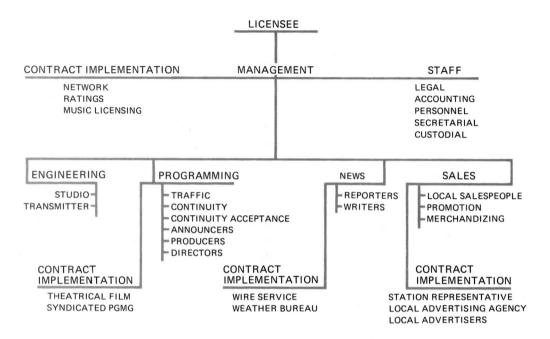

Fig. 8.1

Station Organization and Contract-Implementation Function. (There will be some
variations in organization and contract implementation among stations.)

Since television stations are owned primarily as an investment on which
to make profits, managers tend to be those who have been successful in
sales and who know how to work with budgets. In fewer instances a general
manager will have come up through the ranks of programming, and even
more rarely will he or she have been an engineer. Each year there seem
to be more and more station managers who have not had broadcasting
experience but who have been trained in management directly and had
successful experience managing in other kinds of business.

One management function unique to broadcasting is the "ascertainment" process that is vital in the renewal of the license every three years.
It implies getting to know all segments of a community and understanding
their needs and interests that must be considered by a station operating
in the public interest. Ascertainment primarily involves discussions with
community leaders by the manager and by some of the station's personnel.

Engineering

In fifty years of broadcasting there has been less change in the organization and function of the engineering department than in any other division of the station. This is true in spite of great changes in equipment as the emphasis moved from radio to television.

A station's technical staff is headed by a chief engineer who knows how to install, repair, and operate equipment and, most important, knows how to work with people. The chief engineer works out of an office and personally accepts no operations shifts, but can fill in anywhere if needed. Among the functions of the chief engineer are to (1) keep an inventory on equipment and know when to reorder, (2) take responsibility for tracking down anything that goes wrong on the technical side of the station, (3) know the capabilities of individual engineers and assign them to specific duties on specific shifts, (4) get along with unionized personnel who are protective of the rights they have won through collective bargaining. It would probably be difficult to say exactly what a chief engineer does, but he or she always seems to be busy.

The chief engineer's staff has two branches—studio and transmitter. The division is required because the studios and transmitter are usually separated geographically and because the qualifications for working in the two locations are different. While some engineers will be able to work in either area, many will be trained and qualified for only one or the other.

Studio technicians maintain all the equipment used in producing television programs—in studios, remote units, and control rooms. In many unionized stations technicians also operate the production as well as the control-room equipment.

There is a geographical separation because studios are normally near the center of a community where they are easily accessible to staff, talent, and advertisers. A transmitter will normally be top of a mountain or high building. Across the northern parts of the country, transmitter buildings are equipped with sleeping and living facilities so the engineers can stay several days in case of bad snowstorms. The transmitter of a station licensed to operate in Poland Springs, Maine (with studios in Portland), is located on the top of Mt. Washington, New Hampshire, which in much of winter is completely isolated. Engineers may stay there for several weeks before replacement staff arrives.

A transmitter operator is required to hold a license from the commission and to keep the station's signal compliant with commission requirements. No one else in the station except the owner is required to have a license from the FCC.

Programming

The average television station is a network affiliate that operates for approximately 133 hours a week (19 hours a day from 6:00 A.M. to 1:00 A.M.). A program director heads a small staff responsible for scheduling and local production. Among the functions to be fulfilled at all stations are those of the traffic manager who makes up the daily log, or traffic sheet, showing everything that will go out over the transmitter in the coming day down to each ten-second identification; the continuity director who writes some of the local commercials as well as other copy to be read by the announcing staff; the continuity-acceptance person responsible for making sure that all film and other material received from outside meets the station's standards of good taste; and the announcing staff.

The primary responsibility of the program director is to fill the daily schedule from five sources of material: (1) the network feed, (2) local news, (3) theatrical film, (4) syndicated programming, and (5) local (nonnews) programs produced by the program department itself.

The Network Feed

The average affiliate carries about seventy-six network hours per week, or somewhat less than 60 percent of its total schedule. The station manager will make the basic decisions about the affiliation contract and how much network programming will be in the schedule. The master control engineers will press the proper buttons at the proper times to feed network programs to the transmitter. The details of the network-affiliate relationship are described in Chapter 9.

Local News

The program director depends on the news department to fill from one to two hours a day in the schedule. There may be short newscasts at sign-on in the morning, at sign-off the next morning, and at noon. The primary news effort will be the half-hour adjacent to the network news feed in the early evening and another half-hour at the end of the network entertainment feed later at night. In the largest markets some stations are scheduling one or two hours of local news early in the evening.

Theatrical Film

The program director will schedule film that was made for showing in theaters but becomes available to television stations after there is little chance for more profits at the box office or in sale to the networks. Theatrical film is appropriate for filling fairly long periods of the schedule—from ninety minutes to two hours or more. It can be scheduled around the network programs in the morning, at noon or late afternoon, in the early evening or late at night.

Syndicated Programming

Because theatrical film normally comes in fairly long units of time and the supply is comparatively limited, a vital source of material is the syndicated television program. Syndicated programs may have once appeared on the networks or they may have been prepared for sale directly to stations without prior exposure in the community.* They normally come in lengths of thirty minutes or an hour (minus time for commercials) and are important to affiliates and indispensable to the independent stations. (Syndication in its various forms is discussed in Chapter 10.)

Local (Nonnews) Programs

Finally, there is the programming and other material produced by the program department itself. In the average station local origination falls into the following categories:

1. Children's programs.
2. Women's service programs.
3. Public affairs programs.
4. Religious programs.
5. Public service announcements (PSAs).
6. Local commercial announcements.

It must be remembered this discussion concerns the "average" station. The smallest ones may locally produce only a discussion or two in a week while the largest may do their own "specials" involving substantial investments.

Children's programs produced locally are less prevalent than they were in the early days of television when viewers were less discriminating and there was less outside programming available. It was not unusual then for a station to hire a woman experienced in working with children to do a program of activities that could be carried on at home. Many stations relied on syndicated formats like "Romper Room" in which the station would receive help in finding the talent and the talent would receive ideas and materials from the company that had originated the program concept. With the growing pressure for ratings it is far more likely that the average station will buy some cartoons that have been successful over the years and will look to its network for more creative offerings.

Women's programs have been traditional in television, as they were in radio. There seems to be a trend away from the typical interview and feature programs in mid-morning to a more widely based women's service show around the noon hour. Development of the VTR has been a great boon

---

* Some movie companies that make theatrical film also package programs specifically for television.

in permitting a hostess to tape at convenient times for the interviewees and then combine the interviews with other materials at airing time.

Public affairs programs are usually in the form of discussions of topics of current interest. A member of the program or news department or an outsider will serve as moderator to put together a panel each week to talk about a different subject. Because it is inexpensive programming, and since the FCC does insist on a minimal coverage of local opinion, every station will do some such programs.

Locally produced religious programs may consist of taking a remote unit to a church and broadcasting the service. More frequently, local clergy will be invited to the studio for a special short message. The bulk of religious programs are provided by national sects that purchase the time.

Public service announcements are provided ready to air by national organizations like the Red Cross, the Boy Scouts, and the Cancer Society. Although national PSAs are carried, stations feel a special responsibility to help local organizations. Considerable assistance in both writing and production will be given by the station in preparation of local PSAs.

Local commercial announcements are prepared by a station for local advertisers, especially those who do not work through advertising agencies. In some instances the station receives still pictures and writes copy to be read by an announcer. Some commercials will be prepared in the studio on videotape. All commercials for national advertisers and most large local advertisers will be delivered ready to run on film projector or videotape playback.

In summary, it should be noted that while the program department is responsible for organizing the schedule and filling all the time, it does comparatively little production itself—possibly as little as an hour a week.

The News Department

Although the program director looks to the news department to fill an hour or two a day, there is actually very little news gathered directly by the local news staff. There is a heavy reliance on the following three outside sources.

The Wire Services   Companies like the Associated Press (AP) and United Press International (UPI) operate a twenty-four-hour service that is available to stations at prices ranging from two or three hundred dollars up several thousand dollars a month, depending on the size of the market and the number of stations subscribing in one contract. In each station a news-teletype machine provides five-minute news summaries, business news, sports news, and features on a variety of subjects. The wire services also provide television stations with still photographs, national weather maps, and satellite weather photos. These visuals can be shown on the screen while a newscaster is giving the related story. There are also organizations providing daily news film footage to stations that do not get such service from their networks.

The U.S. Weather Bureau   Stations supplement nationwide weather reports from the wire services with specific local forecasts from the nearest office of the U.S. Weather Bureau.

The Network Feed   Affiliated stations may contract with their networks for permission to tape the regular evening newscasts as well as a special twenty-minute feed that comes through in the afternoon. Taped segments from the afternoon feed and the evening newscast can then be inserted into the "local news" program.

The typical half-hour of local news (twenty-eight and one-half minutes), may contain the following:

  6 minutes of commercials

  5 minutes of wire copy on major stories

  4 minutes of sports news from a wire service

  2 minutes of weather information from the U.S. Weather Bureau

  1 minute of business news from a wire service

  _5 minutes of footage from the network feed

23 minutes from outside sources

Five to six minutes are left for local coverage where a local reporter goes into the field with a crew to make a visual record for showing on the air. This emphasis on how little local news is gathered by the news department is not intended as a criticism of the average station. Indeed, there are viewers who want the weather reports, business news, sports, and other materials that are quite beyond the capacity of the local news staff. If one wishes a much heavier emphasis on local news, it is available in the local paper and on local radio stations. Even the largest stations in the country will not produce more than some twenty minutes of totally local coverage in an hour-long local news program.

In the early days of radio the news operation was usually part of the program department. As news became more important in the late 1930s, it seemed inappropriate to have newspeople responsible to the "show business" people in programming. Almost every station today will have its news department reporting directly to management. In spite of critics, the commitment of most broadcast news people (network and local) to accurate and complete reporting is very strong. The errors in fact and judgment that are inevitable are more apt to be due to human frailty than to conscious bias. Many station managers will admit they wouldn't dare try to tell the head of the news department how to handle a particular story.

Increased Importance of Local News

Station managers in the 1970s learned two things they had not suspected about their local news programs: first, they contributed greatly to the prestige of a station within the community and had a major influence on ratings in the time slots that followed. Secondly, as more emphasis was placed on local news programming, it became the most profitable part of a station's operations. It was reported that a single rating point for local news in the largest markets was worth a million dollars a year in revenues. As a consequence the ratings wars at 6:00 PM became as intense at the station level as they were during prime time among the networks.

Over thirty consultants or "news doctors" became successful advising stations on news formats, the hiring of anchorpersons and other factors related to the popularity of news programming. News departments have grown in size until they are among the largest in the stations. Up to a third of television stations have either purchased or leased helicopters and practically all are making investments in electronic news gathering (ENG) equipment that makes easier the covering of more material outside the studio. As ABC's rising ratings enabled it to replace some of its weaker affiliates by choosing stronger stations that had been affiliated with CBS or NBC in certain communities, one of the primary criteria used was the strength of the local news operation.

The Sales Department

Sale of time for advertising is a station's only significant source of revenue and for the average affiliate falls into three categories:

Network business = 9.5 percent.

National spot business = 51.4 percent.

Local business = 38.9 percent.

Network business is obtained by network salespeople dealing with advertising agencies in New York City and other major centers. National spot business is obtained by salespeople for the station representative dealing with the same agencies who make network purchases. The station sales manager is in constant touch with the station rep but the local salesperson does not participate in the effort. (National spot business is discussed in more detail in Chapter 10.) The local salespeople are responsible for securing local business.

8.6 LOCAL ADVERTISING

A station differentiates between local and national advertisers by matching their distribution areas with the circulation area of the station. If all of a client's business is conducted within the area where the station has a consistent audience, it is considered a local advertiser. If the product or service is distributed in other markets, the station considers it a national advertiser.

In the early days of radio there was a standard 30-percent discount offered by a station to the local advertisers. This was justified on the ground that the ad was probably reaching audiences at the outer edges of the circulation area who were not potential customers. Furthermore, local advertisers frequently could not afford to pay the higher national rate and the station would rather receive a smaller amount than have the time unsold. It is not possible to generalize that all television stations give a 30-percent discount to local advertisers, but most will differentiate and charge less than the national rate to local businesses.

Control of Rates

The FCC has no regulatory power over the rates a station charges and does not even have a record of what they are. The station is free to raise or lower its rate structure whenever it wishes. Nevertheless, there is among stations a high degree of uniformity in the cost of reaching a thousand homes because so much buying is done by national advertising agencies that deal with many stations and work from formulas relating charges to audience size. If a station raises its rates to the point where the agencies consider the time a poor buy compared with the competition in the same or in a similar market, the station will have so much unsold time it will lose money. The practice is to keep rates at the highest possible level while still selling most of the available spots.

The Rate Card

When a salesperson visits a client the primary reference document is the station's rate card or list of prices. It contains basic data about the station—how long it has been operating, its network status, the equipment it has for special programming, and other information the advertiser might seek. In addition, the rate card has a complete breakdown on the prices of different units of time in different periods and in different quantities.

The modern television rate card bears little resemblance to that of the traditional radio station in the mid-1940s. Yet, since the current practices grew out of the earlier methods of operation, the rate cards of today will have more meaning in view of the differences from the traditional and an understanding of how they came about.

The price an advertiser used to pay a radio station was a function of three factors:

The Class of Time   More people used to listen to radio in the evening than during the day, so the evening prices were higher. The hours from 6:00 P.M. to 11:00 P.M. were called "prime time" and on the rate card appeared as "Class A." The hours from 9:00 A.M. to 6:00 P.M. were called "Class B" and cost half as much as prime time. Before 9:00 A.M. and after 11:00 P.M. was usually labeled as "Class C" and cost half as much as "Class B," or 25 percent as much as prime time. The lack of logic in the price structure is clear. The audience did not suddenly double at 9:00 A.M. and again at 6:00 P.M. Neither was it reduced by half at precisely 11:00 P.M. Furthermore, the audience was not constant between 9:00 A.M. and 6:00 P.M. or between 6:00 P.M. and 11:00 P.M. Broadcasters were not then as committed as today to making sales on the basis of formulas relating prices to cost-per-thousand homes.

The Unit of Time   Until 1950 practically all purchases (in both radio and television) were for program-length units of time. What we now call "commercial minutes" (of sixty or thirty or ten seconds) were sold only at station breaks between programs or within the few "participating" programs produced by stations. An advertiser was always called a sponsor and would purchase an hour or a half-hour or a quarter-hour or five minutes of time. The ratio of prices between the units was uniform among stations:

$$60 \text{ minutes } = 100 \text{ percent}$$
$$30 \text{ minutes } = 60 \text{ percent}$$
$$15 \text{ minutes } = 40 \text{ percent}$$
$$5 \text{ minutes } = 25 \text{ percent}$$

Again, it should be kept in mind that these prices were for the time only, and the sponsor still had to pay for the program to be placed in the unit that had been purchased.

The Length of the Contract As with other things for sale, the price for a unit of radio time declined as more was purchased. The highest price was for buying just one unit. The most common lengths of contract were thirteen weeks, twenty-six weeks, and a year. As one bought more, the cost per unit was less.

Comparing Rate Cards

One major advantage of the old rate card structure was that it was an excellent method for comparing the prices charged by different stations. It was fairly easy to find for each station the charge for one hour Class A time purchased just once (1 Hr–ClA1) from *Broadcasting Yearbook*, or *Standard Rate and Data Service* (S DS) or from the rate cards themselves. If two stations charged the same amount for that highest-priced unit, their rates would be approximately equal for all other units of time.

Today's rate cards are nearly impossible to compare. Few will even list the 1 Hr–ClA1 rate because they never make that kind of sale. Even if that figure is given, one can make no generalizations from it when considering the cost of the thirty-second spot that is the most frequently used unit. There are a number of factors that make such an estimate impossible.

First, the quoted rate by any station is frequently only a beginning point for negotiations to determine how much an advertiser will actually be required to pay. If the station is coming out of a period in which its ratings slipped somewhat, and if it has a large number of available spots, it will rather accept a lower rate than leave the time unsold. If the ratings have been good and if most of the time has been sold, the quoted rate may be the one the advertiser will have to pay.

Second, one never knows what external factors go into determining the actual price. A good customer who buys consistently through the years can get a better break than someone who is purchasing for the first time.

Third, one never knows if an advertiser has a nonpre-emptible ("fixed") spot or not. If the purchase is being negotiated well in advance, a lower price may be offered with the understanding that if someone comes along who will pay the rate card price, the latter will get the time.

Finally, the time may have been purchased on a run-of-schedule (ROS) basis. This means that the advertiser purchased a large number of spots but does not control when they will be aired. When the traffic sheet for a day is prepared and there are unsold spots, the ROS commercials will be inserted. The advertiser likes a certain amount of ROS spots because the price is much lower. The station likes ROS because it provides flexibility in scheduling and unsold time can be filled at the last minute.

The Local Salespeople

Local sales people use their time in the same ways as people who sell medical supplies or industrial equipment. They work out of offices where they can make phone calls to customers and they travel throughout the city seeing people in their offices. Knowledge of sales technique and the ability to sell are far more important to a salesperson than understanding broadcasting. If a sales manager has to choose between two applicants who appear to be identical in all respects, except that one has had successful experience selling shoes while in college and the other has completed a college broadcast curriculum with a straight-A average, the former will usually get the job.

Salespeople have an up-to-the-minute listing of all the "availabilities" or unsold spots at a station. Salespeople also have the latest rating information indicating how many viewers an advertiser might hope to reach in each spot. And, of course, they always carry a rate card, along with contract forms.

The challenge of television salespeople today is identical to that of the radio salespeople in the earliest days of broadcasting. They have three objectives: first, to sell themselves and establish their credibility with the advertisers with whom they would like to do business; second, to sell the medium and persuade a potential customer that television is a good advertising buy (the salesperson who criticizes a competitor station is really saying the medium is not always a good buy and has partially lost the second mission of making television advertising look attractive); finally, to sell the salesperson's own station and persuade the advertiser to buy some of the availabilities.

The selling of the medium today is a little easier than it was in radio in the 1930s and 1940s when most retailers had been brought up in the tradition of advertising in print—newspapers and circulars. They liked the permanence of the printed page that could be put in a scrapbook or cut out and pasted in a store window. It was a tangible piece of evidence that the advertising dollar had been well spent.

Servicing the Account

After a local sale has been completed, a salesperson must be concerned with "servicing" the account. Most new advertisers come into broadcasting hoping they will get immediate results while fearing they are making a mistake. Someone has to "hold their hands" and keep reassuring them that television advertising is doing some good, that it is a long-term proposition, and that patience is in order. Servicing the account also means making sure the advertising copy is at the station on time, because if the commercial is not aired, the advertiser doesn't pay. There may be no problem for a few weeks because the sponsor enjoys the novelty of advertising on TV and gives high priority to providing material to the station's continuity writer who puts the script into final form. But then other things command attention and more of a salesperson's time may be spent making sure a contract will be carried through to its conclusion.

An effort of the sales department related to servicing the account is its merchandising that seeks to relate broadcast advertising to the point of sale. Stores are persuaded to feature a product on their shelves along with a poster for the program in which it is advertised. Since it is not possible to offer equal services for all products, merchandising is a service offered to those whose business the station especially wants.

The point to remember is that when a station sells directly to local advertisers, it encounters fairly heavy sales expenses and there may be substantial costs in servicing these accounts.

The Local Advertising Agency

The first "space brokers," forerunners of the modern advertising agency, appeared in the 1840s. These "space brokers" would buy large amounts of advertising space in newspapers at a discount and then sell the space to individual retailers. In the 1860s and 1870s advertising agencies as we know them evolved. In all but the smallest markets today there are agencies who work for clients in all media—print, broadcasting, direct mail. When advertisers buy time through an advertising agency, they pay exactly the same price they would pay if they bought directly from a station. But the station gets less because it gives an automatic 15-percent discount to an agency. To illustrate, if an advertiser buys $1,000 worth of time on a station through an agency, the agency will be paid the full $1,000. But the agency will pay the station only $850. In effect, the station is paying the agency for its services. But the agency's only responsibility is to serve the client. The obvious question is why the station encourages the practice, as indeed it does.

First, the agency is acting as a salesforce for the station. Because an agency makes money as a client does more advertising, it will encourage the increase in expenditures as long as they can be justified. (No intelligent station manager wants money spent on the station if it would really be wasted by the advertiser. When one expects to be in business a long time, one's best asset is a satisfied customer.) Because advertisers picked their agencies in the first place, they have confidence in these agencies' judgment. It would take much of the station salesperson's time to reach a comparable position of confidence. In short, for a 15-percent discount, a station is getting a salesforce that requires no out-of-pocket expense.

Second, the agency will then service the account. It will handle the psychological problems if an advertiser gets discouraged. It will also make sure the copy or the filmed commercials are prepared and delivered to the station before the deadlines. (The agency gets no commission if the ad does not run as scheduled.) Again, these are services the station would otherwise have to provide but now gets without having to pay for them.

Finally, there is an advantage many overlook. The station bills the agency and the agency is responsible for payment. If a new business gets started in a community and wants to buy time directly, the station would have to run a credit check on it and hope the business was successful enough so the station would get its money at the end of the month. If advertising is handled through an agency, the station does not bother with the client's credit—that is the agency's problem. The station is thus saved the cost of making a credit check.

What does an advertiser get from an agency in return for the 15-percent commission allowed by a station? The agency will advise a client generally on how to divide advertising dollars among the various media (e.g., newspapers, radio, television, direct mail, hand bills, posters). The agency will give further advice on types of commercials and perhaps even come up with "story boards" (line drawings of various stages in a television commercial), or rough layouts of print ads. The agency will then purchase time from the station.

Since this is valuable assistance that the advertiser gets for free, one would wonder why all sponsors do not work through agencies. Why bother with station salespeople at all? The answer is that a very small advertiser may spend so little that 15 percent of it is too little to be worth an agency's effort. An advertiser must have a business of a certain magnitude before it becomes attractive to an agency.

If a client wants an agency to go further and execute or produce commercials, billing is on a cost-plus basis. This means the agency will charge the client for all costs incurred in doing the commercial plus enough to constitute a reasonable profit.

There is one other category of local business that has been solicited by radio stations for years, although it is only recently that television stations have started to concentrate on it as a comparatively untapped resource. Some national advertisers have a standing offer to their retailers. If a store will buy time locally and use it to run a commercial for a national product with a "trailer" telling the name of the retailer, the national advertiser will pay half the cost. For example, a thirty-second commercial for a General Electric dishwasher ending with the announcement that it is available at the Blank Department Store is called a cooperative ad. It provides additional exposure for a product and gives a local merchant the chance to get the store's name on the air at a reasonable price.

From cooperative business has come an illegal practice that has plagued broadcasters for years—double billing. It is stimulated by the fact that a local advertiser is often entitled to a local discount of up to 30 percent. When a cooperative commercial has been run, the station makes out two bills. One is for the full national rate and the other is for the lesser local rate. Both of them are receipted. The merchant pays the smaller bill and then sends the larger one to the national company asking that half of it be reimbursed. Instead of receiving a check for half of the 70 percent actually paid, the local merchant gets a check for half of the full national rate. The practice is now punishable by fines and has resulted in nonrenewal of station licenses, but the problem still exists.

8.7 STATION CONTRACTS WITH OUTSIDE ORGANIZATIONS

The fourth element in a station consists of the contracts the licensee signs with outside groups to acquire various services. The following are some types of contracts that either have been mentioned or will be discussed later:

1. With a network for affiliation (Chapter 9).
2. With a station rep for sales service in the national spot market (Chapter 10).
3. With a ratings service for audience measurement (Chapter 11).
4. With a company selling rights to show theatrical film.
5. With a syndicator selling rights to show television programs (Chapter 10).
6. With an advertising agency for barter syndication (Chapter 10).
7. With a news agency for wire services.
8. With Broadcast Music Incorporated (BMI) and the American Society of Composers, Authors, and Publishers (ASCAP) for the rights to use copyrighted music.

The National Association of Broadcasters (NAB)

The networks and most major and many smaller stations belong to the NAB, which was formed in the early 1920s to represent broadcasters in their confrontation over payments for airing copyrighted music. Over the years the NAB has added many functions and is perhaps best known as broadcasters' lobby with Congress and the FCC. At the same time it provides a number of services valuable to the individual stations:

1. The NAB organizes national and regional conferences where the licensee and his or her management team can meet with their peers and discuss mutual problems.

2. The NAB circulates information about actions by the FCC and other governmental agencies pertaining to broadcasting. It also provides management and engineering advice on various problems.

3. The NAB sponsors codes of good practice for both radio and television. From the codes a licensee can obtain guidelines that will help in problem programming areas. The Television Code Authority also reviews programs and commercials about which questions of good taste might be raised.

4. The NAB has organized the Television Information Office (TIO) which tries to serve all stations as a public relations office disseminating favorable publicity to opinion makes. TIO material are also available to stations for local distribution.

5. The NAB has organized the Television Bureau of Advertising (TVB) and the Radio Advertising Bureau (RAB), which offer help to stations with sales problems.

8.8 UNIQUE CHARACTERISTICS OF RADIO STATIONS

With the advent of format radio and program-syndication services there are a number of ways in which today's average radio station differs from the television stations described above.

1. It is not possible to make an accurate preliminary radio station analysis based on a handful of criteria. There are so many stations that audience trends are unpredictable. The earlier advantages of power and frequency in AM stations have lessened as most people have tended to tune to local outlets. There never was an important difference in FM facilities. Affiliation with a network is no longer an important determinant of popularity.

2. The typical radio station staff is much smaller, especially if the format music is provided by a syndicated service.

3. In AM radio the engineering staff will not be as neatly split between studio and transmitter branches. As many stations have moved all operations under one roof, the control room engineer may also be responsible for the transmitter.

4. Many radio stations will have no local news operation but will depend entirely on the wire services or a radio network.

5. Since a radio station is far more dependent on local business than is a television station, the local sales staff needs to be larger and more aggressive in proportion to the size of the station.

SUMMARY

The central role of stations in our system of broadcasting and their heavy dependence on outside organizations for much of their programming and services emphasize the importance of understanding the relationships among the various units of the system in order to understand broadcasting.

GLOSSARY ITEMS

The following words and phrases used in Chapter 8 are defined in the Glossary:

Area of Dominant Influence (ADI)

Availability

Class of Time

Commercial Minute

Compensation

Continuity

Cooperative Advertising

Cross-Ownership

Designated Market Area (DMA)

Double Billing

Electronic News Gathering (ENG)

Fixed Rate Price

Fringe Time

Grandfather Clause

Group Owner

Independent Station

Licensee

Market

Merchandising

National Spot Business

Network Affiliate

Network Feed

Network-Owned-and-Operated (O&O)

Participating Advertiser

Pre-emptible Rate

Prime Time

Public Affairs Programming

Public Service Announcement (PSA)

Public Service Programming

Rate Card

Remote Unit

Run-of-Schedule

Servicing an Account

Station Representative (Rep)

Syndication

Theatrical Film

Traffic

Ultra High Frequencies (UHF)

Very High Frequencies (VHF)

Wire Services

PREVIEW

Networks were formed in the 1920s because they were advantageous to advertisers, group owners, and affiliated stations. By 1945 traditional radio networks reached their peak. In the late 1940s networks moved to gain control of their entertainment schedules. In the first half of the 1950s TV networks largely displaced radio networking. NBC was number one under the leadership of Sylvester L. "Pat" Weaver. In the second half of the decade CBS became equal to NBC, ABC started moving up, and DuMont went out of business. More and more programs were produced by outside packagers who sold part ownership of series to the networks in return for developmental money. Through the 1960s the networks owned most of their prime-time programming. In the 1970s the FCC sought to limit the power of the networks but the TV network today is surprisingly similar to the radio network of 1945.

CHAPTER 9

THE NETWORKS

In television the primacy of the networks is unquestioned. Network programs fill somewhat less than 60 percent of the time in an affiliated station's schedule. To that amount of network exposure must be added the repeat programs that were first seen on the networks and subsequently carried by individual affiliated and independent stations. Of even greater significance is the almost total dominance of the networks during the hours when they are distributing programs. This sets the style for all programming.

From any point of view, network programming is where the action is. Understanding television programming requires understanding the television networks. Understanding the television networks is easier if one starts with the beginning of radio networks, traces their development to a peak in the 1940s, watches the transplanting of their form without change to television, and then sees the adaptations that have been made to meet changing conditions.

9.1 THE THEORY

For some four decades after their beginnings in the late 1920s networks did not expect to make significant amounts of money from their network operations. The profits they realized came from the O&O stations and other activities that are described in the following chapter. The yearly network operation was considered a success if it produced no deficit while servicing the affiliated stations and the advertisers. The motivation for forming networks in the first place came from two sources—advertisers and group owners seeking better programs for their stations.

The Advertiser and the Network

Assume that in 1925 a dairy processing plant distributes cheese in its own city and in two other communities that are perhaps a hundred miles apart. The dairy operator decides to use the new medium called radio to let more people know the company's name. By enlisting the gratitude of listeners for a presentation of enjoyable programming, the dairy operator hopes to sell more cheese.

DEFINING A "NETWORK"

The phrase may be used to describe different arrangements in broadcasting:

1. The technical definition of "network" is two or more stations carrying the same program simultaneously.

2. For practical purposes the word is applied to an organization with an ongoing arrangement whereby it supplies a substantial amount of programming on a regular basis to a lineup of interconnected stations known as affiliates—i.e., ABC, CBS, NBC, and PBS. There may be delays in showing programs in different parts of the country to comply with time-zone differences.

3. An "ad hoc network" is a special arrangement whereby a number of stations carry only a single program or event. Following the program feed, each station proceeds with its own programming and may or may not join the lineup of stations in the next presentation. "Operation Prime Time" and certain sports events come under the ad hoc rubric.

It should be noted that the airing of syndicated programs does not constitute networking even though many stations may carry the same program at the same time, as with "Wild Kingdom" or "The Lawrence Welk Show." Such stations are not interconnected.

The first step is to go to a station in each of the three cities and purchase time. Assume that our entrepreneur buys a half-hour in the early evening on each station. The next step is to arrange for programs to fill the time. This was normally done in 1925 by working with each station's programming department. The cheese maker would be aware of a generalization that had emerged—that one should plan to spend for one's programs an amount approximately equal to the expenditure for the time in which the programming would be heard. This was not the result of scientific study or any particular wisdom on the part of an expert. The medium was new and so was the idea of using it for advertising. One had a total budget to spend on two elements—the time and the program. Why not split the amount equally between them?

That the rule made good sense is indicated by the fact that even through the 1960s there was a close relationship between the two figures in television advertising. What a network was willing to pay for a program was approximately equal to the value of the time on all the stations that would carry it. Even today when networks charge all that the traffic will bear, it is frequently the case that the program budget is very close to half of what advertisers will be paying for all the commercial spots in a program.

The hypothetical cheese maker in 1925 purchased time on three stations and had a program budget on each that was roughly equal to the time charges.

CITY	TIME CHARGES	PROGRAM BUDGET	TOTAL
A	$1,000	$1,000	$2,000
B	300	300	600
C	500	500	1,000
Totals	$1,800	$1,800	$3,600

Even a novice at radio soon learns that the audience appeal of a program is apt to be closely related to the amount of money spent on it. In a given community a program that cost $800 would normally get more listeners than one that cost only $500; and if one were to spend $1,000, the audience would be even larger.

The cheese maker would also be informed that even with the limited technology of the time, it would be possible to originate a program in a studio in one city and relay it to other cities for simultaneous broadcast. Thus, instead of spreading the $1,800 among three programs in three cities, the cheese maker could spend it all on one program that would be broadcast in all three communities without a significant increase in cost to the advertiser. The people in City A would have a program costing nearly twice as much as they would normally expect, and the people in City B would have a program six times as expensive as its size justified. Without realizing it, the cheese maker would have participated in starting a small network.

The Group Owner and the Network

The theory is further illustrated by considering a hypothetical group owner with five stations in large markets throughout the country. In each market there is competition for the audience and the owner wants to present the best possible programming. By purchasing time on the five stations as a package, the advertiser would be justified in preparing a program at a cost equal to the value of the combined station charges. Since the group owner must rent distribution facilities (phone lines from AT&T) from coast to coast, the program will be passing by many stations that belong to others who are also seeking to improve the attractiveness of their schedules. If buying time on the five stations would justify the advertiser's paying $5,000 for the program, the addition of another fifteen stations along the line may justify increasing the program costs to $10,000. This would make the original group owner even more competitive in those cities where his or her stations were located. Why not go out and actively seek stations that would like to carry the program and continue to increase their number so the advertiser would continue to increase the program budget?

On the face of it, this move appeared to be perfect for everyone. The group-owned stations were getting better programs. The advertiser was getting wider exposure on better programming. The stations owned by others were particularly happy becuase they, too, were getting better programs and more audience without any effort beyond agreeing to have an engineer push the proper button at the proper time.

Fairly soon, however, group owners began to realize that there were problems and expenses. Other group owners were doing the same thing, and it required hiring an expensive sales staff to persuade sponsors to buy time on one network rather than another. The AT&T line charges for connecting stations became substantial. It took secretarial help and a lot of someone's time to keep in constant contact with the stations carrying the programs. As the programs got bigger, it was necessary to build new studios that could accommodate them.

Network-Station Relations

The solution was to formalize the network structure and to ask the stations carrying the programs to share in expenses. Various arrangements were tried until the structure evolved that existed in the late 1930s when the networks had stabilized.

Networks dealt with national advertising agencies, selling them time on a large number of stations (O&Os plus affiliates who had signed contracts agreeing to participate). The sale was for time only—an advertiser was wholly responsible for providing the program, so program dollars were not included in the computations. Networks billed the agencies for the combined value of the time on all the stations that had carried the program. Assume this figure was $20,000.

1. A sponsor paid an agency the full amount of $20,000.

2. The agency took advantage of the 15-percent discount and paid the network $17,000.

3. The network retained the money it needed to cover the costs of personnel, studios, line charges, and other items. The network kept a little over 50 percent of the original amount—in this case over $10,000.

4. Each station received a proportional share of the remaining $6,000 as its compensation for carrying the program. The station whose rate card called for $1,000 got $300; the station with a rate card for $400 received $120.

To recapitulate:

$20,000 was paid by a sponsor to an agency.

3,000 was retained by the agency.

17,000 was paid by the agency to the network.

10,000 or more was retained by the network.

6,000 was paid by the network as compensation to the participating stations.

Viewed from another perspective, and assuming the advertiser put another $20,000 into its program, the total advertiser cost would be $40,000 and the stations would share 15 percent of the larger amount.

Station Compensation It should be noted the networks did not disburse money to the stations on individual programs. Books were kept by the month, and the network did its accounting as follows: it required from each station about twenty-four free hours to cover line charges; it then figured compensation on a sliding scale. For example, it might pay the station 10 percent of its rate card for the first ten hours, 20 percent for the next ten hours, and so on until it reached a maximum of about 70 percent for the final hours carried in the month. (The sliding scale was abandoned by the television networks around 1960 when the Department of Justices ruled it constituted unfair pressure on affiliates to carry more programming.) When all the computations were completed at the end of the month, the station (either O&O or affiliate) compensation came to about 30 percent of its rate card.

We now see the simplest definition of a network—it is a time broker. Through contracts it collects time from O&Os and affiliates. The collected hours are combined into a package that is sold to a sponsor. Particularly in the days of traditional radio through the 1940s, everything else a network did was peripheral.

Financial Benefits to the Affiliate

Why were stations willing to carry network programming when they received in return such a small percentage of their rate cards? The answer involves several considerations.

First, a station never got full rate-card prices on anything it sold. If a local sale occurred without an advertising agency, the station got 70 percent. If a local sale occurred through an agency, the station got just under 60 percent. If national spot business was done through a station representative (see Chapter 10) the station received about 70 percent. The 30 percent from the network did not appear quite so small compared to revenues from other sources.

Secondly, a station received the 30 percent without corresponding expenses. It did not have to hire salespeople or use its studio or service the account. The income received was also for time that the station would not have been able to sell locally since retailers could not afford to buy the whole schedule.

Third, a station was selling to the network the audience for which the network was primarily responsible. If the station had no network programs, its audience might have been so small that it would not be able to justify a full rate card of more than one-third of what it was entitled to with the affiliation.

The value of network programming to a station is illustrated by comparing the prices quoted by the VHF network and independent television stations in New York City. About 1970, when stations were still giving one hour–Class A–once prices, the following rates were quoted:

STATION	CHANNEL	NETWORK STATUS	1 HR–CI A1
WABC-TV	7	O&O	$10,000
WCBS-TV	2	O&O	10,000
WNBC-TV	4	O&O	10,000
WNEW-TV	5	Independent	3,600
WOR-TV	9	Independent	3,000
WPIX-TV	11	Independent	2,500

WNEW-TV is one in a group of stations owned by Metromedia, Inc., and is probably being run as well as an independent station can be operated. If Channel 2, 4, or 7 were to have no network programming, the prices on its rate card would probably be about those of WNEW-TV's rate card, or only 35 percent of current prices.

Public Service Benefits to the Affiliate

There was a further advantage that was very important for a station concerned about the service it could render to its listeners. A network served a station as its news and public service departments at the national and international level. The network made it possible for the station to broadcast the news to a degree the station could never afford alone. The network maintained a news staff around the world and had the ability to bring listeners up to the minute on what was happening in other parts of the country and around the world. While many of the news programs were sponsored, advertising dollars did not fully cover all the expenses of the network news operation. Stations, by taking only a portion of rate card for all programs, were sudsidizing network news that rounded out the local news coverage they could offer to their listeners.

A network brought to stations programs in which national and international issues were discussed in an attempt to make people aware of various points of view and the arguments on different sides. Networks also presented religious programs representing the major faiths. There were cultural presentations by the world's great orchestras and opera companies, all beyond the reach of a station and all needed if the station were to give its audience a well-rounded service.

Having pointed out these advantages to the stations, this discussion must add that too frequently stations failed to clear the time in their schedules to carry programs that some of the listeners wanted very much but which the majority would reject in favor of more entertainment. It is customary to blame the networks because there is not more "good" programming in the areas of culture, discussion, and documentaries. The fact is the networks have always had a higher sense of responsibility than many of their affiliates and they have many times distributed excellent programming that was carried by so few stations that the programming just could not be continued.

9.2 CRITICISM OF THE NETWORKS

By the mid-1930s radio had grown big enough to attract the attention of critics who thought it was failing to make its potential contribution to our society. They felt there was too much emphasis on entertainment, that the advertisers were too dominant, and that there was too little local programming to meet local needs. As they looked at the medium closely, they saw that the networks exerted nearly total control. The FCC was shortly to document how dominant the networks had become. In 1938 there were 660 commercial stations of which 341 were affiliated with the four national networks. More important than the number of affiliates (and O&Os) was the fact that they were by far the most powerful. The network stations accounted for more than 97 percent of the night-time broadcasting power in the country. NBC was not only the licensee of ten stations and operator of five more under contract with their owners, but it also had two networks—NBC Red (the old AT&T) and NBC Blue (the old RCA).

There was ample evidence that the network system had circumvented the theory of the Communications Act as originally conceived by Congress. The heart of the commission's power was the choice of licensees who were expected to use their own judgment to operate their stations in the public interest. Yet, after getting authorization to broadcast, the licensee frequently signed away control over much of the schedule to the network. Since the networks were also licensees who had passed commission scrutiny, such transfer of control might have been to a degree acceptable. But the networks then sold time to advertising agencies who made all the programming decisions on behalf of their sponsor-clients. The agencies had no formal responsibility to anyone but the advertisers and had never been required to persuade the FCC that they should be fiduciaries of the public airwaves. The figures above indicate that during the evening hours of greatest listening, it was the agencies who determined what the vast majority of the American people would hear.

Networking practices were a natural outgrowth of unrestricted development within the free enterprise system. The tie between network and affiliate was by contract and differed little at that time from other contractual relationships. As with any other agreement, it was written to favor the more dominant of the two partners. While it was true that no network can function or even exist without affiliates, it was also true that no network needs a single affiliate as much as the affiliate needs the network. Each station negotiated individually with the network. When contracts were written, the network had far more leverage and used it. The affiliates were not unhappy with the arrangement. None complained to the commission about loss of freedom. But when there was criticism about lack of variety in the schedule and the failure of the station to do more local programming, the licensees would respond that they were doing the best they could under the limitations of network contract provisions.

The 1941 Chain Regulations

After studying the situation for two years, the commission wrote regulations that would not force different programming on the local stations, but which would remove their excuse of blaming the networks when there was justifiable criticism. There were eight "Chain Regulations" whose purpose was to free the stations from network dominance if they wished such freedom.

Recounting some of the regulations serves to indicate the extent to which radio in the 1930s had become primarily network programming.*

Exclusive Affiliation of Stations

The NBC and CBS contracts provided that an affiliate of either might not carry any programs from another network. The result of such a provision became evident in the fall of 1938 when the Mutual Broadcasting System obtained exclusive broadcasting rights to the World Series. Since there were great gaps in Mutual's nationwide coverage, the games were offered to affiliates of NBC and CBS. The people not ordinarily reached by Mutual wanted to hear the series. CBS and NBC stations in cities without Mutual affiliates wanted to carry the games. The network wanted to provide the signal to those stations and the advertisers wanted to pay for the additional coverage. Even though everyone directly involved wanted to have the series on some non-Mutual stations, the contracts those stations had with CBS and NBC made it impossible. Many people never did hear the World Series because of the exclusive-affiliation provision of the contracts.

Since the stations had clearly bargained away their rights to broadcast in the public interest in this and other situations, the FCC ruled that such arrangements were not acceptable. It is important to note that traditionally, the FCC had no power over networks. It is only the stations that are subject to commission regulation. Therefore, it was necessary to write this and the other regulations as though the stations were being restricted even though the purpose was to free them from network domination. The first Chain Regulation was worded as follows:

> *No license shall be granted to a station having any contract, arrangement, or understanding, express or implied, with a network organization under which the station is prevented or hindered from, or penalized for, broadcasting the programs of any other network organization.*

The networks were thus put on notice that if they kept the exclusive-affiliation provision in the contract, no stations could sign and there would be no networks.

This rule acquired great significance in the 1950s when there were many major communities with only two television stations that were affiliated with CBS and NBC. As ABC was trying to become competitive, it was vital that at least some of its programs be aired in the cities where it had no affiliates of its own. Under this first Chain Regulation, the CBS and NBC affiliates were free to carry ABC programming if they wished.

---

* For a description of all eight Chain Regulations and their rationale, see *National Broadcasting Co., Inc., et al. v. United States et al.*, 319 U.S. 190, May 10, 1943.

When ABC started its "Disney" series in 1954, it was able to get coverage throughout the country although it had not nearly enough primary affiliates for such extensive reach. Without the prohibition against exclusive affiliations, it is quite likely that ABC would have needed another ten years to achieve parity with the other television networks, and it might never have been able to make it.

Right to Reject Programs

Existing contracts gave stations the right to reject individual programs from the networks but put on the licensee the burden of proving that the rejected program was not in the public interest or that another program being substituted was more beneficial to the audience. The commission felt this, too, was an abdication of responsibility and ruled that stations must have the right to reject programs without having to demonstrate to the network anything beyond their desire to carry something else. Although the impact of this provision was not obvious, it did take away from the stations a convenient excuse for questionable programming practices. For example, if there are only two television stations in a community and both were carrying professional football on a Sunday afternoon, there would be justifiable criticism that the people of the area were entitled to more choice than picking one of two games. The stations could not respond by saying they were required by contract to carry the games and the blame should be placed on the networks. This regulation very clearly places responsibility for the schedule on the local licensee. If questioned, he or she must be willing to state on the record that the public interest is best served by scheduling professional football when the one competitor is doing the same thing.

Dual Network Operation

Feeling that it was unhealthy for one organization to operate two of the four national networks, the FCC ruled that no license would be granted to a station if it signed a contract with a company that operated more than one network. This effectively told NBC to relinquish either the Red or the Blue network. Since the Red was much stronger than the Blue, NBC sold the Blue network to Ed Noble who had made a fortune producing Lifesavers candy. The Blue network was renamed the American Broadcasting Company (ABC).

Network Fear of the Chain Regulations

The Chain Regulations were promulgated in 1941 and were immediately appealed by the networks to the courts. There were statements by leaders of NBC and CBS that they constituted a "death penalty" and that there could be no continuation of the networks if the regulations were permitted to stand. In 1943 the Supreme Court rejected the networks' objections and affirmed the commission's power to impose the Chain Regulations.* That they have not been a death sentence is an indication that even the networks failed to realize the strength of the structure that had evolved in the first ten years and how beneficial it was to the affiliates as well as to themselves. Network leaders truly believed they would be unable to continue if current restrictions in the contracts were removed. Yet, when the Chain Regulations were affirmed and enforced, the affiliates continued much as they had in the past. To this day, network practices carried over to television have changed little in spite of different conditions and frequent regulatory changes. It can be concluded the relationship is good for both parties and will continue for the foreseeable future.

9.3 THE TRADITIONAL RADIO NETWORKS

Traditional network radio reached its peak in 1945. The schedules were largely sold out. The networks' ability to bring war news to the people rapidly and dramatically made the radio receiver an important center in the home. Networks accounted for well over 90 percent of radio listening through much of the day. There were two primary sources of the programs that emanated from the networks—advertising agencies and the networks themselves.

Programming by Advertising Agencies

Virtually all network entertainment programming was conceived, written, produced, and directed by the agencies who purchased time for their clients. Advertising was characterized by "sponsorship" in which a company paid for a unit of fifteen, thirty, or sixty minutes and occupied all the commercial time in the unit for its own products. It was the sponsor who, through the agency, made all the program decisions and, on most occasions, actually owned the program.

Indicative of the degree of sponsor control was a story in *Broadcasting* June 12, 1944, in which General Foods announced "a series of network program time changes precipitating a major revamping of CBS and NBC summer and fall schedules." The press release came from the sponsor through its advertising agency and there was no indication the networks themselves had been involved in the decision or even knew about the changes until the story was published.

---

* *Loc. cit.*

The only control networks exerted over sponsored entertainment programs was the requirement that scripts be submitted in advance to a "standards" office. It was the duty of the office to see that entertainment programs included nothing in poor taste. Such censorship was not contested since advertisers did not want to shock or injure listeners' sensibilities. During hearings in Washington, the advertising manager for one of the largest sponsors when asked to give his philosophy of radio programming responded, "Never offend anyone."

Once a script had been cleared by the standards office, the responsibility for representing the network at the airing of the program was in the hands of a network director who would be physically present in the control room. Although the agency director ran the program, the network director had the authority to take over and make sure that network policy was not being violated.

Programming by the Networks

Programming that was completely controlled and produced by the networks was limited to two areas—news and public service.

News Programming

By 1945 the networks had full news organizations with reporters in key centers throughout the country and around the world. There was an increase in the coverage of special events, such as the political conventions and campaigns, inaugural addresses, and presidential appearances before Congress.

This was one area of programming where sponsor control was nearly nonexistent. The first network news reporters tended to be ex-newspaper reporters who were committed to telling their stories without pressures from print advertisers. They would have been unreceptive to the suggestion that sponsors tell them how to cover the news. Even more significant was the fact that the cost of the news operation was greater than the amount received from sponsors. No single advertiser paid wholly for the services received when sponsoring a news program.

Public Service Programming

The network public affairs departments concentrated on discussion programs, religion, and pickups of major opera and orchestra performances. Since it was the philosophy of the day that this type of program should be sustaining (broadcast without a sponsor), and since sponsors could not be persuaded to buy them anyway, they were concentrated in the hours of the week that had the least economic value. Many of the public affairs programs were placed (and neglected) on the Sunday afternoon schedules now occupied by professional sports events.

9.4 NETWORK CONTROL OF PROGRAMMING IN 1948

An important trend in both radio and television starting in 1948 was the assertion by the networks of control over their entertainment schedules. Through the war years the practice of selling time to sponsors who made all program decisions had continued. But in the immediate postwar years the radio networks failed to grow with the economy and with the rest of radio. The situation is illustrated by the experience of the ABC radio network. As the season opened in the fall of 1947, the network was unable to find a sponsor who would purchase the hour from 8:00 to 9:00 on Sunday nights and provide a program to fill it. Sunday night had then (as it has today in television) the biggest audience of the week. ABC presented the Detroit Symphony Orchestra on a sustaining basis.

After several months, when it became obvious no sponsor was going to buy the time, ABC took the initiative. Working with a packager, it developed a program concept that it tried out in small markets and brought to the network schedule in the spring. In April 1948 ABC distributed "Stop the Music," which almost literally stopped America. It was a quiz program for the listening audience. An orchestra played a popular tune until a phone rang and emcee Bert Parks called out "Stop the Music." If a listener could identify the popular tune, he or she received a small prize of perhaps a hundred dollars and the opportunity to guess at the Mystery Tune that was worth up to twenty thousand dollars. The amount increased each week that nobody correctly identified the Mystery Tune.

People became involved. Attendance at movies dropped off on Sunday evenings. People did not go to visit friends as they once had. Anyone who received a call between 8:00 and 9:00 Sunday evening might abruptly say, "Call me back at nine. I want my line clear if Bert Parks calls." "Stop the Music" was first aired in April, opposite Fred Allen's show, which dominated the period with a Hooperating of 16.3, ninth among all network programs. When Allen went off the air for the summer he was in thirty-eighth place and had a lower rating than some of the daytime serials.

Within a couple of months the program had been fully purchased by four advertisers, each of whom took a quarter-hour. They were listed as sponsors, but there was an important distinction—they had no control over the program. The program belonged to ABC and it was to be presented in its time slot whether an individual advertiser agreed or not. Any advertiser who became unhappy could drop out and another would purchase the spot. The significance of this new practice was that ABC had made a virtue of adversity and introduced an entertainment program over which it had complete control. Although it was not then apparent, an important step had been taken toward eventual network control of all programming.

**Agencies and the
Programming Role**

"Stop the Music" aired at a time when the advertising agencies themselves were raising questions about their key role in programming. Their primary concern was the preparation and placement of commercials. When they also did the programming, they were assuming a responsibility that should have been peripheral but for which they might be dismissed if they were not successful. There were profits to be made in packaging programs. But there were also profits in being the broker who purchased from program specialists. Then if a program failed, the onus would to a degree be elsewhere and the agency could recommend dealing with another packager.

Since 1946 there had been an upsurge in the number of program packagers who were making "audition platters" (sixteen-inch half-hour electrical transcription discs) and trying to sell them to agencies for their clients. They did not approach the networks at first because they were distributing only what the agencies brought to them.

**Networks and the
Programming Role**

The networks had become increasingly unhappy with agencies and sponsors controlling entertainment scheduling. Not only were the networks unable to change the schedules when it seemed advisable, they were also at the mercy of the sponsors with the most successful shows and had to give concessions to them. For example, it was very important to NBC that the Jack Benny program should start the Sunday evening block of programs. It was well known that CBS would welcome Benny and his sponsors, so when General Foods made requests of NBC, there was always the implication that failure of the network to be "reasonable" might result in moving the Benny program. CBS had been working since 1940 to break the hold of the sponsors by packaging its own programs. Nevertheless, it still produced only for sale to sponsors and did not put its own entertainment programs into the schedule until they had been purchased.

In the fall of 1948 CBS took another significant step toward controlling its own schedule. Williamm Paley was ready to make a major effort to catch up with NBC in radio and to lay the groundwork for television. He wanted the best programs on the air, but he wanted them on his own terms so there would be no reliance on sponsors in scheduling. He wanted to be able to put each program where it would do the most good for the entire schedule and to be able to move programs as needed.

Paley's strategy was to introduce to radio talent the concept of "capital gains." For example, he wanted Jack Benny but knew it would do no good to offer more money than Benny was getting from his sponsor—the tax structure was such that most of the increase in salary would have been taken by the government. So he suggested that Benny incorporate himself and sell the stock to CBS. The profit from the sale would be taxed at the 25-percent capital-gains tax rate instead of the 80–90 percent he would have had to pay if the money were considered personal income. The biggest radio news in the fall of 1948 was that CBS had purchased Jack Benny for $2.5 million. The "Amos 'n Andy" show was bought for $2 million and there were several other capital-gains deals. NBC resisted the temptation to raid CBS, although there were rumors that Arthur Godfrey would have been available.

Ready for New Challenges

The traditional radio networks had grown vigorously during the two decades since their establishment in the mid-1920s. In two or three years after the war they diminished to the point where their eventual irrelevance was fairly obvious. They had become caught up in negative currents as inexorable as the positive climate that had made their dominance inevitable. With hardly a pause, the network organizations transferred their attention and their energies to television and entered a new era.

9.5 1949–1955 EMERGENCE OF THE TELEVISION NETWORKS

It is logical for two reasons to start the story of television networks in 1949. First, 1949 was a year of solid growth for television from almost nothing to the point where it was approaching significance.

1. The number of stations on the air grew from forty-one to ninety-eight.
2. The number of markets with television grew from twenty-three to fifty-seven.
3. The number of television receivers in American homes tripled from under one million to more than three million (compared with forty-one million radio homes).
4. Total television revenue tripled from an estimated $8 million to $24 million (compared with $425 million radio revenues).
5. Network revenues increased from less than $1 million to more than $10 million (compared with $129 million radio network revenues).
6. AT&T expanded its facilities so a television signal might be sent from the Northeast to Chicago, Milwaukee, St. Louis, and other cities in between. Establishment of network connections encouraged stations to go on the air as soon as possible.

Secondly, Sylvester L. ("Pat") Weaver, generally considered the most imaginative and innovative television programmer of all time, was named in that year to the vice-presidency of NBC in charge of the television-network organization.

In spite of these favorable factors, the networks still faced a multitude of problems. Sponsors were very reluctant to make heavy investments in network television because there were so few homes that could view it. The three million television homes were miniscule compared with the forty-one million radio homes (90 percent of the total), yet television costs were already soaring beyond radio expenses. Advertisers preferred to wait until they could see more return on their expenditures.

Advertising agencies were reluctant to be as active in packaging television programs as they had been with radio. They were already starting to leave radio packaging to program specialists and had found it most difficult to prepare television programs. Because the medium was so new, it was impossible to maintain a budget through a series. Even if a program were as simply produced as covering a radio variety show with a TV camera, it seemed that each week brought a new complication for which no plans had been made. Labor-management relations were especially difficult because both sides realized that decisions made in these early days would become precedents that would bind them for years to come. Program packaging was a money-losing proposition during this time. When sponsor and agency reluctance were combined, it is easy to understand why network television was off to a slow start.

AT&T was still far short of its goal of providing coast-to-coast interconnecting facilities for all of the networks. It was to be another two years before programs could be sent from New York City to California. Even then, there was only enough capacity to relay one program at a time through much of the nation, so the networks had to share the cable.

The networks were still trying to determine what constituted a good television program. The stations had pioneered in televised wrestling but had showed it so much that it had lost its appeal. A television program had to be more than a simple simulcast of radio where cameras were merely placed in a radio studio to show the viewers what radio listeners were hearing. But how much more a television program needed to be was not clear.

Among the most popular programs of 1949 were simple productions like the Ed Sullivan "Toast of the Town" and the comedy-variety hour of comedian-host Milton Berle, "Texaco Star Theater." There was also the first experimentation with live drama that in two or three years would constitute the most exciting television of the early years. Domestic-situation programs such as "I Remember Mama" and "The Goldbergs" provided a foretaste of TV's most popular series ever, "I Love Lucy," which premiered two years later.

The Television Networks in 1949

Near the end of 1949 there were four networks struggling to get started—ABC, CBS, DuMont (DuM), and NBC—Mutual did not enter the field. They were competing in a nation where ninety-eight stations were operating in fifty-seven markets. If one compared only the number of affiliates each network claimed, the networks appeared to be on even grounds.

ABC—52

CBS—56

DuM—53

NBC—55

But when one looked at the estimated revenues for sale of time in 1949, the apparent equality of the networks quickly disappeared.

NETWORK	REVENUES IN 1949 $ MILLIONS
ABC	1.2
CBS	2.7
DuM	0.9
NBC	5.5

NBC was receiving more revenues for its time than the other three networks combined.

Comparing the Networks in 1949   ABC was the former NBC Blue radio network that had never been as powerful or profitable as the Red. In radio markets where two stations were carrying NBC programs, the Red affiliates had usually been the stronger. The Blue network had included some strong stations in markets where the Red affiliates provided only fringe coverage. But when the contracts of those stations with ABC had expired, they sought and received an NBC affiliation. E. J. Noble, in buying the Blue network, had purchased the weaker components of NBC and left the stronger ones with their original network.

The comparative strength of the radio affiliates was important to television networking because it was the most powerful and lucrative radio stations that moved first into television. If the licensee of an NBC radio affiliate built a television station, the licensee would normally affiliate it with the NBC television network. There were fewer ABC radio affiliates capable of entering television early.

The reasons for the CBS lag being NBC television were different. In radio it had been highly competitive in most markets and the CBS lineup of stations had as much capacity as the NBC affiliates for an early entry into television. But CBS gambled that its system of color would be substituted for monochrome at the end of World War II. If that had happened, all stations would have been starting anew in applying for licenses in the UHF. When the FCC rejected the CBS color proposal in 1947, the CBS stations had lost valuable time. In 1949 when NBC had its full complement of five television O&Os and ABC had four, CBS had only two plus a 45-percent interest in a third.

DuMont was never a competitive network. Allen D. DuMont was one of the early pioneers in television broadcast technology and had three stations—in New York City, Washington, D.C., and Pittsburgh, Pennsylvania—upon which he tried to build a network. In 1955 the DuMont network was doing so little business and had such poor prospects that it gave up its effort, leaving the other three networks (ABC, CBS, and NBC) that are still operating.

Most of NBC's early strength as a television network could be traced to the fact that it was owned by RCA, which had been heavily involved in the technical development of television from the beginning. It was RCA that held the first significant public demonstrations of television at the New York World's Fair in 1939. The system of television approved by the FCC in 1941 was largely pioneered by RCA. It was RCA that was making more television receivers than any other company and was willing to have NBC subsidize program service in order to increase sale of sets. NBC affiliates had been urged by their network to go into television just as soon as possible.

Closer examination of the data under the heading, **The Television Networks in 1949**, reveals the sources of NBC's lead over its rivals in 1949. Each of the networks had between fifty-two and fifty-six affiliates among the ninety-eight stations on the air. The usual practice for a station in a market with fewer than four outlets was for it to sign a "primary affiliation" with one network and a "secondary affiliation" with one or more of the others. If a station were a primary CBS affiliate, it was committed to carrying most of the CBS schedule. During some hours of the week, however, it might carry programs from NBC or ABC. The critical question concerned the primary affiliations of the licensees in the one-station markets.

An analysis of the stations and their markets in 1949 shows the following:

37 markets had one station each.

8 markets had two stations each.

12 markets had three or more stations each.

(New York City and Los Angeles each had seven stations.)

ABC, CBS, and NBC had twelve primary affiliations or O&Os each, since there were that many markets with three or more stations. Among the eight two-station markets, it is probable that NBC had five primary affiliations and that ABC and CBS shared the rest. The attraction the networks had to the one-station-market outlets is indicated by the following data submitted to the FCC when DuMont was pleading for more opportunity to have its programs distributed. DuMont analyzed the programming of stations that were alone in markets and reported the following percentage of programming from different sources.

	NBC %	CBS %	ABC %	DuM %	LOCAL %
Afternoon	31.9	17.0	7.3	6.9	36.9
Evening	47.8	20.2	8.9	4.3	18.8

The DuMont figures combined with other calculations indicate that a more accurate comparison of affiliations among the four networks would be the following:

	PRIMARY PLUS O&Os	SECONDARY
NBS	42	14
CBS	33	22
ABC	10	43
DuM	8	44

It was clear that NBC had a big lead, CBS was in second place, and ABC and DuMont brought up the rear. As long as advertisers followed the "rule of thumb" of allocating program dollars equivalent to their time charges, the best programs would wind up on NBC or CBS.

The Program Problem

The major problem facing the television networks in 1949 was how to break the vicious circle in which UHF stations found themselves some five years later. Until there were more highly attractive (expensive) programs, the number of stations and viewing homes would continue to grow slowly. Advertisers would be willing to pay for more attractive programs when the number of viewing homes was much larger. If television networks were to show significant growth in the immediate future, nonadvertising money would be needed to subsidize popular programs until the sponsors were willing to pay the bills.

NBC took the lead in breaking through the programming barrier when it hired "Pat" Weaver. Weaver realized that the traditional and slow way of building NBC television would be simply to keep ahead of the other three. This meant concentrating on the affiliate lineup, waiting for the end of the Freeze and the acquisition of more stations, and depending on a slow accretion in the number of television homes and the subsequent willingness of sponsors to finance better programs. However, he saw the future more clearly than some others and realized that waiting for sponsors meant a delay of several years. Since RCA had the speculative dollars and wanted to use them to boost the sale of receivers, he set out to break the impasse with bold new concepts.

In January 1950, shortly after joining NBC, Weaver made his first major program announcement. NBC had budgeted $50,000 per week for a Saturday night program to last two-and-a-half hours and to be called the "Saturday Night Review." The first hour was to come from Chicago (starring Jack Carter) and the last ninety minutes were to originate in New York City with Sid Caesar and Imogene Coca. The show was classified as comedy-variety. The program would be available for sponsorship in segments or in rotating commercial minutes, but it was an NBC show that would stay under NBC control. Weaver was jumping to the third step in progression of advertising patterns even before the second stage had become wholly established.

Advertiser Relationships to Programs

The first step was traditional sponsorship in which an advertiser buys a time segment, provides a program to fill it, and uses all the commercial time for its own products or services. A variation was the situation where the advertiser bought the time but put its commercials in a program produced by the network to its specifications. The important factor of traditional sponsorship is advertiser control of the program.

The second step, which was just getting started, was called "alternate sponsorship." In this phase, two advertisers joined forces in purchasing a time segment and then agreed on the program. During one week Sponsor A would have two of the three commercials (in a half-hour prime-time program), while Sponsor B would have the other. The situation would be reversed in alternate weeks, with Sponsor B having two commercials and Sponsor A having one.

This step came as the cost of television time and programs rose to the point where few advertisers were willing to risk the dollars for singly sponsoring a program. Even in 1949 with the few stations available, the cost of time plus program for a half-hour drama was approaching $50,000 per week. Over a year this could mean a commitment of over two million dollars. For a small network advertiser this might mean "putting all of one's eggs in one basket." Even the largest advertisers were reluctant to pay that much money when there was no guarantee of size of audience. All recalled that Fred Allen had been a highly desirable radio program for its advertiser until "Stop the Music" had come out of nowhere to steal the audience and make the investment in Allen an extremely poor one.

SYLVESTER L. ("PAT") WEAVER, JR. b. 1908

Courtesy: NBC

In the first half of the 1950s "Pat" Weaver, more than any other individual, molded network television into the medium that so dominated the attention of Americans for the next quarter-century.

Born in Los Angeles in 1908, he was a 1930 Phi Beta Kappa graduate of Dartmouth College in New Hampshire with a major in philosophy. For a year he leisurly toured Europe and the Mediterranean area. Returning to America he tried selling magazines door-to-door in the New York City area before going to California to embark on a writing career. After three years as a writer and program manager for the Don Lee regional radio network, he went to New York as a free-lance writer, producer, and director. In 1935 he went to the Young and Rubicam advertising agency to produce the Fred Allen network program, and two years later was named head of the radio department.

In 1938 he joined the American Tobacco Company to take charge of the advertising for Lucky Strike cigarettes. He was shortly made advertising manager for the whole company under its eccentric president, George Washington Hill. From 1941 to 1945 he was in the armed services with such disparate duties as commander of a patrol craft in the South Atlantic and program manager for the Armed Forces Radio Service. Following the war he returned briefly to the American Tobacco Company before going back to Young and Rubicam as vice president and director of radio and television. From that job he went to NBC in 1949 to build up the television network.

In a matter of weeks he had announced the "Saturday Night Review" that would change the concept of sponsorship to participation advertising in commercial minutes. In the next few years he introduced other programs that were not only innovative but far too expensive for individual or alternate sponsorship. These were the "Today" show, "Tonight," "Home," and "Wide Wide World." He also introduced the "Spectaculars," which became "Specials," and he was the first to evict programs that failed to provide sufficient lead-in audiences for the next time periods.

He resigned from NBC in 1956. For a brief time he explored the possibilities of setting up a new network that would concentrate on a program service primarily for independent stations in fifteen of the largest cities, but noth-

ing came of it. Until 1963 he spent several years as a marketing consultant to Kaiser Industries and in various capacities with the McCann-Erickson advertising agency. He then became head of STV, a pay television enterprise in California. The company was off to an auspicious start when a referendum item was placed on the state ballot in the fall of 1964 asking the voters whether they wanted "pay TV or free TV." The company was abandoned after a resounding defeat in the referendum. (The courts later ruled the referendum unconstitutional, but the harm had been done and STV was abandoned.)

Although it is more than twenty years since Weaver left network television programming, he is still remembered as the most imaginative and innovative man the field has ever known.

Participation Advertising

Weaver was entering the third stage, where the network would provide the program without prior consultation with advertisers, place it in the schedule, and then make it available on a "participating" basis where the advertiser could buy single commercial positions rather than the whole program or even segments of it. ("Stop the Music" had been sold in quarter-hour segments.) Some advertisers bought segments of the NBC "Saturday Night Review," but others bought only commercial minutes. This gave each the opportunity to buy as much or little as fit their advertising budget, yet each was paying a proportionate share of the total costs.

For example, *Broadcasting* estimated the total budget for time and program for the two-and-a-half hours at $90,000.* The program was at first carried on only twenty-one stations.) In the five half-hour segments there was room for fifteen one-minute commercials, and each was priced by the network at $6,202.

Participation advertising was also called the "magazine concept" because of its similarity to typical magazine advertising where an editor puts the editorial content together without knowing who the advertisers will be or where their messages will be placed. During the next few years Weaver added more programs of the same nature. There were the "Today" (early-morning) and "Tonight" (late-night) shows that have been highly successful. There was the "Home" program, somewhat similar to the traditional morn-

* Ibid., February 6, 1950, p. 122.

ing women's programs on radio with news, interviews, and features. There was also the most exciting program of all, "Wide Wide World," a ninety-minute trip across the continent to see what was going on in various places. The June 27, 1955 show included live segments from a bullfight in Mexico, a Shakespeare rehearsal in Ontario, Canada, urban sequences from New York, Chicago, and San Francisco, with an idyllic pastoral scene in Iowa. It closed with simultaneous pickups of the Golden Gate Bridge in San Francisco and the lights of New York City.

The Specials

The final program innovation by Weaver is still with us today in the "specials" presented by every network. Weaver started by calling them "spectaculars" but changed the title when it was obviously impossible to be spectacular at all times. The first one, in the fall of 1954, starred Betty Hutton in "Satins and Spurs." It had lavish publicity and dominated in ratings. Although the reviews were less than enthusiastic (most commented on the poor quality of the color) the program was still so far superior to the average series episode, it was obvious people would want more. Another early special that was much more successful was Mary Martin in "Peter Pan."

The special fills a number of needs. It gives a network a chance to put on programs that can be highly publicized and that will, it is hoped, help to pull up ratings for the time period.

The special is also very important for the advertiser with a seasonal product or with a product that needs extra advertising at certain times of the year. There are some who use television only at these particular times, such as the Hallmark Greeting Card Company. Cards are sold year-round, but there are peak selling periods for Christmas, St. Valentine's day, and June weddings. It is at such times the Hallmark "Hall of Fame" aired its excellent dramatic programs.

Other sponsors who advertise on the networks throughout the year have certain times when they need to advertise more heavily. Makers of cold remedies like to advertise heavily during late fall and winter as do the makers of snow tires and antifreeze. Automobile manufacturers usually buy time on specials in the early fall when they are introducing new models. For example, it was the Ford Motor Compnay that made history by paying the unprecedented price of $1 million to show the movie *Bridge on the River Kwai* in the fall of 1966.

There is another advantage of the special sometimes overlooked. Some regular series advertisers may want to sign a fifty-two-week contract to obtain the advantages of being annual customers, but the total cost for the year may be somewhat more than they can afford. It is possible for a network to sign a fifty-two-week contract with them and guarantee that they will be preempted four times in the year for specials. This cuts an annual network budget by one-thirteenth.

By introducing participation-advertising programs ("Saturday Night Review," "Tonight," "Today," "Home," "Wide, Wide World," and specials), Weaver was able to move NBC into a clearly dominant role in the early 1950s. Although DuMont was headed for extinction as a network, both ABC and CBS were laying the groundwork to provide strong competition to NBC.

ABC Merger with United Paramount Theaters

The first move came from ABC, which was in great need of cash to invest in programming. ABC had a comparatively short list of primary affiliates and was not able to place many programs on its secondaries because the schedule was not of NBC or CBS caliber. The station lineup for ABC would increase as programs improved, but advertisers would not pay for more expensive programming until the number of stations was assured.

LEONARD H. GOLDENSON b. 1905

Courtesy: ABC

Leonard Goldenson, chairman of the board and chief executive officer of ABC, came to broadcasting from a background in motion-picture theater management. He was educated at Harvard College and Harvard Law School and in 1933 joined Paramount Pictures, Inc. Five years later he was named vice president with full responsibility for 1,700 theaters. As a giant in both production and distribution, Paramount, after World War II, was forced to break up into separate companies. Goldenson became president of United Paramount Theaters which had received a hefty amount of cash in the split.

At the same time ABC was trying to improve itself so that it could compete with NBC and CBS in television. One of its greatest needs was money with which to provide programming more costly than advertisers were willing to finance. Goldenson had become interested in the field by observing an early television station operated by Paramount and saw the advantages for both Paramount and

ABC in a merger. Under his leadership the merger took place and he became chairman of the board and chief executive officer of the new company.

Over the next three decades he led the network from its rather dismal third place to a strong first in the late 1970s. Indicative of his leadership strength was the 1979 report by *Dun's Review* listing the American Broadcasting Company as one of the five best-managed companies in the country. *Dun's* attributed the network's success to astute leadership. "Starting from scratch in the 1950s,

Goldenson built up each part of ABC one by one, using profits generated by one victory to finance an assault on the next hurdle. At the same time he set up a system of decentralized entrepreneurial management that has been a key ingredient in ABC's success."

Among Goldenson's other accomplishments was breaking down the Hollywood resistance to production of programming for television, the reorganization of ABC radio into four networks for different segments of the station spectrum, and the separation of AM- and FM-radio operations.

Since ABC did not have a wealthy parent corporation (as did NBC in RCA) it sought to merge with a company with cash that might be used for programming and other improvements. In the late 1940s Paramount Pictures, responding to pressure from the government, agreed to separate its production and its theater ownership. The company owning the theaters was called United Paramount Theaters and, in February 1953, it merged with ABC to form AB-PT. (We will still refer to it as ABC, as do most people.) This merger gave ABC the cash with which to provide programs that would attract a bigger lineup of stations.

It took nearly three years to get the stockholders' and the FCC's approval for the merger (the new organization had to be approved as the licensee of the O&Os), to finish the paper work, and to make arrangements for the first program. In April 1954, ABC announced a multimillion-dollar contract with Walt Disney studios for twenty-six one-hour programs per year to be aired on Wednesday evenings. Disney had for several years refused to sign any television contracts until he saw where the medium was going. Once he had made up his mind to try television, an important consideration in signing a contract was his need for cash with which to build the Disneyland amusement center in southern California. ABC agreed to invest in it, but was not enthusiastic and sold off its interest at the earliest opportunity.

In the fall of 1954 the Disney programs came on the air. The series was so attractive that many of the ABC secondary affiliates carried it. For the first time ABC could present a full complement of stations from coast to coast.

For the next twenty years ABC engaged in a series of shrewd and imaginative moves that helped it become a competitive network. ABC continued to invest in a few highly attractive programs and used them as leverage to extend its lineups for less popular shows. For example, one fall ABC signed a contract with Frank Sinatra to do a weekly program. It attracted almost as much excitement as had the first Disney contract because Sinatra had not done any regular television. When both outlets in a two-station market wanted to carry Sinatra, ABC chose between them by seeing which was also willing to carry the "Mickey Mouse Club" (another Disney program) in the afternoons. When it was necessary to choose between two stations to carry NCAA football in the 1950s, the winner was the one that also agreed to carry the "Gillette Saturday Night Fights."

ABC was the first network to make a conscious drive to attract the younger (up to forty-nine years old) audience with its considerable purchasing power. ABC consistently emphasized sports over the years and appears now to have somewhat more than its share of popular games and meets. It was very successful in building a schedule to exploit the deficiencies of the competition in the race for ratings. For example, at one time the Sunday evening audience from 8:00 to 9:00 was split evenly between "Ed Sullivan" on CBS and "Steve Allen" on NBC. Both involved variety and comedy. Western programs were just starting to hit their peak in popularity, so ABC commissioned a new one, "Maverick," and scheduled it in the fall of 1958 from 7:30 to 8:30 on Sunday nights. It soon dominated the ratings.

CBS Gains Momentum

In 1955 CBS not only achieved parity with NBC but even took a slight lead in the ratings. This occurred three years after the Freeze ended when CBS had its own primary affiliates in most markets. CBS had continued to build on the appeal of stars that had motivated its talent raids on NBC back in 1948. By the fall of 1955 many of CBS's most popular programs were built around stars. Its schedule included:

Sunday Jack Benny, Ed Sullivan, "GE Theater," and "Alfred Hitchock Presents"

Monday "Burns and Allen," "Arthur Godfrey Talent Scouts," "I Love Lucy," and "Studio One"

Tuesday Red Skelton and "The $64,000 Question"

Wednesday "Arthur Godfrey and His Friends"

Thursday Bob Cummings, "Shower of Stars," "Four Star Playhouse," and Johnny Carson

Friday "Our Miss Brooks" and a number of other sitcoms, followed by Ed Murrow's "Person to Person"

Saturday Jackie Gleason and "Gunsmoke"

Program Evictions

In retrospect, 1954 was an especially significant year in the history of the television networks. We have noted the introduction of specials on NBC, the Disney program on ABC, and the CBS star-based schedule that in the following year would put it ahead of NBC for the first time. Even more important was a particularly dramatic move the networks took to establish control over their own schedules. Again, it was NBC that moved first.

Since 1928 the NBC radio network had carried "The Voice of Firestone," an orchestral program with semiclassical selections. Since 1948 the program had been simulcast on Monday evenings on NBC radio and television. The sponsor was happy with the television programs even though they got low ratings. The advertising was largely institutional, and its purpose was to stimulate good will.

"The Voice of Firestone" was prestigious, and NBC liked its presence in the schedule. The sponsor was paying the full rate for the time. But the sponsors of the programs following "The Voice of Firestone" were very unhappy because they had to start with a low "lead-in" audience. It was discouraging to start a program knowing that very few people were watching and having to hope the audience would reach the desired size by the time the first commercial was aired.

"The Voice of Firestone" on NBC Monday evenings from 8:30 to 9:00 was followed by Dennis Day (a tenor for Jack Benny) and then "Robert Montgomery Presents" (a dramatic anthology program). CBS had "Arthur Godfrey's Talent Scouts" from 8:30 to 9:00, followed by "I Love Lucy" and the Red Buttons comedy-variety program. For Dennis Day to build a respectable audience from scratch against "I Love Lucy" was impossible.

In April 1954 NBC regretfully informed Firestone that "Voice" could not stay in the schedule the following fall (regretfully, because no one likes to "discharge" an old friend who pays the bills promptly and adds luster to one's business). "Voice" got additional chances on CBS and ABC, but eventually all three networks refused it prime time because of its low ratings.

Later in the same spring, CBS also evicted some programs and refused to reconsider even when the sponsors threatened to take the matter to the courts. A year later, in the spring of 1955, as CBS was making its major bid to take the lead, it demonstrated its determination to take full control over its schedule. The issue involved the time from 7:30 to 8:00 P.M., Monday through Friday. The schedules on CBS and NBC were as follows:

TIME	CBS	NBC
7:30–7:45 P.M.	News	Music
7:45–8:00 P.M.	Music	News

The CBS reporter involved was Douglas Edwards and the NBC reporter was John Cameron Swayze. The CBS music quarter-hours involved Perry Como, Jo Stafford, and Jane Froman. The NBC programs were built around Tony Martin, Dinah Shore, and Eddie Fisher. The two networks had almost identical ratings and the sponsors were completely satisfied because they were buying what amounted to a guaranteed circulation. They saw little risk in buying during this time period.

In its move to the front of the ratings, CBS announced it was changing the pattern by scheduling a different half-hour program each night. The old sponsors were invited to bring in their own programs if they had something that met the network's specifications. If they had no programs of their own, they could have first chance to sponsor what the network chose to schedule. But there was no question about the network's intent to make the final decision itself.

In spite of strenuous objections from the sponsors, the evening 7:30–8:00 periods on CBS the next fall contained the following programs, some of which were provided by sponsors and some by the network:

Monday "Robin Hood"

Tuesday "Name That Tune"

Wednesday "Brave Eagle"

Thursday "Sgt. Preston of the Yukon"

Friday "The Adventures of Champion"

Not all were sponsored as the new season opened, but as they did well in the ratings participating advertisers eventually purchased all the commercial availabilities.

Network Studies by FCC and Congress

The overpowering foothold of NBC and CBS and the concomitant difficulty of UHF stations led to a two-and-a-half-year series of government inquiries into their practices. First, the Senate Interstate and Foreign Commerce Committee held hearings to determine whether the 1941 Chain Regulations had accomplished their goals and whether the networks were at least partially responsible for the problems of UHF. In February 1955 the committee released the Plotkin (majority) and Jones (minority) reports. Both generally criticized the networks for not giving more of their programs to UHF stations in mixed markets. The networks countered by pointing out that the choice of stations in a market was up to the advertiser.

In June 1957 the "Cellar Report" appeared, summarizing a study made by the House Antitrust Subcommittee. The following October the "Barrow Report" was issued by an FCC network study staff that had been working for two years. Both reports were sharply critical of network practices.

From the release of the Plotkin and Jones reports in early 1955 to a year after the Barrow Report in late 1957, the networks were subjected to a constant barrage of criticism. It was a troubled time for the networks since all the reports were by groups in positions of great power. Minor new regulations were imposed that had little effect on the networks in the long run. Again, their basic structure had been proven sound and no one could figure out a way to replace or even substantially change them.

9.6 1955–1960 GROWTH OF PROGRAM PACKAGERS

The most significant trend between 1955 and 1960 was the move of production responsibility away from both networks and advertising agencies. As "program plus time" became too expensive for one or even two advertisers, there was less opportunity for an agency to package a program itself even if it wanted to. Network attitudes paralleled those of the agencies which ten years earlier had decided program production was a peripheral activity that added unnecessary risks to an already risky business. Although the networks had been successful at doing some of their own production, they were still primarily in the business of being time brokers. For the networks to produce the whole schedule would have called for major organizational changes that did not seem justified.

The mid-1950s brought a plethora of would-be packagers who offered to bring in series of programs all produced and ready for airing. To some it seemed that everyone who had ever had a program idea was wandering up and down Madison Avenue in New York City with a 16-mm pilot (sample program) ready for display. People descended on the networks and agencies trying to sell series of thirty-or-so programs based on the pilots.

For a brief period the agencies and networks financed program series based only on their evaluation of the pilots. But they soon learned that while many people could produce an acceptable pilot and some might be able to produce eight or ten good programs based on the pilot, few indeed could maintain the quality for thirty programs.

By the end of the 1950s the networks were making all the program decisions and purchases. Some agencies remembered the "good old days" when life had been more exciting producing programs and they complained of the new trend, but the networks had gained firm control and would never again hand it back. The networks were now dealing only with those packagers who had been most successful in the past or who had contracts with the biggest stars, so they had reason to believe that a series would be as good as its pilot.

Problems of Producing and Selling Pilots

By 1957 and 1958 the networks were becoming more competitive, as CBS and NBC were approximately equal in the ratings and ABC was drawing closer to them. Each felt the need for more complete treatment in pilots to give more information about the potential of a series. At that time the average half-hour program was being budgeted at about $50,000, though it might cost five times that much to do a good pilot. The reason was that in doing a series many of the costs can be divided among all the programs, but in a pilot one must speculate large amounts of money that can be divided among programs only if the series is sold. For example, if a series is built around a railroad or a western town or a colonial home, one must build the set in order to make the pilot representative of the whole series. Making a pilot also requires an investment in costumes and other items that will be reused only when the series has been purchased.

More important is the fact that a producer must ensure that a star will be available later if the series featuring that performer is bought by the network. Assume, for example, that a packager has a series idea starring Henry Fonda. It may be in September that Fonda agrees to do the pilot. It may then take anywhere from six to nine months to get the script in satisfactory condition, to line up the location for shooting, build the set, and hire and prepare the talent. After shooting the pilot it may take another three months to edit it and get it ready for presentation to the networks. The networks used to make their final decisions on fall schedules in February or March. In this example, perhaps eighteen months will have elapsed between the time Fonda agrees to do the series and the time when the network makes its final decision. In the meantime, Fonda would be getting other offers for television programs or motion pictures or roles on Broadway. He must be paid for an option so that if a packager calls on him, he will be available.

Taking all these things into consideration, packagers found they were spending up to a quarter-million dollars producing a half-hour pilot.

After completing a pilot, the speculating packager headed for New York City to see three potential customers, probably already knowing which network might be most interested and which would be second choice if the sale to the first network didn't work out. The procedure would be to screen the pilot for the program personnel of the first network and then make the sale on the spot or perhaps receive enough encouragement to decide not to show it further. Or, the pilot might be turned down for no better reason than that a key member of the network staff may have had a "bad day" personally. (It may also be that the pilot wasn't very good or didn't fit in with the network's plans.)

On leaving the office of the first-choice network to visit the next one, a packager may or may not have understood that there are no secrets in broadcasting. There is a constant shifting of personnel among networks, agencies, and other companies. It is quite likely that before the elevator reaches the lobby, the people at the next network will already know that the pilot has been turned down. When the second network screens the pilot, those watching will be looking for the reasons the first network did not take it. If it becomes necessary to go to the third network, there will truly be two strikes against the pilot before it could even be shown.

The "Step" Process

The packagers failed to see the wisdom in speculating so much money under such high-risk circumstances and changed their approach. When the program idea was first conceived, a packager went to the network most likely to be interested and "talked it through," giving only verbal details on story line, settings, star, etc. If the network was enthusiastic about the presentation and asked for a written story treatment, the response was, "Fine, advance me $5,000 to get it done." At that point, if the idea seemed good enough, the packager received the $5,000. Two months later, when the packager returned with the rough treatment, if the network asked for a sample script or two, perhaps $20,000 more would have to be advanced. At each step when the network indicated it was interested and asked that more work be done, the packager asked for and received more money. Quite logically, this joint progressive development of program pilots was called the "step process." In the end, there might be a half-hour pilot on which $250,000 had been spent, some by the network and some by the packager— in different ratios depending on the circumstances.

Obviously no network (or other business organization) ever hands out money without getting something in return. In helping to finance pilots, the network was, with each payment, buying "a piece of the action" and becoming a joint owner with the packager. If profits were made on the series, they would be shared between network and packager according to the arrangement made during the step process.

Working this way has obvious advantages for the packager. When it is time to make a final decision on using a series, the network is considering an idea in whose development it has been involved for a year or more and through which it stands to make money if it is successful. Although the packager has had to share the ownership, the initial investment has been smaller and the chances the series will be used by the network have increased immeasurably.

A typical half-hour taped comedy program premiered on one of the television networks in September 1975 after progressing through the following steps.
August 1974—Producer and star of show get idea for half-hour situation-comedy series.
November 1974—Presentation made to network that approved idea and gave producer $20,000 to hire writer for pilot script.
January 1975—Script completed and presented to network.
February 1975—Network approved script and gave producer $250,000 to shoot the pilot.
March 1975—Pilot completed.
May 1975—Network commitment made to air series in fall.
July 1975—Production started.

The budget for each episode was about $95,000. The above-the-line budget to cover the creative aspects was $54,000. Among the larger items above the line were:

Cast	$19,000
Packaging fee to production company	5,000
Writing staff	10,000
Individual script	4,500
Royalties	2,000
Executive producer	4,500
Producer	3,000
Director	3,000
Associate director	900
Taxes and insurance	2,000

The below-the-line budget to make the program once the creative costs were paid came to $41,000. Among the major items were the following:

Stagehands	$5,500
Live studio rental	7,750
Assistant director/stage manager	2,000
Basic crew	4,500
Videotape, recording, and editing	5,080
Studio overhead	10,000

Miscellaneous below-the-line items included scenery, construction of sets, drapes, rental of stock scenery, scenic painting, costumes and wardrobe handlers, makeup, and rental of rehearsal space.

An important advantage for the network is its ability to exert a measure of control over the series if the ratings are not satisfactory. There have been instances where, when the network suggested changes, the packager refused to listen. If the network is part owner, the packager must be cooperative. Financially, the network could realize impressive profits from successful series when they went into later syndication (see Chapter 10).

In the early 1960s the networks owned (either wholly or in part) over 80 percent of their prime-time programming, and the amount rose to over 90 percent by the end of the decade. Each of the networks had a "house packager," a wholly-owned subsidiary that worked with the outside packager when both owned part of the program.

9.7 1960—1970 FCC ATTEMPTS TO DIVERSIFY NETWORK PROGRAM SOURCES

Network ownership of programming was a matter of concern to members of the FCC and in 1964 Chairman E. William Henry decried the situation. It was his thesis that the program chiefs of the networks exhibited bias when they were choosing among pilots, some of which they owned themselves. He proposed that aside from news and commentaries, no network be permitted to have any ownership in more than half of its prime-time programming. It was called the "fifty-fifty rule." All the rest of the programming would have to come completely from outside sources.

A year later the matter was put on the FCC agenda but was never brought to a resolution. By then network programming was so expensive that no one could imagine who would specifically underwrite the other 50 percent. No agency could recommend that its client spend the money to speculate on a program and then support it throughout the year. By the mid-1960s the cost for time and program for a half-hour came to about $150,000. This meant that a series of thirty programs alone would represent an investment of about $2,250,000 (at $75,000 each) and time for fifty-two weeks would cost an additional $3,900,000. Since the FCC could find no one except the networks prepared to make such an investment in programming, the idea was dropped.

The 1970 Chain Regulations

In 1970 the FCC finally moved to lessen the hold of the networks on program production. Three new Chain Regulations were passed:

The first forbade the network from acquiring any ownership in programming done by outside packagers. This failed to change the step process with outside packagers, however, since the networks were still the only organizations prepared to spend millions of dollars in program development. Instead of spending the money and getting part ownership, the dollars they advanced toward pilots were applied against the right or license to show the program on the network.

The second regulation barred the network from any syndication of programs to individual domestic stations whether the programs were owned by the networks or not. The importance of this regulation will become clearer in the next chapter.

The third regulation was known as the "Prime-Time Access Rule" (PTAR). It limited the access a network might have to time on its O&Os and affiliates.

> *No television station assigned to any of the top-fifty markets in which there are three or more operating commercial television stations, shall broadcast network programs offered by any television network or networks for a total of more than three hours per day between the hours of 7:00 P.M. and 11:00 P.M. local time. . . .*

Excluded from the regulation were news broadcasts or coverage of news events or political broadcasts by legally qualified candidates.

The normal scheduling pattern for all three networks had been to feed programs from 7:30 P.M. to 11:00 P.M. for a total of three-and-a-half hours. PTAR cut that total by a half-hour each night. After a period of indecision, the networks all decided to drop the half-hour from 7:30 to 8:00 P.M., Eastern and Pacific Time, and to continue feeding from 8:00 to 11:00 on weekday evenings.

The regulation has been highly controversial. NBC and CBS opposed it. ABC was neutral since the regulation came just as cigarette advertising was banned from the air by Congress and it meant seven fewer half-hours for which programs would have to be developed. Syndicators like it. Stations accepted it after they found it to be helpful in the profit-and-loss statements. The FCC twice modified PTAR without announcing a firm decision to keep it or drop it. Ten years later the rule was still in effect and popular with stations and syndicators for whom it is very profitable. It diversified program sources as the FCC hoped, but most now feel it has also decreased program quality and originality.

9.8 THE CURRENT TELEVISION NETWORKS

Network Pricing Practices

The most significant trend in the 1970s has been the sale of commercial minutes (and "thirties") in individual programs with the price determined only by the laws of supply and demand. No longer is there any uniformity of prices throughout a period like prime time from 8:00 P.M. to 11:00 P.M. Rather, each program is evaluated in advance in terms of expected ratings and the probable price agencies would recommend their clients pay. In a single evening on a given network, prices per commercial minute might range from $50,000 for the average program to $100,000 for one that is leading in the ratings. When NBC paid $10 million for the right to show *The Godfather*, it priced its commercial minutes at $225,000 each. (On computing the price-per-thousand viewing homes, it might turn out to be only slightly more expensive than any other prime-time programming.)

The networks do not offer circulation guarantees. The advertisers cannot get their money back if the rating of a program is less than expected. If ratings are seriously off, however, a network will frequently give additional commercial minutes without charge until the advertiser has reached approximately the number of homes expected when the contract was signed. This practice would be used only with the largest advertisers and is the sort of understanding that is never written into a contract.

Over a period of only two or three years in the early 1970s the most commonly sold unit changed from the commercial minute to the "commercial thirty," or half-minute. Advertisers have found the thirty-second spot to be almost as effective as the full minute and prices have tended to be only half the price for one minute.

Network-Affiliate Compensation

All three networks compensate their affiliates about the same amount, although they use different formulae to calculate the amounts. Since advertisers are no longer billed separately for time and program, it would be meaningless to try to compare the percentage of its rate card that a station receives as could be done with traditional radio networks in the 1940s. Rather, the best comparison is in terms of percentage of total advertiser network expenditures passed on to affiliates. In 1945 this was approximately 15 percent (half of the 30 percent time charges).

According to FCC figures the networks in 1972 paid to their affiliates 15 percent of their revenues (network revenues were equal to total advertiser expenditures). Since 1972 there has been a steady decrease in the percentage. In 1977 it was down to 10 percent and has declined further in subsequent years.

Barter Arrangements

However, reported compensation is only part of the story. Throughout the 1970s there was an increase in bartering that brought in added revenue for the stations as a result of their network affiliations. Since sporting events are regularly presented, it is worthwhile to consider the arrangements for carrying them. In the late 1950s ABC was faced with the problem of bidding for renewal of the rights to carry NCAA college football on Saturday afternoons. It knew the price of the rights would be much higher than in the current contract and could see no way of making money if stations were to continue receiving compensation for carrying them. (The top figure that ABC or any other network can bid is determined by the amount of money advertisers are willing to pay for all commercials combined.) ABC communicated with its affiliates its inability to bid for a continuation of college football if stations were compensated for carrying the games. The network then asked if the affiliates wanted the games badly enough to carry them without compensation.

FRED SILVERMAN b. 1937

Courtesy: NBC

In June 1978 Fred Silverman set a record that is unlikely to be challenged for many years. While others have worked for all three major networks, none has done so at his level of title and responsibility and at such young ages. Silverman was forty-one when he was named

president and chief executive officer of NBC. Prior to that he had been president of ABC Entertainment, the programming entity of the network. He had joined ABC after being vice president for programming of CBS-TV.

A key to his success may lie in his reputation for being "the best viewer working in television." He genuinely enjoys watching television and will view even when it is not necessary in his job. Silverman seems to have an uncanny ability to know the tastes and desires of that elusive person, the average viewer. In all of Silverman's positions he read all pilot scripts and paid meticulous attention to casting and other aspects of programs in their developmental stages.

Born in New York City, he was a radio-television major at Syracuse University. For his master's thesis at Ohio State University he did a study of ABC programming and prospects in the 1950s. His first job in broadcasting was at WGN-TV in Chicago, one of the nation's most prestigious independents and a current superstation for cable importation. He is best remembered there for his packaging of movies in the film library. For example, he combined the children's film titles in the collection into a "Family Classics" series that greatly increased the ratings. After a few weeks at WPIX-TV, an independent station in New York City, he joined CBS-TV where his thesis had been noted. He was director of daytime programming until he became vice president.

At that time CBS was number one in the ratings and ABC was getting ready to make its move to first place. Silverman was president of ABC Entertainment from 1975 to 1978

and it was during that period that ABC became the strongest of the three networks.

Although he initiated many series that were highly successful, he will be longest remembered for his contribution to the miniseries concept. It was his decision to schedule "Roots" during eight consecutive evenings. He was also responsible for "Shogun," another miniseries that in the fall of 1980 brought NBC out of its ratings doldrums.

The response was overwhelmingly affirmative since the stations liked the prestige and other advertising business the games attracted. Furthermore, ABC agreed to leave some open commercial spots in the coverage that the stations could sell at the high prices warranted by appearing during the broadcast of a popular sport. Actually, stations probably made more money by waiving compensation for the games and having spots to sell than they could have made going out to buy a program and then trying to sell spots against the competition of football on another network.

There are also "barter" agreements, as on the "Today" and "Tonight" programs. The network sells all the commercial minute spots and keeps all the revenues from some of the half-hours while leaving all the commercial spots and revenues in the other periods to the stations. No money changes hands between network and stations.

One network executive has speculated the time will come when networks will offer no dollar compensation to affiliates for carrying its programs. Rather, he predicts, there will be a percentage of commercial minutes left open for station sale to provide the source of station compensation for network affiliation.

How do television networks of the 1980s compare with the radio nets of 1945? It is amazing to see how many similarities there are. Stations are highly dependent on them for building the increased audiences that justify higher rates and profits. No station has voluntarily given up an affiliation to operate as an independent station. Network compensation appears to be decreasing but the increasing prevalence of bartering has at least partially offset this decline.

Ad Hoc Networks

There have for years been *ad hoc* or special networks for the coverage of certain sports events. Stations carried the events for which the networks were established and then had no further relationship with them until another event that might have the same or a different station lineup. In May 1977 the airing of David Frost's interviews of President Nixon was considered barter syndication (see Chapter 10) but was, in effect, an *ad hoc* network. The programs were fed by satellite to key stations around the country and then relayed to other cities by regular land lines and microwave relay. About half the commercial spots in the programs were sold nationally and the rest were sold locally with the stations keeping the revenues as their pay. In the same year several of the large independent stations got together to form "Operation Prime Time" (OPT) and commit major budgets for programs of high quality that would also be distributed by satellite with some commercials sold nationally and the rest locally. Subsequently, other *ad hoc* networks have been formed by program packagers and by advertisers with similar arrangements. It is important to note that these *ad hoc* networks are carried in many cities by stations affiliated with the regular networks but who are willing to pre-empt the usual programs because the stations can make so much more money on the barter arrangement.

The Outlook in the 1980s

What does the future hold for the conventional television networks? Their profitability increased steadily through the 1970s except for the recession year 1975. However, there are hints that the networks may be past their peak and that there may be increased erosion of their dominance. The network share of audience (the percentage of all viewers turned to one of the networks) declined some 5 percent in the late 1970s. This can be attributed to a number of factors:

1. Pay cable has grown as people have shown their willingness to pay for recent movies and other attractions without commercials. According to Nielsen estimates the growth in one year (February 1979–1980) has been phenomenal:

	FEBRUARY 1979	FEBRUARY 1980
Pay-Cable Homes	3,550,283	5,750,650
STV Homes	173,628	376,500
Total	3,723,911	6,127,150

Although the number of STV homes will probably never become very significant (unless there are spectacular developments in direct-broadcast-satellite transmission), the growth in pay cable will probably continue apace as more and more services are offered.

2. The "superstations" and origination by satellite (see Chapter 6) have been increasingly popular—especially since they provide a lot of sports programs.

3. More and more television-set time is being devoted to playing video games and viewing cassettes purchased for home video recorders and video discs.

4. The *ad hoc* networks have double impact; not only do they take away network audience in the markets where they are carried by independent stations but they also are carried in other markets by network affiliates and so the regular network program is not even in competition.

None of these factors is expected by itself to make a significant difference but each is nibbling away at the amount of network viewing, and momentum seems to be growing. While dramatic changes are not forecast in the near future, there is little doubt in the minds of most people that another ten years will see great changes in network prospects. In recognition of these probable changes, all three networks are planning to provide program services for cable.

GLOSSARY ITEMS

The following words and phrases used in Chapter 9 are defined in the Glossary:

Ad Hoc **Network**

Alternate Sponsor

Barter

Chain Broadcasting

Chain Regulations

Commercial Minute

Compensation

Mixed Markets

National Spot Business

Network Affiliate

Network Cooperative Programming

Network-Owned-and-Operated (O&O)

Network Primary Affiliate

Participating Advertiser

Pilot Program

Prime-Time Access Rule (PTAR)

Exclusive Affiliation

Fifty-Fifty Rule

Lead-in Audience

Line Charges

Magazine Concept

Program Packager

Public Affairs Programming

Public Service Programming

Simulcast

Special

Sponsorship

Station Representative (Rep)   Syndication

Step Process   Television Freeze

Sustaining Program

NETWORKS CHRONOLOG 1923–1980

1923	First network connecting WEAF with other stations in AT&T network.
1926	Formation of NBC and its Red and Blue networks.
1928	William S. Paley became president of CBS.
1934	Formation of Mutual Broadcasting System.
ca.1937	Networks had evolved to modern form.
1941	FCC passed the Chain Regulations.
1943	Supreme Court upheld Chain Regulations. NBC Blue network sold to Edward J. Noble and later became ABC.
1945	Peak year of traditional radio networks.
1948	Radio networks moved to assert control over their own program schedules: 1. ABC and "Stop the Music." 2. CBS and talent raids on NBC via capital gains.
1949	Sylvester L. ("Pat") Weaver joined NBC to head television network.
1950	NBC-TV inaugurated "Saturday Night Review" to be followed in next three years by other participating advertising programs—"Today," "Tonight," "Home," and "Wide, Wide World."
1951	ABC and United Paramount Theaters agreed to merge. AT&T inaugurated coast-to-coast network TV facilities.
1953	FCC approved merger of ABC and UPT.
1954	NBC evicted "The Voice of Firestone." NBC offered first "spectacular," later known as "special." ABC offered first Walt Disney programs.
1955	DuMont network ceased operation. CBS drew even with NBC in TV ratings. First of network studies by Congress and FCC.
ca.1956	Emergence of outside program packagers.
ca.1958	Beginning of "step process" in financing pilots.

1959   FCC ruled networks could be station representatives only for stations they owned.

1960   Network controlled 80 percent of prime-time programming by owning them either wholly or in part.

1962   Networks had to give up sliding scale of station compensation.

1963   Option time eliminated by FCC.

1964   FCC Chairman proposed "fifty-fifty rule."

ca.1965   Preponderance of network buys were for commercial minutes.

1970   FCC passed three more Chain Regulations:
    1. Networks may not acquire ownership of programs brought in by outside packagers.
    2. Networks may not engage in program syndication.
    3. Networks may not feed more than three hours of prime-time programming to affiliates per night.

1977   ABC broadcast of "Roots" miniseries.

1978   Fred Silverman named president of NBC.
    Networks began to increase affiliate compensation.
    Independent stations began "Operation Prime Time."

PREVIEW

Advertisers turn to national spot advertising because their needs vary with the seasons and among markets and because there are limited commercial availabilities on the networks. In national spot business an advertiser buys time on individual stations through the station representatives (reps) who serve as the stations' sales agencies in the national market.

Stations turn to syndicated programming because they need more nonlocal material than they are willing to accept from the networks. They purchase from syndicators who sell programs specifically made for television (as opposed to theatrical film) at prices geared to the size of each market. Syndicated programming falls into three categories: off-network, original, and barter. In the 1970s there has been a marked increase in original and barter syndication due to FCC regulations.

CHAPTER 10

NATIONAL SPOT ADVERTISING AND PROGRAM SYNDICATION

10.1 OVERVIEW OF NATIONAL ADVERTISING

National spot advertising comes into focus as one looks at the overall efforts of the national advertiser. FCC figures for 1978 showed the following distribution of advertising expenditures in television:

DOLLARS (IN BILLIONS)	CATEGORIES
3.0	National advertisers to networks
2.3	National advertisers to stations (nonnetwork)
2.0	Local advertisers to stations
7.3	Total

The nonnetwork expenditures of national (and regional) advertisers are known as national spot business, which accounted for roughly 40 percent of the national television dollars and 30 percent of the total.

While the viewer at home sees only individual commercials on the screen, the advertiser thinks in terms of a "campaign" in which television is only one aspect. The airing of a single commercial is a very small part of the television effort. An advertiser's strategy is planned by the year so that everything is part of a unified effort. Before thinking about using television in a campaign, an advertiser must make several basic decisions.

1. A Campaign for Each Brand

Many major companies sell more than one brand in a product category, such as automobiles, soaps, cereals, and drugs. A company starts by separating its brands for advertising purposes and giving to each a large measure of independence. For example, there are separate advertising campaigns for each of the automotive divisions of General Motors—Chevrolet, Pontiac, Buick, e.g. The campaigns are approved by corporate headquarters. Although there may be common themes among them, they are planned and conducted individually. Similarly, Procter & Gamble and General Foods have different staffs working on the campaigns for their different brands.

2. Selecting the Advertising Agency

The advertising department for each brand works with an advertising agency. Unless there has been some unusual development in the past year, the brand will continue with the agency it selected some time earlier. If a change is required, the advertising manager will always select a new agency that does not have a competing brand in the same product category. Chevrolet, for instance, would never hire an agency that was also serving a Ford, Chrysler, or foreign model. An agency might be willing to terminate a brand in favor of a competing one, but that would be rare and would take place only if the new brand were an account substantially larger than the one it replaced.

Agencies are highly competitive. Each of the major ones has a full line of services, including research to evaluate campaigns and provide data and guidelines for decision making. Each has experts in all of the media and creative personnel for conceiving print and broadcasting advertisements. Brand-advertising managers select an agency from those available largely on the confidence they have in the people who head it and the "feel" the agency seems to have for the kind of advertising desired.

3. Setting the Advertising Budget

An advertiser has to make one more corporate decision (perhaps in consultation with an agency)—the total amount of money to be spent on a brand's campaign. To decide, it is first necessary to determine the optimum point at which:

1. All the advertising dollars will bring in more business.
2. Any additional dollars would bring in too little business to justify their expenditures, based on the law of diminishing returns.

The decision may be complicated by other factors such as a lack of credit or cash to advertise as much as may be desirable, or the inability of a plant to produce all the items that might be sold with additional advertising. After taking everything into consideration, the advertiser gives the agency the final decision on how much to spend in the campaign for the coming year.

4. Allocating Dollars to Media

The next decision is the first where an advertiser may lean heavily on the agency. There must be a division of the dollars among the media—radio, television, newspapers, magazines, direct mail. The proportions vary among products since each medium has unique abilities to reach given audiences and to use different persuasive devices. The large advertisers seek a "mix" to take advantage of several or all media simultaneously.

A typical over-the-counter drug product had a total annual advertising budget in the late 1970s of $11,832,000 divided among the media as follows:

$10,800,000 for television

1,000,000 for print

32,000 for radio

Of the television dollars, $8,700,000 were spent with the networks and $2,100,000 went to "spot" advertising. Of the network dollars, about two-thirds were spent for prime-time commercial openings. All of the radio dollars went to buy spots. The expenditures were divided evenly throughout the year.

How heavily advertisers will rely on an agency will depend partly on the number and caliber of people in their own advertising departments.

Each of the major advertisers with many brands maintains an advertising department with, perhaps, a hundred or more personnel. Many of them have worked with agencies and are as knowledgeable as the current agency executives. The advertiser's dependence on the agency is less in such a case, and the division of dollars among media may be made internally. On the other hand, a small national advertiser with only a few million dollars to spend may have an advertising department consisting of only an advertising manager and a secretary. Such a manager leans very heavily on an agency to present various options and to suggest how to make decisions.

The Television Campaign

Once an agency has been selected for a brand and informed of the amount of money to be spent in television, the agency can proceed with specific planning. Again, there is a decision-making process that develops in logical sequence.

Dividing the Television Dollars

Aside from production of commercials, there are two broad categories of expenditures in television—network and nonnetwork, or national spot. How much goes to each category will depend on the capacity of each to meet an advertiser's specialized needs. The role of national spot business becomes apparent as we look more closely at network advertising.

Purchasing Network Time

Money for network advertising will be committed first for a number of reasons. Networks try to sell their commercial minutes and commercial thirties on an annual basis. In the spring of each year the prime-time schedule is announced for the fall and advertisers are asked to contract for their purchases. (Contracts for advertising other than at prime time are made through the year.) The most desirable locations in the schedule will be sold first to those who sign annual contracts. The advertiser who waits until the last minute will have to be satisfied with time of marginal value as it is available or with time within specials. This situation may vary when a network is having trouble with the ratings. Its availabilities may be more numerous—but, of course, they are then not as attractive.

The network-time purchasing decision will normally be made at the executive level of an agency because so much money is involved with each contract and because of the inevitable risk. Even buying only one thirty-second spot a week in prime time involves committing some two million dollars or more a year—at $40,000 to $50,000 per spot. Then, if the competing program on another network turns out to be an unexpected smash hit (as happened with "Stop the Music"), the expenditure may be unproductive.

An advertiser will normally buy more than one location in the weekly network schedules. Since one commercial by itself is likely to have little influence on buying habits, only when there are larger numbers can each reinforce the other so that the television commercial becomes effective. An agency for large accounts will, therefore, probably place its commercials throughout the schedules of all the networks in an effort to extend the messages to more people and to spread the risk so that the failure of one network program will not be disastrous.

Production of Commercials

It is the responsibility of an agency to see that commercials are prepared and delivered to the networks (and to the stations in national spot business) for airing. This is a function the agency will perform for a client at an additional cost beyond the 15-percent commission allowed on the purchase of media. There will first be a general agreement on the kind of advertising and then discussion of commercials at the "story board" stage. At that point there is a series of drawings and words in "comic book" style (balloons with lines to show who is speaking) to illustrate the idea. Then the agency will be asked to execute the commercial by preparing or contracting for the actual film or tape that is sent to stations and networks. Normally the agency will deal with a production house that specializes in the making of commercials.

It is easy to see that a commercial produced with a big star in some exotic location costs a lot of money. Some of the most expensive have run to well over $100,000 each. What is more difficult to realize is that the simplest of the national commercials will cost $25,000 to $35,000 each without using any big names or going to special locations. (Local commercials, on the other hand, may be videotaped in a local station at a cost of only $2,000 to $3,000 each or less). Following is a typical budget of a production house for doing two thirty-second national spots. The budget does not include writing the script or the principal talent who is under contract with the advertiser or the final editing of the film. The breakdown is as follows:

Shooting footage (6,000 feet)	$3,200
Production, direction, and shooting crews	14,632
Performing talent (extras)	562
Wardrobe	500
Studio, set, and props	2,458
Location costs	5,637
Rental of equipment	818
Editing costs	500
Miscellaneous	250
Overhead and profit to production house	8,567
	$37,124

Limitations of Network Advertising

Network advertising has several limitations that force virtually all major brands to use nonnetwork advertising also.

First, there is limited network time available. The television day is of a fixed length and cannot be expanded the way a newspaper or magazine can to add more pages when there is more advertising to be accommodated. There are only so many hours, and stations will carry no more network feed once they have accepted the normal sixty/seventy hours a week. The number of the most attractive locations in a schedule is even more limited. Only about a third of network programming carried by the typical affiliate falls within prime time, and the commercial spots between programs are controlled by the stations.

Second, a network purchase is comparatively inflexible throughout the year. We have already noted the desire of the networks to sell on an annual basis. While there may be a limited number of spots opening up during the year, there is little opportunity for advertisers to make major changes in their schedules of commercials from week to week.

Third, a network purchase is even less flexible in terms of the markets an advertiser can reach with commercials. Each of the networks has about 200 affiliates throughout the country. Major national advertisers want to reach viewers in all markets, and the networks prefer to sell all the stations in one package since it is the most efficient way of doing business. The opportunity to use a network for only a few markets is very limited. From a network an advertiser normally buys a "uniform blanket" of coverage across the country.

10.2 TELEVISION NATIONAL SPOT ADVERTISING

The jobs of a brand-advertising manager and agency would be easier if three things were true: if the needs for advertising were the same every week of the year; if the needs were the same in every market; and if there were unlimited first-rate availabilities on the networks. Since none of these conditions is met, problems remain after network utilization, and there is a place for "national spot business."

By definition, national spot advertising means nonlocal purchases of time for commercials on individual stations. It involves both regional and national advertisers, all but a local retailer whose business does not extend beyond the circulation area of a station. They want to "spot" their advertising instead of buying a network lineup. National spot business enables an advertiser to meet those needs that cannot be satisfied by network purchases. The largest brands use it to supplement network buys. Regional advertisers—like most beer companies—may use it for all their television coverage.

The biggest single advantage of national spot business is its flexibility. The brand manager constantly watches sales figures in every market and is prepared to move more advertising into those with problems on very short notice—a week or a month, perhaps. (With some major accounts 25 to 30 percent of national spot sales for an average month are placed after the month begins.) The "flights," or spot-advertising contracts, are becoming shorter and more frequent. Whereas once an agency would buy spot advertising for a year or six months, many now buy for only a month or two at a time, thus getting maximum flexibility.

Assume an automobile company has decided to spend $500,000 in spot television during the last two weeks in September in fifty markets. The budget is divided among them in specific amounts. The agency knows from experience that it will probably buy time from 125 of the 180 stations in those markets. Assume the decision on the "flight" was made well in advance, so the purchasing takes place in June and July. The agency's problem is to decide on the best buys on each of the 125 stations in fifty markets and to sign contracts for airing the commercials.

One can immediately see two impractical solutions. First, an agency could assign fifteen or twenty of its staff to go out by train, plane, or bus to each of the markets. There they would visit each station to find what commercial locations were available during the last two weeks of September and to sign contracts for those they wanted. The purchasing effort would be extremely expensive and the resulting flight might suffer from the difficulty of supervising all those buyers in the field.

A second impractical solution would be to invite each of the 125 stations in the fifty markets to send a salesperson to New York City (or to Detroit) to discuss the availabilities and to make sales presentations. Stations could not afford to have their salespeople on the road for individual accounts and the agency would get little work done if over 100 salespeople were invading the premises, each trying to get in before the competition. (It must be remembered the agency has other accounts and other campaigns. At the moment it is handling the September flight for the automobile company, it may also be involved in five more flights buying time on 500 stations in 200 markets.)

The Station Representative

The solution lies in bringing an agency and a station together through an intermediary organization called the station representative (rep). A rep is a company with headquarters usually located in New York City and with branch offices in other advertising centers around the country. The rep serves as the station's salesperson in the national spot (nonnetwork) market precisely as a local salesperson works the local market. The local salesperson works with local advertisers and agencies; the rep salesperson works with national and regional agencies.

The majority of national spot television business is handled by some twenty reps who sell time for the 520 largest stations. The twenty will vary in the number of stations each represents and in the volume of business. About half are subsidiaries of station groups (e.g., Westinghouse, Metromedia, the networks) and represent only or primarily the stations owned by the parent groups. Of the remaining reps, the two with the most stations also had the largest billings:

Blair—90 stations—$311 million estimated billings in 1979

Katz—115 stations—$243 million estimated billings in 1979

The three network-subsidiary representatives are at about the midpoint in terms of estimated dollars billed in 1979, although each represents only five stations.

ABC—$121 million

CBS —$ 95 million

NBC—$ 88 million

Regardless of its size, no rep will serve two stations in the same market. The importance of a rep to a station is indicated by the fact that national spot sales account for about half of total revenues to stations.

The rep has contracted with each of its stations to sell time on a commission basis. In radio the traditional rep commission was 15 percent and it is still approximately the same today. As television time became more expensive, stations thought they should pay lower commissions. The lead in lowering the commissions was provided by the group owners. If a company with five stations asks a rep for a somewhat lower rate in return for all its business, the rep will be inclined to accept. Through negotiations over the years the point has been reached where the normal television rep commission is 8 to 10 percent.

Theoretically, reps get a percentage of all national spot business on a station whether their sales forces actually complete the contract or not. In recent years more advertising agencies with regional accounts have tended to deal directly with stations and most reps acknowledge they probably do not get all the commissions to which they are entitled. They are philosophical about it since there is no way to police the stations and they hope the lost amounts will stay relatively low.

Just as a local station hires a sales staff to visit local advertisers and their agencies, so does a rep hire a staff to visit national agencies. Some reps will assign an individual salesperson to a few agencies seeking to sell them time on all the stations represented. Other reps will assign an individual to sell time for a few stations (in a geographical area, for example) to all of the agencies.

The National Spot Campaign

Return to the example of the agency that has a half-million dollars to spend on a September flight in fifty markets. Instructions are passed on to "time buyers" who purchase station time to implement national spot campaigns. This is their sole responsibility and they become specialists in working with the reps. They may receive instructions to spend $8,000 in Denver, Colorado and be told what portions are to go for day time, prime time, and fringe time (4:30–6:00 P.M.). Time buyers will know the "efficiency level" (cost per rating point) at which they are expected to purchase. They should pay the same approximate price to reach a thousand homes in Denver during the day that they would pay in Chicago or Sacramento. This is the factor that keeps station rates uniform around the country. A station manager may raise prices, but if they reach the point where a buyer in New York cannot achieve the required efficiency level, the time will be unsold. Since buyers work constantly with stations in all markets, they quickly recognize the stations whose rates may be getting out of line.

Traditionally, time buyers turned to *Standard Rate and Data Service* (SRDS) for preliminary information about stations and markets. This is a monthly publication, with data provided by each station, that reflects the individual rate cards carried about by salespersons. Comparing SRDS entries over a four-year period tells a good deal about changes in national spot business. Looking under Denver, Colorado, the twenty-seventh largest market in the country with about 600,000 television households, a time buyer would have found the following in January 1976:

> KBTV, *Channel 9, rep is Peters, Griffin, Woodward, Inc., ABC affiliate, highest quoted 30-second spot in prime time is $900.*
> KMGH-TV, *Channel 7, rep is Katz Television, CBS affiliate, highest quoted 30-second spot in "The Waltons" is $1,200.*
> KOA-TV, *Channel 4, rep is Blair Television, NBC affiliate, highest quoted 30-second spot in prime*
> *time is $1,500.*
> KWGN-TV, *Channel 2, rep is WGN Continental Sales Co., no network affiliation, highest quoted 30-second spot in prime time is $140.*

In June 1980 each of the stations has the same network or independent status. KWGN-TV is still represented by WGN Continental Sales, but each of the three network affiliates has changed its station rep: KBTV to Blair; KMGH-TV to Harrington, Righter and Parsons; KOA-TV to Telerep. The competition among reps was very intense during the last of the 1970s.

More significantly, none of the stations quotes any prices for time periods or spots within individual programs. (This situation is true of many other stations throughout the country.) This failure to give prices reflects a trend that started in the early 1970s with the establishment of time-buying services, companies that contracted to make spot purchases. Traditionally, all time buying was (and still is for the most part) done by advertising agencies. However, new companies came along and claimed they could buy spot time more cheaply and they usually did by bargaining strenuously with stations. Whereas agency time buyers had tended to pay published rates or to bargain only modestly, the new services successfully negotiated for much lower prices. This brought agency time buyers under pressure to do the same thing until no published rate was taken seriously by anyone. In addition, fluctuations in audiences meant corresponding fluctuations in prices, so that even if a station were determined to stick with its rates, it would have to publish a new card every time new ratings were taken. Even under such a situation, if the spot market were "soft" at a given time, with fewer purchases being made, the station would still make accommodations in prices to meet changing supply-and-demand conditions.

A time buyer who has $8,000 to spend in Denver may turn to SRDS to make sure he or she has the right station rep for each station and will then call each of the four reps listed to ask for their "availabilities" or unsold commercial positions in the day-part wanted—for example, "early fringe," 4:30–6:00 P.M. Each of the reps will then deliver to the time buyer a computer printout of the available spots with the latest rating for each in numbers of both households and persons in various demographic groups (see Chapter 11).

From the quoted rating and charge for each availability, the time buyer can very quickly calculate whether the price is reasonable in terms of the efficiency standard the buyer has been given. It is quite possible that a spot has been quoted at $275 whereas the buyer's guidelines indicate paying only $235. At that point the buyer calls the rep salesperson to say, "You have quoted me $275 for the spot on Mike Douglas at 5:00 P.M. I'll take it if you can make the price $235." Then the rep has to decide whether to wait for another buyer to pay the full price or take the firm offer for a lesser amount. Similar bargaining is carried on simultaneously with reps for other stations in Denver and all the other markets covered in the flight.

Another factor influencing price is the category of spots in the purchase:

"Fixed" means the buyer has a guaranteed spot. This is the most expensive category.

"Pre-emptible" spots are those that sell for a lower price but which the buyer knows may be replaced if another advertiser is willing to pay full price.

"Run-of-Schedule" (ROS), as noted in the discussion on local sales in Chapter 8, refers to the least expensive purchases that provide no guaranteed position in the schedule.

Reps in the 1980s are regaining much of the status they had with stations in the early 1950s. In the early days reps were especially important as the primary circulators of information and ideas about what other stations were doing. They could advise on rates and programs and network affiliations because they were the only ones in close contact with many stations in different situations. Their influence declined in the 1960s and early 1970s as the stations became well-established and reasonably close to being sold out at satisfactory rates. By the end of the 1970s, however, stations found more and more need for outside advice in many areas. Since nearly all time purchases were being negotiated, stations needed help in establishing rates and knowing how firmly they should stick to them. Stations also turned to the reps' extensive research and computer capability for help in programming, network affiliation details, news policy, and a number of other matters.

10.3 RADIO NATIONAL SPOT ADVERTISING

Except for the complexities of computer operations and the fact that nearly all prices are negotiated, television spot advertising today is very similar to radio spot advertising in the traditional days of the 1940s. However, the changes in radio in the last three decades have led to corresponding changes in station representation. As the number of stations has increased so greatly, the dollar value of individual spots has decreased. Today, it is quite possible to find many stations where spots are sold for $2.00 each. Since an agency gets its primary revenue from taking a 15 percent commission on time purchased, it is obvious that receiving thirty cents for buying a $2.00 spot is not viable. The paper work alone would cost more than that. Consequently, it has been estimated that perhaps as many as half of the 8,000 commercial radio stations receive no national spot revenues at all.

Some of the radio spot money is still handled traditionally in the largest markets—a time buyer wanting coverage in New York City will buy time on individual stations through their reps. However, much more radio spot money is going to "unwired nets." These are made up of stations associated with a single rep who sells their time as a package. Thus a time buyer can sign a single contract with a rep for a group of stations across the nation efficiently enough to make the 15 percent commission worthwhile. Purchases are rarely made within specific programs—the emphasis is on saturation buying that involves large numbers of commercials spread throughout a day.

10.4 TELEVISION PROGRAM SYNDICATION

As the typical affiliated television station depends on national spot business for nonlocal and nonnetwork advertising dollars, so does it depend on program syndication for nonlocal and nonnetwork programming. The independent station, which gets no programs from the network, leans even more heavily on the syndicator. By definition, program syndication is the sale of programs directly to stations, either individually or as groups. It normally refers to programs that were specifically produced for television as opposed to theatrical film, and is in units of thirty, sixty, or ninety minutes with open time for commercials.

The price a station pays for syndicated programming is related to the size of its market. In the 1950s prices were usually quoted with reference to the rate card. A program director might be told that the cost of an episode would be the price the station charged for a single half-hour of Class B time. When large units of time disappeared from rate cards, syndicators charged according to the size of the market alone. For example, a half-hour program designed for use in prime time might cost a station in New York City between $5,000 and $6,000, while a station in one of the smallest markets could buy the same series for $100 per episode. An independent station is frequently at a disadvantage since its lower rate card does not justify an expenditure as high as affiliates are willing to pay. The independent can bargain for more realistic prices only when the syndicator is certain there is no chance of selling to one of the affiliates.

Program syndication falls into three categories: off-network, original, and barter.

Off-Network Syndication

Off-network syndication is sale to stations of programs that were shown earlier on a network. The packager of an entertainment series sells to the network only the right to show the programs during a given broadcast season. At the end of the network run all rights in the series revert to the packager. The normal procedure is to place the programs in syndication and offer them to individual stations. The network on which the program was first seen has no bearing on the affiliation status of potential purchasing stations. A program originally shown on CBS might be purchased in syndication by ABC and NBC affiliates as well as by independents.

Although there was great station demand for program materials in the early 1950s, there were few off-network series available. Of the top ten syndicated programs in 1954, "Badge 714" (called "Dragnet" when it was on the network) was the only one that first had network exposure. When program packagers proliferated in the mid-1950s, the amount of off-network products increased rapidly. Indeed, a major motivation of the packager was the expectation of great profits in later syndication sales. If a network contracted with a packager for a series at $50,000 an episode (a typical half-hour price in 1960), the entire amount and sometimes more would be spent on production. At the end of the network run the packager would have been reimbursed for approximately all expenses and could do as he or she wished with the programs. This also explains in part the willingness of the networks to invest in packaged series through the step process. They would then share in the syndication profits.

The availability of off-network syndicated series has declined in the 1970s as the networks have revised some of their programming practices. In the early 1950s the television networks followed the radio pattern in that a year of programming consisted of thirty-nine original programs plus a summer replacement. By 1960 it became clear that there was a greater audience than anticipated for reruns. Many who missed a program the first time around would choose to tune in when it was offered again. There was also the chance of some people watching the program a second time if they had liked it enough on the first showing. As programming costs rose, networks began to save money by buying fewer programs and showing them more often. From the 39-13 pattern the networks gradually shifted to a 24-24-4 typical series year: to cover a period of fifty-two weeks there would be twenty-four original programs, each would be rerun once, and the time period would be pre-empted four times for specials.

It normally takes a package of about a hundred espisodes to offer an off-network series in syndication successfully. This is because a station does not typically buy off-network with the intention of running one episode a week as the show was originally broadcast. Instead, a program director "strips" the program in a time period five days a week. For example, the "Perry Mason" programs appeared on CBS weekly, but a station might use them from 4:00 to 5:00 P.M. (or 10:00 to 11:00 A.M., or any other time) Monday through Friday. To make it worthwhile for a station to schedule such a show, there should be enough programs so that by running each episode twice, a time period can be filled for up to a year.

When the networks were buying over thirty episodes a year, a successful packager might have enough for syndication after three years or so. As the number of purchases dwindled to twenty-four, it would take four or five years on a network to accumulate enough episodes. The problem became especially acute in the mid-1970s as the three networks became highly competitive, changing series much more frequently than they did earlier. Very few current series are expected to last for five years and the prospects for a continuing supply of off-network products are poor.

Off-network series have several advantages for a station. First, it is buying programs that were successful on the network and are, therefore, known to viewers through extensive network promotion. It is not necessary to introduce a newcomer to the schedule and wonder if it will be accepted. Some original viewers will be glad to see the programs again and, since the program is normally shown in a different time slot than when it was first aired, there is a chance to get a whole new group of viewers.

Second, a program director can make a purchase on the basis of a complete rerun "track record" in the ratings. Brochures for a series will not only give the successful ratings history on the network but they will also show how the series has done in various markets where it has been used in syndication against different types of competitive shows. For example, a program director might be looking for a half-hour program when the other stations in that market are running a game show and a sitcom. By checking with the syndicator, the program director can probably find other situations where the proposed program has run against just such competition and have an idea as to its probable success. Since the early 1960s it has been possible for a program director to schedule highly successful network reruns like "I Love Lucy" and "Gunsmoke" ("Marshal Dillon" in syndication) and others that dominated the networks a few years earlier.

Original Syndication

Original syndication is sale to the stations of programs that were designed only for syndication and thus not earlier shown on networks. For several years off-network syndication was a station's primary and almost only satisfactory source of outside programming beyond the network feed and theatrical film. In the late 1960s original syndication, which had not been very successful in the earlier days of television, reemerged.

Original Syndication by Station Groups
The first significant moves were taken by group owners seeking for their stations programming that was unique and more attractive than network reruns and theatrical film. Group W (Westinghouse) was a pioneer in the field with its "Merv Griffin" and "Mike Douglas" programs. The rationale behind such programming was almost identical with the thinking of the groups when they were starting the networks.

The program director of a station group at the company level might have received an assignment to devise a program to fill ninety minutes a day on the five owned stations with a budget roughly equivalent to the combined value of the time on the stations where it would be shown. This was in accordance with the old rule-of-thumb that said program and time charges should be approximately equal. Assume for illustrative purposes that the figure was about $5,000 per program.

In working with a program idea like the "Merv Griffin Show," the program director might discover that what he or she would like to do would cost $7,500 and that cutting the figure by a third would make a substantial difference in quality. Then employing the logic that had led to formation of the networks, groups saw that adding more stations would justify expenditure of more program dollars. The next step would be to go to other stations, especially independents in the major cities, to see if they would be interested in the proposed series. When enough responded affirmatively, the group would be able to proceed with its plans to develop the more expensive variation of the program.

The "Merv Griffin" program can also be used to illustrate how a program can remain essentially unchanged while being presented under different conditions. It was started and placed in syndication by Group W. In the late 1960s the CBS affiliates were putting pressure on their network to enter the late-night programming field. There was a diminishing supply of good theatrical film and they wanted more direct competition with Johnny Carson on NBC and Dick Cavett on ABC. When Griffin's current contract ran out with Group W, he was hired to do a late night (11:30 P.M. Eastern time) program on CBS. When the program was unsuccessful and dropped by the network, another group owner, Metromedia, produced and placed the Griffin program in original syndication again.

The Prime-Time Access Rule and Original Syndication

Aside from a few programs by group owners, the supply of original syndication material was quite limited until the Prime-Time Access Rule became fully effective. It was noted in the chapter on networks that the FCC ruled in 1970 that a network affiliate in one of the top fifty markets could not broadcast more than three hours of network feed in an evening. A subsequent paragraph in the rule said that the "access time" of the affiliates in the top fifty markets:

> *may not after October 1, 1972 be filled with off-network programs; or feature films which within two years prior to the date of broadcast have been previously broadcast by a station in the market.*

The average affiliate in the eastern time zone had been carrying three-and-a-half hours of network feed between 7:30 and 11:00 P.M. plus a half-hour that was apt to come from off-network syndication. Each affiliate in the top fifty markets was, after October 1, 1972, forced to seek a full hour of nonnetwork material. The other time zones were similarly affected.

The FCC had hoped some of the time would be devoted to local productions that might be related to local interests and needs. However, the economics of the medium led stations to seek other entertainment programming that would be less expensive and that would be better as a vehicle for commercials in prime time. At first there was great confusion and expectation that a court test might return the situation to its earlier status. When it became apparent the rule would not be overturned by the courts and that the FCC had no intention of dropping it precipitously, program packagers began providing original syndication for the access hour. The series were mostly low-budget and somewhat similar to network programming with an emphasis on game shows and wildlife programs. By the mid-1970s the production values of the programs came closer to network quality.

The established packagers have become the leaders because only they can get stations to make commitments based on presentations. Until a series is purchased by a number of stations, it will not be economically worthwhile to go into production. Advance commitments are sought from the network O&Os and from other group owners who are willing to agree to buy only if they have complete confidence in the packager and the stars that are under contract.

Barter Syndication

Barter syndication is the donation of an original syndication program by an advertiser to a station in return for free commercial time within it. Although there were barter syndication programs for many years, the Prime-Time Access Rule made them more prevalent and successful. This is illustrated by the experience of Mutual of Omaha and its "Wild Kingdom" program. For several years "Wild Kingdom" had been on NBC Sundays at 7:00 P.M. eastern time, sponsored by Mutual of Omaha. When the Prime-Time Access Rule became effective, NBC decided not to include "Wild Kingdom" in its schedule.

Mutual of Omaha liked the early evening hour and wanted to continue placing its commercials in the context of "Wild Kingdom" which reached the kind of audience it needed and permitted an excellent commercial lead-in by host Marlin Perkins. If Mutual of Omaha were to go directly into the national spot market, it might not be able to get spots where it wanted them, and they might be located in programs less conducive to the success of the commercials. So Mutual of Omaha decided to place "Wild Kingdom" in barter syndication.

The first problem was to obtain from the FCC a waiver that would permit stations to carry a series that had been on the network. The waiver was granted after assurances that the programs would be new and not repeats of what had been presented on NBC. Through its agency, Mutual of Omaha approached stations individually with the following proposition: "If you will put 'Wild Kingdom' in your schedule in the early evening, we will give it to you for free. What we ask in return is that you give us two-and-a-half of the five commercial minutes." Since "Wild Kingdom" had a good ratings history and some characteristics the stations wanted in their schedules, nearly 200 accepted the offer. Because there was no exchange of money between the advertiser and the station, it was a typical case of barter syndication.

The station, by giving away half of the commercial minutes in the program, was adhering to the old formula of equal valuation of time and program. If the value of one of the minutes was $300, the value of the half-hour (time and program) was $1500. By giving the sponsor two-and-a-half commercial minutes, the station was in effect paying $750 for the program and retaining $750 for the time by selling the other commercial openings. (The Mutual of Omaha barter arrangement was a little better for the sponsor than most; the more standard arrangement is for an advertiser to get only two free commercial minutes.)

Barter syndication can be identified by the viewer in two or three ways. When the program is introduced, there will usually be the statement, "Sponsored by ———." Some of the commercials will be for the advertiser who claims sponsorship and others will be completely unrelated. When the commercials are specifically introduced or given completely by the host, it is also an indication of barter syndication.

At the time that the Prime-Time Access Rule led to the growth of half-hour barter syndication programs, network evictions of longer shows also encouraged the trend. The "Lawrence Welk Program" had been in the ABC Saturday night schedule for years and was evicted in the early 1970s for a reason similar to that which led to NBC's replacement of "The Voice of Firestone" in the 1950s—it was not providing the proper lead-in audience for later programs. When Welk went to barter syndication, the program had an even longer list of outlets than it had had on the network. He persuaded advertisers to pay him for inclusion of their commercials in the programs so that he might pay all his production costs. Then he persuaded the stations to accept the programs for free with the commercials that were already included. The station revenues were made by selling the other commercial spots.

10.5 RADIO SYNDICATION

As noted earlier, the primary emphasis in radio syndication is in the provision of a total schedule—normally a special music format. There is limited syndication of old off-network dramatic series. It might also be said that some of the network-station deals approach barter situations in that there is an exchange of programming without any cash flow in either direction.

10.6 SUMMARY CHARTS

At this point it is appropriate to summarize three sets of interrelationships that have been developed over several chapters:

1. The functions of the Television Network in the early 1960s.
2. The flow of dollars from advertiser to station.
3. The flow of programs from various sources to station transmitter.

ANOTHER LOOK AT THE TELEVISION NETWORK

In the early 1960s a discussion of networks would have covered at least five major aspects:

1. The network was a *time broker* collecting time from stations and packaging it for sale to advertisers. Associated activities were carried out by its news, sports, and public affairs divisions.
2. The network was a *licensee* of five stations in the largest markets.
3. The network was a *station rep* for its O&Os and some of its affiliates.
4. The network was a *program packager* with at least partial ownership of over 90 percent of its prime-time product.
5. The network was a *program syndicator* selling to stations the programs it owned either by itself or in conjunction with outside packagers.

Various Chain Regulations have ruled out both the representation by networks of any stations except its O&Os and participation in program syndication. At the same time, by assuming heavier risks in program development, the networks have been more than compensated by the profits from network operation itself for losses in representation, packaging, and syndication.

A DOLLAR FLOW REVIEW

The figure below shows the four routes by which dollars flow from advertisers to stations:

1. Local advertiser deals directly with station and pays approximately 70 percent of the national rate card.

2. Local advertiser buys time on station through advertising agency which retains 15 percent of the 70 percent and pays the station approximately 59 percent of the national rate card.

3. National advertiser buys time through agency on the network and pays 100 percent of rate card to agency; agency pays 85 percent of rate card to network; network gives station about 15 percent of the original charge to the advertiser, or 30 percent of time charges.

4. National advertiser buys time on the station through agency and the station rep. Advertiser pays 100 percent of rate card to agency; the agency pays 85 percent of rate card to the rep; rep gives station about 79 percent of the original charge to the advertiser.

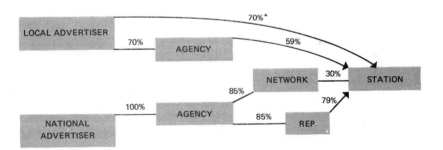

A PROGRAM FLOW REVIEW

As shown on page 314, programs flow to a station's transmitter from the following sources.

1. Stations provide local news programs, some participating women's programs, and some discussion and other public affairs programs.

2. Networks themselves specialize in news, sports, and public affairs.

3. Most entertainment programming specifically for television comes from program packagers. Some programs are delivered to the networks for showing in a season and then returned to the packagers for syndication. Other programs go directly from packagers into original or barter syndication.

4. Theatrical film may go to the networks for showing and then return for distribution to stations through syndication. Other movies go directly into syndication after theatrical showings.

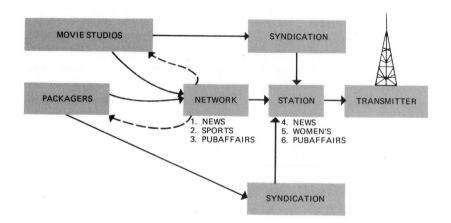

SUMMARY

National spot advertising and syndicated programming are among the lesser-known aspects of broadcasting. However, they are essential to the operation of a station and to meeting the needs of advertisers. Without them the whole industry would become vastly different.

GLOSSARY ITEMS

The following words and phrases used in Chapter 10 are defined in the Glossary:

Access Hour

Advertising Mix

Availability

Barter

Demographics

Fixed Rate Price

Flight

National Advertiser

National Spot Business

Network

Off-Network Syndication

Original Syndication

Pre-emptible Rate

Pre-emption

Prime-Time Access Rule (PTAR)

Program Packager

Run-of-Schedule (ROS)

Special (Spectacular)

Station Representative (Rep)

Stripping a Program

Syndication

Time Buyer

PREVIEW

Broadcast ratings figures are a response to advertiser needs for information about audiences. There are three basic concepts underlying all measurements: homes (or persons) using television (sets-in-use for radio), share of audience, and rating. Because a continuous census is impossible, figures are estimated from samples. So many questions are raised about sampling that broadcasters and advertisers joined to form the Broadcast Rating Council that audits both figures and methods of measurement firms. Advertisers use ratings figures to calculate the cost of reaching 1,000 homes (or persons) in planning their campaigns. They realize all figures are estimates and depend upon a consistency of measurement to enable them to make valid comparisons among commercial availabilities.

CHAPTER 11

RATINGS

Success in American broadcasting is spelled "R-A-T-I-N-G-S." As ratings rise, so do the fortunes of networks, stations, program packagers, talent, and syndicators. Money from advertisers flows to highly rated time periods. When stations cannot achieve competitive ratings they go off the air. When program chiefs produce schedules with high ratings, they get promotions, raises, and bonuses. When their schedules fail in the ratings, they may be fired.

Some of those dissatisfied with broadcasting feel the ratings are a convenient scapegoat for whatever is wrong. People may say ratings are valueless, that they are based on inadequate samples, that they give inaccurate results, and that the broadcasters misuse them. Ratings are blamed when a "good" show is dropped and those of lesser quality are retained. The skeptics ask, "How can anyone possibly tell about more than seventy-five million homes by surveying only twelve hundred?" "How can broadcasters say some programs are highly rated when everyone knows they are junk?"

Advertisers are ultimately responsible for the importance of the ratings. It is the agencies that buy time by the ratings book to be sure commercials are seen by audiences large enough to justify their cost. Broadcasters and advertisers spend millions each year for ratings figures on which they base decisions involving billions of dollars. If ratings were of no value, one of two reasons for their use must be given: either those who pay for them are naive or they are perpetrating a fraud. Neither explanation is acceptable.

11.1 BASIC MEASUREMENTS

Households versus Persons

Traditionally, all measurement of radio and television audiences was in terms of households. A rating of 20 meant that 20 percent of homes heard or viewed a station. From scanty audience-composition estimates, advertisers would project the household ratings to make rough guesses of the numbers of persons in various demographic categories. As radio family audiences dwindled in the 1960s radio ratings figures were given in terms of people rather than homes. In the late 1970s refinements in television measurement made possible the direct reporting of demographic ratings (measurement of persons viewing), which enabled the advertisers to be more precise in calculating the viewing audience as composed of different groups. Although household figures still account for some 75 percent of television ratings usage, the trend in ratings to using the number of persons is growing.

The difference between the figures for households and persons lies in the definition of the "universe" with which measurement companies work—the group chosen for study, the population from which the sample is drawn. A universe may be the households or the persons in an area. Normally, an advertiser is not concerned with all the persons, only those in the demographic group where most of the advertiser's customers are found; for example, teens from ages thirteen to seventeen or women eighteen to forty-nine. Once the universe has been defined, the basic terminology and methodology remain the same for both kinds of ratings.

Measuring Households

The first questions asked by broadcasters and advertisers about audiences are reflected in three basic concepts: homes using television (HUT), share of audience (share), and rating.

Assume there is a market containing about 140,000 television homes served by three VHF commercial television stations. Also assume that someone wishing to measure the audience at 7:30 P.M. on a typical winter evening could instantaneously check on the receiver in each home. One might find the following:

1. There are a total of 140,000 television homes (homes with television sets).
2. Of the 140,000 television homes, 90,000 have their sets turned on.
3. The 90,000 homes that are using their sets are divided into three groups:
   a) 40,000 are tuned to WXXX.
   b) 30,000 are tuned to WYYY.
   c) 20,000 are tuned to WZZZ.

These figures, diagrammed in Fig. 11.1, are all one needs to compute the three basic ratings figures.

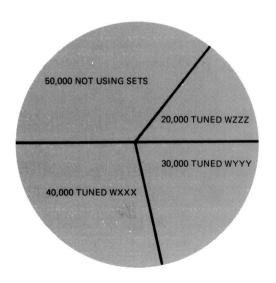

Fig. 11.1
Pie chart showing use of television in 140,000 homes.

1. Homes Using Television (HUT)

HUT is the percentage of television homes that have their sets turned on. (The equivalent concept in traditional radio was "sets-in-use" or "SIU.") It is computed by dividing the number of homes using television by the total number of television homes. In our hypothetical market the computation would be:

$$\text{HUT} = \frac{90,000}{140,000} = 0.642 = 64.2\% = 64.2$$

In common usage, the percentage symbol is dropped from all ratings figures and one would simply say, "the HUT is 64.2."

During the day the HUT figures early in the morning hover around 5 and rise to a high of 50–70 in prime time depending on the time of the year. (See Fig. 11.2.) HUT figures are comparatively constant from week to week and will not normally reflect programming changes. Although a particular special feature like "The Godfather" or "Roots" may cause a slight increase in the HUT, most shifts in audience are among people who were planning to watch television anyway.

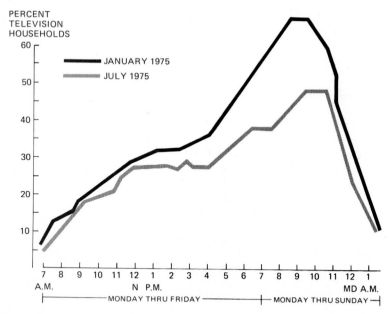

PERCENT HOUSEHOLDS USING TELEVISION

NIELSEN ESTIMATES
TOTAL U.S.

Fig. 11.2

Nielsen chart reflects difference in HUT figures between mid-winter and mid-summer.

Used by permission. A.C. Nielsen Company

2. Share of Audience (Share)

Share is the percentage of those homes using television that are tuned to a given station. It is calculated by dividing the number of homes tuned to each station by the HUT number (not the HUT percentage).

$$\text{WXXX Share} = \frac{40,000}{90,000} = 0.444 = 44.4\% = 44.4$$

$$\text{WYYY Share} = \frac{30,000}{90,000} = 0.333 = 33.3\% = 33.3$$

$$\text{WZZZ Share} = \frac{20,000}{90,000} = 0.222 = 22.2\% = 22.2$$

At any given time in a market the shares of all stations combined should equal 100 percent after making allowances for rounding off the percentages.

The share is of value to broadcasters primarily because it is a quick way of comparing the audience of one station with the competition at the same time. In a three-station market where each is a VHF network affiliate, each station would like to have at least a thirty share at all times to feel it is holding its own. If the share falls substantially lower, it is probably necessary to make programming changes. Obviously, Station WZZZ above would be in trouble at 7:30 on the night that was measured.

3. Rating

To this point the word "rating" has been used as a generic term to denote all figures obtained by audience-measurement organizations. Technically, a rating is the percentage of all television homes tuned to a given station or program. It is computed by dividing the number of homes watching the station by the total number of television homes.

$$\text{WXXX Rating} = \frac{40,000}{140,000} = 0.285 = 28.5\% = 28.5$$

$$\text{WYYY Rating} = \frac{30,000}{140,000} = 0.214 = 21.4\% = 21.4$$

$$\text{WZZZ Rating} = \frac{20,000}{140,000} = 0.143 = 14.3\% = 14.3$$

When all the ratings for a given time are added, they should equal the HUT after making allowances for rounding off the percentages.

The rating is valuable for comparing a station's audience at one hour of the day with that at another time, or for comparing the audience of one program with that of another at a different time. Advertisers are less interested in knowing how a station compares with its competition than they are in knowing how widely their commercials will be seen. A rating point represents the same number of homes in a market whenever it is delivered by the station. For example, in the market of 140,000 television homes one rating point represents 1,400 viewing homes whether the measurement is made at noon or at 4:00 P.M. or at 9:30 P.M. But it might represent different numbers of viewers as the audience composition changes.

To summarize: in the hypothetical situation above, the three basic ratings figures are:

1. HUT—the percentage of television homes where the set is being used at a given time.

2. Share—the percentage of viewing homes tuned to a given station at a given time. It is most useful in making comparisons with the immediate competition.

3. Rating—the percentage of television homes tuned to a given station at a given time. It is most useful to advertisers who want to know how large an audience has seen their commercials.

Measuring Persons

The trend to demographic ratings (based on the number of persons) can be traced to advertisers' interest in reaching potential customers—a program's audience other than potential customers is considered "waste circulation." This interest in potential customers is evident as an advertiser makes the original choice of different media. One rarely sees television commercials for extremely expensive items like yachts, antiques, rare stamps, or for specialized sports equipment such as scuba gear. The potential customers for these items are more effectively reached through direct mail, specialized magazines, or other media. Using television would mean the vast majority of the audience for which the advertiser is paying would be of no value to the advertiser whatever.

The advertiser who buys television availabilities wants the commercials to be seen as much as possible by those who are most apt to be customers. For purposes of advertising, an audience is divided according to sex and age groups. The following list shows current Nielsen estimates of the population percentages of persons in each of several demographic groups that would be meaningful to advertisers:

15%	Children	2–11
11	Teens	12–17
25	Women	18–49
24	Men	18–49
25	People over fifty	

An analysis of products advertised on television will show that the majority are purchased primarily by women ages eighteen to forty-nine. (Obviously the division by years is arbitrary—there will be a spillover into higher and lower ages as well as purchases by men.)

Nielsen estimates for January 1980 indicate the country had 76.2 million television households with a total number of 206.8 million persons, or an average of 2.71 persons per household. In the hypothetical community of 140,000 homes, the 379,400 persons would be divided into the following categories:

56,910	Children	2–11
41,734	Teens	12–17
94,850	Women	18–49
91,056	Men	18–49
94,850	People over fifty	

Assume an advertiser buying time is selling cosmetics that are purchased primarily by women from the ages of eighteen to forty-nine. If it were possible to know what every one of the 94,850 women in the group was doing at 7:30 on a typical winter evening, the breakdown would resemble the following:

40,500 are watching television. The rest are not at home, are in homes where the set is not being used, or are doing something else while the set is being viewed by other members of the family.

22,000 are viewing Station WXXX.

10,300 are viewing Station WYYY.

8,200 are viewing Station WZZZ.

These are all the figures one needs to complete the basic measurement of persons for the selected universe of women eighteen to forty-nine.

1. Persons Using Television (PUT)

PUT is the percentage of the chosen population segment watching television. It is computed by dividing the number of viewers by the total number in the universe.

$$PUT = \frac{40,500}{94,850} = 0.426 = 42.6\% = 42.6$$

2. Persons Share of Audience (Share)

The "persons" share of an audience is the percentage of the viewing persons watching a particular station. It is computed by dividing the number of persons viewing a given station by the total number of viewers.

$$WXXX \text{ Persons Share} = \frac{22,000}{40,500} = 0.543 = 54.3\% = 54.3$$

$$WYYY \text{ Persons Share} = \frac{10,300}{40,500} = 0.254 = 25.4\% = 25.4$$

$$WZZZ \text{ Persons Share} = \frac{8,200}{40,500} = 0.202 = 2.02\% = 20.2$$

3. Persons Rating

The persons rating is the percentage of the chosen population viewing a particular station. It is computed by dividing the number of persons viewing a given station by the total number in the selected universe (women eighteen to forty-nine, in this case).

$$WXXX \text{ Persons Rating} = \frac{22,000}{94,850} = 0.232 = 23.2\% = 23.2$$

$$WYYY \text{ Persons Rating} = \frac{10,300}{94,850} = 0.108 = 10.8\% = 10.8$$

$$WZZZ \text{ Persons Rating} = \frac{8,200}{94,850} = 0.86 = 08.6\% = 8.6$$

To summarize the hypothetical situation above, the three basic ratings categories for the group of women ages eighteen to forty-nine are:

1. PUT—the percentage of the chosen population segment viewing television.
2. Persons Share—the percentage of viewing members of the population segment watching a given station at a given time.
3. Persons Rating—the percentage of the population segment watching a given station at a given time.

11.2 SAMPLING

These definitions of HUT, share, and rating are accurate in the hypothetical situation because it was assumed one could "instantaneously check on the receiver or the persons in each home." Such a check would constitute a census in which information is obtained about the chosen universe or every unit in which one is interested. But taking a census of television homes or persons is impractical on a day-by-day and hour-by-hour basis. Because they cannot conduct such a census, broadcast-measurement firms base their calculations on information taken from a sample or small group that represents the total. Therefore, in practical situations the word "estimated" should be inserted in each of the above definitions to reflect the way in which they are calculated. While people generally drop the word in conversation, it is significant that in print, the major rating services always indicate their figures are "estimated." Thus, it is correct to say, "HUT is the estimated percentage . . . ," share is the estimated percentage . . . ," or "rating is the estimated percentage. . . ."

Possible Sampling Errors

Since few take the time to understand sampling theory, some critics feel free to say that ratings can have little value. Their doubts generally focus on two questions:

1. Is the sample large enough?

2. Is the sample sufficiently representative?

Is the Sample Large Enough? Nielsen network ratings are based on data from a sample of about 1,200 homes. Thus, the company is generalizing about more than 75,000,000 homes based on what it learns from fewer than two thousandths of one percent. Is that reasonable? The question really is, "how certain can one be that the ratings are accurate?"

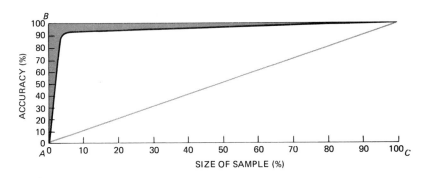

Fig. 11.3

The answer to that question may be found in a chart (Fig. 11.3) that compares the size of a sample with the expected accuracy of a generalization about the total group. On the *A-B* vertical axis is plotted the accuracy one can expect from certain estimates or generalizations. On the *A-C* horizontal axis is plotted the size of a sample in terms of its percentage of the total.

On this chart two positions can be plotted by use of common sense alone. If the sample is zero in size so that information has been obtained from nobody, then there would be zero expectation of accuracy about any generalization. On the other hand, if one conducts a census and gets information from everybody, then one would expect 100 percent accuracy. It is no longer an estimate, it is a truth of which one is sure.

The key to the acceptance of generalizing from sampling is that the line connecting the two positions already plotted is not a straight line. It is not necessary to have a sample of 10 percent in order to achieve 10-percent accuracy. Neither does it require a 50-percent sample to achieve 50-percent accuracy. Rather, the line goes up very steeply at first until it reaches a point above 95-percent expected accuracy and then rises very gradually until reaching the second known point where there is 100-percent accuracy as one takes a census.

Drawn for **Broadcasting** by Jack Schmidt

"There's no talking to him today....He got a call from a rating firm last night."

Reprinted, with permission, from Broadcasting

The accuracy of a generalization made from a sample is determined by application of probability statistics formulas. These formulas are the bases on which many decisions are made in other areas of life besides audience measurement. If an automobile manufacturer receives a shipment of a million small parts, they will be subjected to a sampling examination or inspection. If a sample of a given size yields satisfactory results, the whole shipment will be accepted. The U.S. Census Bureau uses sampling techniques to keep its data current during the ten-year intervals between each census. The dependability of the statistical formulas is a matter of faith that must be accepted unless one is prepared to study the subject intensively enough to perform independent calculations. (Measurement firms will provide the figures on which the statistics are based if a purchaser of the ratings wants to check them.)

Nielsen response to criticism of sample size

To answer those who say a sample of 1,200 homes is too small, the Nielsen Company prepared a graph showing the margin of error (possible inaccuracy) expected in samples of different sizes. Since the margin of error associated with a given sample size is related to the size of the ratings it produces, Neilsen has selected as an illustration a rating of 20 which is about average for prime-time programs. (See Fig. 11.4.) The chart can be read, "If there are a hundred homes in the national sample, a rating of 20.0 would have a possible inaccuracy of plus or minus four. There would be confidence that the true rating was between 16 and 24." As the sample gets larger, there is a smaller spread in the limits within which one can confidently say the true rating lies. When the sample size is 1,000, one can say with confidence the true rating is between 18.7 and 21.3. When the sample is increased to 4,000, the possible inaccuracy is reduced by one-half and the true rating would be between 19.4 and 20.6.

Sample size a compromise

The size of the Neilsen sample (and of the other rating services) is the result of the compromise advertisers and broadcasters make between their desire for accuracy and their willingness to pay for it. All ratings firms would gladly double or quadruple their sample sizes if the purchasers of their services were willing to pay sufficiently higher prices. In effect, advertisers and broadcasters are indicating that the degree of accuracy given by ratings companies is good enough for their purposes and that a higher degree would not be worth what it would cost.

The broadcast rating council

All major measurement organizations employ statisticians to advise them on the sample sizes necessary for varying situations. However, the public is not forced to put its confidence entirely in the ratings firms themselves. In the early 1960s congressional hearings were held that raised significant questions about audience measurement. Broadcasters and advertisers realized that since ratings figures were so widely used, it was to everyone's advantage that they be as accurate as possible. The NAB and the networks, in cooperation with other industry-wide broadcasting and advertising organizations, formed the Broadcast Rating Council (BRC) for the specific purpose of auditing and accrediting those companies engaged in continuous audience measurement.

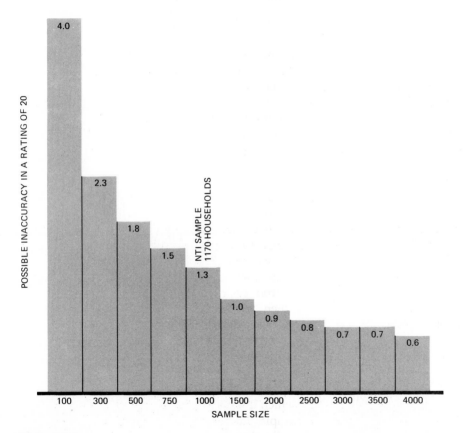

Fig. 11.4
Nielsen graph shows estimated standard error for 20 rating. *Used by permission.*
A.C. Nielsen Company

The BRC hires independent auditing companies that study the records of the raters to verify that they are complying with the most stringent standards, not only in the matter of sample size but in all other regards as well. The BRC now evaluates and accredits three major firms that provide most of the audience information regularly used by broadcasters and advertisers:

The Arbitron Company, which provides the "Arbitron" ratings for local television and radio stations.

A. C. Nielsen company, which provides the television network ratings as well as figures for local television stations.

Statistical Research, Inc., which provides network radio ratings.

The measurement companies would quickly go out of business if they were not able to answer the questions of skeptics. Faulty ratings are of value to nobody. Broadcasters and advertisers depend on them to make their most critical decisions. The care that is taken to provide accurate estimates is at least as great as the care taken to turn out safe automobiles, safe foods and drugs, safe cosmetics, and many other items, all of which are also tested by sampling techniques. The person who denigrates ratings on the basis of sample size alone would, if floating on a raft in the middle of the ocean, probably proclaim with assurance, "the world is flat."

Is the Sample Representative? If one wants to make a generalization about all the students in a college (concerning their political preferences, for example) but obtains information only from the students majoring in one department, the generalization will be highly suspect. Not only must the sample be large enough to satisfy statistical requirements, it must also be representative of the whole student body. If there are equal numbers of students in the various years of study, there should be equal numbers from each class in the sample. If two-thirds of the student body are men, then two-thirds of the sample should also be men. The sample should also reflect accurate proportions of students from different income-level homes and from different areas of study. The sample should be identical with the whole student body in every important characteristic except size.

A ratings company must also be sure that its sample is representative of the total population about which it wishes to make generalizations. Given the sizes of population and samples involved, the representative characteristics of the sample are primarily assured by random selection of sample participants. Homes and individuals are selected at random when every unit of the population (the group about which the generalization is to be made) has an equal chance of being chosen. If there has been any limitation on the random selection of a representative sample, the ratings company is expected to define the situation and how it was handled so that the purchaser of the ratings can decide if the limitation is significant.

ARTHUR C. NIELSEN, SR. 1897–1980

Courtesy: A.C. Nielsen Company

The man whose name is synonymous with success in television programming entered the field of audience measurement to supplement the market-research services he was supplying to clients in the 1930s. Even today the television "Nielsens" account for only about a tenth of his company's total business.

His father was a Danish immigrant who learned to speak English in night classes at a business college, married his teacher, and later became manager of the General Accounting Division of the Quaker Oats Company. Born in 1897, A. C. Nielsen was graduated from the University of Wisconsin in 1918 with the highest grades ever given in engineering. He inherited from his father a skepticism about the values of advertising and a desire to learn why people bought certain products. In 1923 he formed his own market-research company servicing a growing list of clients until the Depression years of the early 1930s. By 1933 the staff of forty-five employees had been reduced to the original six with which he started and his company was in danger of folding.

In 1936, as business was improving, Nielsen became interested in measuring the radio audiences that were so important to his clients. Three years were spent researching a method of learning about listening without relying on questions and answers. Another four years were devoted to a pilot project. In 1942 he first installed his "Audimeters" to record radio listening in 800 homes in the eastern and central states. By 1947 he had 1,100 homes in his sample from coast to coast, and in the following year 1,500. (As he measured listening, he was also correlating the advertisements heard in a home with an inventory of brands in the pantry.)

In 1950 he bought out the network radio measurement service of C. E. Hooper, who used a system of coincidental telephoning and who had run for several years the best-known of the ratings companies. In 1963 Nielsen, along with other raters, went through intensive investigation by a congressional committee. His service was strengthened by the experience, and there are many people today for whom the word "Nielsens" is synonymous with "ratings."

His company has grown from the original 6 employees to over 12,000. It is the world's largest marketing-research organization serving some 3,700 clients in twenty-two countries on six continents.

Possible Nonsampling Errors

After the questions about sampling have been answered, there are two nonsampling error possibilities about which questions can also be raised:

1. Are the sample data accurate?

2. Are the data correctly interpreted?

Are the Sample Data Accurate? Most of the data collected by audience-measurement firms are verbal in that the respondents answer (either orally or in writing) questions or make choice among possible alternatives. There are three questions that should be asked in evaluating the accuracy of the generalizations to be made later.

a) Did the respondents clearly understand the question and the instructions? Was it clear when they were to make notations in the diaries? Should it be every time the program changed, or when the dial was changed, or when the composition of the audience before the set changed? Or was it acceptable to fill in the information at the end of the evening?

b) Is one response more socially acceptable than another? In the 1930s there was great criticism of the soap operas and respondents were reluctant to say they listened to them until the interviewers had taken enough time to establish rapport and understanding. When people are asked to talk about their favorite program they are tempted to elevate to a high priority the news, documentaries, and cultural programs they rarely bother to watch. They may indicate that their favorite station is the educational outlet because they think there may be social prestige associated with viewing it. One should assume that if one answer is more acceptable than another, some people are going to be less than completely truthful.

c) Do the respondents know or can they accurately recall the information being sought? It would be simpler if a person were to be asked only to describe what he or she is actually doing at the moment. Unfortunately, it is occasionally necessary to ask what happened a few hours or a day earlier. Even when people are asked to write down what they are seeing at the moment, they may forget to do so and fill in the information later based on recall. People have difficulty when they try to remember what they ate at the evening meal last night, unless it was an unusual day or unless the meal was unusual. It takes only a little while to forget what happened in the past.

Recognizing the danger of depending on verbal responses, Nielsen has for many years concentrated on behavioral data where there is no need for recall and less chance a respondent will feel impelled to give socially acceptable answers to an interviewer in a face-to-face situation. The Nielsen data, as will be seen, come from a meter attached to the receiver and require no effort on the part of the viewer.

Are the Data Correctly Interpreted? Finally, it is possible to get accurate information from a good sample only to have the measurement company or purchaser draw conclusions that are not warranted. Homes that figure in a rating will range in degree of attention to the program all the way from 100 percent to zero. Some viewers will do nothing but watch carefully to catch every detail, others will be casually attentive while reading or carrying on a conversation. Some will leave the room and pay no attention to various portions, most likely the commercials.

In summary, criticism of the ratings is not limited to size of sample. There are several legitimate questions to be raised. There are experts who raise them and insist on acceptable answers. But if there were faults as obvious as some think, the ratings companies would long since have disappeared and made room for those who would do better.

Importance of Consistency

The broadcaster and advertiser accept a margin of error (both sampling and nonsampling) because they are more interested in comparative estimated data than in the true figures that could come only from a census. It would not bother them too much to learn that all ratings figures are too high or too low so long as the error were consistent and they still had a valid comparison of program and station popularity on which to base the expenditure of their program development and advertising dollars in television.

Similarly, broadcasters and advertisers accept the possibility that some data are inaccurate or that they are not perfectly interpreted. There is the assumption that nonsampling errors also are consistent throughout the data and do not seriously impair the ability to make program and advertising decisions.

11.3 MEASURING THE TELEVISION AUDIENCES
Television Network Ratings

Broadcasters and advertisers depend on the A. C. Nielsen Company for TV network rating services. Data are collected from a sample by means of an Audimeter, the automatic meter that Nielsen pioneered in the 1930s. When a home has been selected as a member of the sample, it receives $25 upon its agreement to participate and then gets $1 per month per TV set and an agreement that Nielsen will pay half the costs of future television repairs. The home is visited by a technician who installs the Storage Instantaneous Audimeter (SIA), a unit that is connected to the set but remains inconspicuously in a closet or some other out-of-the-way place. It stores the information concerning the precise times the set is turned on and the channel to which it is tuned.

Each Audimeter (there is one for each set in a sample home)* is connected by a special phone line to a central office in Florida. At least twice each day a signal is sent to the SIA commanding it to transmit the stored data about viewing since the last check. As all the data from all the homes are received, they are fed to a computer that can then calculate for each national program the standard HUT, share, and rating, even when a program may have been aired at different times in different markets. The great advantage of the current system is the speed with which the computers can process the data. It is even possible to locate terminals in a client's own office so that he or she can receive in the morning a printout on the ratings for two nights earlier. The Nielsen ratings are the lifeblood of the network and network advertising decision making and very important to the affiliates and O&Os who want rough indications of how their schedules are doing.

Television Station Ratings

From the network ratings a national advertiser can make some educated guesses about how individual stations around the country are drawing audiences during the hours they carry network programs. There will, however, be some variation in network program preferences from market to market. More important, the network ratings give few clues about station audiences during nonnetwork hours. For that reason it is necessary to have station ratings compiled separately from network ratings.

Both Nielsen and Arbitron provide station ratings for some 200 markets around the country. Both use the diary method. Arbitron offers a service whereby each market is normally measured from three to five times a year depending on its size. The New York City and Los Angeles markets are covered almost continuously (thirty-three weeks a year). The audience in a market is measured during four consecutive weeks that constitute a

---

* Note: If either or both sets are turned on, the home is counted only once in the HUT calculations. If both sets are turned on, each is counted in calculations leading to the share and ratings figures. It would be possible in that situation for the combined share figures to total more than 100 and for the combined ratings figures to total more than the HUT.

"sweep." The schedule of sweeps is published so that the stations in every market will know when they are due and the advertisers will know when sweeps were taken. During the sweep periods stations and networks will carry especially strong programs to improve their ratings.

The Arbitron process starts by calculating the number of homes needed in each week of each sweep in each market to give statistical reliability. Specific names are selected at random from a mailing list that includes all homes with listed telephone numbers and additional nonlisted numbers are called at random to ensure that the sample is representative. If a family agrees to participate, it receives a "diary" or booklet with the hours of each day for a week conveniently laid out. (See Fig. 11.5)

The sample home is instructed to keep a diary for each television set and the members of the family are asked to indicate in it each time the set is turned on, the programs to which it is tuned, and the members of the family watching. The biggest question related to the diary method concerns the known fallibility of human beings. Some people will forget to fill in the diary at a given moment and may complete it later from imperfect recall.

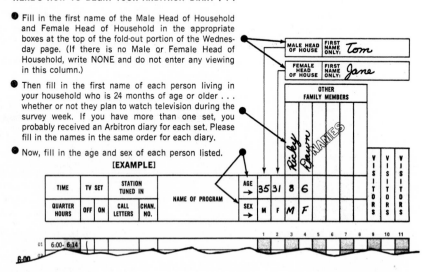

Fig. 11.5
Arbitron Diary *Courtesy: The Arbitron Company*

HERE'S HOW TO MAKE VIEWING ENTRIES . . .

The example in the lower part of this page shows you how to make the entries.

When the set is OFF . . .

❶ Draw a line in the "Set Off" column for ALL quarter-hours the set is OFF.

When the set is ON . . .

❷ Draw a line in the "Set On" column and ask yourself these questions:

What Station?

❸ Opposite the correct time period, write in the station call letters, channel number and the name of the program, whenever this set is on for 5 minutes or more in a quarter-hour.

Who is watching?

❹ **Household Members**

Put an X in the proper columns to indicate the persons who are watching or listening to this set for 5 minutes or more in a quarter-hour.

❺ **Visitors**

If a visitor watches or listens to this set, fill in the visitor's age and sex in a VISITORS column (see example).

❻ **No one watching or listening but the set is on.**

If the set is on but no one is watching or listening, opposite the correct time period, write in the station call letters, channel number and "0" under all family member columns (see example).

How long?

❼ When the information from one quarter-hour to another remains the same, draw lines or use ditto marks (") . . . as shown in the example.

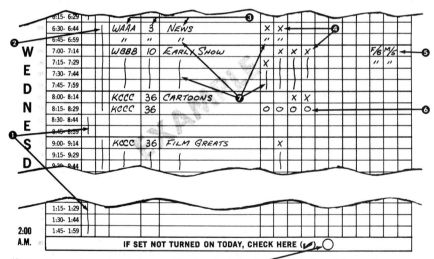

If your **set** was not turned on during an entire day, check the **circle** at the bottom of the **evening** page.

© 1975 ARB (American Research Bureau), Inc.

YOUR ARBITRON DIARY STARTS ON THE NEXT PAGE . . .

At the end of its week participating in the sample, the home mails the diary to Arbitron where it is checked and all the data fed to computers. At that point the computers deliver for each station in each market the HUT, share, and rating figures that are sold to broadcasters and advertisers.

The Arbitron and Nielsen diary reports are the "bible" of the time buyer implementing a national spot campaign and of the station salesperson and national spot rep.

In addition to the market reports based on diaries in sample homes, Nielsen and Arbitron also deliver station data from meters in the largest markets such as New York City, Chicago, and Los Angeles.

11.4 MEASURING THE RADIO AUDIENCES

All television-ratings figures described above have used the television home as the basic unit for all calculations. With the change in radio-listening patterns since the 1940s, the basic unit in measuring the radio audience has become the individual person.

Radio Network Ratings

Network audience estimates are provided by Statistical Research, Inc., under the name "Radio's All Dimension Audience Research" (RADAR). Respondents come from households chosen by the random digital dial (RDD) method. A computer is used to select households in an area from all possible combinations of telephone numbers, thus including the unlisted as well as listed phones. Within each household reached, one person is selected at random and asked to become a member of the sample. If the person agrees, he or she is called daily for a seven-day period to describe radio listening. Statistical Research, Inc., reports that the degree of cooperation from panel members is very high.

Radio Station Ratings

Through the 1970s there were two major companies providing radio station ratings: Arbitron with diaries similar to those used in television surveys and Pulse, which used the roster-recall method. The latter involved personal interviews in which a person was given a radio listing for the previous day and asked to indicate what he or she had heard. The method was criticized for its dependence on memory and when it became so expensive that stations were unwilling to support it, Pulse dropped its service leaving Arbitron alone in measuring audiences for radio stations.

SUMMARY

The major measurement organizations are:

1. The Arbitron Company, which uses the diary method to provide ratings for radio and television stations.

Drawn for BROADCASTING by Sid Hix

"To which audience do you credit a teen-ager watching TV, a transistor radio at one ear and a telephone at the other, with a record player on in the background?"

Reprinted, with permission, from Broadcasting

2. A. C. Nielsen Company, which uses the diary method to provide ratings for television stations and the Audimeter to provide television network ratings.

3. Statistical Research, Inc., which uses the telephone-recall interview method (based on a random digital dialing method) to provide radio network ratings.

THE TELEPHONE-COINCIDENTAL METHOD

In the 1940s the most-quoted network radio figures were the "Hooperatings" that were obtained from coincidental telephone interviews. C. E. Hooper had a corps of interviewers in thirty-six key cities. During the hours when the networks were feeding the stations, Hooper employees in each of the cities would dial numbers selected at random from telephone directories and ask three basic questions:

Were you listening to the radio just now?

To what station were you tuned?

What program were you hearing?

When the results of all the interviews were collected, Hooper would calculate the basic SIU (sets-in-use), share, and rating figures.

Currently there is no major measurement organization accredited by BRC to use the telephone-coincidental method but it remains an excellent device for anyone wishing to do occasional television surveys at low cost and with a reasonable degree of accuracy. A station or advertiser or college class can organize a group of people to use their own phones and to choose telephone numbers at random. During the time period in which the group is interested, each person can make calls asking the above three basic questions plus others if desired. The standard HUT, share, and rating figures can be calculated. The coincidental survey draws on one of Hooper's strongest claims: it asks people about their activity at a given moment and without any dependence on recall.

11.5 HOW ADVERTISERS USE RATINGS

This chapter began by noting that ratings have come under a barrage of criticism and sought to encourage an intelligent appraisal rather than a blanket condemnation based on the apparent inadequacy of sample size. It is time now to raise the question, "how good are the ratings?" One can evaluate audience measurement (or banking, or schools, or government or anything else in our society) only with reference to the purposes for which the evaluation is intended. Its failure to be perfect is important only if perfection is necessary to fulfill its function.

Ratings services were started in the 1930s in response to demands from advertisers. The advertisers who today support the ratings do so to help them make important decisions. For example, assume an agency executive has $25,000,000 to spend in the coming broadcast year on network advertising. Which of the availabilities should be purchased? Or, assume a time buyer has instructions to spend $15,000 next September in Little Rock, Arkansas. Station reps report the availabilities on each of the stations there. Which availabilities should be bought?

Audience measurement figures are simply a tool in the decision-making process which resembles a consumer's decision-making process in choosing among varying brands. An advertiser could have more accurate estimates if he or she were willing to pay for them. Advertisers maintain that the ratings as they are now provided are good enough to help make advertising decisions. Why pay for something that would be more precise but no better for the purposes?

Cost Per Thousand (CPM)

In the hypothetical case illustrating basic measurements, a community of 140,000 homes had its viewing audience divided as follows:

Station WXXX = rating of 28.5 = 40,000 homes

Station WYYY = rating of 21.4 = 30,000 homes

Station WZZZ = rating of 14.3 = 20,000 homes

On the face of it, the first station is the one that an advertiser should use. However, the popularity of WXXX has enabled it to raise its rates considerably while the law of supply and demand has brought lower rates to the others. Assume the rates for a thirty-second spot in fringe time are as follows:

Station WXXX = $90.00

Station WYYY = $60.00

Station WZZ = $35.00

(Actual differences would not normally be as drastic.) How does a time buyer in New York City decide which station is the best buy? The answer lies in calculating the cost per thousand (CPM) homes for each station. This is done by dividing the cost of station time by the number of thousands of homes in the audience:

$$\text{Station WXXX CPM} = \frac{\$90.00}{40} = \$2.25$$

$$\text{Station WYYY CPM} = \frac{\$60.00}{30} = \$2.00$$

$$\text{Station WZZZ CPM} = \frac{\$35.00}{20} = \$1.75$$

From an efficiency point of view Station WZZZ is clearly the best buy.

Cost Per Point (CPP)

Agencies geared to time buying in terms of demographic ratings (the number of persons) have found it more satisfactory to work with "ratings points" or percentages of the target audiences. For example, the illustration of a persons rating was a situation in which there were 94,850 women ages eighteen to forty-nine in a market. One percent of that number or a "point" would be 948. One can calculate the cost per point (CPP) by dividing 948 into the cost of the spot. Again, assume the prices just used for the three stations and the persons ratings used earlier as follows:

STATION	COST	PERSONS	POINTS	COST PER POINT
WXXX	$90	22,000	$\dfrac{22,000}{948} = 23.1$	$\dfrac{\$90}{23.1} = \$3.89$
WYYY	$60	10,300	$\dfrac{10,300}{948} = 10.8$	$\dfrac{\$60}{10.8} = \$5.55$
WZZZ	$35	8,200	$\dfrac{8,200}{948} = 8.6$	$\dfrac{\$35}{8.6} = \$4.06$

If one were primarily interested in women eighteen to forty-nine, Station WXXX would now be the best buy, followed closely by Station WZZZ with WYYY being least valuable. On the other hand, if one were primarily interested in teens thirteen to seventeen and if Station WYYY had a game show built around rock stars, that show might be by far the best buy.

It should be noted that the sole purpose of calculating costs per thousand (CPMs) and costs per point (CPPs) is to assist a time buyer in making purchasing decisions. The same logic and methods would be used in selecting among network availabilities.

Cumulative Audience (Cume)

An advertiser knows that a single exposure to a commercial means very little. He or she wants to buy time in such a way that prospective customers will receive multiple impressions. The advertiser is, therefore, interested in knowing to what extent individuals receive repeated exposure of the same program week after week. For example, assume there is an average network prime-time TV program with a rating each week of about 20. When the base of 76.2 million total United States TV homes is multiplied by .20, this calculation provides an estimate of 15,240,000 homes tuned to the program each week. An advertiser wants to know whether those homes are the same ones each week, in which case the same people are receiving multiple exposure to commercials, or whether they are a different 15 million each week, in which case the commercial is seen only once in each home.

To answer this question, the ratings firms can provide a cumulative audience figure ("cume") that will estimate the number of homes that saw at least part of the program at least once. In Fig. 11.6 Nielsen has estimated that in a four-week period 33.5 million homes will see at least one general drama program out of a series of four. The cume is then broken down into categories showing what percentages of the 33.5 million saw one program, two programs, or more than two. This breakdown shows the advertiser what the extent of audience duplication is. Most advertisers try to establish a suitable balance between "reach" (unduplicated cumulative audience) and "frequency" (multiple exposure of duplicated audience).

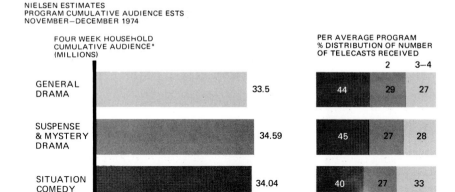

NIELSEN ESTIMATES
PROGRAM CUMULATIVE AUDIENCE ESTS
NOVEMBER–DECEMBER 1974

Fig. 11.6

Nielsen-estimated average program cumulative audience. *Used by permission. A.C. Nielsen Company*

Demographics

As noted, demographics refers to audience-composition data: when a home is included in the HUT or rating, how many people are viewing, what are their ages and sexes, what are their income levels, and so on.

At an elementary level, Nielsen has used demographic information to chart the differences in weekly television usage among households with different characteristics—the size of the households, the presence of non-adults, and household income. (See Fig. 11.7.)

Figure 11.8 shows the estimated millions of persons in various categories (children, teens, men over eighteen, and women over eighteen) viewing television during prime time on various evenings during the week.

The division into categories is much broader than Nielsen would provide for an advertiser. One could with equal ease have divided the men and women into groups from eighteen to twenty-four, twenty-five to forty-nine, and fifty and over.

Figure 11.9 shows the three categories of age viewers of two typical television programs. The point to note is that all rating services ask many questions about the characteristics of household members and can then use

HOURS/MINS, MONDAY—SUNDAY, 24 HR TOTAL

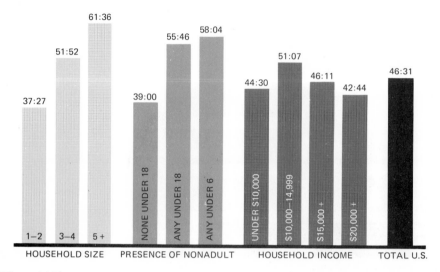

Fig. 11.7

Nielsen-estimated hours of television usage per week by household characteristics.
Used by permission. A.C. Nielsen Company

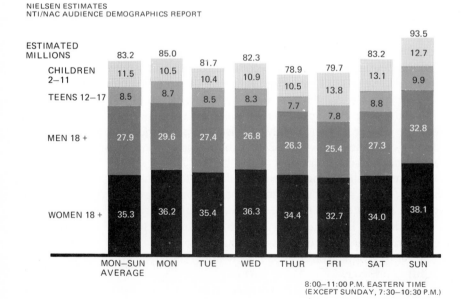

8:00—11:00 P.M. EASTERN TIME
(EXCEPT SUNDAY, 7:30—10:30 P.M.)

Fig. 11.8

Nielsen-estimated persons viewing by night of week. *Used by permission. A.C. Nielsen Company*

the information to give very detailed audience-composition or demographic information.

THE HOUSEHOLD AUDIENCE DOESN'T TELL THE WHOLE STORY!

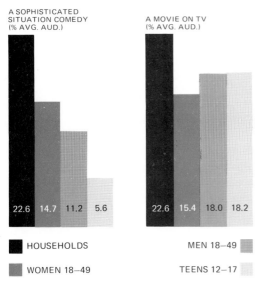

A SOPHISTICATED SITUATION COMEDY (% AVG. AUD.)

A MOVIE ON TV (% AVG. AUD.)

22.6 14.7 11.2 5.6

22.6 15.4 18.0 18.2

■ HOUSEHOLDS   MEN 18–49 ▨

■ WOMEN 18–49   TEENS 12–17 ▨

Fig. 11.9
The three categories of viewers to two typical television programs. *Used by permission. A.C. Nielsen Company*

A Hypothetical Illustration

Demographic data are important to an advertiser trying to reach a specific segment of the population. A cosmetics company, for example, may be advertising a line priced for sale to women in middle-income families ($10,000 to $15,000). It is anticipated that the brand will appeal most to women between twenty-five and forty-nine years of age since it is too conservative for teenagers and young adults and not conservative enough for women over fifty. Obviously there will be some sales to high- and low-income women and to older and younger women than the intended audience, but the bulk of the sales will determine the target audience sought on television. Except for certain gift-buying seasons, all sales are expected to be made directly to the women who are the users. Both housewives and working women are important to future sales.

Assume the advertiser has allocated $5 million a year for network television—about $100,000 per week. The objective is to buy thirty-second spots as efficiently as possible, despite the fact that there will be "waste circulation" to the extent that the audience will include men and others who are not potential purchasers. This makes it all the more important that the campaign be carefully planned.

When the agency talks with the networks, it finds that there are spots available throughout the schedule. The prices for prime-time thirties range from $30,000 to $60,000 each, while daytime spots range from $2,000 to $8,000. (For simplicity, fringe time will not be considered.) The problem is how to spend $100,000 per week most efficiently. Three prime-time spots would reach too few women for the price, since children and men outnumber women in the audience during the evening. The money might be spent for fifty of the cheapest daytime spots, which would insure a larger number of impressions but would mean missing out on working women, who are among the best potential customers because they consider cosmetics part of daily attire.

The probable attractiveness of the various programs in which the availabilities are found must also be considered. Some of the programs have track records since they have been on the air before. If the programs competing on the other networks are changed, however, the rating of a show being considered may also change. A new program must be evaluated not only in terms of the appeal it should have to the target audience but also in terms of the competition from the other networks and the lead-in from the show that precedes it.

Although the explanation is complicated, this is the kind of problem a big advertiser faces all the time. A solution emerges by feeding all the demographic data into a computer and asking for the expected cost-per-thousand women between twenty-five and fifty for each program type in each period. Then the "mix," or combination of daytime and prime-time programs, is determined that will give the largest cumulative audience. The advertiser will then be able to make a decision on what spots to buy to come as close as possible to the maximum number of exposures to the maximum cume among the target audience.

When stations purchase syndicated programs, they are aware of advertiser problems and seek shows that will appeal to the audiences most desired by spot buyers. The problem is essentially the same in planning a national spot campaign except that similar decisions must be made in 200 markets that have different program schedules and different availabilities. Nielsen or Arbitron diary surveys contain the audience-composition figures from which the most efficient mix from the availabilities in each market is determined.

With the development of format radio stations and specialized programs for homogeneous audiences, it is possible to buy radio time with even more precision and less waste circulation than can be achieved in television. For example, the advertiser who wants to reach teenagers buys time on a rock station. If the target is women ages twenty-five to fifty, an MOR station is chosen. If the advertiser wants to reach men ages twenty-five to fifty, all-news and MOR stations are combined. A major difference from television is that instead of buying spots in specific programs, on radio many more spots throughout the day are bought in a saturation campaign that will reach the largest possible audience to the particular station.

SUMMARY

Ratings are obtained by sampling techniques, and the most crucial questions about them concern the size and representative characteristics of the sample. Ratings calculations yield estimates of the true audience figures that could be obtained only through a census. Current ratings are of great importance to our system because broadcasters and advertisers consider them good enough for their purpose—making choices among various alternatives. Those who have great concern about the role ratings play can more profitably level their criticism at those who use ratings than at those who produce them.

GLOSSARY ITEMS

The following words and phrases used in Chapter 11 are defined in the Glossary:

Advertising "Mix"

Availability

Cost Per Point (CPP)

Cost Per Thousand (CPM)

Cumulative Audience (Cume)

Demographics

Diary

Homes Using Television (HUT)

Margin of Error

Persons Using Television (PUT)

Prime Time

Random Digital Dialing

Random Sample

Rating

Representative Sample

Roster Recall

Sampling

Saturation Campaign

Sets-in-Use Index (SIU)

Share

Storage Instantaneous Audimeter (SIA)

Sweep

Telephone Coincidental

Telephone Recall

Time Buyer

"Waste Circulation"

PREVIEW

Section 315 of the Communications Act applies to the use of stations by political candidates themselves while the Fairness Doctrine applies to all other aspects of campaigning and to the airing of controversy about subjects of public importance. Under Section 315 broadcasters are required to give candidates reasonable access to the air waves and to afford equal opportunity to all aspirants for a given office. A broadcaster is not permitted to censor what a candidate wishes to say. While Section 315 was clearly stated in the Communications Act and has been comparatively unchanged in three decades, the Fairness Doctrine grew step by step from almost unnoticed beginnings through winding paths that were far from clear at the time. It is, therefore, difficult to define, open to many interpretations, and troublesome both to those who enforce it and to those to whom it applies.

CHAPTER 12

SECTION 315 AND THE FAIRNESS DOCTRINE

The most intense clashes between the functional- and literal-free-speech points of view have come in the context of Section 315 and the Fairness Doctrine. In the former, Congress applied a fairness concept to the use of broadcast facilities by political candidates. In the latter, the FCC extended that fairness concept to all political campaigning not covered by Section 315 of the Communications Act and to all other situations where broadcast schedules enter the field of controversy. Under each, a station is required to extend time to political candidates or to spokespersons for different ideas. Under each, the station much then permit other candidates or spokespersons to respond. In each there is the feeling that freedom of speech has been impaired because broadcasters cannot program as they wish during periods when they must air political and controversial programming under prescribed conditions. Though Section 315 and the Fairness Doctrine are both implementations of the same fairness concept, their applications are quite separate and distinct and are treated seriatim in this chapter.

12.1 BROADCASTING AND THE ELECTORAL PROCESS

This country is and will remain democratic to the extent that its government is responsive to the will of its citizenry. The primary check people have on their elected officials is the ballot, which gives them an opportunity to determine who shall occupy local, state, and federal offices. This makes the electoral process the most sacred of all American possessions and one that cannot be violated with impunity.

When Americans look at the potential impact of broadcasting on this society, they turn to politics first. In his campaigns of the 1930s, Franklin D. Roosevelt used radio to appeal directly to the people and to bypass the printed press that reported the mostly negative reactions of reporters and editors to his candidacies and programs. By the late 1940s many of those running for office were using radio, and it had been clearly demonstrated that use of the medium could be critical. Today it is known that while radio and television are incapable of converting the vote of a committed individual from one candidate to an opponent, broadcasting can still be a crucial factor in determining the outcome of an election.

Broadcasting's strength lies in the fact that many elections are determined by the votes of large numbers of people who are either neutral in preference or so close to being neutral that radio and television can be effective in swaying them. There have been presidential elections in which the shift of only 50,000 votes throughout the country would have produced a different winner. Those 50,000 and perhaps millions more are apt to be swayed by the candidate who employs the best makeup artist, has the most pleasing speech, or is the most appropriately dressed. Candidates know that the vote of the person who is barely beyond the point of neutrality when entering the polls counts as much as the vote of someone who is very heavily committed. This fact helps explain why so much political advertising appears to be lacking in logic. Decisions by those in the middle of the political scale frequently depend on small factors, and recognition alone may be the most important.

Section 315 and the Electoral Process

It was with appreciation of the sanctity of the electoral process and from fear that broadcasting might somehow be used to pervert it that Congress enacted Section 315 of the Communications Act. Its purpose was to minimize the possibility that broadcasters might swing elections through unregulated use of their stations. Its method was to ensure that all candidates for an office have equal opportunity to use a station's facilities.

The "Equal-Time" Law

It is common practice to refer inaccurately to Section 315 as the "equal-time" law. In actuality, it rarely (perhaps in 2–5 percent of the cases) requires equal time. In the great majority of instances there is provision for equal opportunity, which in our society is a very different matter.

12.2 THE ORIGINAL LAW, KEY AMENDMENTS, AND INTERPRETATIONS

Some provisions of Section 315 can be confusing. This discussion starts by looking at it as originally enacted and then moving on to changes that have been made by congressional action and by FCC and court interpretations.

Congress repeated in the 1934 Communications Act a section of the earlier Radio Act that covered use of stations by candidates in political campaigns:

> *Section 315. If any licensee shall permit any person who is a legally qualified candidate for any public office to use a broadcasting station, he shall afford equal opportunities to all other such candidates for that office in the use of such broadcasting station, and the Commission shall make rules and regulations to carry this provision into effect:* Provided, *That such licensee shall have no power of censorship over the material broadcast under the provisions of this section. No obligation is hereby imposed upon any licensee to allow the use of its station by any such candidate.*

In understanding Section 315 as enacted, amended, and interpreted, there are five major considerations:

1. Broadcaster's discretion to permit political use.

2. Definition of "candidate."

3. Definition of "use."

4. Definition of "equal opportunity."

5. Prohibition of censorship.

Broadcaster's Discretion

As pointed out in the Prologue, the broadcaster's right to use his or her best judgment is at the heart of the literalist-functionalist free-speech controversy. As written, Section 315 seemed to place congressional confidence in licensee judgment, by starting with the word "if." This implies that broadcasters may or may not extend the use of their facilities to political candidates. At the end of the paragraph is a very explicit statement that a licensee is under no obligation to permit political use of its station in a campaign. As a practical matter, however, a station would have to find unique circumstances to justify "sitting out" an election. Every station is required to return to the FCC sooner or later for a renewal of its license that says it must broadcast "in the public interest." Since our system of government is rooted in the electoral process, it would be difficult to persuade the commission to renew a license if the station had refused to permit the use of its facilities in campaigning.

Broadcaster's Discretion— Partially Removed in 1972

In spite of a high degree of participation in political broadcasting by radio and television stations, Congress amended Section 312 of the Communications Act in 1972, adding the following to the list of reasons for which the commission may "revoke any station license or construction permit:"

> *For willful or repeated failure to allow reasonable access to or to permit purchase of reasonable amounts of time for the use of a broadcasting station by a legally qualified candidate for Federal elective office on behalf of his candidacy.*

Although the above was not part of Section 315, it had the effect of removing some of the broadcaster's discretion. In itself, it did not, however, materially change the situation since most stations had been and continued accepting candidates in their schedules.

Broadcaster's Discretion Further Limited by FCC Interpretation

In 1976 the FCC issued a ruling that further violated the concept of licensee discretion in political broadcasting. For two decades WGN in Chicago had followed a policy of refusing to sell political time on its television and AM radio stations in units of less than five minutes each. The management shared with others the feeling that it was inappropriate to merchandise candidates as one sold soap—in thirty- and sixty-second spots. WGN's policy, therefore, was to sell them time only in units large enough to make possible discussion of the issues.

During the 1976 Illinois primary for the Republican nomination for the presidency of the United States, President Ford's committee complained to the FCC that it had not been able to buy the short spots it wished. The Ford committee was joined in its complaint by the National Black Media Coalition and the United Auto Workers who felt that requiring a minimum purchase of five minutes was unfair to the poorer candidates. The commission in a 5–2 decision ruled that the Communications Act as amended required the stations to sell the short announcement time to "allow reasonable access."

In 1979 the FCC went further in imposing on the broadcasters its own judgment in the highly subjective matter of defining reasonable access. The Carter-Mondale Committee asked each of the networks for a half-hour of prime time in December to announce that Carter and Mondale were running for reelection. Each of the networks denied the request on the grounds that it was too early. The election was nearly a year away. The first primaries would not be held for another two or three months. Aside from the Iowa caucuses there was no immediate vote pending and certainly nothing that justified reaching the entire nation at that moment. It was also significant, as will be noted shortly, that giving access to Carter and Mondale would have required giving equal opportunities to all other presidential candidates that could have seriously interfered with the regular program schedule. The networks felt it would be more appropriate if the announcement were made at a press conference that could then be reported on tape in the evening newscasts.

The FCC ruled that the networks had failed to give reasonable access and an appeals court upheld the decision. By then the Iranian hostage crisis had led President Carter to withdraw from overt campaigning and the request for time was withdrawn. However, the decision was most troublesome to broadcasters as one more instance of refusal to accept their judgment, which had been a fundamental part of the broadcast regulatory system.

Definition of "Candidate"

Section 315 refers only to broadcasts of the candidates themselves. If a supporter appears in a candidate's behalf or if there is a political announcement in which the candidate does not appear, the broadcaster is guided by the Fairness Doctrine, which is treated later in this chapter. Generally, the Fairness Doctrine has been extended to all political broadcasting except when the actual candidate is involved.

Through many decisions and guidelines the commission has very specifically defined the three characteristics of candidates who require Section 315 treatment by stations.

1. Candidates must have made a public announcement of candidacy. This can be done in a public speech or in a news conference or in a letter to a newspaper or in some other public manner. The fact that everyone assumes a particular office holder will run for reelection is not significant—he or she must have made a public announcement. Even saying that one

is planning to run is not enough to entitle a candidate to 315 status; it is necessary to make an explicit declaration of candidacy.

2. Candidates must have met the requirements making it possible for people to vote for them. The requirements vary from state to state, but they must have done whatever is necessary either to get their names on the ballot or to be write-in candidates.

3. Candidates must be eligible to serve if elected to office. If after election they would be found to lack an age or residence or other requirement, they are not legally qualified candidates, even if the laws of their particular states make it possible for people to vote for them.

The size of one's constituency or one's chances of winning are of no significance whatever. In many elections there are those whose names may be known to virtually none of the electorate and who are completely ignored by the press and the odds makers. But, if they meet the above criteria, they are entitled to exactly the same treatment as an incumbent who is expected to be reelected by a landslide.

An illustration of the importance of the public declaration of candidacy is frequently found in the experience of legislators, governors, and mayors as they near the end of their terms. It may be that everyone in a constituency assumes an incumbent will run for another term and the individual may, in fact, have said he or she expected to be a candidate. Many have been given time by a station for a regular "report to the people" in which they chat about what they have been doing on the job and interview colleagues and voters. Such reports can be kept on the air up to the moment that the office holder officially announces his or her candidacy and must then be removed unless the station is prepared to give equal opportunity to all the other candidates.

Definition of "Use"

The definition of "use" extends well beyond the obvious situation where a candidate enters the studio and asks for voter support at the polls. The commission has ruled repeatedly that a candidate "used" a facility even though no plea for votes was made. In fact, any appearance by a candidate during a campaign, where he or she was readily identifiable, means that the opposition has guarantees to equal opportunity under Section 315. It does not matter that the candidate claims there is no political motivation for an appearance. Neither does it matter if the appearance is in a dramatic production, a weathercast, or an old movie.

In the winter of 1972 Pat Paulsen, actor and comedian, announced that he was a candidate in the New Hampshire primary for the Republican nomination for president of the United States. He not only made the required public announcement, it was possible for the people in New Hampshire to vote for him, and he was qualified to serve as president if he were elected. In the eyes of the commission he was a "legally qualified candidate." The immediate consequences of his candidacy were as follows:

1. NBC-TV informed him that it would not go through with a commitment to use him in two upcoming specials.

2. The NBC O&O stations decided not to use two segments of a syndicated series, "The Mouse Factory," in which Paulsen had been the host.

3. NBC-TV extended thirty seconds of free time to two other candidates after it had inadvertently shown the movie *Where Were You When the Lights Went Out?* in which Paulsen appeared for half a minute.

In 1976 Ronald Reagan was a candidate for the Republican nomination for the presidency and in 1980 he was also the final Republican candidate. In both instances, broadcasters were informed that if they broadcast his old movies, they would be liable for equal-time demands by his opponents.

"Use" by a Station Employee

A problem can arise if a station performer decides to run for office within the circulation area of the station, no matter how obscure the place of the election might be. His or her appearance constitutes use. If an on-the-air reporter is running for a seat on the local school board in a small suburb of the city in which a station is located, the station has three alternatives:

1. It can suspend the reporter from on-air duty for the duration of the campaign.

2. It can offer to each of his or her opponents as much time on the air as the reporter uses.

3. It can seek a waiver from the opponents in which they agree they will not seek equal time, provided the reporter makes no mention over the air of being a candidate or in any other way uses the appearance to further his or her election. In practice, most broadcast performers will not seek public office unless they are sure the waivers will be forthcoming.

Emergency Incumbent Reports and "Use"

There is no question about the application of Section 315 if an incumbent candidate uses broadcast facilities to report to the people on routine matters—all opposing candidates would be entitled to the same opportunity. But the first time an incumbent president running for reelection sought to report on an extremely urgent crisis, the FCC found itself in a position of not knowing how to respond. In 1956, the major candidates for the presidency were incumbent Republican Dwight D. Eisenhower and challenger

Adlai Stevenson. There was a crisis in the Middle East climaxed by a joint Israeli-French-British invasion of the Sinai peninsula and occupation of the east bank of the Suez Canal.

On Wednesday, just six days before the election, President Eisenhower was given time from 7:00 to 7:15 P.M. on all networks to explain our government's interpretation of and position on events. Immediately Stevenson and a minor-party candidate sought equal opportunity or equal time since the president had not been charged for his usage of the networks.

In response to network requests for a ruling, the FCC said the question was too important to answer on short notice and thus left the networks with no guidance. Later in the month, after further consideration, the commission ruled that the president's address had been exempt from Section 315 since he was using facilities to report to the people on an international crisis. Eight years later the FCC reaffirmed the principle and ruled that Barry Goldwater was not entitled to equal opportunity to respond to a preelection speech by President Johnson concerning a crisis in American-Russian relations.

Candidate "Use"— Not Applicable to News Programs

The most important change in Section 315 came in 1959 when Congress passed an amendment that has led to many questions and problems. In the winter and early spring of that year there was a primary campaign for the Democratic nomination to the Chicago mayoralty. One of the candidates was Lar Daly, a "perennial candidate." He has run for the presidency of the United States (and many other offices) and achieved minor recognition as a Johnny Carson guest in Uncle Sam costume. His opponent was the incumbent, Mayor Richard Daley.

Throughout the primary campaign the local television stations covered incumbent Daley in such noncampaign activities as welcoming the visiting president of Argentina and opening the March of Dimes campaign. Lar Daly protested to the FCC that incumbent Daley was getting an unfair advantage from news coverage of mayoral duties and asked that the Chicago stations be notified they must report equally extensively on his (Daly's) activities.

Matters can pend before the FCC for months and years under normal circumstances, but the commission is aware that when a Section 315 issue is raised, it must be handled immediately or irreparable harm may be done. On receipt of protests and inquiries, it acts with the utmost speed. The Chicago stations explained their position to the FCC and emphasized that the film clips of Daley were included in their regular newscasts and were the kind of thing they would normally carry about the mayor at any time of the year.

Legally qualified Candidate Lar Daly making television appeal. *Photo courtesy of Broadcasting*

By the narrow margin of 4–3 the FCC agreed with Daly that appearance of a candidate on a news program constituted "use" under Section 315. Telegrams were sent to the Chicago stations and for the remainder of the primary campaign the stations were required to give equal news coverage to candidates Daley and Daly.

The FCC decision was especially stunning to broadcasters because it reversed a unanimous ruling of two years earlier. A candidate for judge of the Detroit Common Pleas Court complained that his opponent had received exposure on local news programs when he was given a temporary appointment pending outcome of the election. The FCC responded that there was no evidence ". . . that the broadcast was more than a routine news broadcast by Station WWJ-TV in the exercise of its judgment as to newsworthy events." The line of reasoning seemed to have no bearing on the Lar Daly case.

Whatever the reason, the FCC had reversed itself and had created an intolerable position for major incumbent candidates. In less than two years the country would be choosing a president, one third of the senators, and all members of the House of Representatives. If the Daly decision were to stand, no network or station would cover the newsworthy activities of any of the candidates for the above offices or for a host of state and local positions. If there is one thing that will move Congress and the administration to swift action, it is the threat that they may be deprived of all news coverage of their activities when seeking reelection. With dazzling speed, both houses of Congress passed bills, a joint conference committee worked out a compromise that was passed by both houses, and it was sent to the president, who signed it on September 14, 1959. The amendment read:

Appearance by a legally qualified candidate on any—

1. bona fide *newscast,*
2. bona fide *news interview,*
3. bona fide *news documentary (if the appearance of the candidate is incidental to the presentation of the subject or subjects covered by the news documentary), or*
4. on-the-spot coverage of bona fide *news events (including but not limited to political conventions and activities incidental thereto),*

shall not be deemed to be use *of a broadcasting station within the meaning of the subsection. Nothing in the foregoing sentence shall be construed as relieving broadcasters, in connection with the presentation of newscasts, news interviews, news documentaries, and on-the-spot coverage of news events, from the obligation imposed upon them under this Act to operate in the public interest and to afford reasonable opportunity for the discussion of conflicting views on issues of public importance.*

The intent of the amendment is clear: broadcasters are to be free to use their own judgment about what is newsworthy and should be included in news programs. If a station deems one or some candidates more newsworthy than others, it may report on those it wishes and omit coverage of the others.

The biggest problem with the amendment was the definition of bona fide news interviews and events. Two criteria have emerged from FCC decisions and statements:

In the presidential election of 1960 the situation was unique in several respects. Neither of the major candidates (Richard M. Nixon and John F. Kennedy) was an incumbent. Each wanted all the television exposure he could get. Each was a skilled debater with confidence in his own ability. When the networks asked the candidates if they would engage in televised debates, each responded affirmatively.

Broadcasters made a request to Congress, and Congress acquiesced because each of the candidates had signified his approval. The outcome was the following:

> Resolved . . . *That that part of Section 315 (a) of the Communications Act of 1934, as amended, which requires any licensee of a broadcast station who permits any person who is a legally qualified candidate for any public office to use a broadcasting station to afford equal opportunities to all other such candidates for that office in the use of such broadcasting station,* is suspended for the period of the 1960 presidential and vice presidential campaigns . . .* (emphasis added)

The resulting Nixon-Kennedy confrontations were known as "The Great Debates," and many feel they were significant in Kennedy's victory at the polls. It is certain that all heavily committed party members felt that the winner in the debates was the one whom they already favored. Most observers feel that neutral viewers were favorably impressed with Kennedy's bearing and that Nixon's "five o'clock shadow" and general lack of poise during the first of the four confrontations worked against him.

Broadcasters were hopeful that the 1960 experience might be a breakthrough possibly leading to a total repeal of Section 315, certainly relaxing it with respect to major candidates for the top offices. In subsequent presidential election years Congress failed to take similar action because there was no unique situation where both major candidates favored the debates. In 1964 Lyndon Johnson was an incumbent who had profited from presidential exposure and did not feel great need for more. In 1968 and 1972 one of the candidates was Nixon who had been the debate route before and would have no part of it again.

Equal Opportunity— Debates as News Events

After the 1959 amendment excluding *bona fide* news programs from Section 315 there were new questions raised about broadcasting campaign events. In 1962 broadcasters in Michigan and California asked if they might air as news coverage debates between major candidates that had been arranged

---

* Public Law 86-677, 86th Congress, August 24, 1960.

by others. The commission responded that, regardless of who made the arrangements, debates still constituted "use," and minority candidates would be entitled to equal opportunity. In July 1975 the commission was asked to take a new look at the question. The FCC changed its position and said stations might carry such debates with one important stipulation: the events must have been arranged by someone other than the broadcasters or the candidates. Thus, if the League of Women Voters or some similar organization arranged for a debate between the major candidates, broadcasters might decide to cover it as a news event without having to give equal opportunity to minority candidates.

The first airing of such debates came in the 1976 presidential campaign. While it appears that there will be more "debates," a number of questions are still unresolved. For example, does the principle extend to other federal and to local elections? If so, does it mean that the public will have significantly less opportunity to hear minority points of view? Second, the commission stressed that the debates not be under control of either broadcasters or candidates. But no candidate will go into a debate without being sure that he or she faces no inherent disadvantage in the format. In 1976 the two major candidates had their representatives negotiate with the League of Women Voters concerning the arrangements. Does this violate the stipulation that candidates not "control" the debates?

Prohibition of Censorship

Section 315 is very specific in stating that a licensee "shall have no power of censorship over the material broadcast under the provisions of this section." There are no qualifying phrases and there are no exceptions.

For many years this provision placed some stations in an untenable position, a "damned-if-you-do-and-damned-if-you-don't" dilemma. The problem was that laws in some of the states held a broadcaster liable for everything that went out over the airwaves, and if an individual said something for which he or she might be sued, the station could be sued also. The existence of this dilemma was considered a good reason for broadcasters to argue that Section 315 should be abolished entirely.

The problem was resolved by some stations in an illegal fashion that they didn't like but considered essential under the circumstances. In the studios of a radio station might be found a sign announcing that all political scripts had to be submitted forty-eight hours in advance and that a candidate was not permitted to deviate from the script by a single word. (The commission later ruled that scripts could *not* be required in advance.)

Most candidates complied with a station's rules without too much opposition. When a script was submitted, the station lawyer would read it to see if there were any possible provocations for a lawsuit. If any such material was found, the candidate would receive a friendly call indicating that a casual legal glance over the script had revealed that it was possible that the candidate could be sued for something he or she had planned to say. (It was not indicated that the station could be included in the suit also.) Upon hearing about it, nine times out of ten, the candidate, wanting to avoid a lawsuit, would take it out of the script, no matter what he or she thought the occasion really merited.

On rare occasions a candidate would insist upon the right to say what he or she pleased and would claim to welcome a court case to bring everything out in the open. The station's lawyer would not argue and the candidate would come into the studio, eyes ablaze with anticipation of all the trouble about to fall upon the head of the opposition. As the candidate read the script the control room engineer would be following along. Just about the time the legally dangerous words or sentences were to be spoken, the engineer would reach for a cigarette or a cup of coffee and carelessly happen to hit a switch that kept the studio feed from going to the transmitter. By the time the difficulty was repaired, the candidate was beyond the danger spots and few in the audience would have any idea what had happened.

The WDAY Case

The dilemma was finally resolved by a Supreme Court decision. In a North Dakota senatorial race in 1956 one candidate had time on station WDAY and accused his opponent of "conspiring to establish a Communist Farmers Union Soviet right here in North Dakota." Suit against WDAY was brought in the courts of North Dakota and appealed to the Supreme Court which ruled that "Section 315 grants a licensee an immunity for liability for libelous material it broadcasts."* The Court pointed out that to rule otherwise would mean that states could punish licensees for actions required by federal law. Since the WDAY case in 1959 stations have not had to worry about the legal consequences of uncensored speeches by candidates.

Offensive Material

There still remains the problem of political material that might be in such poor taste that it would offend members of the audience or even lead to riots or other disturbances. In the summer of 1972, J. B. Stoner was a candidate in the Georgia Democratic primary for nomination as a United

---

* *Farmers Educational and Cooperative Union of America, North Dakota Division* v. *WDAY Inc.*, 360 U.S. at 535, June 29, 1959.

States senator. He bought time on several stations for the following thirty-second political announcement:

> *I am J. B. Stoner. I am the only candidate for United States Senator who is for the white people. I am the only candidate who is against integration. All the other candidates are race mixers to one degree or another. I say we must repeal (Georgia Senator) Gambrell's civil rights law. Gambrell's law takes jobs from us whites and gives these jobs to the niggers . The main reason why niggers want integration is because the niggers want our white women. I am for law and order with the knowledge that you cannot have law and order and niggers too. Vote white. This time vote your convictions by voting white racist J. B. Stoner into the run-off election for United States Senator. I thank you."*

Stations were reluctant to run the spot, but they had no alternative under Section 315. A petition was filed with the FCC by the Atlanta chapters of the National Association for the Advancement of Colored People and the Anti-Defamation League. The commission responded that censorship might be justified only if a speech represented a clear and present danger. Unless there were near certainty that the airing of a spot would cause riots or other disorders in a matter of hours, the freedom of the candidate to speak uncensored was paramount.

Theoretically, candidates can use any offensive language they wish and be as obscene or indecent as they deem desirable. One might, for example, make a campaign speech against pornography and proceed to show the most explicit scenes from the most objectionable films. Without doubt the response of the commission would be that it would permit station censorship only in the presence of clear and present danger. (Fortunately, most candidates would regard objectionable material as highly ineffective and will avoid it in their desire to win votes.)

Summarizing—Broadcasters and Campaigns

The following major generalizations may be made about the responsibilities of broadcasters in political campaigns:

1. Although Section 315 says that broadcasters may use their own discretion about allowing time to candidates during campaigns, the practical truth is that they must make their facilities available if asked. The Communications Act permits the commission to revoke a license if candidates

---

* In Re: Complaint by *Atlanta NAACP*, Atlanta, Georgia, 36 FCC 2d 636.

for federal office do not receive reasonable access, and the commission would also find it difficult to renew a license in the public interest if licensees refused to be part of the electoral process.

2. Section 315 applies only to the candidates themselves. To be a legally qualified candidate, one must have made a public declaration, have done whatever is necessary so people can vote for him or her, and be qualified to serve if elected. All noncandidate uses of broadcasting are covered by the Fairness Doctrine which in campaigns implements the philosophical approach of Section 315.

3. A candidate has "used" broadcast facilities whenever he or she appears in readily recognizable form except in news-type programs.

4. All candidates are entitled to equal opportunity except in news-type programs. If broadcasters decide to cover press conferences or debates arranged by outside groups, there is no requirement that other candidates be given the same coverage.

5. The only justification for censoring candidates would be the overwhelming evidence that a clear and present danger will exist if they are permitted to say what they want.

12.3 CONTINUED CONTROVERSY ABOUT SECTION 315

Section 315 will continue to be controversial. Philosophically, the broadcasters consider it an infringement upon their freedom of speech to be required to afford reasonable access to all federal candidates and to be required to give equal opportunity to minority candidates of whom few have heard and for whom fewer would vote. When broadcasters are required to carry certain materials they are denied the right to exercise their own guaranteed freedom of speech.

Pragmatically, broadcasters point out that in many elections there are large numbers of fringe candidates who meet all the legal requirements and are entitled to an equal opportunity along with the two or three who have the best chance of winning. Broadcasters claim they could better serve the public if they could offer free time to the leading candidates without having to extend equal opportunity to all the others.

Without question, broadcasters will continue to press for change, but there appears to be little chance that Section 315 will be entirely repealed. Broadcasters are opposed by an unexpected and somewhat unnatural alliance between groups at the two extremes of the political spectrum. Conservatives so distrust the networks that they will insist on keeping Section 315 as a way of preventing the "eastern liberal establishment" from expanding its influence. At the same time, liberals have so little confidence in the smaller stations throughout the country that they believe Section 315 is necessary to protect the free circulation of ideas by candidates in small communities.

Even though broadcasters may try to argue that the original scarcity of the airwaves that prompted regulation in the first place no longer exists, broadcast media have now become so influential that few outsiders want to see them free of restraint with regard to the most important aspect of this democracy—the political process.

SECTION 315 CHRONOLOG

1934   Section 18 of the Radio Act of 1927 became Section 315 of the Communications Act of 1934.

1956   Incumbent presidential candidate Eisenhower reported to the nation on the Suez Crisis and the FCC ruled that opposing candidate Stevenson was not entitled to equal opportunity.

1957   In *WWJ* case FCC ruled that candidate for judge may not demand equal opportunity if opponent appears in newscast.

1959   In *WDAY* case Supreme Court ruled that station may not be sued in state courts for carrying alleged defamatory material uttered by candidate it was not permitted to censor.
FCC ruled that Lar Daly was entitled to equal news coverage in Chicago mayoral primary.
Congress amended Section 315 to remove *bona fide* "news-type" programs from equal-opportunity requirements.

1960   Congress passed resolution suspending Section 315 equal-opportunity provisions from presidential and vice-presidential elections in 1960, thus making possible the Kennedy-Nixon "Great Debates."

1962   FCC ruled against further debates between major candidates at state level because they would violate equal-opportunity provision.

1964   FCC ruled that broadcasts of presidential press conferences were not *bona fide* news-type programs exempt from equal-opportunity provisions.

1970   In letter to Nicholas Zapple, Senate Communications Sub-committee counsel, FCC extended to supporters of candidates the equal opportunities of candidates themselves.

1971   Congress amended the Communications Act:

1. To permit revocation of license for failure to afford reasonable access to candidates for federal elective office.

2. To require stations to charge candidates only lowest unit charge for purchased time.

3. To set limits on campaign expenditures.

1975 FCC reversed two rulings related to the 1959 amendment:

1. Presidential (and other) debates might be carried as news events by broadcasters without extending equal opportunity to all candidates if:

a) The broadcasters had neither arranged the debates nor held them in studios.

b) The candidates had not arranged the debates.

2. Presidential (and other candidate) press conferences might be carried as news events without equal-opportunity requirements for other candidates.

1976 In *WGN* case the FCC ruled that "reasonable access" meant willingness to sell thirty- and sixty-second spots.
Carter-Ford presidential debates sponsored by League of Women Voters and carried by the networks.

1979 FCC ruled networks failed to give reasonable access to Carter and Mondale.

1980 Appeals court upheld FCC on Carter-Mondale ruling.
Presidential debates between Reagan, Anderson, and Carter.

12.4 THE FAIRNESS CONCEPT LEADS TO THE FAIRNESS DOCTRINE

The Fairness Doctrine, like Section 315, illustrates the conflict between the literal and functional points of view with respect to the issue of free speech. It represents an extension by the FCC of the Section 315 philosophy to other areas of controversy. The lines were first drawn in the late 1920s. Broadcasters were emphasizing the Federal Radio Act mandate that the commission "not interfere with the rights of free speech by radio communication." The commission was enunciating a "fairness concept" that extended beyond political campaigning the implication that in controversial matters broadcasters should refrain from imposing their own views on the public. In the 1929 *Great Lakes* statement, the commission said,

> *It would not be fair, indeed it would not be good service to the public to allow a one-sided presentation of the political issues of a campaign. Insofar as a program consists of discussion of public questions, public interest requires ample play for the free and fair competition of opposing views, and the commission*

believes that the principle applies not only to addresses by political candidates but to all discussions of issues of importance to the public.* (emphasis added)

The difficulty in applying philosophical abstractions to specific situations ensured that the struggle would be long, confusing, and frustrating to all.

The *Mayflower* Decision

Throughout the 1930s the issue was dormant. The commissioners were so busy regulating the traffic and investigating the networks that they had little time to seek out the implications of the right to freedom of speech as applied to public-issue programming. Broadcasters were so busy developing the medium that they for the most part failed to enter areas of controversy in their programming that would have forced the matter to the attention of the commission. The modern history of what was to become the Fairness Doctrine started in the early 1940s with the *Mayflower* decision.

In 1939 station WAAB in Boston submitted to the FCC a routine application for renewal of its license. The Mayflower Broadcasting Corporation, also of Boston, filed a challenge to the renewal. The challenger claimed WAAB had not been operating in "the public interest" and requested that its frequency be assigned to the Mayflower Corporation. A principal ground for the challenge was the undisputed fact that WAAB had aired "so-called editorials" in 1937 and 1938. These were statements broadcast by the station taking the same kind of one-sided stand that would be found on the editorial page of a newspaper.

In 1941 the FCC denied the Mayflower challenge, partly because it was not deemed financially qualified to construct and operate the station, and partly because it had made misrepresentations of fact to the commission.

In renewing the license the FCC took note of the fact that WAAB had been editorializing, that it had stopped of its own accord before its license was due for renewal, and that it had no intention of resuming the practice. Then, without any indication of breaking new ground and almost as though in passing, the commission indicated its disapproval of broadcast editorials:

> *A truly free radio cannot be used to advocate the causes of the licensee. It cannot be used to support the candidacies of his friends. It cannot be devoted to the support of principles he happens to regard most favorably. In brief, the broadcaster cannot be an advocate.†*

---

* In the Matter of the Application of *Great Lakes Broadcasting Co.*, FRC Docket No. 4900, 3 FRC Ann. Rep. 32 (1929).

† In the Matter of the *Mayflower Broadcasting Corporation* and the *Yankee Network, Inc.,* (WAAB) 8 FCC 333, 338, January 16, 1941.

In the *Mayflower* decision the FCC was stating what it felt was a logical implementation of the fairness concept. It was better that the public should hear no discussion than to hear one side only. Because there were not enough frequencies to permit all persons who wanted to broadcast their opinions to build their own stations and because the public was entitled to a presentation of all sides of a controversy, the FCC concluded that it was only fair to prevent those who did own stations from using them to give their own opinions—thus editorializing was prohibited.

Prior to the *Mayflower* decision few broadcasters had shown any desire to editorialize. Now, however, they considered the ban an unwarranted intrusion on their freedom of speech. Following the end of World War II broadcasters brought increasing pressure on the commission to reverse the *Mayflower* decision.

In the meantime, the attitude of the commission toward the fairness concept was becoming more sophisticated. The prohibition of editorials to protect listeners against one-sided broadcasts had been a negative approach. The commission began to view fairness more affirmatively, and in two or three decisions stimulation of discussion became a paramount regulatory objective.

Mayflower Revised

Because of pressures from broadcasters and because of its own change in views, the FCC in 1948 held hearings "In the Matter of Editorializing by Broadcast Licensees." A year later it issued a report that became known as the "Revised *Mayflower* Decision," although neither the Mayflower Corporation nor station WAAB was involved in it. The report reviewed the commission's desire to encourage debate and then concluded that editorializing could be an effective stimulant for initiating broadcast discussion of controversial issues.*

There was still concern with the fairness concept and the inherent danger when an audience was exposed to a one-sided discussion. Therefore, the FCC ruled that editorializing was acceptable (in the public interest) provided licensees made an "affirmative effort" to see that the other side of an issue was also presented. The editorializing broadcaster had to accept the responsibility for permitting the other side to respond. If necessary, a broadcaster must actively seek out such a speaker. It was left to individual licensees to use their own judgment in selecting representative speakers for the other side, but licensees could not "stack the deck" by choosing persons obviously incompetent to make the best possible response.

---

* In the Matter of Editorializing by Broadcast Licensees, 13 FCC 1246, June 1, 1949.

The Fairness Doctrine

This requirement that the broadcaster provide response *to* broadcast editorials was the original Fairness Doctrine. Although the hearings had been called to consider only editorializing, the report went into other areas. There was an overall statement defining freedom of speech in terms of circulating ideas as opposed to simply speaking one's mind.

> *It is this right of the public to be informed rather than any right on the part of the Government, any broadcast licensee or any individual member of the public to broadcast his own particular views on any matter, which is the foundation stone of the American system of broadcasting.* *

The report went on to emphasize an affirmative responsibility on the part of the licensee to provide a reasonable amount of time for the presentation of programs on public issues. After reviewing a number of its decisions the commission generalized:

> *And the Commission has made clear that in such presentation of news and comment the public interest required that the licensee must operate on a basis of overall fairness, making his facilities available for the expression of the contrasting views of all responsible elements in the community on the various issues which arise.†*

In a concluding paragraph, the report sought to recapitulate what had been implied in fifteen confused and confusing pages. Three points seemed to emerge: (1) a licensee must devote a reasonable amount of time to discussion of issues, (2) the discussion must give the public a chance to hear all points of view, and (3) the licensee may choose the appropriate formats, including editorials if he or she wishes. Because the report was so muddled few read it carefully, and most attention was focused on the issue that had led to the hearings in the first place—editorializing. The rest of the report was buried until the FCC exhumed it more than a decade later.

Slow Growth of Editorializing

Throughout the 1950s the Fairness Doctrine was discussed only with reference to editorial responses. At first few stations took advantage of the opportunity to express their opinions on controversial issues. Some licensees

---

* Ibid., 13 FCC at 1249.

† Ibid.

had nothing they wanted to say or were afraid they might make enemies and drive away advertisers. Others were genuinely concerned that the commission might make it impossible to justify their choices of opposition representatives.

The few who did try editorializing learned that all the commission required was evidence the licensees had used their best judgment in choosing among opposing speakers or that they had made a good-faith effort to find such a person if none appeared voluntarily. No broadcaster experienced difficulty with the FCC over editorializing. Then managers of a few stations like WDSU in New Orleans began speaking at meetings saying they had tried editorializing and found it to be good for business. It had increased their audiences and had not offended or driven off advertisers, even when there were editorials urging southern citizens to abide by unpopular court desegregation rules. They also reported that editorializing seemed to give them a prestige in their communities that they had not enjoyed before. With such favorable reports, more stations began the practice. By 1960 about seventy-five television stations were editorializing regularly and the number doubled in the next couple of years.

12.5 EXPANSION OF THE FAIRNESS DOCTRINE

In the early 1960s the commission emphasized its interest in editorializing and expanded the Fairness Doctrine into other programming areas. In its 1960 programming policy statement the FCC listed fourteen elements usually necessary to meet the public interest.* One of the elements was "editorializing by licensees."

In 1962 the FCC staff reviewed two documentaries about which Fairness Doctrine complaints had been made. A CBS documentary, "Biography of a Bookie Joint," had shown film of a police raid on a bookmaking establishment and it was alleged that Boston had been singled out unfairly in national publicity concerning a problem that extended well beyond that city. An NBC documentary, "The Battle of Newburgh," reported on a controversial welfare program. The Newburgh city manager claimed the program was "biased, misleading, and lacking in objectivity." In both instances the commission found that the networks had sought to be fair and had afforded a reasonable opportunity for presentation of other points of view. While broadcasters hailed these decisions, there was concern that the Fairness Doctrine was being expanded into the field of news programming.

In 1963 the commission took under advisement the question of whether a dramatic program had violated the doctrine. Armstrong Circle Theater

---

* Report and Statement of Policy re: Commission *en banc* Programming Inquiry, 25 Fed. Reg. at 7295, July 29, 1960.

had done a play entitled "Smash-Up." It was in dramatized documentary style and dealt with fraudulent claims in automobile accidents. The National Association of Claimants Counsel of America protested the program might have prejudiced jurors in accident cases. Lawyers wrote in to complain the program had portrayed their profession in an unfair light. After four months the FCC ruled the drama had not violated the Fairness Doctrine, but the fact that the question was considered at all by the FCC indicated that the doctrine might be applied to entertainment programs.

In 1965 station KTLN in Denver, Colorado ran an investigative documentary on persons engaged in "debt adjusting" and titled the show "The Gougers." The station concluded that debt adjusters used immoral methods and performed no useful purpose in society. A Fairness Doctrine complaint was made to the FCC which asked the station to justify the show's title and one-sided view of debt adjusters. The station replied to the commission that debt adjusters "were no more entitled to broadcast time than dope peddlers." The response of the FCC was that as long as debt adjusting was a legal activity in Colorado, those who practiced it could not be put in the same category as those who were clearly criminal. The commission said an attack had been made on the honesty and integrity of those in the debt-adjusting business and it was the duty of the station to give them a chance to respond.* So commissioners were prepared to extend the doctrine wherever it seemed appropriate.

The 1963 Advisory

As the commission expanded the Fairness Doctrine, there was growing confusion on the part of broadcasters who complained that they did not know what was expected of them. To combat the confusion, the FCC in July 1963 issued an "advisory" to stations. The opening paragraph called attention to a statement in the 1949 policy ". . . that the licensee has an affirmative obligation to afford reasonable opportunity for the presentation of contrasting viewpoints on any controversial issue he chooses to cover."† Reference was then made to three recent FCC rulings holding that the licensee had a Fairness Doctrine responsibility beyond editorial responses:

1. When a program involves attack on a person or organization.

---

* "In re: 'Fairness Doctrine' Requirements." Letter to *Radio Station KTLN*, FCC 65-681, July 21, 1965.

† In re: "Broadcast Licensees Advised Concerning Stations' Responsibility Under the Fairness Doctrine as to Controversial Issue Programming." Public Notice—B. FCC 63–734, July 26, 1963.

2. When a noncandidate takes a partisan position on either issues or candidates during a campaign.

3. When a licensee permits use of his or her facilities for the presentation of views on controversial issues such as racial segregation.

The 1963 document was probably more significant than most people realized at the time because it was a major expansion of the Fairness Doctrine beyond its apparent original position. The commission realized it was moving well beyond broadcasters' understanding that the Fairness Doctrine was related primarily to editorializing, for the commission added:

> *It is immaterial whether a particular program or viewpoint is presented under the label of "Americanism," "anti-Communism" or "states rights" or* whether it is a paid announcement, official speech, editorial, or religious broadcast. *Regardless of label or form, if one viewpoint of a controversial issue of public importance is presented, the licensee is obligated to make a reasonable effort to present the other opposing viewpoint or viewpoints.* (emphasis added)*

Free Response to Controversy in Paid Program

Two months after the July advisory, *Broadcasting* headlined a story, "More FCC Confusion on Fairness."* Two radio stations in Alabama had asked the FCC for a ruling on their Fairness Doctrine responsibility when carrying a sponsored syndicated program, "Life Line," in which there had been attacks on a nuclear test ban treaty then being debated in the Senate. The syndicator had advised the stations that they need not permit answers to the program if there were no local chapter of an organization wishing to respond and that, in any event, they would not have to give free time for such a response. In a letter (called *Cullman* after the name of one of the licensees) the FCC ruled:

> *But, it is clear that the public's paramount right to hear opposing views on controversial issues of public importance cannot be nullified by either the inability of the licensee to obtain paid sponsorship of the broadcast time or the licensee's refusal to consider requests for time to present a conflicting viewpoint from an organization on the sole ground that the organization has no local chapter.†*

---

* *Broadcasting* September 23, 1963, p. 72.

† In re: "Responsibility Under the Fairness Doctrine." Letter to *Cullman Broadcasting Co., Inc.,* FCC 63–849, September 18, 1963.

This was an amplification of the previous advisory passage giving licensees Fairness-Doctrine responsibility for anything aired even though their only involvement might have been the sale of time and even though they might personally disagree with the viewpoint expressed. *Broadcasting* had cause less for confusion than for concern that the functional-free-speech point of view appeared headed for an indefinite extension.

The 1964 Fairness Primer

The 1963 advisory was followed by a 1964 fairness primer that was more extensive. It was a digest of cases divided into categories and was designed to answer questions that might arise about either broadcaster rights or responsibilities. The primer came at a time when Congress was considering whether the fairness concept needed to be written into law in order to eliminate the confusion that attended evolutionary development by the FCC. The House Commerce Committee asked the commission to take no disciplinary action against stations on Fairness-Doctrine grounds until there had been time for further consideration. The commission responded that it had not to that point taken any such action but refused to make a commitment it would not do so if the need were to arise.

The *Red Lion* Case

In the fall election of 1964 there was a small incident that eventually reached the Supreme Court and became the ultimate peg on which the Fairness Doctrine survived. Station WGCB, located in the town of Red Lion, Pennsylvania, was owned by Reverend John M. Norris, an ardent conservative and supporter of Barry Goldwater. During the Johnson-Goldwater election campaign Reverend Norris continued carrying a syndicated program called "Christian Crusade" on time purchased by Reverend Billy James Hargis, another political conservative.

In one program Reverend Hargis made a personal attack on Fred Cook who had written a book, *Barry Goldwater—Extremist of the Right*, and an article for the *Nation* magazine, "Radio Right—Hate Clubs of the Air." The book and the article expressed an anti-Goldwater point of view that was most unacceptable to those who shared the political beliefs of the two ministers. In the program attacking Cook, Reverend Hargis charged, among other things, that Cook had been fired from a newspaper job after falsely accusing a public official of attempted bribery.

Cook asked the station for time to respond to the attack. He was informed that since the Hargis time had been purchased, he (Cook) would also have to buy time if he wished to respond. (This was a year after the FCC had clearly stated in *Cullman* that licensees could not charge for time to respond even though the attacking program had been sponsored.) Cook protested to the FCC.

A year later the commission informed station WGCB it had violated the Fairness Doctrine and directed that time be given to Cook so he might respond to the Hargis attack. Norris decided this was a matter of principle on which he would not compromise. He appealed the FCC decision to the courts on the grounds that the FCC had gone beyond its authority as granted by the Act of 1934 and that the Fairness Doctrine was an infringement on his freedom of speech. In June 1967 the court of appeals upheld the FCC's judgment on WGCB. More important than the effect on WGCB itself was the interpretation of observers that the court was at the same time upholding the constitutionality of the Fairness Doctrine and the right of the FCC to establish and implement it.

FCC Fairness Doctrine Rules and the *RTNDA* Case

Until the summer of 1967 no aspect of the Fairness Doctrine had been written into specific rules. There were only FCC statements and individual decisions. Encouraged by the June decision of the appeals court in the *Red Lion* case, the FCC moved in July to "codify" the Fairness Doctrine and to "elevate it to rules status." The purpose, according to the commission, was to eliminate some of the confusion and to emphasize the importance of complying with the doctrine in two specific situations: in the case of personal attacks and when editorials were aired favoring or opposing a political candidate. A further motivation was that once rules were adopted by the FCC, a station could be fined for failing to follow them. A month later the proposed rules were amended to exclude the personal-attack requirements from *bona fide* news-type programs.

As soon as the rules were announced, the Radio Television News Directors Association (RTNDA) announced that it would appeal their constitutionality to the courts. Most observers of American broadcasting felt that newspeople had a high degree of commitment to fair coverage of news and the news directors' organization had great prestige generally. From the broadcasters' point of view it was an ideal group, compared with WGCB, to go to the courts against the FCC. The RTNDA filed its appeal with the court of appeal in Chicago, which it felt was more apt to be sympathetic than the Washington court that had just upheld the FCC in the *Red Lion* case.

While the *RTNDA* case was pending in Chicago, the Supreme Court agreed to hear the *Red Lion* case. Knowing of the RTNDA case and being aware that the loser would inevitably seek review, the Supreme Court held the *Red Lion* case in abeyance until it might be heard with the second case.

As the RTNDA had hoped, the Chicago court ruled against the Fairness Doctrine. It said that the FCC had exceeded its authority in promulgating the Fairness Doctrine, that the doctrine was "burdensome and unconstitutionally vague," and that the doctrine was an infringement on freedom of speech. The court also cited some of the FCC's own statistics: there were 6,253 commercial radio and television stations in the country compared with 1,754 daily newspapers. Its conclusion was that "scarcity of the frequencies" could no longer be used as a basis for applying more regulation to broadcasting than to the print media. In brief, the RTNDA and the broadcasters won a complete victory at the appeals-court level.

The confusion of the 1960s was probably never more apparent than at this point. In the *Red Lion* case the court of appeals in Washington had upheld the Fairness Doctrine. In the *RTNDA* case the court of appeals in Chicago had struck it down. The two decisions were diametrically opposite.

The *Red Lion* Decision

In 1969 the Supreme Court handed down a landmark decision in the *Red Lion–RTNDA* case. It unanimously upheld the FCC and affirmed its authority to enforce the Fairness Doctrine. This decision reinforced the fear of broadcasters that even more extensions would be forthcoming shortly.

Scarcity of the Frequencies

In two other respects the *Red Lion* decision clarified concepts that had been developing over the years. First, the Supreme Court laid to rest the argument that the increased number of stations meant there was no longer any scarcity of the frequencies. Rather, it defined scarcity as the situation "where there are substantially more individuals who want to broadcast than there are frequencies to allocate." Thus, even though there might be fifty or a hundred stations in a market compared with a handful of newspapers, there was still a scarcity if there were more who would like to have stations but who could not be assigned spectrum space.

Functional Free Speech

Secondly, there was a definitive expression of the functionalist-free-speech point of view. In comparing the right to speak with the right to hear, the Court said:

> Because of the scarcity of radio frequencies, the Government is permitted to put restraint on licensees in favor of others whose views should be expressed on this unique medium . . . It is the

right of the viewers and listeners, not the right of the
*broadcasters, which is paramount.**

Countercommercials

Compounding the confusion and frustration of broadcasters in the second half of the 1960s was another extension of the Fairness Doctrine into an area that few imagined the commission would enter. It concerned cigarette commercials. In 1964 the Surgeon General, at the direction of Congress, submitted a report on smoking. It found that "cigarette smoking may be hazardous to your health," and the following year Congress passed an act providing that cigarette packages must carry a warning to that effect.

In 1966 John F. Banzhaf III, a lawyer in New York City, became concerned about the number of cigarette commercials on television. He reasoned that while each was on the surface only a plea to buy a particular brand, all were, in effect, messages persuading viewers to smoke cigarettes. The commercials featured happy, youthful, and vigorous people in pleasant surroundings who were made even happier when they could enjoy· their favorite brands. Although none of the commercials said in so many words, "Cigarettes are wonderful, you really ought to try them if you want to be happy," all of the commercials rather clearly implied this sentiment. (Advertising experts and psychologists had maintained for years that the steady increase in cigarette consumption was in part due to the combined results of all advertising for individual brands.)

Banzhaf wrote to WCBS-TV in New York City citing three specific commercials that indicated that smoking was "socially acceptable and desirable, manly, and a necessary part of a rich full life." He requested that free time be given to responsible groups opposing smoking. He asked that such groups receive time approximately equal to that which was spent on the promotion of "the virtues and values of smoking."

WCBS-TV did not question the premises on which Banzhaf had argued but pointed out that over the years it had aired the negative aspects of smoking both in regular newscasts and in special programs. Since the station felt it had adequately provided contrasting viewpoints on the subject, it refused Banzhaf's request. Banzhaf protested to the commission which, in June 1967, responded in a letter to WCBS-TV. It reviewed the situation and came down squarely on Banzhaf's side in the particular instance, but added that its action was not to be taken as a precedent.

We hold that the Fairness Doctrine is applicable to such
advertisements. We stress that our holding is limited to this

---

* *Red Lion Broadcasting Co., Inc., et al.* v. *Federal Communications Commission et al.,* 395 U.S. at 390, June 9, 1969.

> *product—cigarettes. Governmental and private reports . . . assert that normal use of tis product can be a hazard to the health of millions of persons. The advertisements in question clearly promote the use of a particular cigarette as attractive and enjoyable. Indeed, they understandably have no other purpose. We believe that a station which presents such advertisements has the duty of informing the audience of the other side of this controversial issue of public importance—that however enjoyable, such smoking may be a hazard to the smoker's health.**

The FCC's action was upheld in a court of appeals. In 1969 the Supreme Court refused to review it.

A Review of the Situation at the End of the 1960s

In 1949 the Fairness Doctrine appeared to call only for responses to editorials. Twenty years later it seemed to have reached the following proportions:

1. *Editorial Response:* The concept had been clearly established and there was a minimum of confusion about it. More and more stations were editorializing and there was little dissatisfaction with the requirement that time be made available for response.

2. *Personal Attack:* This was the specific item that led to the *Red Lion* case. Although there were still questions about what might constitute a personal attack liability under the Fairness Doctrine, no further cases had arisen to demonstrate that broadcasters found the provision troublesome.

3. *Extension to Political Campaigns:* The FCC had specified that presenting an editorial in favor of or opposing a candidate incurred an obligation to give time for response. It had also ruled that if a noncandidate used station facilities to take a stand on a candidate or on a campaign issue, then time must be given to another noncandidate for response. (If a candidate were to demand and receive time to respond, Section 315 would require that all other candidates for the same office might also demand equal opportunity.) Yet to come was the Zapple ruling of 1970 that extended the Fairness Doctrine to everything in a campaign not already covered by Section 315. In effect, the commission was to rule that use of facilities by a political party or by a committee for the election of a candidate was subject to the equal-opportunity principle already discussed. The extension of the Fairness Doctrine added few problems for broadcasters since they were so accustomed to working with Section 315 and since most of them wanted to observe the fairness concept in political campaigns anyway.

---

* Letter from Federal Communications Commission to Television Station *WCBS-TV*, 8 FCC 2d 381, June 2, 1967.

4. *Free Time to Respond:* The commission had established the principle that if a Fairness Doctrine obligation is incurred in a sponsored program, free time must be given for the response.

5. *Countercommercials:* The courts had upheld the FCC requirement for cigarette countercommercials, but the commission had stressed it would not consider its action in the field a precedent. It clearly did not wish to extend the doctrine in this area.

6. *Program Types:* In its 1963 statement the FCC said a station had a Fairness-Doctrine obligation whenever it permitted use of its facilities for views on controversial issues. The commission said the form did not matter—whether or not a controversial statement was an editorial was insignificant. There were no specified limitations on program types.

7. *Bona Fide News:* The commission had granted Fairness-Doctrine exemption to personal attacks very similar to the exemption granted to political candidates appearing on news-type programs in the amendment to Section 315.

12.6 THE 1970s QUESTIONS

When the Supreme Court in 1969 upheld the Fairness Doctrine in the *Red Lion–RTNDA* case and refused to review the Banzhaf cigarette-commercial ruling, broadcasters felt the commission had been given a green light on the doctrine, that the commission would continue the pressure and whatever happened in the 1970s would probably be worse than the confusion of the 1960s. The first few months of 1970 provided evidence that these fears were justified. The *Red Lion* decision opened the floodgates; the flow of complaints was stimulated by the climate of the times with the emergence of consumer, environmental, and antiwar advocacy. By 1971 Fairness-Doctrine protests and petitions were coming in to the commission at an annual rate of over 2,000.

The FCC staff appeared ready to extend the Fairness Doctrine into new areas. In the fall of 1969 the NBC Huntley-Brinkley evening news had done segments on the perils of aviation in which some thought the "ability of private pilots was put in an unfavorable light." Although NBC pointed out that it had only done interviews with typical commercial and private pilots to show the difference in experience and training without generalizing about all private pilots, the commission's staff ruled that the contrasting view on private aviation had not been represented. It ruled, therefore, that the newscast segments were a violation of the Fairness Doctrine and ordered NBC to indicate how it would balance the broadcasts.

It was not until several years later that broadcasters could see that just when the situation had appeared darkest, it was about to improve. Of the thousands of complaints received by the FCC in the early 1970s, not one was carried to a conclusion that significantly expanded the Doctrine. Courts that had supported expansion of the Fairness Doctrine in the 1960s began to have second thoughts and the tide of judicial support turned in favor of broadcasters. Commissioners themselves realized that the situation had to be stabilized. In 1971 FCC Chairman Dean Burch called the implementation of the doctrine "a chaotic mess" and two years later said in a speech to the Federal Communications Bar Association, "I am not prepared to rewrite the book, and I have no power to rewrite the Act, but I confess to a growing perplexity about the foundations of the Fairness Doctrine and its role in the regulatory scheme." Events were to persuade commissioners that the 1967 cigarette ruling had been a mistake.

Another indication that the FCC would draw back from further expansion came in September 1970 when the commission reversed its staff's recommendation on the NBC news ruling and said:

> *A policy requiring fairness, statement by statement or inference by inference, with constant governmental intervention to try to implement the policy would simply be inconsistent with the profound national commitment to the principle that debate on national issues should be wide open and robust.*

To summarize the development of the Fairness Doctrine in the early 1970s several cases have been selected that illustrate three questions about its extension into new areas. Each involves judicial reversals of the FCC, and one involves a double reversal where the Supreme Court, by reversing a court of appeals decision, upheld the FCC.

1. Must broadcasters sell time to initiate controversy?
2. Must the opposition be given time to respond to a response?
3. When do commercials violate the Fairness Doctrine?

Must Broadcasters Sell Time to Initiate Controversy?

In its 1949 statement of the Fairness Doctrine the FCC required each station to devote a reasonable amount of time to discussion of issues but said broadcasters could use their judgment on format and choice of spokesperson. Acceptance of broadcasters' judgment was at issue when two organizations went to the FCC with essentially the same issue: could broadcasters be compelled to sell time for controversy? Each organization was asking the commission to take the doctrine a step further. Rather than giving the broadcasters responsibility for selecting a speaker to balance points of view, each wanted the right to demand access to the airways to respond to materials that had been aired.

The first group was Business Executives Move for Vietnam Peace (BEM), an organization of some 2,500 business executives who felt people should be able to hear points of view about the Vietnam war other than those expressed by the government. Specifically, BEM thought the armed forces recruiting spot announcements carried by radio station WTOP-AM in Washington, D.C. presented an attitude toward the war that should be balanced by giving the other side. BEM taped spot announcements against the war and sent them to WTOP and other stations around the country. WTOP refused to air them as public service announcements (PSAs). When BEM asked to purchase time for the spots, the station still refused. BEM appealed to the FCC, arguing that if the commission upheld the station's right to refuse to sell time for the tapes, such a ruling would constitute a situation where an agency of government was acting to suppress an antigovernment policy.

The other group was the Democratic National Committee (DNC). It had asked to buy time from CBS for two purposes: to comment on public controversial issues in response to presidential speeches and to solicit funds. When CBS refused the request, the DNC went to the commission asking for a declaratory judgment that the network had an obligation to sell the time for both purposes.

The FCC first disposed of the DNC request for a ruling on buying time to solicit funds, agreeing that the network was required to permit such purchases. The commission then considered simultaneously the DNC and BEM demands that they be permitted to purchase time to air their views on controversial issues. It rejected the two requests and ruled that the Fairness Doctrine required broadcasters to decide when it was necessary to balance viewpoints and to find the speakers for the other side.

BEM and the DNC appealed the decision to the court of appeals in Washington. A year later the court shocked both the commissioners and broadcasters by ruling that the FCC had been wrong. The gist of the court decision was that if a station sold time for the purpose of selling products, it could not refuse to sell time for the discussion of public issues. The court said that licensees were trustees for the people in use of the public airwaves and might not arbitrarily decide what issues were important enough for debate. Broadcasters felt the court ruling would have altered the entire philosophy of broadcast operation and regulation. Assuming the Fairness Doctrine still held in a revised form, broadcasters would have had to sell time for controversy and then make free time available to answer the paid statements. By the time licensees had put into the schedule all those who wanted to buy time to talk about the many controversial issues and then accommodated all those who wanted to respond, the licensees would have no freedom left to program what they wanted. They would have approached being a common carrier like the telephone company with no control over the content of the transmissions.

Two years later the Supreme Court reversed the appeals court decision and returned the situation to what it had been when the FCC rejected the BEM and DNC requests.* The Fairness Doctrine had not been extended into the new dimension that had been so feared. Balancing viewpoints was still broadcasters' responsibility and they were not required to sell time to those who wished to enter a controversy.

Must the Opposition Be Given Time to Respond to a Response?

In the early months of 1970 the DNC was keeping a tally on President Nixon's television usage and brought to the attention of broadcasters what they had already noted—that in the sixteen months since his inauguration President Nixon had been carried by the networks a total of twenty-one times. There had been eleven speeches and ten news conferences. No previous president had requested nearly that amount of exposure. (Congressional Democrats were also concerned and had asked the networks to give them time to respond to the President.)

Frank Stanton, president of CBS, responded to the DNC and Democrats in Congress with a dramatic announcement. Because of its concern with possible presidential domination of the airwaves (not only immediate but long-range) CBS proposed setting aside time for a program to be called "The Loyal Opposition." There was no commitment to offer it on a regular basis, but when it seemed that a current or future president had used so much time that response was needed, the facilities of the network would be extended to the opposition.

Early in July 1970 Lawrence O'Brien, DNC Chairman, took advantage of the offer and appeared on CBS-TV making a slashing attack on the administration and many of its policies—in the Vietnam war, civil rights, the environment, and the economy. There was an immediate demand from the Republican National Committee (RNC) for time in which to respond to those items in O'Brien's speech that had not been included in earlier presidential speeches. The RNC claimed that because O'Brien had discussed issues not introduced by the president, the Fairness Doctrine required that the Republicans have a chance to answer. CBS refused the request and the RNC complained to the FCC.

---

* *Columbia Broadcasting System, Inc.* v. *Democratic National Committee*, 412 U.S. 94, May 29, 1973.

The following month the FCC held that since O'Brien had commented on issues not raised in presidential speeches, CBS should give the RNC an opportunity to respond. The obvious result of such reasoning, if carried to an extreme, would be that if the RNC raised new issues, the DNC could ask for more time and so long as each continued to break new ground in the debate, it would never end. The FCC took note of such a possibility but held CBS to be at fault for not restricting O'Brien to those issues that had been raised in the president's speeches. However such restriction could have been made only by asking O'Brien for a copy of his script in advance and then censoring inappropriate material. Such action would have been quite inconsistent with the principle that stations should not censor discussion on issues.

In November 1971 the appeals court, to which CBS had gone for relief, reversed the FCC. It pointed out that censorship of the O'Brien speech would be much worse than having a speaker bring up new areas. The court also stingingly suggested that the Republicans on the FCC might have been more interested in protecting the president than in regulating broadcasting in the public interest. Unfortunately, "The Loyal Opposition" was discontinued by CBS.

When Do Commercials Violate the Fairness Doctrine?

It was noted in Chapter 7 that one of the important constraints on commissioners is the need to be consistent with precedents. Nowhere is this more clearly illustrated than in the applicability of the Fairness Doctrine to commercials. When the FCC in 1967 extended the Fairness Doctrine to cigarette advertising, it stressed that the extension was not to be a precedent since the situation was so unique. On several occasions in subsequent years when there were protests against commercials for various products, the commission repeated its assertion and refused to act. Three years after its Banzhaf ruling, the commission found that it was not always possible simply to declare that a decision was not to be a precedent.

In April 1970 (about the time of the BEM and DNC petitions) the FCC received a complaint from an ecology group, Friends of the Earth (FOE). FOE contended that serious health problems were caused by high-powered automobiles and leaded gasolines that polluted the atmosphere. Since these hazards were not totally dissimilar to those associated with cigarette smoking, FOE felt broadcasters should be required to give time for countercommercials pointing out the danger in the products being advertised. It made such a request of WNBC-TV in New York City and, upon being refused, went to the FCC.

The FCC dismissed the FOE petition referring to its earlier statements that the Banzhaf ruling was not a precedent. FOE then appealed to the courts. A year later a decision was handed down that just as the FCC had once decided that cigarettes were a Fairness-Doctrine issue, so now the court found that high-powered cars and leaded gasolines were also controversial in the area of health. The court suggested, however, that countercommercials might not be the only recourse. The FCC was told to decide whether or not WNBC-TV in its overall programming had adequately presented the other side.*

The commission called on WNBC-TV and FOE to discuss procedures. Both agreed that a study of programming over a twelve-month period would be reasonable. WNBC-TV went through its schedule for the year preceding the FOE complaint extracting all news and other items that had presented the health hazards in the products under consideration. When the results of the study were presented, the commission decided that both sides had been adequately represented and again dismissed the FOE complaint.

A somewhat different issue concerning commercials was raised in 1971 when FOE joined with the Wilderness Society to protest some Exxon commercials on NBC that had argued the need for immediate implementation of plans for the Alaska Pipeline. This was shortly after the discovery of large oil reserves on the Alaskan North Slope. The only way the oil could be efficiently transported to civilization was by pipeline. Many conservationists were saying the pipeline and accompanying roads would seriously injure the environment and that if there were a break in the pipeline, the impact would be disastrous. Specifications for the pipeline were at that moment a subject of court review and action by the administration. In short, the pipeline was highly controversial.

The two conservation groups asked NBC for time to respond to the Exxon commercials. When the network refused, they went to the FCC. The commission held that when a commercial entered areas of controversy (other than the value of the products) the Fairness Doctrine was applicable. NBC was directed to supply a record of all its news and other programming presenting the dangers of the pipeline. After considering the report, the FCC relieved the network of need to broadcast further material.

The principle of keeping controversy out of commercials seemed to be clearly established and broadcasters themselves policed commercials to make sure no Fairness-Doctrine issues were being raised. When something did get on the air, the situation was remedied without recourse to the FCC. For example, a year after the Exxon controversy, a complaint was sent to WRC-TV (NBC O&O in Washington, D.C.) about commercials it had been carrying for the Association of American Railroads. Wally Schirra, the former

---

* *Friends of the Earth* v. *Federal Communications Commission,* 449 F. 2d (D.C. Cir.), August 16, 1971.

astronaut, was acting as spokesman for the association and in one commercial spoke favorably of a transportation bill then pending in Congress. Since the bill was highly controversial and still in legislative discussion, NBC agreed tht countercommercials should be aired and voluntarily made time available for them.

During the oil crisis in the spring of 1974 the Mobil Corporation wanted to use some of its commercial time to defend the role of the major oil companies in the situation. Commercials were prepared in which Mobil sought to give its position relative to American efforts to cope with the problems. The commercials were considered controversial and all networks refused to carry them, even when Mobil offered to buy additional time in which others might give countercommercials.

12.7 THE 1974 FAIRNESS DOCTRINE REPORT

In June 1974, twenty-five years after it issued the Fairness Doctrine, the FCC attempted to clarify its position in light of the confusion that had grown through the years. The 1974 "Fairness Report" resutled from an inquiry begun in 1971. From it the following points emerge:

1. The goal of the Fairness Doctrine is to foster "uninhibited, robust, and wide open" debate on controversial public issues.

2. The Fairness Doctrine calls for balance in overall programming rather than in each individual program. There is no need for a precise balancing of time on both sides so long as a licensee feels there is a balance in the schedule.

3. It is a licensee's responsibility to determine when there is need for balance and to pick the speakers.

4. A licensee must provide a reasonable amount of time for the presentation of discussion of controversial issues. Such presentation must include the opportunity for opposing viewpoints. If no speaker for an opposing side appears, the licensee has an affirmative responsibility to seek one out.

5. The FCC will not examine any charges of misrepresentation in news programming unless there is evidence of a deliberate attempt to distort information.

6. There was an attempt to lay the Banzhaf ruling to rest for all time by saying it had been a "serious departure from the ruling's central purpose—an informed public." The commission criticized its own 1967 ruling by saying, "While such an approach may have represented good policy from the standpoint of the public health, the precedent is not at all in keeping with the basic purposes of the Fairness Doctrine." Henceforth it was to be assumed that standard commercials for products made no meaningful contribution to informing the public on issues.

7. Commercials that enter into controversial matters of public importance incur a Fairness-Doctrine responsibility.

8. The report rejected a suggestion by the Federal Trade Commission (FTC) that the Fairness Doctrine be invoked when commercials made claims based on scientific premises that were in dispute and when commercials were silent about negative aspects of the advertised products.

9. The right of access to the airwaves was rejected while broadcasters retained responsibility for seeing that there are spokespeople who would provide balance in the schedule. "Thus, while no particular individual has a guaranteed *right* of access to the broadcast microphone for his own self-expression, the public as a whole does retain its 'paramount right to receive suitable access to social, political, esthetic, moral, and other ideas and experiences' " (emphasis in original).

10. The report restated the principle enunciated in the letter to Nicholas Zapple to the effect that the Fairness Doctrine applied to all aspects of campaigning not covered by Section 315. The one departure from Fairness-Doctrine precedent was that there was no obligation on a broadcaster to give free time to respond to a paid political program or announcement.*

12.8 THE "FORGOTTEN HALF" OF THE FAIRNESS DOCTRINE

In its 1974 report, the commission reiterated (paragraph 4 above) the responsibility of a licensee to provide a reasonable amount of time for the presentation of discussion of controversial issues. This principle dated back to decisions made in the mid-1940s and was clearly enunciated in the original 1949 Fairness Doctrine. It had been honored in the breach, however, as the commission focused its attention on trying to ensure fairness once a field of controversy had been entered. *Broadcasting* referred to it as the "forgotten half" of the Fairness Doctrine when reporting on a 1976 FCC letter to WHAR(AM), a top-40 radio station in Clarksburg, West Virginia.

In 1974 Congress was considering legislation on strip mining. Representative Patsy Mink (D-Hawaii) sent to a number of stations a tape she felt was needed to counter a program that had been provided by the U.S. Chamber of Commerce. WHAR refused to carry the tape on the ground that it had not been carrying any programs on strip mining and, therefore, did not need it to balance something that had already been aired. The station later specified that it had not been carrying any "local" programs but it was also unable to document any outside items on the subject.

A complaint about the station's refusal to carry the tape was filed with the FCC by lawyers for the Media Access Project (MAP). After consideration,

---

* In the Matter of the Handling of Public Issues Under the Fairness Doctrine and the Public Interest Standards of the Communications Act. FCC Docket No. 19260. June 27, 1974.

the FCC informed the station that it had violated the Fairness Doctrine by failing to cover an issue that was of great importance to its community and gave it twenty days in which to report on its plans to remedy the defect. This case puts all licensees on notice to honor their responsibility to provide time for treatment of locally controversial issues, even if they have not been treated previously.

SUMMARY

The road from the fairness concept underlying portions of the 1927 Radio Act to the Fairness Doctrine of the 1980s was long and difficult. Since 1940 the commission has been consistent in its search for guarantees of the public's right to receive a balanced presentation of different points of view. The *Mayflower* decision reflected the FCC's view that if different sides were not presented, there should be no discussion at all. Editorializing and allowing response amounted to a better way of meeting the commission's objective. The functionalist-free-speech approach led to attempts to ensure that broadcasters would provide access to controversy even beyond those areas they entered of their own volition. Broadcasters were consistent in their opposition to all actions likely to affect their freedom to program in the public interest as they saw it.

The Fairness Doctrine is no longer the source of great controversy it was in the early 1970s. It poses a serious threat only to those broadcasters who are extreme in their disregard for the need to air controversy and to give the public an opportunity to hear opposite points of view. In its 1976 *WHAR* decision, the FCC indicated that strict adherence to the Fairness Doctrine was the single most important requirement for operation in the public interest. The continuing problem for both commissioners and broadcasters is the application of that abstraction to specific programming practices.

GLOSSARY ITEMS

The following words and phrases used in Chapter 12 are defined in the Glossary:

Bona Fide News	**"Great Debates"**
Clear and Present Danger	**Lowest Unit Charge**
Countercommercials	**Public Service Announcement (PSA)**
"Equal-Time Law"	**Zapple Doctrine**
Fairness Doctrine	

FAIRNESS DOCTRINE CHRONOLOG

1941   Mayflower Decision—Broadcasters cannot editorialize.

1949   Issuance of "Fairness Doctrine"—Broadcasters may editorialize if they assume affirmative responsibility to give opposing speakers a chance to respond. Must also devote reasonable amount of time to discussion of issues.

1963   Fairness Doctrine Advisory issued by FCC mandated
1.   opportunity for response to personal attack,
2.   opportunity for response when noncandidate (including broadcaster) takes partisan position in political campaign,
3.   opportunity for response when programming touches on controversial issue such as segregation.
Extended Fairness Doctrine to all controversy, regardless of program type.
Broadcaster must provide free time for response to attack in paid program.

1964   Fairness Doctrine primer issued by FCC.
Origin of the *Red Lion* case.

1965   FCC ruled WGCB must give equal opportunity to respond to personal attack.

1967   Washington appeals court affirmed FCC stand in *Red Lion* case.
FCC raised Fairness Doctrine to level of rules:
1. In case of personal attack,
2. In editorials endorsing or opposing political candidates.
RTNDA appealed to court to invalidate Fairness-Doctrine rules.
Bona fide news programming exempt from personal-attack aspect of Fairness Doctrine.
FCC ruled in Banzhaf case that cigarette commercials are covered by the Fairness Doctrine.

1968   Chicago appeals court upheld RTNDA in ruling out Fairness Doctrine.

1969   Supreme Court decision in combined *Red Lion–RTNDA* cases affirmed the FCC's Fairness Doctrine.

1970   FCC staff ruled NBC violated Fairness Doctrine in Huntley-Brinkley newscast on private pilots.
FCC reversed staff ruling on NBC newscast on private pilots.
Origin of *BEM* and *DNC* cases. FCC said stations and networks not required to sell time for controversy.

Origin of *FOE* case. FCC said Fairness Doctrine not applicable to product commercials since cigarette ruling was unique.

"The Loyal Opposition" on CBS. FCC said RNC had right to respond to O'Brien comments not pertinent to presidential remarks.

FCC in Zapple letter said Fairness Doctrine covered everything in political campaign beyond scope of Section 315.

1971   Appeals court reversed FCC in "Loyal Opposition" case and said RNC not entitled to opportunity to respond.

Appeals court reversed FCC in *BEM* and *DNC* cases and ruled that stations and networks must sell time for controversy.

1973   Supreme Court reversed appeals court on *BEM* and *DNC* cases and upheld FCC stand that time need not be sold for controversy.

1974   NBC issued Fairness Doctrine report summarizing its position on many issues.

1976   FCC said WHAR had violated Fairness Doctrine by failing to program on the controversial subject of strip mining.

1978   Supreme Court upheld FCC policy of not considering Fairness-Doctrine application to product commercials.

PREVIEW *There was an abortive attempt to start educational radio in the 1920s but it was not until the reservation of FM channels in 1945 that substantial progress was made. In the early 1950s educators realized that decisions with long-range implications were being made in television and persuaded the FCC to set aside reserved channels for educational institutions. Throughout the rest of the 1950s progress was slow and disappointing in spite of massive assistance from the Ford Foundation. In the 1960s the federal government committed funds to public broadcasting and there were reasons to hope that public television would shortly become quite significant. The expectations with which the medium entered the 1970s foundered on a confrontation with the Nixon administration which, in turn, caused former allies CPB and PBS to oppose each other in the area of program control.*

CHAPTER 13

PUBLIC (EDUCATIONAL) BROADCASTINGS

When the Freeze ended in 1952, commercial television grew steadily until it became the dominant mass medium. Public (educational) television, on the other hand, started slowly and developed erratically in an atmosphere of constant crisis. To participants and observers alike, educational television was both exciting and disappointing. Its current status is controversial and defies precise description. The situation was a continuation of the history of educational radio whose roots go back to 1920.

13.1 1920–1935 THE BEGINNINGS

Among those claiming to be the first radio broadcasters was the University of Wisconsin at Madison. Its professors were operating a transmitter before Dr. Conrad's 1920 experiments that led to KDKA in Pittsburgh. When the scientists at Wisconsin and other institutions had developed a technical capability, other faculty members wanted to use it for educational radio. Some institutions entered the field with great enthusiasm, seeing radio as a way of giving everyone the equivalent of a college or high school education. It was assumed that if a microphone were placed in a classroom, people in their homes would want to listen and benefit from the lectures and discussion. By 1925 there were about 170 stations operating at various educational levels. But it became clear that the public would not tune in to academic programs of the kind being offered and that operation of stations that would attract audiences required both skills and dollars that were not available to educators. Aside from a handful of midwestern stations, where radio was part of the extension services to rural audiences, most educators were disappointed in their broadcast efforts and ready to give up.

At the same time it had been demonstrated that profits could be made from commercial stations. As soon as a frequency was released by an educator, someone else applied for it. By the early 1930s only a couple of dozen educational radio stations remained on the air and the dream of formal home instruction by radio had proved to be unrealistic. Some were still convinced that educational radio had an important potential and on several campuses there were faculty members who were studying the medium, working with commercial stations, and acquiring the skills needed for successful educational operations. But when they went to the Federal Radio Commission for new licenses, they were informed there was no longer any available space on the spectrum for them.

When Congress passed the Communications Act of 1934 it responded to pressure from educators by directing the new FCC to report on the advisability of setting aside some frequencies for use by educational institutions. After hearings the FCC recommended there be no educational reservations since commercial stations were required to operate in the public interest which would require cooperation with educators.

13.2 1935–1945 EDUCATORS ON COMMERCIAL STATIONS

For the next ten years most educators could broadcast only in time provided by commercial stations. In some instances an excellent cooperative arrangement existed. One of the most prestigious discussion programs of the time was NBC's "University of Chicago Roundtable." In central New York two commercial stations paid two-thirds of the construction costs of a radio workshop on the campus of Syracuse University which then served as the public service department of each of them.

But in far too many instances the results were disappointing. Part of the fault lay with some educators who went to stations with the condescending attitude that they knew more about broadcasting than those who were doing it all the time. Those educators implied that if the commercial broadcasters would step aside, the educators would show them how it should be done. The response of station personnel was to withdraw and let the educators proceed without any of the advice and help they really needed. It was in those years that educational programs received the reputation of being extremely dull. It was also a time in which an unhealthy antipathy was built up between educators and broadcasters.

The FCC was kept aware of educators' desire for their own frequencies and in 1938 set aside space for them on the VHF spectrum. It could not be used at the time since there were no appropriate receivers, but the ruling heralded a continuing regulatory interest in educational broadcasting. When FM radio was authorized in 1940, five of forty channels were assigned to educational institutions but they remained comparatively unused due to wartime shortages of materials.

In 1945 the FCC was making plans to move FM radio to a higher spectrum position where there appeared to be room for some 4,000 stations, compared with the fewer than 1,000 AM outlets at the time. Under the leadership of the U.S. Office of Education, educators petitioned the commission to set aside a sizable portion of the new channels for their exclusive use. Because the FM spectrum appeared to be almost infinite, there was no opposing voice urging the FCC to deny the educators' application. Thus, when 100 FM channels were assigned from 88 mHz to 108 mHz, the twenty channels between 88 mHz and 92 mHz were reserved for educational institutions wishing to use them without advertising support.

13.3 1945–1950 GROWTH OF EDUCATIONAL FM

In the early postwar years between 1946 and 1950 educators paid little attention to television; they were too busy thinking about FM, which assured them ample opportunity for broadcasting. The number of educational stations grew slowly from six to over sixty during the five years, although many of them were low-powered having only ten watts. At the same time, there was an increased availability of time on commercial FM stations which were having trouble finding program material. Educators were highly enthusiastic about radio.

13.4 1950–1952 ASSIGNMENTS FOR EDUCATIONAL TELEVISION

It was in 1950, when the Freeze was two years old, that educators realized the FCC was about to establish a pattern for national television and that it was a medium in which they should be involved. They wanted television channels set aside for education as they had been reserved in FM some five years earlier. There was, however, a significant difference in the two situations. No one had actively opposed the assignment of FM channels to education, but there was strong opposition to a similar reservation of TV channels. By 1950 it was becoming clear that not only was television the medium of the future, but also that there was a scarcity of desirable channels. Operators of AM radio stations who wanted to get into television realized that every TV channel assigned to education meant one fewer available for commercial operation. It was inevitable that the NAB, consisting of commercial broadcasters, would oppose educational-television assignments.

Although educators had a reputation for being ineffectual in political situations, they were able in 1950 to organize more effectively than anyone would have expected. Seven educational groups of national scope cooperated to form a new organization called the Joint Committee for Educational Television (JCET).

The initial problem of any new organization is raising money. The JCET was among the first to receive grants from the Ford Foundation. Henry Ford's will had provided that control of the company would remain in the family but that the bulk of his holdings would, for tax purposes, be given to a foundation for use in nonprofit activities. After his death it had taken time to settle his estate and it was 1950 before the foundation was ready to start thinking about how to use its money. Few at that time had any idea of the eventual stature the Ford Foundation would reach, but it became clear five years later when there was a series of grants to the endowment funds of over 4,000 private colleges, universities, and hospitals. The foundation's purpose was to disburse dollars that had accumulated faster than they could be spent. The total amount given away at one stroke to use up income without touching the capital was $500 million.

The JCET was able to interest the Ford Foundation in its problems and received a small organizational grant with an invitation to return when more was needed. (During the next two decades educational television was to receive more than $250 million from the Ford Foundation and its subsidiary Fund for Adult Education and Fund for the Advancement of Education.)

The next problem was employment of a lawyer. Theoretically, any person or group can go directly to the FCC and present arguments and petitions. Nevertheless, as in a courtroom situation, it is wise to have a lawyer who knows his or her way around and can organize materials in the most effective way. One difficulty in selecting a JCET lawyer was that all the experienced attorneys of the Federal Communications Bar Association already had commercial broadcasting clients and would have a conflict of interest if they represented the JCET. It might have been possible to hire some young person who had just been admitted to the bar and would work cheaply, but such a move would have been to invite failure in a very difficult undertaking.

The JCET finally employed Telford Taylor as its attorney. Taylor had been general counsel to the FCC from 1940 to 1942 and had then entered the Army. He had served as United States chief of counsel for war crimes trials from 1946 to 1949. Not only was he thoroughly at home with the FCC, he was also one of the most respected lawyers in the country. Furthermore, he represented no commercial broadcaster and would have no conflict of interest.

In their preliminary deliberations the educators calculated they needed 10 percent of all television assignments reserved for their use. Realizing one rarely gets everything requested, they drew up a petition asking for 25 percent. When the petition for a quarter of the channels was presented to the FCC, the stage was set for a confrontation between the JCET and the NAB.

The NAB was not motivated solely by the fact that commercial radio operators wanted Television channels—it had a genuine philosophical disagreement with the educators. The NAB argued, as the FCC had in 1935, that all licenses are granted "in the public interest." The NAB argued further that every commercial operator realized this fact and was fully prepared to cooperate with educators. Furthermore, by putting a few programs on commercial stations, educators would reach much larger audiences than they could hope to achieve all day long on their own stations. Commercial operators would build up audiences and then deliver them to educators so they might do truly significant programming. The few educational radio stations on the air had done very poorly in attracting audiences and it was not in the public interest to let some of the television channels remain practically unused in terms of the numbers of people who would view them.

The arguments of the JCET started from quite different premises. Attention was called to public education generally throughout the country. For three reasons it appeared that schools were going to need outside assistance to an extraordinary degree if they were to meet the coming challenges. First, the postwar baby boom would greatly enlarge school enrollments. Second, education had become increasingly complex; from 1939 to 1949 humanity had doubled its entire store of knowledge and would probably redouble it again by 1959. There was much to be taught beyond the three Rs. Third, there was an anticipated shortage of teachers. During the war many industries paid more than schools, and teachers left their profession. It appeared there would not be enough of them to serve the huge numbers of students who would need to learn so much.

The thesis of the JCET was that the educators were not in need of a half-hour here and a quarter-hour there. Rather, they needed their own stations so that during the day they could help meet the needs of public and private schools and colleges and during the evening present adult education.

One of the most significant persons in the fight for educational stations was Frieda Hennock, the first woman to serve on the FCC. She had been a lawyer in New York City and was appointed to the FCC by President Truman. She made no secret of her interest in educational television. In the hearings the JCET organized the educators who were to testify and the NAB coordinated the appearances of commercial broadcasters. Hennock usually asked educators questions that would elicit the most favorable responses. Commercial broadcasters had cause to suspect that she and the JCET had worked together on questions to ask the commercial representatives. After a broadcaster had made the statement that educators had no need for reserved channels because time would be made available for them to reach large audiences on the commercial stations, Hennock might ask about the broadcaster's personal experience during the ten years from 1935 to 1945, when the relationship between educators and broadcasters had been so unsatisfactory. She was able to present affidavits from educators stating that the broadcaster had usually denied them time on a radio station when they had asked for it.

When the hearings and deliberations were ended, the FCC announced that it had reserved 12.5 percent, or 242 out of 2,000 channel assignments, for education. Technically, the channels were labeled "noncommercial." But in response to an inquiry from the city of New York, the commission specified that they would be licensed only to *bona fide* educational institutions or organizations. Some of the reservations were extremely valuable— VHF channels in Boston, Pittsburgh, Chicago, and San Francisco. Two-thirds were in the UHF band, which eventually turned out to have little commercial value. Educators immediately began to receive warnings from commissioners that they should start making plans to use the reserved channels or they might lose them.

In April 1952 the FCC announced the Freeze would end in June. Because there was such a backlog of applications, the FCC also announced that for the next year it would devote all its efforts to granting licenses in accordance with its table of assignments and would consider no applications for changes in the table. At that point, the NAB said it agreed that one year was a reasonable length of time to give educators to apply for licenses. At the end of the year commercial broadcasters would feel free to apply for any educational reservation on which no action had been taken. The issue was clarified a year later.

John Doerfer had been nominated to be a member of the FCC in the spring of 1953. He routinely appeared before a Senate subcommittee as a prelude to a vote on confirmation. A member of the subcommittee was Senator Tobey of New Hampshire who had become well known through televised hearings on organized crime. When Doerfer was asked for his reaction to the proposition that if no action were taken on an educational reservation for one year, commercial broadcasters should be permitted to apply for it, he indicated that he could see nothing wrong with it. At that point Senator Tobey proclaimed that those reservations should be maintained forever, that education was too important to be shunted aside just because it could not move in a short time. He called upon the FCC then and there to make it clear that those reservations had been made "in perpetuity" and said if he did not immediately get such reassurances he would call a meeting of his Senate Commerce Committee and demand an accounting from the commissioners. Shortly thereafter, Acting Chairman Rosel Hyde announced that the educational reservations had indeed been made in perpetuity and the commission had no intention of turning them over to commercial use. Thus, whether it took an educational institution or group one or five years to make application, the channel would be there for its use.

13.5 1952–1960 LAYING THE GROUNDWORK

In June 1952, when the Freeze was lifted, there was speculation as to how rapidly educators would be able to move in activating their stations and which would be first on the air. It was estimated that the cost of each would be about $250,000 and few institutions could afford to spend that amount. The Ford Foundation offered a matching grant to help any educational group get started. For every dollar raised or committed to a new station, Ford would add another 50 cents up to a maximum of $150,000. Thus, if an institution had $200,000, Ford would add another $100,000, pushing it over the top.

Patterns of Ownership

The commission made it clear that competing applications would not be entertained for an educational channel in a community. If more than one institution or group were interested in getting a construction permit, the FCC would wait until they had worked out some kind of cooperative arrangement and could submit a joint application. In the next decade three patterns of educational-station ownership emerged.

1. Some stations were licensed to a single private institution, such as a college or university. If money were available to that single body, it would be able to move much more rapidly than if it were cooperating with several

others, and the first stations were started in this manner. The drawback to having a station operated by a single institution was that the operating budget loomed rather large in the expenses of the college or university and if there were hard times, television was one of the items easiest to cut.

2. Some stations were licensed to governmental agencies, either a state commission or university or a municipal board of education. It was in the midwest that educational radio had been most satisfactory and it was there also that states began making the first of the governmental plans for educational television. A state university can move with reasonable speed (although it must work through the state legislature) and a state university's television budget is not as conspicuous as it would be when included in the expense of a private institution. Generally, the state-operated stations and systems appeared later than those licensed to private institutions.

3. The type of organization that emerged latest but was in many respects the most successful involved organizing a new community group for the purpose of building and operating a station. It took time to bring together representatives of public and parochial schools, colleges and universities, art museums and historical associations, and other cultural components of a community. However, once they were organized, the new entity had a broad base of support.

Such groups normally started by asking the local board of education to set aside money for daytime operation of in-school programs. Then large gifts would be sought from corporations, businesses, and wealthy citizens while small five- and ten-dollar donations would be solicited from the other citizens. While they never seemed to be fully free of financial problems, the community stations had such a wide range of support that they nevertheless weathered their crises. As a matter of fact, the community stations generally were more outstanding and significant on the national scene than the other types.

The First Stations

In 1953 the first two educational stations came on the air. Each was licensed to a single private institution; KUHT to the University of Houston, and KTHE to the University of Southern California. A couple of years later the danger of station operation by a single institution became apparent when the University of Southern California lost the support of the wealthy oilman who had given money for the station. He stopped his donations, the university was unable to get community funding, and the station went off the air.

Programming was an even more important problem. The first stations appeared to be very amateurish when compared with the commercial network and station offerings seen in their communities. This situation was to be expected. Even the wealthiest commercial stations today with their VTRs and ample funds rarely produce more than an hour a day of completely local programming. When educational stations came on the air they were forced to fill three or four live hours a day without any recording capacity and without adequate funds or experienced personnel. The result was predictable—as educational radio programming in the late 1930s was written off as dull, so educational television in the mid-1950s received the same label. Televised lectures and panels discussions simply did not have wide audience appeal.

National Educational Television

The Ford Foundation had anticipated the problem and had moved to fill the need by funding the National Educational Television and Radio Center (NETRC). (In 1959 it became known as simply National Educational Television [NET] and for simplicity that appellation will be used throughout.) Money was provided for purchasing a kinescope recorder (at about $50,000) for each educational station and for several colleges that had their own production facilities. Each was then invited to submit proposals on programs it would be able to produce well if there were money available. For example, a station in Texas might submit a prospectus for doing a thirteen-week series on the culture of Indians in the Southwestern United States at a total cost of $39,000. If the NET program staff in Ann Arbor, Michigan approved the proposal, it would contract with the station to produce the programs in its studios and to make a kinescope recording of each. The kinescopes would be sent to Ann Arbor for duplication and distribution to other educational stations around the country.

NET then organized a "bicycle network" that worked as follows: The first program in a series would be mailed to Station A which would show it and then mail it to Station B. In the second week Station A would show the second program while Station B would show the first. Each would mail its copy to the next station, and in the third week Station A would be showing the third program, Station B the second, and Station C the first. In this fashion, each series would eventually be seen in its entirety on all stations in the group. Such programming had to be comparatively "timeless" in character since some episodes would not be shown on some stations until a year or more after production. A few outstanding programs are still remembered: "Japanese Brush Painting," which stimulated such interest that it became difficult to find necessary painting supplies; "The Great Plains Trilogy," which gave the history of mid-America; and "The Religions of Man," which led to searching discussion among viewers. Among the best children's programs was "The Finder" with Sonny Fox.

Two important limitations plagued the NET bicycle network in the mid-1950s. First, too many of the programs were done by local stations with local production standards and too frequently were of more local interest than national. While local production was not necessarily a fatal flaw, it did mean that in comparison with the schedules of the commerical networks, the educational programs were poorly produced and uninteresting to the majority of the viewing public. Local production did little to lift from educational television its reputation for presenting dull material.

Even more significant was the fact that the programs were being circulated by kinescope film recordings which are inherently limited in quality to the point that one immediately knows if a program has been recorded rather than presented live. Although NET took every possible precaution to maintain high kinescope quality, it could never eliminate the basic technical inferiority. Viewing was therefore restricted to those whose interest in the subject matter was intense.

When the Ampex Corporation demonstrated its new videotape recorder in 1956, all networks and some stations immediately placed orders for the first models which cost about $75,000 each. Shortly thereafter, the Ford Foundation donated funds to purchase a VTR for every educational station plus several more at Ann Arbor for duplicating purposes. By the end of the 1950s NET had overcome one of its two major deficiencies and was distributing technically superior program recordings on videotape. Its next step was aimed at improving the program schedule—it moved its headquarters to New York City, the heart of television production and criticism. It heralded the hope that in the 1960s educational television would move to more significant levels.

13.6 1960–1970 GREAT EXPECTATIONS

Aside from educational reservations made during the Freeze and the early support of the Ford Foundation, there was little about educational television in the 1950s to ignite either excitement or enthusiasm. The medium made only slow headway and had little impact on the public. In the 1960s some of the earlier efforts came to fruition and there was help from other sources.

Educational Station for New York City

NET felt it could achieve significant program advances only if it had a strong affiliate in New York City that could draw on professioanl talent and attract the attention of the major newspaper and magazine critics. Channel

25 had been reserved for educational use in the city, but by 1960 it was clear that a UHF station could do comparatively little in competition with VHF stations, and there were seven commercial VHFs in New York.

One of the seven was Channel 13, assigned to Newark, New Jersey. It had been activated in 1948 by Atlantic Television, Inc. (WAAT-TV), and its transmitter was located with those of the New York stations on the Empire State Building. In 1958 the sale of WAAT-AM, -FM, and -TV to National Telefilm Associates (NTA) for $3.5 million was approved by the FCC. Channel 13 became WNTA-TV but over the next two years did very poorly and eventually was on the air only eight hours a day.

In the early months of 1961 NTA announced that Channel 13 was for sale and several commercial groups expressed an interest in purchasing it. In March the FCC announced its intention of locating educational stations on the VHF band in New York and Los Angeles. It was apparent that there would be no approval for sale of WNTA to a commercial company and negotiations were halted. A community group was formed in New York City, headed by John White, president of NET, that entered into negotiations with National Telefilm Associates.

Later in the year the station was sold to Educational TV for the Metropolitan Area (ETMA) for slightly over $6 million. (This was the same television station that along with associated AM and FM radio entities was sold for $3.5 million three years earlier.) ETMA received major grants from the commercial networks ($500,000 each) and the independent stations in New York. The rest of the money was raised from corporations, individuals, and, of course, the Ford Foundation. A waiver was received from the FCC permitting location of the main studio in New York City, although it was also necessary to maintain a smaller studio in Newark.

NET Programming

WNDT (TV), *New Dimensions in Television*, came on the air in 1962 and in the following year there was a significant change in NET's programming. To that point, practically all programs on the bicycle network had originated as concepts with the individual stations. In 1963 NET formed its own programming staff that took over the function of originating program ideas, some of which were produced by NET staff personnel and some of which were still contracted out to the strongest of the educational stations. It then became possible for NET to build a network schedule with programs that constituted a unified whole. Production values gradually approached those of the commercial networks since NET was able to hire personnel with commercial experience who wanted to work in a situation free of commercial pressures.

NEWTON N. MINOW b. 1926

Courtesy: Chicago Public Television

When Newton Minow joined President Kennedy's "New Frontier" in 1961 as chairman of the FCC, he was practically unknown to either broadcaster or critic. Three months later his name was familiar to both and he had coined a phrase that became a rallying cry to those who felt television was ignoring society's needs. Accepting an invitation to address the annual convention of the NAB, Minow challenged broadcasters to take time off to watch a full day of their own programming.

He then assured them that if they did so, they would observe "a vast wasteland."

Born in Milwaukee, Wisconsin, he obtained undergraduate and law degrees from Northwestern University. For two years he was a law clerk to Chief Justice Vinson of the Supreme Court. He then became a special assistant to Governor Adlai Stevenson of Illinois and worked on the latter's campaign for the presidency of the United States. From his campaigning and later work in the Democratic party Minow developed ties that led to his selection as chairman of the FCC.

Minow was given much credit for making commercial Channel 13 in the New York City area available for purchase by a community educational group. As FCC chairman he let it be known that the creation of VHF educational stations in New York and Los Angeles was of the highest priority and that if there were an application to transfer Channel 13 to a commerical operator, it would be subjected to the most intense scrutiny and exhaustive hearings. Purchase by community interests was thus facilitated making feasible the subsequent movement of NET to New York and its resources.

Following his years with the FCC Minow became executive vice president, general counsel and a director of Encyclopaedia Britannica, Inc. At the same time he was chairman of the Chicago Educational Television Association and an important force in bringing WTTW (TV) in Chicago to its current status as one of the half-dozen strongest public television stations in the country. In addition to his continuing interest in WTTW, he also served as chairman of the Public Broadcasting Service in the late 1970s.

This situation represented the breakthrough that made educational television a significant factor in the American system of broadcasting. Among the outstanding NET offerings of the 1960s were "Spectrum," a series presenting science topics for laymen; "The Great American Dream Machine," a magazine format series; "An American Family;" and "VDBlues." Some of these programs were carried on the PBS interconnection in the 1970s. There were also individual dramas presented in a series called "Playhouse." The network schedule was better organized, programs had national interest and were produced to high standards, and they were distributed on videotape which was technically equivalent to live presentations. Since the bicycle network still took time for distribution, there was no capacity for doing up-to-the-minute programs that would be feasible only with an interconnected network.

The Educational Television Facilities Act of 1962

During the 1950s about forty-seven educational television stations had come on the air financed by state and local governments, educational institutions, foundations, corporations, and individuals. However, there were many more ready to join the ranks as soon as money could be raised. In 1962 the federal government made its first financial commitment to educational television. Congress amended the Communications Act to provide grants that could be used for educational television facilities. The amount, $32 million dollars over five years, was not large in terms of the total federal budget, but it did provide an important impetus for stations that had completed everything but the final funding. The Secretary of Health, Education, and Welfare was authorized to grant up to 75 percent of the total cost of a project to activate a new station or improve the facilities of an existing operation. The 47 stations at the beginning of the 1960s nearly doubled to 92 in 1965 and redoubled to 190 by the end of the decade.

Ford's Domestic Satellite Proposal

Toward the second half of the 1960s, the Ford Foundation continued to be educational television's major patron and stimulant of exciting ideas. Most foundations prefer to make "seed money" grants to enable a recipient to start an activity that will then become self-supporting. Ford had been the major contributor to educational television for sixteen years and felt the time had come to use more of its resources for other purposes. It therefore proposed in 1966 that the Foundation spend $80 million to finance a domestic satellite system that could distribute network television programming throughout the country less expensively than could AT&T with its co-axial lines and microwave relays. The profits of the system were to be turned over to educational television. Although the plan was not accepted by the FCC, it was heartening to know that attempts were being made to solve both the distribution and long-range financial problems of educators.

The Carnegie Commission on Educational Television

In January 1967 the Carnegie Commission on Educational Television issued a report that was expected to be significant. It had been studying the future of the medium for over a year under a $500,000 grant from the Carnegie Corporation. Its membership was distinguished under the leadership of James Killian, president Emeritus of MIT and a long-time public servant. President Johnson and key congressional leaders had indicated their interest in the report as a basis for possible legislation.

The report started with a new name for an old concept. In an effort to eliminate the unfortunate connotations of the word "educational," the Carnegie Commission referred to the medium as "public television."

The Carnegie Commission noted that the annual budget for all public television was about $58 million exclusive of the current grants to support NET. These dollars came from the federal government under the facilities act, from state and local governments, foundations, and others. The commission concluded that it would require a massive infusion of federal funds if public television were to approach its potential. The commission saw the federal government as the major source of new funds and proposed the creation of a group to be known as the Corporation for Public Television that would be nonprofit and nongovernmental. It was to be the channel for federal and other dollars going to program development, research, production, and support of individual stations.

To avoid political interference with public television, the commission recommended "permanent funding" whereby the government would impose an excise tax of 2–5 percent on new television sets. The dollars would be collected by the government and turned over to the corporation without requiring congressional action beyond passage of the original act. To further separate it from government there was to be a board of twelve members, six to be appointed by the president and confirmed by the Senate and the other six to be chosen by the original appointees.

The corporation was to make provision for a live interconnection for programs to all public television stations. NET was praised for its contributions to past efforts and designated as one of at least two major program suppliers for the corporation.

Reaction was generally favorable. The Ford Foundation praised the report since it promised that government would take over some of the heavy burden of supporting educational television. CBS was so enthusiastic that it pledged a gift of one million dollars on the day the new Corporation became operational. The individual public stations felt this was what they had long needed to give them relief from their financial crises. NET was less enthusiastic since it anticipated becoming one of several rather than the only program supplier.

The Public Broadcasting Act of 1967

In February 1967, President Johnson recommended legislation to Congress based on the Carnegie report and signed the new legislation into law that November. However, there were two areas in which the new law deviated from the Carnegie recommendation. First, its concern was broadened to include radio as well as television. The central group was known as the Corporation for Public Broadcasting (CPB) and some of its efforts were directed to the older medium.

More significantly, there was no provision for "permanent funding" or an excise tax or any other source of income dedicated for the CPB. Instead, the law provided that CPB be given nine million dollars for the first year and that further funds be appropriated by Congress in the future. The Board was to include fifteen members to be appointed by the president and confirmed by the Senate, with no more than eight from one political party.

The failure to include permanent funding was not surprising in view of the doubts many members of Congress had about governmental involvement in communications. Even though the 1967 act contained safeguards against political interference, the current Congress would not commit funds for the indefinite future in an area where there were no precedents. There was a split among educators. Some assumed that things would still work out in the long run. Others felt it would be better for educational television to continue in its current state of uncertainty than to permit the building of a system whose future would be at the whim of politicians each year.

The Public Broadcasting Laboratory

In 1967 the Ford Foundation granted ten million dollars to Columbia University for a two-year "Public Broadcasting Laboratory" (PBL). The laboratory was to consist of Sunday night programs distributed live to all the educational stations in the country. Emphasis was to be on news and public affairs. PBL was beset by problems from the start.

Ford had announced the Columbia University grant before the university had fully agreed to take on the project. Thus, there was the highly unusual case of an institution refusing to accept such a grant, largely because it was planning a new fund-raising project and was afraid that a hard-hitting news program might scare off some of its corporate donors. Ford then announced the grant would be administered through NET but the network was to have no control over the content. This was offensive to the group that had done all of the national programming for educational television over the past ten years. However, NET could not refuse to cooperate with the foundation which had provided all of its money and so agreed to be a bookkeeper for the operation to be run by outsiders. The stations around the country were not entirely enthusiastic because they were being told they were expected to carry a program fed to them live without any opportunity to preview the material. Most of them were engaged in perpetual fund-raising activity and they were afraid, like Columbia University, there might be segments that would alienate some of those on whom they depended for donations. Furthermore, the stations felt this to be an abdication of their programming responsibility.

Finally, on the day of the first broadcast in the fall of 1967, full-page ads in some of the leading newspapers around the country proclaimed that people would have a chance to see the news covered in a way that commercial television would never dare to handle. The programs themselves were reasonably good but failed to come up to the standards of the advertisements. The series was on the air for two seasons. It was satisfactory, but when the two years and the ten million dollars had been expended, PBL left the air with comparatively little impact. It was important as the first live interconnection of educational television stations and as a preview of the problems in getting cooperation between divided central authorities and the growing number of diverse educational stations.

The Children's Television Workshop and "Sesame Street"

While the CPB was being organized the big news in 1968 was the formation of the Children's Television Workshop (CTW). Until that time children watched either cartoons, which were excellent "baby sitters," or "educational" programs, which were usually dull. Joan Ganz Cooney saw the need for a preschool program that would give young children (especially those in deprived neighborhoods) a head start on elementary education and that would entertain at the same time. Over the years, commercials on television had been more heavily researched than had programs; the technique of communication by short segments was well developed. It was Cooney's intention to use the techniques of commercials in preparing children for school.

In March 1968 she received grants totalling between six million and eight million dollars for a two-year project to go on the air in the fall of

1969. The major donors were the Carnegie Corporation, the Ford Foundation, and the U.S. Office of Education. The resulting "Sesame Street" programs were among the highlights of public television, although they have been subject to criticism from some educators who have disagreed with certain aspects of the pedagogical approach.

In retrospect, most of the developments in educational (public) television were favorable in the 1960s. NET became a far more effective network, the federal government in two significant pieces of legislation assumed a commitment for advancement of the medium, and the CTW won accolades for the most exciting educational programs yet known.

13.7 1970–1975 CONFRONTATIONS

The 1960s appeared to have paved the way for great advances in the following decade. It looked as though all elements were ready to fall into place so public television could begin to achieve its potential. In the fall of 1971 events began to press upon each other. A *dramatis personae* of various participants would interact during the next few years in a highly complicated situation that must be followed step by step to understand the outcomes.

1. *CPB, the Corporation for Public Broadcasting:* It was dependent on Congress for annual funding and had yet to receive as much as the Carnegie Commission recommended. The funds for 1971–1972 had not been appropriated by the fall of 1971, but were to come to only $35 million (far less than requested). The organization of the corporation had been completed. The chairman of the board was Frank Pace, who had been secretary of the army and director of the budget for the federal government. CPB's president was John Macy, who had also had a long and distinguished career in government.

2. *PBS, the Public Broadcasting Service:* The Public Broadcasting Act of 1967 had directed CPB to assist in development of an interconnection system (the technical part of a network) but had specifically forbidden it to own or operate such an interconnection or a production facility. In 1969 CPB had fostered the organization of PBS to operate the interconnection. Although most of its funds were to come from CPB, PBS was designed to be autonomous. The original nine-member board consisted of five selected by the stations themselves, one each from CPB and NET, and two more chosen by the first seven to represent the public. PBS had planned for the fall 1971 season a ten-hour interconnection schedule each week—two hours a night, Sunday through Thursday. Its budget for the year was only seven million dollars, which accounted for the limited schedule. Its president was Hartford Gunn, who had built and managed WGBH-TV in Boston, one of the first and most prestigious of the educational stations.

3. *NPACT, the National Public Affairs Center for Television:* It was organized and funded by the Ford Foundation to serve as the source of news and public affairs programs for PBS. It came into being in the summer of 1971 and had hired two top newsmen to provide leadership. Sander Vanocur had been on the NBC news staff for fourteen years. Robert McNeil, who had earlier been with NBC in Chicago, had spent the preceding three years with the BBC in England. They were to head a staff of fifty-five to sixty people and to receive salaries commensurate with their earlier earnings. Vanocur was hired at $85,000 per year, and McNeil at $65,000.

4. *NET, National Educational Television:* After more than fifteen years as the only network for educational television, it was to become one of the PBS program suppliers. NET's president was James Day, who had organized and operated for many years KQED in San Francisco, one of the most successful community stations in the country.

5. *OTP, the Office of Telecommunications Policy:* It was organized in 1970 as a branch of the White House to speak for the administration on all matters having to do with broadcasting. Its director was Clay T. Whitehead who had been with the Nixon administration from the beginning as an advisor on communications matters. He had previously been with the Rand Corporation, a "think tank" in California.

6. *The Ford Foundation:* It had continued its grants to public television, filling in the gaps where CPB had received too little from Congress to accomplish its goals. Ford's main efforts were to support programming by NET and NPACT and to help fund the PBS interconnection costs that CPB was unable to meet.

The FBI Segment of "The Great American Dream Machine" —October 1971

A taste of future turmoil in public broadcasting came on Sunday, October 3, 1971, when PBS started its fall season. It scheduled "The Great American Dream Machine" which had been highly successful on NET. It had a magazine format, stimulated much discussion, and was acclaimed by the critics. In the first program of the new season was a twelve-minute segment that "contained interviews with three young men who asserted they had been assigned by the FBI to provoke violence within radical organizations." The tape for the whole program was sent by NET to PBS well in advance of air time. PBS previewed it and decided the FBI segment was insufficiently documented and asked NET to provide something else to fill the twelve minutes.

The NET reaction was that it had for over fifteen years been the network of educational (public) televsion and certainly knew as much about what was appropriate as did the new PBS. Furthermore, PBS was supposed to be only an interconnection, not a network that would control its programming. Therefore, PBS would either carry the segment as delivered or "go black" and present nothing for the period. The program was carried without the FBI segment and controversy erupted. NET announced plans to play the segment on Channel 13 in New York City the following Friday night and have the producers and critics discuss the censorship of its program. PBS President Hartford Gunn was invited to appear and he responded that not only would he be there, PBS would also schedule a live interconnection so stations across the country could carry this response.

It was then learned that the director of the FBI had written to NET protesting the segment before it had been sent to PBS. Although Gunn claimed he had not known of the FBI protest, this event appeared to confirm the fears of those who said taking federal money for public television would lead to censorship. The results of the Friday night debate were inconclusive. The participants were persuasive in explaining their positions and it was clear each side would have acted in the same way if the program were to be done over. The tensions were reminiscent of the PBL squabbles in 1967.

Whitehead's Speech to the NAEB October 1971

Later that month Whitehead, director of OTP, was a featured speaker at the annual convention of the National Association of Educational Broadcasters (NAEB). His topic was decentralization and it was obvious he had read the report of the Carnegie Commission more carefully and selectively than had his listeners. In presenting its report in 1967 the Commission emphasized that it had visited 92 of the 124 educational stations then on the air and had been in touch with the rest. Apparently it had been more impressed with the needs of the stations than with the need for strong central leadership for the report included the following:

> *The Commission believes that the first task, upon which any further accomplishment must be built, is the strengthening of the local stations. (p. 33)*
> *The local stations must be the bedrock upon which Public Television is erected, and the instruments to which all its activities are referred. (p. 36)*
> *Educational television is to be constructed on the firm foundation of strong and energetic local stations. The heart of the system is to be in the community. Initiative will lie there, the overwhelming*

*proportion of programs will be produced in the stations,
scheduling will be performed by the local station and staff.
(p. 87)**

It was Whitehead's premise that Congress in 1967 had intended a system
of public television founded on the "bedrock of localism" and he was supported by the individual statements cited above. His attention was especially
riveted on NPACT which was designed to be a news arm of PBS and which
was drawing very heavily on those trained in the commercial networks then
under attack by the Nixon Administration. The specific issue was whether
PBS was to be a network with control of its programs or simply an interconnection providing technical facilities by which the stations would exchange programs.

Whitehead's speech was depressing to public broadcasters, since it pre-
saged their being joned with commercial television as a target of administration antagonism and pressure. Furthermore, in his position of formulating administration policy, Whitehead was a most important individual
in determining White House recommendations to Congress on CPB funding.

Budgeting by Congress

In February 1972 the White House submitted OTP-proposed legislation to
Congress calling for allocation of $45 million to CPB in the coming fiscal
year with the condition that one-third of this money be immediately handed
over to individual public radio and television stations. For the next few
months intense debate about the future of public broadcasting centered on
the issues of "localism" and whether PBS should be a network or an interconnection agency. The principal protagonists were, on one side, CPB
and PBS supported by NET and most of the stations and, on the other side,
the OTP supported by President Nixon and the conservative "silent majority."

It was the OTP thesis that the Public Broadcasting Act of 1967 had
been designed to strengthen public television at the local level and that
CPB's primary function was to channel federal dollars to the stations. It
was argued that the three commercial networks were covering national
news and issues and that public stations should emphasize other areas. The
act had mentioned "interconnection" and PBS should, therefore, be a device
for selecting the best programs being done by the stations, helping them
with the financing, and then distributing them to the rest of the public
system. In effect, OTP was arguing for a return to the programming phi-

---

* Carnegie Commission on Educational Television. *Public Television: A Program for Action.*
New York: Harper, 1967.

losophy of the original NET in the mid-1950s when programming concepts were originated at the local level and the distributed programs had been produced to local standards. The only difference would be live distribution as opposed to the bicycle network.

CPB and PBS, on the other hand, believed that public television stations should present a balanced service, that local stations should not only engage in local programming, but should also have access to coverage of national issues and events in ways not presented by the commercial networks. History had shown that broadcasting became significant only when there was centralized networking. If public television were to make an impact on society, it needed its own network. CPB and PBS argued, furthermore, that public broadcasters themselves should be permitted to make the final decisions about programming emphasis.

Disposition of the Budget—Spring and Summer 1972

Congress was persuaded by CPB and PBS and passed a two-year bill that would have given CPB $64 million in 1972–1973 and $90 million in 1973–1974. But in July 1972 President Nixon vetoed the bill with a restatement of his belief that CPB had assumed too much control over local stations. Presidential news secretary Ron Ziegler announced that CPB would continue on year-by-year funding until there was some kind of reorganization that would free the stations by lessening the control of CPB and PBS.

Changes in CPB Leadership—September 1972

Following the Nixon veto, CPB Board Chairman Pace and President Macy resigned their executive posts saying it was essential for the CPB leadership to be more closely attuned to the administration. For the next month the picture was bleak and confused.

In September 1972, with a Republican majority for the first time, a new CPB leadership team was installed. The chairman of the board was Thomas B. Curtis, vice-president and general counsel for *Encyclopaedia Britannica* and a former Republican congressman from Missouri. The new CPB president was Henry Loomis, who had been deputy director of the United States Information Agency (USIA). In the 1940s Loomis had been an assistant to MIT President Killian. In the early 1950s Loomis had been one of the first Eisenhower supporters and went to Washington in 1953 as an assistant to the president. He later became director of the Voice of America and was retained in that position by Presidents Kennedy and Johnson until he split with Johnson on news policy about Vietnam. He took office as CPB president professing no expertise in public television but with a conviction that tax dollars should not be used for controversial programming. It was his belief that CPB should use most of its dollars to help stations and to provide instructional and cultural programs. It appeared that in the coming months PBS would be more closely aligned with the stations than with the CPB in the fight for congressional funding.

Following Nixon's landslide victory in November 1972, the OTP appeared to have more power than ever. In December Whitehead delivered his "carrot-and-stick" speech in which he offered commercial stations longer licenses if they would assume more local control over the news they broadcast. There was clearly an attack on television over a broad front that included both the commercial and public sectors.

Control of the Interconnection

As 1972 came to an end, CPB moved to assert some control over national programming that had previously been left entirely in the hands of PBS. CPB did so by naming specific programs it was prepared to fund for another year and omitting several that had been produced by NPACT along with others that were known for their "liberal bias." Since the earlier practice had been to give money to PBS and let it make all programming decisions, a showdown was imminent.

CPB vs. PBS—Winter 1973

During January and February 1973 a struggle took place between CPB and PBS. Attempts were made to work out an acceptable compromise on control of the programs to be distributed, but by March the prospects for settlement were dim. CPB issued a statement pledging to carry on in a "spirit of maximum cooperation" with PBS. But it added that "the ultimate responsibility and accountability to Congress for the proper use of the interconnection facilities funded by CPB" rested with the Corporation.

At this point PBS was in danger of being ignored to the point of oblivion. There were two centers of power: CPB with the money appropriated by Congress and the individual stations that broadcast the programs from whatever source. PBS had been strong because of its association with CPB and now feared that CPB might bypass it and start working directly with the stations. The prospect of losing all national programs frightened the stations who wanted to be able to include in their schedules programs with a broad orientation that would lend balance. Each station wanted a maximum degree of autonomy but not so much that it couldn't draw upon programs of broad scope.

The solution was for PBS to take over representation functions, thus speaking for the public stations in addition to providing the interconnection service. If the stations were to refuse to cooperate with CPB, the corporation might become obsolete and meaningless. While this outcome was unlikely, it was real enough so that CPB had to deal with PBS in a new light when the latter organization became the official representative of the stations. At the same time, Whitehead's localism demands were being partially met. PBS decisions in the future were to be considered actions of the stations it represented.

Search for Funding—Spring 1973

While CPB and PBS were trying to work out a compromise on program control of the interconnection, both joined in trying to persuade Congress again to pass a bill providing enlarged funding for two years. Whitehead opposed any funding beyond a single year at a restricted level. He made two primary points about public broadcasting as he saw it:

> *The distribution of programming over the interconnection system by PBS amounted to precisely the kind of federally funded "fourth network" which the Congress sought to avoid. . . .*
> *Another problem area is the funding of public-affairs programs. . . . Reliance on federal monies to support public-affairs programming is inappropriate and potentially dangerous. Robust electronic journalism cannot flourish when federal funds are used to support such programming*

These comments were made in the spring of 1973 when the Nixon administration was still basking in the glow of its great landslide of the previous November election and before Watergate began to occupy its attention and sap its power.

Attempts at Compromise—Spring 1973

In April a CPB negotiating committee headed by Chairman Thomas B. Curtis worked out a compromise with PBS for presentation to the full board. PBS would continue its responsibility for scheduling the interconnection; PBS could schedule programs that were not funded by CPB. If there were controversy about such a program it would be referred to a "monitoring board" made up of three CPB trustees and three PBS trustees. A majority vote (four of the six) would be required to keep a program off the network. CPB would continue funding the programs it wished to sponsor. If the stations disagreed with any program decision of the CPB program department, there was a complicated ritual that would leave matters ultimately in the hands of the respective chairmen of CPB and PBS.

As with any compromise, this one left neither side completely happy, although PBS could feel it had gained a minimal victory. Chairman Curtis had every reason to believe he would be supported by the entire board when the compromise was presented. To his surprise and dismay the board deferred action and voted to disband the old negotiating committee while forming a new one and asking for a "cease fire" until something could be worked out.

Chairman Curtis bitterly submitted his resignation amid talk that the OTP had killed the compromise by telephone calls to board members urging them to vote against it. Reportedly, Curtis had accepted the chairmanship during the preceding year only after assurances from the White House that he would be free to use his own judgment in the office. While it is probable that President Nixon may not have known the details of the situation, most observers had little doubt that the president's Office of Telecommunications Policy had sabotaged the compromise.

The only man to whom CPB could turn at such a time was Vice-Chairman James Killian who had chaired the original Carnegie Commission that had recommended the corporation in the first place. He enjoyed the confidence of everyone involved and, in spite of ill health, agreed to become the chairman. In June 1973 a second compromise was announced and approved. It was essentially similar to the one turned down by CPB two months earlier. PBS maintained control of the interconnection subject to elaborate schemes to resolve controversies, but it was to receive no money from CPB to spend for programs. Program dollars were to be spent by CPB itself or given directly to the stations to pay for the programs they wanted on the interconnection. This was the localism for which Whitehead had been fighting so hard.

The Outlook in January 1974

At the start of 1974 public broadcasters hoped that the worst was behind them. The cooperation between CPB and PBS was working reasonably well. President Nixon had finally signed an authorization of $47.5 million for the current year. In January congressional leaders came to a Washington conference sponsored by PBS and vowed to keep fighting for long-range funding. Vice-President Gerald Ford attended and praised public television for meeting needs overlooked by commercial broadcasters.

PBS could point with pride to a number of series that has attracted favorable reviews. The science series "Spectrum" of the 1960s had been replaced with the even more impressive "Nova." From the BBC had come "Masterpiece Theater" and "Civilization." "Washington Week in Review" and "Wall Street Week" were analyzing the general and economic news. There was excellent cultural programming on "Theater in America" and "Dance in America."

The Station Program Cooperative

An essential element in the 1973 compromise between CPB and PBS placed more responsibility for program selection in the hands of the local stations. Stations used their CPB funds for programs on the interconnection through a mechanism called the Station Program Cooperative (SPC) that was unveiled in early 1974. The SPC gives stations an opportunity to make interconnection program decisions by indicating what they are willing to purchase for their program dollars. In the beginning of the planning period of each year PBS circulates to the stations a long list (perhaps a hundred) of programs that will be available. All stations go through the list and indicate which ones they are willing to buy at the quoted prices. Then the list is pared down by eliminating those with the fewest station votes. After going through several rounds of station choices, PBS finally has a list of programs to be distributed and the income from individual stations to pay for them.

Those skeptical of this plan feared that local station managers worried about losing support from local donors might avoid all public-affairs programs and choose only the safer cultural and instructional offerings. While some controversial programs were left out of the schedule, from the beginning NPACT programs were represented as well as other series touching on current issues. A more serious deficiency has been the tendency of stations to spend their money for acceptable series programming that will fill more hours than outstanding documentaries or specials. If PBS lists two possibilities at the same cost to a station—a one-hour documentary and a series of thirteen half-hour programs—most stations will opt for the latter which, with repeats, will fill thirteen hours in a year as opposed to only two hours that would be filled by the former offering.

Funding Sources for Programming on the Interconnection

Since the compromise of 1973 the PBS schedule has consisted of programs funded from four distinct sources:

1. Programs chosen by the stations and paid for through the SPC with CPB and local dollars.

2. Programs funded directly by CPB. For the most part, these are pilots of series that CPB thinks would be appropriate for the interconnection in

subsequent years. By funding the first programs, CPB gives the stations an opportunity to see and evaluate them and to decide if they would like to pay for them through the SPC later.

3. Programs funded by the Ford Foundation (through NET and NPACT), by other foundations, and federal projects.

4. Programs funded by commercial companies through the "patron plan." Although a public station can carry no advertising, it can carry programming funded by a commercial company. Furthermore, FCC regulations require it to give courtesy announcements at the beginning and end to the effect that "presentation of this program was made possible by a grant from ————." Among the most prominent of the patrons providing programs in the early 1980s were the large oil companies. Mobile, for example, purchased rights to the British "Masterpiece Theater" and Gulf paid for a series of National Geographic specials after none of the commercial networks would carry it.

The patron plan is controversial. Commercial broadcasters feel that it is a form of commercialism and that the patrons are interested only in generating goodwill among certain people who can be better reached by public stations than by the commercial outlets. Critics of public television wonder whether the public broadcasters can be objective in producing shows about business after becoming dependent on commercial dollars for some outstanding programs.

The Public Broadcasting Financing Act of 1975

The 1973 compromise between CPB and PBS over control of the interconnection and the Station Program Cooperative that emerged from it seemed to satisfy the Nixon administration. In 1974 Whitehead suggested a plan that would fund CPB for a five-year period. Among Nixon's last actions in the summer of 1974 was sending the Whitehead proposal to Congress with his endorsement. The result was the 1975 Public Broadcasting Financing Act.

The original plan was for Congress both to authorize and to appropriate funds for five years with gradually escalating amounts. Congress, however, removed the appropriation item so the authorized dollars would have to be voted on separately every one or two years. To encourage the solicitation of other money Congress authorized only one federal dollar for every $2.50 raised from other sources. It also mandated that some of the money voted to CPB must be used for instructional television.

Although public broadcasters felt that five years was medium-range funding and would have preferred long-range or permanent funding, and although there was disappointment that the whole appropriation was not actually made, a mood of optimism did prevail after the passage of the bill. It was assumed that under a new president the days of confrontation were past and that the medium could proceed with its plans for the future.

13.8 1975–1980 MINIMUM PROGRESS AND DISAPPOINTMENT

The latter half of the 1970s did see some encouraging progress in public television. Budgets were gradually increased, but they failed to keep pace with inflation and there was a significant increase in audiences—although not enough to be reported by Nielsen and Arbitron. Unfortunately, most of the outstanding programs were acquisitions from other sources that were funded by corporations under the patron plan and thus did not signify that the system itself was improving.

PBS on the Satellites

The movement of PBS to satellite distribution led to a reorganization of its services into three parallel networks:

PTV 1—the "Blue" service—responsible for prime time programming in culture, public affairs, and entertainment.

PTV 2—the "Red" service—to handle special events and other programs that did not fit neatly into one of the other two services.

PTV 3—the "Green" service—to present instructional programs for school and college students.

Thus, with simultaneous transmissions, the stations had a greater selection of programs that might be taped for inclusion wherever most desirable in the schedule although it was hoped that prime-time programs would be carried live, making possible more effective advertising to build audiences.

Cultural Threat from Cable

Although the PBS audiences were small, comfort could be taken from their loyalty as evidenced by their participation in fund raising—both by making donations and by working on drives. This loyalty stemmed mostly from the fact that public television was the only regular source of cultural programming of a high order. Two fall 1980 announcements in the field of cable may presage even more difficulty for PBS than lack of funding.

Warner-Amex announced that its satellite cable transponder, used during the day for "Nickelodeon" children's programming, would be used at night to transmit a cultural service produced by ABC. Almost simultaneously, a new venture, Rockefeller Center Television, announced a pay-cable program service concentrating on "high-quality entertainment." Its first acquisition was an exclusive contract for all BBC programming. Although PBS gets only about 4 percent of its schedule from the BBC, there is still concern because that small amount has included the most attractive programs on public television. The question is the degree to which the entry of cable into cultural programming will take away a significant portion of the audience that has been so loyal and so essential to PBS and its affiliates.

Carnegie Commission II

The disappointments in public television were spelled out by a second Carnegie Commission labelled Carnegie II. It was formed at the request of those who felt the promises of Carnegie I in 1967 had been unfulfilled and that it was time to take another long-range look at the problems and possible solutions. Very early in its 1979 report, Carnegie II generalized, "We find public broadcasting's financial, organizational and creative structure fundamentally flawed." Referring to public television's "attempt to invent a truly radical idea," it continued, "sadly, we conclude that the invention did not work, or at least not very well." The demise of the dream was traced back to the confrontations of 1972 and 1973.

The report indicates the commission felt it was CPB and the stations that had most seriously failed in their responsibilities and focused little blame on PBS, which had been buffeted between them. The most significant error of CPB was seen as its participation in the programming process—a constant source of tension between CPB and PBS. Carnegie I felt that CPB's first function was to insulate the system from politics. However, dating back to the first CPB-PBS confrontation of 1973, CPB had also maintained a complete program department and had directly funded productions of which it approved. The Carnegie commissioners thought this situation was not only an unhealthy split in programming responsibility, but also a hindrance to CPB in its primary mission of keeping politics out of public broadcasting. In addition, the board "took action to downplay public-affairs programming in order to avoid placing the entire federal appropriation in jeopardy."*

At the same time the stations were faulted for being too concerned with surviving and not rocking the boat. "Stations have found that the best vehicles for fund-raising have been programs that do not threaten the audience's sense of well-being. . . . It is not the programs that are made, but

---

* Carnegie Commission on the Future of Public Broadcasting, *A Public Trust*, (New York: Bantam Books, 1979).

the programs that are not made, that cause concern. . . . The system of dependence on underwriters has created little incentive for local public-affairs programs, for programs that serve small or less affluent audiences, or for controversial programs that may offend." To the extent that most of the stations' boards of directors and most of the contributing audiences came from the more affluent in the community, it is easy to see that most programs will have as their first requirement not to offend the establishment. Not only in public stations' local programming but also in their voting in SPC, there has been the tendency to play it safe and opt for quantity over quality.

It was noted that while the stations were responsible for the survival of PBS in the 1973 confrontation with CPB, they still did not want a strong central network. Whitehead's emphasis on a bedrock of localism had struck a responsive chord in station managers and they were not about to surrender control to the "Washington-Boston axis." As a consequence, there was little in either local or national programming that might have qualified as providing leadership for society.

The recommendations of Carnegie II focused on the need for more money and "tinkering" with the system to lessen the possibility of political intervention. CPB was to be replaced by a Public Telecommunications Trust with primary responsibility for being a fiduciary agent of funds and insulating the system from political pressures. There was to be a separate Program Services Endowment to undertake preparation of national programs, presumably to be distributed by PBS although the programming role of the interconnection was not spelled out.

Proposed Cut in CPB Funding

Public television's problems of the late 1970s were compounded with the election of the Reagan administration in 1980. Early in the budgeting process it was proposed that the subsidy to CPB be cut by 25 percent. In a period of high inflation, that would amount to a "real" cut of over a third from levels that CPB had been planning on. Since the original projections had never been overly generous, the cuts will make for very real difficulties in the coming years.

13.9 NATIONAL PUBLIC RADIO

The 1967 Carnegie Commission report was devoted entirely to educational television and its long-range development. When they saw that radio had been ignored, the educational radio stations circulated information about the background and importance of their medium and persuaded Congress to pass a Public *Broadcasting* Act rather than a Public *Television* Act. CPB had found ample guidance for its television activities in the Carnegie Commission report but had no corresponding basis for proceeding in radio.

In 1969 CPB commissioned a study of educational radio that uncovered several discouraging facts. Although there were more than 400 educational stations on the air, there was great diversity among them. About half operated with a power of only ten watts on FM. Many were operated by educational institutions primarily as a training ground for commercial broadcasting. Most had an annual budget of less than $10,000 and no full-time professional staff. Operating hours were few and irregular. There was a program exchange using tape but no centralized authority to provide overall leadership. In short, there was no national educational radio system comparable with the one that had developed in television in the 1950s.

In 1970 CPB identified eighty stations that met minimal criteria in terms of power, personnel (one full-time staff member), and schedule (at least forty-eight hours a week for forty-eight weeks in a year). To these eighty stations CPB made grants to upgrade their facilities and to produce programs. To parallel PBS in television the CPB created National Public Radio (NPR), a program and distribution service controlled by the member stations. Gradually the requirements for membership were increased to five full-time staff members and a minimum schedule of eighteen hours a day for 365 days a year. While public controversy raged about whether PBS should be a network or an interconnection, NPR quietly proceeded to form a network that turned into a strong program service. As the number of its affiliates doubled in the next five years from the original eighty, its audience also increased.

In the mid-1970s NPR was termed one of the best-kept secrets in broadcasting but by 1980 the situation was quite different. Its programs were being carried on 230 stations throughout the country and the combined budgets for NPR and its affiliated stations from all sources were in excess of $130 million per year. Its cumulative audience came to more than five million persons per week. The best-known and most successful program was a daily news magazine show, "All Things Considered," but NPR was pioneering in other ways. To many listeners, a drama series called "Earplay" brought back the glory of early radio that had been lost in commercial broadcast operation.

13.10 ISSUES AND PROBLEMS IN PUBLIC BROADCASTING

As public television enters the 1980s its problems are essentially those it had in the mid-1970s, as highlighted by the Carnegie II report. There are four basic and interrelated questions to be raised and answered:

1. What is public television's identity?

2. Can federal dollars be separated from politics?

3. Which comes first—programming or dollars?

4. Who will provide leadership for public television?

What Is Public Television's Identity?

The overriding problem facing the medium is its own identity and the resulting programming. So long as the label "educational" television was used, there existed a degree of agreement on what it meant. ETV was generally expected to provide instructional programs geared to curricula at various levels, adult education programs (helping listeners solve personal problems, understand the news and civic issues, and make better use of leisure time), cultural programs exposing the audience to the various arts, and programs that would prepare children for formal schooling. It was in those terms that the JCET had argued for educational reservations in 1950 and it was in those terms that the FCC set aside about 250 channels to be used by educational institutions.

When the medium became "public" television, the limits of its concerns and expected programming beyond clear-cut education were no longer so clear. Some people equated public television only with the use of public funds. Some interpreted its mission as providing "alternative programming," which meant analyzing the commercial schedules and filling in the gaps. Might that extend so far as to cover entertainment programming? This view seemed to justify the televising of tennis matches in the early 1970s when there was little coverage of that sport by commercial networks. Is public television justified in continued televising of sports events in direct competition with commercial stations and networks?

Others feel that public television should look at society and program to meet the needs it finds. If one were to program either to fill the gaps in commercial schedules or to meet the greatest needs of the greatest number of people, one of the first priorities would be doing something for minorities. Indeed, specialized programming like "Black Journal" received impressive accolades for public television before being axed by CPB in its fight with PBS over control of the interconnection. In the 1980s many blacks, Puerto Ricans, Mexican-Americans, Chinese-Americans, American Indians, and other minorities feel they have little more hold on public television than on the commercial sector. They are underrepresented in both programming and employment.

Which Comes First—Programming or Dollars?

The failure of public television to do more programming for minorities illustrates the dilemma of the public station. It is never financially secure and must program for those who will reciprocate with membership dollars.

The most obvious potential donors are members of the middle and upper classes who are searching for the culture and ideas that are not presented to their tastes on the commercial channels. Few dollars can be expected from the poor who are most in need of what public television could give. So long as public television stations are desperate for money, they will continue to program so that the rich get more and the poor are ignored.

It would be ideal if important philosophical decisions about identity and mission could be made without reference to pragmatic problems like raising money. From its very beginnings, however, educational television stations secured dollars from whatever sources appeared and then tailored their schedules to their revenues and to the expectations of those who had given the money. When the donors were foundations, programming reflected the interests of foundation executives. When the donors were commercial companies, programming reflected the desire of the corporations to secure a favorable image among certain viewers. When the donors were individual citizens, the programs were designed to so please them that their subscriptions would be continued another year. In effect, stations were forced to play the "numbers game" with an emphasis on demographic statistics related to the potential of raising money for the future.

Can Federal Dollars Be Separated from Politics?

The earliest television stations were dependent on local boards of education and state legislatures (through their university systems) for the part of their budgets that would enable them to get on the air and present instructional materials. So long as they were considered "educational" they were no more affected by political considerations than were the public schools and the state universities. The Carnegie Commission recognized the dangers of accepting federal operational funds and tried to provide safeguards against political interference by specifying a nonpolitical CPB membership and permanent funding.

The story of public television between October 1971 and the end of 1973 showed how completely the desire of the Carnegie Commission could be foiled. The Nixon administration made public television controversial and it is likely that Congress will not for many years enact permanent funding that would permit public television to pursue a philosophy that has not taken politics into account.

Who Will Provide Leadership for Public Television?

At any moment over the first twenty years it was easy to pinpoint the leadership of the medium. Beginning in 1950 the JCET was clearly leading the fight for educational reservations and then assisting educational institutions and organizations to put stations on the air. From the mid-1950s through the 1960s the mantle of leadership was on NET with its programming services and its discussions with stations. By 1968 educational telecasters were looking to the new Corporation for Public Broadcasting to provide leadership with federal dollars. For two or three years, so long as they had compatible philosophies, CPB and PBS worked together spearheading the drive for significance.

Whitehead's October 1971 speech to the NAEB marked the beginning of the end for effective national leadership of public television. The membership of CPB was changed. It and PBS were first split apart and then forced into a confrontation over control of the interconnection. As PBS became the representative of the stations, the confrontation was widened to include the distribution of the limited funds available. Neither party emerged with enough power to lead over 200 diverse stations.

No agency of the federal government has indicated a desire to move into the void. During World War II radio specialists in the U.S. Office of Education provided leadership in the quest for reserved FM frequencies and then stimulated discussion on their use. Today federal dollars for CPB and for facilities are channelled through the Department of Health and Human Services, which has grown so large that any concern it might have for public television is buried under mountains of other activities. The FCC sees itself primarily as a licensing agency and has made no effort to get public broadcasters together to discuss vital problems related to goals and missions. The OTP has shown little interest in public television since winning the fight to emasculate PBS and then initiating a bill to provide five-year funding. Congress has largely ignored public television beyond voting funds.

OTP Director Whitehead was the winner in his fight with the system. Public broadcasting has become a true democracy with power dispersed among the individual stations that have no mechanism for selecting effective leadership for even limited periods of time. In fact, most stations have no desire for such leadership. Each manager is constantly concerned with financial pressures that threaten the station's very existence. Each station manager must work with boards of directors or legislative committees, most of whom want to do the safe (conservative) thing. Station managers are normally cautious in making program selections through the SPC. They are concerned that no program in the schedule alienate those on whom the station is dependent for its funds. They must get as much programming as possible for each dollar they spend, which means choosing an inexpensive series over a more costly documentary or special.

Until effective national leadership emerges that can help public television decide on its identity and mission, formulate policy that stems from philosophical concerns rather than dollar availabilities, and persuade the federal government to keep politics out of funding consideration, there is little hope that the medium will become any more significant in our society than it has been, and it is possible that its importance will diminish.

SUMMARY

Three decades after the FCC set aside reservations for *educational* television at the end of the freeze, the future of *public* television is far from bright. It is impossible to name any one factor which, more than others, was responsible for the fading of a dream. Probably the 1967 change in nomenclature from "educational" to "public" was more important than it seemed at the time because it diffused the focus on the medium's identity. Certainly, it led to the confrontation with the Nixon administration and the intrusion of politics of the worst kind. The specialization in culture during the late 1970s left public television vulnerable to the threat of cable to program sources and to audiences. And the change in political mood leading to a conservative administration and a Congress committed to budget cutting was an additional setback at a critical time.

GLOSSARY ITEMS

The following words and phrases used in Chapter 13 are defined in the Glossary:

Bicycle Network	**Patron Plan**
Channel Assignments	**Permanent Funding**
Educational Reservations	**Public Television**
Educational Television	**Satellite Relay**
Interconnection	**Station Program Cooperative (SPC)**
Instructional Television	
Noncommercial Television	**Television Freeze**

PUBLIC (EDUCATIONAL) BROADCASTING CHRONOLOG

1922   First licenses to educators.

1925   171 educational AM stations on the air.

1935   24 educational AM stations on the air.
FCC recommended there be no special educational allocations. Start of ten-year period of cooperation between educators and commercial stations.

1938   FCC assigned VHF channels to educational radio.

1940   FCC assigned five educational FM channels.

1946   FCC gave educators twenty of one hundred reallocated FM channels.

1950   Educators formed JCET to seek ETV reservations.
JCET hired Telford Taylor as counsel.

1952   FCC assigned 242 educational television channel reservations—80 VHF and 162 UHF.

1953   Educational reservations extended for indefinite period.
First ETV stations start operations.
Organization of NETRC as programming service for educational stations.

1959   NET bicycle network used videotape.

1962   Channel 13 in New York City became educational.
Congress passed the Educational Television Facilities Act.

1963   NET began to produce its own programming.

1966   Ford Foundation proposed domestic satellite service with profits to ETV.

1967   First Carnegie Commission report and passage of Public Broadcasting Act.
Ford Foundation funded for two-year Public Broadcasting Laboratory.

1968   Formation of Children's Television Workshop.

1971   PBS started operation.
Controversy over the FBI segment of "The Great American Dream Machine" and NPACT salaries.
Whitehead's speech to NAEB on "localism."

1972   CPB budget controversy, Nixon veto, Macy resignation.
Loomis appointed president, Curtis chairman, of CPB.

1973   PBS reorganized as representative of educational stations.
CPB-PBS compromise on control of interconnection defeated, Curtis resignation, Killian's appointment to chairmanship, and effecting of new compromise.

1974   Beginning of Station Program Cooperative.

1975   Passage of the Public Broadcasting Financing Act, giving five-year funding authorization subject to periodic appropriations.

1976   CPB and PBS announced plans for interconnection by satellite.

1977   Formation of Carnegie II Commission on Public Television.
Loomis resigned as president of CPB.

1979   Carnegie II Commission published its report.

1980   PBS circulated programs to member stations by satellite.

PREVIEW

The different systems of broadcasting around the world reflect how different governments relate to their citizens, especially with respect to giving them access to a wide range of information and entertainment. The government-licensed free enterprise system in the United States contrasts most noticeably with the government ownership and operation of broadcasting in the majority of nations.

In 1941, the United States government started broadcasting to the rest of the world. The Voice of America and the television branch of the United States International Communication Agency have been the most visible users of broadcasting. Through the Agency for International Development the United States has unsuccessfully sought to encourage systems of effective broadcasting in many Third World nations.

CHAPTER 14

AMERICA AND BROADCASTING AROUND THE WORLD

In the 1950s the United States was the undisputed world leader in television. The British Broadcasting Corporation (BBC) which had begun telecasting twenty years earlier was having difficulty resuming its progress after World War II. Few other countries were even thinking about the new medium. In the ensuing thirty years television has emerged in practically all nations and there are many instances in which programming quality in other countries surpasses that here. Both the BBC and Independent Television in England have made great strides and their programs are among the mainstays of PBS. The NHK in Japan wins many international prizes for its public affairs and documentary programs. Japan has also led the nations in technology such as DBS. Russian television is known for its coverage of cultural events such as the Bolshoi Ballet. The European Broadcasting Union links many nations for sporting and other events.

Most of the progress in the rest of the world is little known to the average viewer in this country since Americans have traditionally had little interest in foreign broadcasting. Since the early 1930s our domestic service has been so extensive that few have felt the need to see foreign entertainment or to hear what foreign stations might want to say to the United States.

For a short distance from this country's northern and southern borders a few people tune to Canadian and Mexican stations. For the rest of the country foreign listening requires short-wave receivers, which have never been sold here in large quantities. By contrast, as World War II approached, people in many parts of the world were hungry for news and either had no domestic radio service or wanted more information than their stations were willing or able to give them. For these listeners international short-wave radio was a primary source of information through the 1940s.

It was not until the 1950s brought a budding dissatisfaction with American television that a few people in this country started looking to the British system as a way of avoiding the negative influences of advertising. At the same time, the United States placed greater emphasis on international broadcasting to implement its foreign policy objectives. As the world has grown smaller people have felt a greater need to know more about radio and television elsewhere and the ways in which to participate in worldwide broadcast communications.

14.1 SYSTEMS OF BROADCASTING

Radio stations now operate in practically every country of the world and only a very few people are beyond the reach of broadcasting. The number of nations without indigenous television is diminishing every year. One of the obvious differences among countries is the way in which each has chosen to control its broadcast facilities. Every country, when it was ready to start radio (and later television), had to make a basic decision about its type of system. This country opted for a government-licensed free enterprise system to which was later added a leavening of public stations that were not to be supported by sale of time for advertising. Frequencies were placed in private hands and the incentive for operation was the chance to make a profit. The majority of countries, however, chose to have their broadcasting under a government-owned-and-operated system. England devised the government-chartered monopoly in which the British Broadcasting Corporation (BBC) operated without competition for many years. A few countries adopted a combination of systems for radio. As television spread rapidly in the 1960s, an increasing number of nations that were reluctant to make the required large investments in the new medium by themselves also used some combination of the three basic systems.

Just as this country's system reflects its basic philosophy about government-citizen relationships and a desire that people have access to a wide range of ideas and entertainment, so do other systems reflect how other countries feel about these basic issues. The American system represents one end of a scale. The government-owned-and-operated system in a dictatorship is at the other end, and the government-chartered monopoly (which in England has become a duopoly) is in-between but reflects concepts closer to the American philosophy than to that of the Soviet Union or other authoritarian countries.

The Government-Owned-and-Operated System

The most prevalent system around the world is government ownership and operation in which facilities are state-owned, all personnel are state employees implementing government policy, and financing comes from government funds. Government ownership and operation derive from the belief that government is best suited to broadcast policy making and management or from a fear of the consequences if ideas inimical to government were permitted to circulate. Depending on which motivation is dominant, program philosophies range between a dictatorial effort to provide only a limited access to ideas and entertainment and a more benevolent attempt to provide the informational and relaxation programming that people may desire.

The Government-Chartered Monopoly System in England

It was natural that the Americans who first studied broadcasting in other countries should find the English system most interesting—in large part because those researchers could understand the programs. The natural affinity of American and English political philosophies meant that Americans were more apt to feel comfortable with the English way of doing things than with the ways of the government-owned systems. Finally, the BBC had no commercials, and some critics were convinced that advertising was responsible for the deficiencies in our system.

In 1927 the English replaced their five-year-old private enterprise broadcasting with a government-chartered monopoly, the BBC, a group of distinguished citizens chartered to operate all stations for a period of ten years. This step reflected a degree of paternalism in which an elite group was to make all programming decisions. It was also a direct rejection of government control, since the citizens on the corporation's board of governors had a ten-year tenure. They were charged with providing a radio service without any machinery for government input or any requirement that the service be popular among listeners.

Under this system the postmaster general had the technical right to censor programs. He did so on only one occasion—there was so much resulting criticism that he never tried it again.

The principal source of financing was a tax on receivers collected by the Post Office and turned over directly to the BBC. The corporation accepted no broadcast advertising but was free to seek money from the sale of its highly popular *Radio Times* magazine that listed the program schedules and contained profitable advertising.

Although the BBC, under its long-time director Sir John Reith, operated according to the principle that it knew better than the people what should be on radio, there was the development of alternative services for different tastes. The "Home Service" provided a general schedule including news, discussion, entertainment, religion, children's, and other programs. In its diversity it was the closest to what the American networks were offering in the 1930s. The "Light Programme" was for that portion of the public that desired mostly entertainment and news in capsule form. The "Third Programme" was highly cultural, including discussion of esoteric subjects such as ancient civilizations and presentation of comparatively obscure classical music. It was matter of pride to the BBC that although the "Third Programme" was aired for several years without substantial audience, it eventually developed a loyal listenership. Since the "Third Programme" was primarily an evening service, its transmitters were occasionally used during the daytime hours for a fourth service broadcasting sports and other special events.

Development of Television Services

In 1936 the BBC unveiled its television system and for nearly twenty years provided the only video service available to the country. In the postwar years television was very low on the priority list of facilities to be rebuilt, and while American television was making great strides in the late 1940s and early 1950s, the BBC was hampered by lack of funds and facilities. As the English became highly critical of the BBC for lagging in television development, a commission was appointed to look into alternatives that would speed up development of the medium. In 1954 the Independent Television Authority (ITA) was chartered by the crown to be financed by advertising as a supplement to the BBC. At the time, American broadcasters claimed the English had finally seen the error of their ways and were adopting the American system. In actuality, the ITA was carefully structured to avoid what was considered the major evil of American broadcasting— advertiser domination of programming.

The ITA was authorized to construct transmission facilities throughout the country for lease to private companies who contracted for specific blocks of time on specific transmitters. Each company was responsible for programming the time it leased and was expected to offer a variety of programs under requirements somewhat similar to the FCC concept of the public interest. Payments by the companies to the ITA were to cover the construction, upkeep, and operation of the facilities. The companies were to obtain their own revenues to cover costs and profits from sale of time to advertisers. At first the ITA leaned over backward to avoid advertiser influence by requiring that all time sales be one a "run-of-schedule" basis where advertisers would not know when their commercials would be aired and hence could not possibly control any program. In subsequent years advertiser resistance to such purchases led to modifications were still intended to keep advertiser influence out of programming.

The ITA has since become the Independent Broadcasting Authority (IBA) with responsibility for both radio and television alternatives to the BBC. However, the charters of both organizations reflect the original concept of the government-chartered monopoly as an intermediate step between free enterprise and government ownership.

American interest in the BBC was stimulated in 1979 with the publication of the Carnegie II report on public broadcasting in this country. Chairman William McGill is said to have wished it were possible to create a BBC for this country but realized it would be impossible in light of the great decentralization that had taken place in the 1970s. Although the BBC has been faced with severe financial problems, it is still considered one of the best broadcast operations in the world and its programs are carried in over ninety countries.

When the ITA came into existence in the mid-1950s, the BBC share of audience slipped to less than 30 percent. In response the BBC formed BBC-1, a new service concentrating on light entertainment while BBC-2 continued its emphasis on culture and minority interests. Currently BBC-2 has somewhat less than ten percent of the audience while the remainder is split between BBC-1 and ITA.

In the 1980s the BBC's greatest problem thus far has been financial. The annual license fee was raised to about $80 which covers an unlimited number of radio and television sets in a household. Revenues from the fees account for nearly all BBC income which has been eroded by inflation and the need to be competitive with the higher salaries paid by the IBA. In early 1980 the BBC announced the elimination of five percent of its more than 25,000 jobs and the dropping of five of the eleven orchestras it maintained.

There are several interesting points of comparison between the BBC and public broadcasting in the United States:

1. In America public broadcasting was the newcomer as a supplement to our commercial system while the British introduced commercial television in 1954 as the supplement to a well-established public operation.

2. Through annual license fees the BBC from the beginning had the permanent funding that has been so elusive for American public broadcasters.

3. Most significantly, the BBC is a highly centralized operation with all decisions made at headquarters. This structure encourages consistency and responsible leadership. By contrast, American public broadcasting is highly decentralized without any effective leadership. As noted in Chapter 13, this situation is the result of pressure from the Nixon administration and the overriding desire of individual station managers to survive in their local environments.

Combinations of Systems

As early as the 1930s a handful of countries adopted combinations of the government-licensed free enterprise and government-chartered monopoly systems. As might be expected, at first these were countries such as Canada and Australia that had strong ties to both the United States and England and had parallel systems operating simultaneously. In Japan in the 1950s a television system evolved similar to the British system in which private companies competed with the government-chartered organization. Comparable arrangements followed in some of the European countries. At the same time when some poorer countries wanted to get into television, they found the heavy expense an incentive to combine various systems. For example, several countries with government-owned radio facilities joined in partnership with American companies to form a chartered monopoly or a private enterprise system. All three American networks were interested in expansion into overseas markets hoping to profit both from station operations and from sale of syndicated programs. A common practice was for a local government either directly or through a chartered corporation to hold 51 percent of the new television facilities while the American network owned the other 49 percent and provided the operational expertise along with much of the programming. This pattern largely disappeared in the late 1960s as countries became more nationalistic and more sensitive about foreign influence over their communications facilities.

14.2 INTERNATIONAL RADIO BY OTHER COUNTRIES

Deliberate broadcasting beyond national boundaries was first tried in the late 1920s when some of the European colonial powers sought through radio to build stronger cultural ties between themselves and the peoples they ruled around the world. England and Holland especially thought it would help to hold their empires together if their subjects overseas listened to the radio programs being heard at home. Early efforts were neither extensive nor effective.

Adolf Hitler of Germany was the first world leader not only to see the potential use of domestic and international radio for purposes of propaganda, but also to have complete control over the medium. He considered every type of program (news, music, comedy, drama, sports, and so on) from the perspective of what it could contribute to his national goals. Only the "good news," from his point of view, was aired; news items were fabricated if necessary. Commentaries told people what to think about the news. Music was selected to stress the military heritage of the country and to build national pride. Comedy poked fun at those who opposed Hitler. Dramas always portrayed the villain as a Jew, a Negro, a Communist, an American, or some other "enemy of the Fatherland." The hero was always the purely Aryan patriotic German.

As he prepared to invade neighboring countries in the late 1930s, Hitler beamed radio programs to Germans in those lands. The difficulties those Germans were suffering were emphasized, and they were told how much better life would be for them when they were reunited with Germany. By the time the military invasion was launched, Hitler could count on so much help from his expatriates that a new phrase entered the language—"the Fifth Column"—the cooperation of which was as valuable as that of a column of infantry or armored vehicles in a battle.

The World War II Battle for People's Minds

During World War II international short-wave radio was a primary weapon in the battle for people's minds. It was not that the combatants hoped to change enemy minds by radio, although there were attempts to destroy morale by broadcasting the "bad" news that the local stations were probably trying to suppress. Programs beamed to the United States were largely ineffective, since Americans paid little attention to short-wave signals. More important were programs for the Africans and Asiatic colonies of the two sides. England broadcast to its colonies trying to enlist their support in the war and to colonies of Germany and Italy trying to neutralize them. This strategy of enlisting the support of their own colonies and trying to neutralize the rest was also followed by the others.

The British were the masters of international radio. The government contracted with the BBC to originate and transmit programs for the rest of the world. The overseas service was financed by government funds quite separate from the income for domestic services. The BBC's primary asset was its credibility—people tended to believe what it said. This was not accidental. There was a conscious effort to give only accurate information, even when it was unfavorable to British interests, and to avoid the possibility of getting caught telling a lie. The BBC developed its reputation to the point where if people heard unexpected and unbelievable news on another service, their first reaction was, "Let's tune to the BBC to find out if it's true."

Few colonial residents had receivers in their homes providing truly convenient reception. But leaders and opinion makers could listen, and there were enough sets in villages and tribes so that news could be received by radio and spread by word of mouth. There were no locally controlled stations, so for most people in the Third World radio was synonymous with short-wave programs from the major European powers.

International Radio by New Nations

An important development of the postwar years was the transformation of colonies into independent nations. When a new country was born, its government had a natural desire to engage in those activities that characterized the major powers. It might first consider building an atomic bomb, but quickly learned that it possessed neither the billions of dollars, nor the hundreds of scientists required. The next item on a priority list might be a major air force but that, too, required much money and a large pool of skilled personnel. Eventually the new government would consider its desire for a powerful radio station and find it was neither too expensive nor dependent on large numbers of educated people. As a consequence, construction of radio facilities proceeded rapidly in the newly independent nations and the airwaves were soon bearing programs aimed not only at domestic audiences but also at people in neighboring countries.

It is axiomatic in broadcasting that when competing services are approximately equal in other respects, people will tend to tune to the station that is most "local," or nearest geographically and spiritually. As new nations built their own facilities, their peoples and those of neighboring states stopped listening primarily to distant European stations. In a few short years global international short-wave radio had become quite regional. For example, Egypt's Radio Cairo has been dominant in the Middle East since the 1950s because it had very powerful transmitters and because Cairo was a cultural and entertainment center making available the best Arabic talent for programming. As President Nasser broadcast his own brand of Pan Arabism, in the mid-1950s, some of his neighbors became concerned about losing control of their own people. The author was enlisted to train Jordanian broadcast executives and to recommend a training program for others in a new station. The avowed purpose of the Jordanian government was to entice its citizens away from Radio Cairo. In the mid-1960s Libya (which borders on Egypt) was considering building a television system with its new petroleum funds. The author was briefly in Tripoli representing the U.S.

Department of State which had been invited to give advice on the training necessary to help personnel run the proposed facilities. On one of my visits to the Minister of Information I inquired into Libyan motivation, hoping that it was a desire to use the medium for bringing an underdeveloped country into the twentieth century sociologically and culturally. Instead, the minister responded it was vital that Libyans no longer listen so much to Radio Cairo, which was broadcasting programs unfriendly to the monarchist Libyan government. The minister said he had noted that whenever television came into a home, people no longer spent as much time with radio. Since Radio Libya had been unable to compete with Radio Cairo for the Libyan audience, perhaps Libyan television could succeed. The wisdom of his concern was demonstrated the following year when there was a coup and a new government closely aligned with Egypt came into power. Radio Cairo had been successful.

The importance of Radio Cairo was also demonstrated by Israeli actions after the "Six Day War" in 1967. Several years earlier the deputy director of Israeli broadcasting had reported his government's plan that television not be started until Israeli radio could complete its work of helping integrate new immigrants into Israeli society. The director felt television would be a distraction and make little contribution to solving national problems. Shortly after the 1967 annexation of areas that included major Arabic refugee populations in Gaza and the West Bank, it became known that Israel was finally going into television. When Israeli broadcasting students in this country went to their consulates to apply for jobs, they were informed that one of the important criteria was the ability to speak Arabic. Like the Libyans, Israel was starting a television service partly to lure its Arab population away from Radio Cairo.

14.3 AMERICAN INTERNATIONAL BROADCASTING

When the United States entered World War II in 1941, it had no governmental international broadcasting. Six companies (General Electric, Westinghouse, NBC, CBS, Crosley, and Worldwide Broadcasting Corporation) owned and operated short-wave transmitters beamed to other countries. By the end of 1942 the United States government had leased the private transmitters and was in the process of building more. The private stations were beamed primarily at Latin America and it was important to get more coverage in the Pacific, in Africa, and in Asia. There were two government organizations responsible for international broadcasts—the Office of War Information (OWI) under veteran newsman Elmer Davis, and the Council of Inter-American Affairs under Nelson Rockefeller. Most of the programming titled "The Voice of America" (VOA) was done by CBS and NBC under contract with the two groups. By the spring of 1943 there were twenty-one trans-mitters in service broadcasting nearly 2,700 programs a week in twenty-one languages. More transmitters were added, but the United States effort did not catch up with that of the European nations. CBS and NBC continued doing the bulk of the programming until 1948.

When the war ended in 1945 there was a rush to demobilize not only military organizations but also everything else related to the war effort. Congress was ready to end funding the VOA, but it became apparent there were to be continuing tensions between the United States and the Soviet Union. As the cold war intensified, the VOA continued its operation from New York City, where it had been placed to be near the center of domestic broadcasting activities. Its distance from Washington was a handicap as people in the VOA felt out of the government mainstream and received less attention and support than they would have enjoyed as a more visible unit with the rest of the government.

In the early 1950s, the cold war was at its height; Senator Joseph McCarthy spearheaded the search for Communists within the country; the containment of communism around the world was a primary objective of United States foreign policy. The United States was heavily involved in helping non-Communist government through foreign aid and mutual-security military treaties. It was clear that America would never return to the isolationism of the 1930s. It was also clear that international radio was important and that the VOA should be brought to Washington and given a more important role.

USIA and USIS

On the recommendation of President Eisenhower in 1953, Congress enacted legislation establishing the United States Information Agency (USIA). It was responsible directly to the president, but had a very close liaison with the Department of State as its source of day-to-day guidance on American policy. The United States Information Service (USIS) was the overseas arm of the USIA. A person might at a given time be assigned a job in Washington as part of the USIA; the next month he or she might be in another country working as part of USIS.

USIS Operations In any foreign country all government employees are under the authority of the ambassador, the president's personal representative in that country. The ambassador is responsible not only for State Department employees, but also for those with the Agency for International Development (AID), the USIS, the military attaches, and advisors and anyone else assigned there.

The ranking USIS officer in an overseas country is the public affairs officer (PAO) of the embassy. Under the PAO will be a staff varying in size depending on the scope of American activities in the country. There may be five or six people (including secretaries) or there may be several times that many. All USIS personnel may be in the capital city working out of the embassy or some may be assigned to individual cities around the country. American USIS employees are augmented by the hiring of foreign nationals.

The most visible USIS activity is normally the library located near the embassy and open to citizens of the country who want information about the United States. It is stocked with standard reference materials plus other books designed to convey impressions and understanding of the United States and its culture. The library is frequently visited by students who have school or college assignments to write about this country. People who are planning trips to this country also go to the library for information. Many friends of the United States in other countries first came to know it through use of the USIS library. But because it is so visible, it is usually the first building to be attacked when anti-American feelings run high.

Many USIS posts, especially in the Third World, include film sections. The USIA maintains one of the largest film libraries in the world with many thousands of educational and entertainment titles. There is usually a theater near the embassy for showing the movies and there may be traveling crews with portable units who will take projectors and films to villages and tribes in the further reaches of the country. The purpose is to show films that will help in basic education and that will give the viewers a better idea of what the United States is like.

There is usually at least one person assigned as liaison with the local radio and television stations and with the newspapers. His or her responsibility is to get to know the media personnel as well as possible and provide them with whatever services might be required. For example, when a new radio station was started in Amman, Jordan, the radio officer of the USIS provided it with a copy of each day's news report from the embassy news ticker until the station could create its own news program. Audio and video tapes and films are received from the USIA in Washington to be offered to the local stations.

The Voice of America

When the USIA was organized in 1953 the VOA became one of its divisions. It was a very difficult period; Senator McCarthy was promising to produce long lists of names of Communists who had infiltrated the military, the State Department, and the public-information staffs. Any attempt to initate major programming activities was made impossible by the climate of the times. The other priority work to be done was building the technical facilities. One of the first VOA directors was Jack Poppele, former chief engineer for WOR in New York City and for the Mutual Broadcasting System. He was also one of the pioneers who had formed the Television Broadcasters Association that later merged with the NAB. While VOA programming was considerably handicapped by McCarthy, the physical facilities were expanded.

Upon entering the White House, President Eisenhower brought with him as a special assistant Henry Loomis, who later became president of CPB. After a brief period in the White House, Loomis went to the USIA to head up its Research and Information Service. He subsequently became director of VOA and filled that position under Presidents Eisenhower, Kennedy, and Johnson. In the late 1950s the VOA began to reflect the results of world-wide research.

The Intended Audience

In earlier days international broadcasts had been beamed to the masses of people throughout the world. With the building of national systems, most listeners tuned to their own stations. The Voice of America began to specialize in broadcasts for the politically curious, people who wanted to know the official American viewpoint on different matters. It was expected that this audience would listen to the VOA news, then tune immediately to the BBC, and then to Radio Moscow and other government voices. The mass audiences were conceded to local stations.

Emphasis on English

The amount of English-language programming was increased for two reasons. First, in many places it would be practical and useful for natives to be able to speak with Americans; a gardener or housemaid who could communicate in English had a better chance at a good job with Americans stationed overseas. A taxi driver who could follow directions in English could earn more. Young people who learned English would later be able to travel to the United States as students. Businesses could expand if their employees could deal with Americans. The increase in English-language programs featured a vocabulary with basic words easily learned and most frequently used.

Second, it was learned that news programs were more authoritative when carried in the language of the country from which they emanated. VOA news carried more authority when it was in English; Radio Moscow news was better received when it was in Russian. Foreign-language broadcasts remained in the schedule, but there was more emphasis on English programming for all parts of the world.

Search for Credibility

The VOA made a conscious effort to achieve the degree of credibility enjoyed by the BBC during World War II. This involved telling the truth at all times, whatever the cost might be. In 1961 Edward R. Murrow, who had organized the CBS European coverage of World War II and then gone on to become this country's best-known and most respected newsman, was appointed by President Kennedy to be director of the USIA. In a statement that is still being used in VOA brochures, Murrow affirmed the search for credibility:

The Voice of America stands upon this above all,
The truth shall be the guide.
Truth may help us.
It may hurt us.
But, helping us or hurting us we shall have the satisfaction of
knowing that man can know us for what we are and can at
least believe what we say.

Newspeople and students understand the necessity for such a policy and the importance of bearing up under the problems it inevitably presents. Some politicians find it most difficult to understand why a costly official voice should be used to spread bad news about this country. A major test came in budget hearings during and after the VOA reports on school integration in Little Rock, Arkansas, when President Eisenhower federalized the National Guard to enable blacks to attend schools to which they were assigned. For a while the three best-known cities in America were Washington, New York, and Little Rock.

When the VOA newcasts covered the integration problems members of Congress kept pressing officials for explanations. They were informed that Radio Moscow and other unfriendly voices were carrying the Little Rock story almost to the exclusion of other items. If the VOA did not cover it, the whole operation would be suspect. Furthermore, by covering it, the VOA could put it in context with the rest of the news.

One of the darkest days in USIA history was when the VOA had to reverse itself on a story about a plane shot down over the Soviet Union. When word first came from Radio Moscow that an American plane had been shot down, the VOA went to the Department of State to find out what had happened. Apparently the advice was sought before the matter had reached the highest levels of government. The VOA was told that an American weather plane operating in Turkey to help the farmers had strayed a short distance over the Soviet border by mistake and had been shot down in a cold-blooded, unnecessary, and uncivilized way.

The next day the VOA had to tell the truth, which had been revealed by the White house. It was not a weather plane; it was a special U-2 spy plane built to fly above the level that might be reached by Soviet missiles. The plane did not stray out of Turkey; it had left Pakistan and was headed for Norway, taking pictures on the way. Furthermore, the Central Intelligence Agency had been operating flights of that nature for some years. The broadcasting of conflicting stories on a single incident can do more to destroy credibility than almost anything else.

Throughout the 1960s the VOA grew in sature and was a reasonably effective voice for the United States. Some are highly critical because there are so many in other lands who dislike the United States government and disapprove of its policies. Critics say that if the VOA had done its job well enough, the United States would not lose so many votes in the United Nations.

It has always been known that broadcasting cannot sell an unpopular product in the marketplace. Franklin D. Roosevelt could persuade the American people to have no fear of fear itself, but he could not muster their support for packing the Supreme Court. The American government could not persuade its own people that Vietnam was a justifiable war, so the VOA should not be faulted for being unable to persuade others to believe what people in this country could not agree on. The VOA probably explained the United States's position as successfully as could be expected under the circumstances.

Through most of the 1970s the VOA was frustrated by the constraints of bureaucratic controls in the airing of news. On occasion it was permitted to give the unvarnished truth regardless of the effect on America's image. For example, a news story in November 1975 started:

> *In Washington, a senate investigation reveals that the United States Central Intelligence Agency was involved in several plots to kill foreign leaders.*

On another occasion in the same year reports about the United States evacuation from Saigon, South Vietnam were limited to official statements from other branches of government. There were increasing complaints both inside and outside the VOA that it was losing its credibility and becoming known as a propaganda tool of whatever administration was in power.

The USICA   There was a reorganization in 1978 and the USIA was replaced by the United States International Communications Agency (USICA). The new agency was established to be far more independent in news and its freedom has been noticed throughout the world. There has been a separation of news programs and the "editorials" that still give the official American policy on daily events.

The Voice of America in the 1980s is a major organization. With a 1980 budget of $85 million it employs over 2,000 persons—about a third of whom are foreign nationals. It broadcasts more than 800 hours a week in thirty-eight languages and theoretically reaches every country in the world. There are twenty-three radio studios in Washington plus five more in New York

City, Miami, Chicago, and Los Angeles. The VOA has forty-one transmitters in the United States beamed overseas and seventy-two more located in other countries. About a quarter of the programming is in English to add credibility and to help people around the world to learn the English language. Officials are especially encouraged by the response in China which has given priority to the learning of English. The VOA offers three half-hour programs of English instruction per day on the Chinese broadcasting service.

The credibility of the VOA has increased under its new parent, the USICA. VOA correspondents no longer travel on diplomatic passports but enter other countries with the same accreditation as other journalists. Neither are they expected to check in at United States embassies for instructions. Plans for the immediate future include new and powerful transmitters connected to Washington by satellite and new programming, including talk shows with listener participation. There is hope that the VOA will before long succeed the BBC international service in influence, as the BBC is currently being hamstrung by restricted budgets.

Russian Jamming   Since the 1950s the Soviet Union has maintained massive "jamming" facilities—some 2,000 transmitters broadcasting loud buzzing noises on frequencies being used by other countries sending programs into the Soviet Union. American signals have been jammed intermittently, usually coincident with low periods in the detente with Russia. Broadcasts from Radio Liberty, Israel, and China have been jammed more consistently. In the summer of 1980 attention was again focused on Soviet jamming when that country went to great lengths to prevent western broadcasts on the workers' strikes in Poland from being heard in Russia. It has been estimated that the Soviets spend more money in a year on jamming than the total combined budgets of the VOA and Radio Free Europe—about $180 million.

USICA-Television

Quite separate from the VOA is the television service of the USICA. Since it is not possible to beam television programs directly to distant points, the emphasis is on preparation of program materials that United States radio-television officers can try to place on local stations. The USICA studio complex in Washington is one of the few facilities in the world where television programs can be recorded on videotape for the use of three (American, British, and French) systems of television. Some programs are produced by agency personnel and some are obtained from stations and networks. The purpose is to circulate materials that will lead to a better understanding of the United States and its people.

The USICA is forbidden by law to circulate its materials in this country. This law reflects the conviction that the government should be completely removed from operating domestic communications. In 1964, after his assassination, the USIA did a film on President Kennedy that attracted much favorable publicity abroad. As a result of special congressional authorization, it was possible for domestic groups to obtain a copy of the film for private viewing, but most Americans never had a chance to see it.

For special events like a walk on the moon or a major presidential speech, the USICA arranges satellite distribution so stations around the world can carry them.

A major disagreement with the Soviets concerns the future use of satellites for international broadcasts directly to homes. An attempt was made to work out an agreement within the United Nations. The technology is ready so that home antennas can be constructed reasonably inexpensively to pick up satellite signals directly. The United States proposed that all nations sign agreements to permit satellites to broadcast international television for home reception. The Soviet Union objected strenuously and it appears unlikely there will be such an agreement in the foreseeable future.

Radio in the American Sector (RIAS)

Ever since the partition of Berlin into four sectors after World War II, the United States has operated RIAS. It broadcasts in German for about 240 hours a week over both medium- and short-wave stations. Its intended audience is in East Germany, although there is extensive listening in West Germany also.

Radio Free Europe and Radio Liberty

On February 17, 1972 Senator Fulbright (D-Ark.) in a debate climaxing discussion of one of the most poorly kept secrets in all of broadcasting, said:

> *Mr. President, I submit that these radios should be given an opportunity to take their rightful place in the graveyard of cold war relics.**

He was speaking of Radio Free Europe (RFE) and its sister operation, Radio Liberty, which were considered among the most effective of all international broadcast organizations. The secret, which had been known to the more sophisticated broadcasters as well as to the Soviet Union and its satellite

---

* *New York Times*, Sec. 6, p. 36, March 26, 1972.

countries, was that RFE and Radio Liberty were organized and financed by the CIA.

In the summer of 1950 the United States was approaching the height of its cold war concern with the advance of communism around the world. The VOA was still an ineffective whisper. On July 4, 1950 RFE began broadcasting to five countries behind the iron curtain—Czechoslovakia, Poland, Hungary, Rumania, and Bulgaria. (Radio Liberty was oranized to broadcst directly into the Soviet Union.) It was announced tht RFE had been founded by a private organization and that it would be supported with donations from the public, and each year there was a plea for funds over American radio and television stations and in the print media.

The programmers were expatriates who had worked in radio in the target countries. They were known to be opposed to communism and were told to broadcast what they thought would be most effective in fighting communism. They were not permitted to use any news item until it had been confirmed by two separate sources, however. Nor were they expected to expound any official American point of view.

Eventually, the organization included over 1,100 employees in Munich, another 350 in Portugal, and 96 in New York. Their broadcasts to the five target countries included:

20.0 hours daily to Czechoslovakia

19.0 hours daily to Poland

19.0 hours daily to Hungary

12.0 hours daily to Rumania

7.5 hours daily to Bulgaria

The purpose was to provide a counterbalance to the news and information available from official sources in those five countries. The emphasis was on items not discussed locally. There was ample evidence the broadcasts were widely received and effective.

The "private organization" that had founded RFE and Radio Liberty was a "front" for the CIA. When there were insufficent donations from citizens, the CIA continued paying all the bills and the fund drive each year was only a token. By the 1970s, with increased business and cultural exchange with the Soviet Union and with President Nixon's visits to Moscow and Peking, there were those who felt operation of RFE and Radio Liberty was not consistent with the changing policy. The CIA involvement was disclosed on the floor of the Senate and the "cover" was blown. The CIA announced it would terminate its funding of the radio operations, and Congress had to decide whether or not to institute open appropriations.

Congress continued RFE and Radio liberty because there are certain ways in which the VOA can never fully gain the confidence of listeners.

The VOA is the official organ of the United States government and must broadcast American policy in a diplomatic context. The expatriate broadcasters of RFE had much more freedom and the audiences respected their views. How much longer RFE and Radio Liberty will continue is an open question today.

Other Clandestine Activity   To what extent has the CIA engaged in other international or foreign broadcasting activities? The whole answer will probably never be known outside the agency itself. It is likely that with broadcasting in the Third World such a critical issue and with the great financial need of newly independent countries in the 1950s and 1960s, there were other ventures. However, following Senator Fulbright's disclosures about RFE and Radio Liberty in 1972, no other such CIA ventures were publiczed until June 1980. At that time a *New York Times* headline read, "U.S. Concedes It Is Behind Anti-Khomeini Broadcasts." The story revealed that an Egyptian transmitter had been used for "The Free Voice of Iran" which featured popular entertainment and anti-Khomeini broadcasts in Persian. The program called on Iranians to avoid fighting Kurdish rebels and to support the exiled former Prime Minister Shahpur Bakhtiar. The story identified a CIA "unconventional broadcasting" section as the sponsor of the station. One would assume that such a section, under the guidance of the national Security Agency, had engaged in other broadcast activities through the years.

The American Forces Radio Television Services

Although the United States military establishment never set out to be active in international broadcasting, it has been making an impact through the programming of stations built for the armed forces overseas. It started in 1941 with an informal radio station to entertain soldiers in an Alaskan camp. As the number of overseas camps grew, the military authorized the Armed Forces Radio Service (AFRS). Small AM stations were built on which military personnel could receive the programs they had heard at home. Most major programs from the networks were transcribed on sixteen-inch discs, and special events like football games and the World Series were sent by short-wave for rebroadcast. As television became widespread in the United States, it was natual that the AFRS should become the AFRTS and build television stations where the United States had large permanent installations. Today the AFRTS (renamed the *American* Forces Radio Television Services) has some 900 outlets around the world (AM, FM, and TV), including 150 shipboard stations.

It was apparent that people living in the vicinity of the military bases were also listening and viewing and beginning to like American radio and television. It is said that in England it was the AFRS that stimulated the most dissatifaction with the rather unexciting BBC. There can be little doubt that the AFRTS stations helped spread American culture and had an influence on listeners in all countries where they were established. It was noted earlier that the Libyan government wanted to start its own television service to keep the people from listening so much to Radio Cairo. The Libyan minister's judgment of what happened to a home with television was based on his observations in Tripoli. Wheelus Air Force Base was about ten miles from the city. It was a training base for American pilots assigned to Europe and it had an AFRTS television station. Traveling throughout the city one could see TV antennas that were oriented toward Wheelus, the only available source of television signals.

In 1980 AFRTS announced long-range plans to distribute programs around the world by satellite. It hoped by means of STRAP (Simultaneous Transmission and Recovery of Alternating Pictures), eventually to be able to send two programs at the same time on a single transponder, thus giving individual stations a greater choice among network and syndicated programs.

American Commercial Programs Overseas

American commercial programs have been aired extensively around the world in addition to their appearance on AFRTS stations. In the early 1960s each of the networks established a foreign syndication unit. Since many stations had American companies as partners who handled much of the programming, it was natural for them to bring in the most popular of the American programs. These proved to be equally popular abroad both in English and in translation to foreign languages. As a consequence, American television programs have been important in establishing and perpetuating sterotypes of the United States around the world.

14.4 AMERICA AND THIRD WORLD COMMUNICATIONS

As former colonies became independent nations after World War II, it became increasingly evident that people must be concerned with what is now known as the Third World. Great segments of the world's population are included within their borders and their people's attitudes and actions are increasingly important to this country. The entry of Third World countries into the United Nations with its "one country– one vote" policy affected international deliberations. These countries also controlled many of the natural resources on which the United States depended. With this fact in mind, it was natural that established nations should seek to influence broadcasting in emerging countries. If a country's radio and television personnel have a political bias, this may well be reflected among their audiences. Hence, the United States and other governments try to make friends with and to influence broadcasters in the Third World.

Third World Disappointment

All former colonies enter nationhood with great expectations of national development and a better life. While broadcasting can be helpful in achieving those goals, many new nations have turned to operating radio stations more as a symbol of prestige and in emulation of the great powers than as a means of accomplishing specific ends. When disappointments exceeded expectations in the independent countries, they became increasingly resentful of western nations who, they felt, had exploited them for so long and were reluctant to release their hold. One focal point in this overall resentment has been the area of communications that is seen as still dominated by the west.

There is resentment against the four biggest worldwide news organizations located in the United States, England, and France. Since each prospers as its services are purchased by western media, each covers most fully the news of interest to western consumers and from their points of view. Since the Third World media also subscribe to these services, the news they received has been tailored for western consumption. Thus, a Latin American country will receive coverage of regional affairs that was prepared for a reader or listener in Chicago, Marseilles, or London.

There is resentment against the American networks on which people depend so much for worldwide perspectives. For months at a time there will be no reports from a country but when there is a catastrophe or uprising, electronic reporters converge in large numbers to cover the story in great detail. When the story is ended, the American audience will get no more information about that country including the mundane items that might have far greater significance.

There is resentment against the increasing use of satellites to which other countries have access only at the pleasure of the United States. When Third World nations attended the World Administrative Radio Conference in 1979, they could see that satellites were a key to the future of information transmission. They saw that western nations were using satellites so extensively that there might be little opportunity for them when they are in a position to do so also.

These resentments have led to a drive, through UNESCO, for a "new information order" in which Third World nations would exercise greater control over the gathering and transmission of news. Obviously, this move distresses the western nations with their tradition of free press and the concept that censorship is unacceptable in any form. Although no important steps have been taken to achieve the new information order, it will be a growing source of tension between the West and the Third World for years to come.

American Interest in Third World Stability and Quality of Life

The United States has had an interest in Third World communication since 1950 but for quite different reasons than those nations themselves. As part of overall foreign policy the United States undertook a massive "technical assistance" program that had two major objectives:

1. To encourage national unity in new countries as a step to government stability.
2. To assist in raising the quality of life by reducing hunger, ill health, and the other effects of poverty.

Both of these objectives were very much in our national interest since their primary objective was to promote a world in which wars would be less likely to occur. It was hypothesized that stable governments of unified peoples would more quickly lead to world order and that well-nourished people would feel less need for aggression. However, both objectives required great effort.

Colonial boundaries were established in the eighteenth and nineteenth centuries reflecting agreements among western nations, frequently with little relationship to natural features that would ordinarily separate peoples. Thus, some new nations found that groups within their populations had little in common and were sometimes mortal enemies. For these countries to succeed there would have to be communication of a sense of national heritage and pride and understanding among different groups. Without such attitudes no government could possibly maintain stability.

The quality of life in much of the Third World was summarized in a number of 1950 generalizations that are still largely true today:

1. More than half the babies born don't live to the age of one year.
2. More than half the people of the world go to bed every night without having had enough food to sustain what is considered normal activity.
3. More than half the people of the world are born, live, and die without attention from a skilled doctor or dentist.
4. More than half the people of the world cannot read or write.

The United States technical assistance program put its primary emphasis on basic education. It is, of course, impossible to eliminate the causes of poverty through education alone. However, it is possible through teaching people how to produce more and take better care of their health to alleviate suffering. As people are better informed, they can better cope with various conditions.

In light of the preponderance of illiteracy in new nations, it appeared that radio provided the best hope in the transmission of basic information and ideas. Even in the 1950s there was scarcely a village or tribe without at least one radio. Within the capital of each country there were specialists in government agencies and universities who had information needed by the people. If that information could be broadcast and received, people would understand their governments and have a better quality of life that might lessen the potential for future wars. The Agency for International Development (AID) looked seriously at broadcasting as one of its important tools for disseminating needed basic information.

American Efforts to Assist Third World Broadcasting

Perhaps the earliest of American efforts to help develop radio in the Third World took place in 1954. The author spent six months of that year in Iran and in subsequent years went to several other middle-eastern and African nations as a consultant for the United States government. The purpose of these trips was to make recommendations to new goverments about facilities and training for using radio (and later television) to raise the quality of life and achieve national unity and stability. The United States government was then prepared to assist in the implementation of long-range planning.

The first problem was to give host governments a new concept of "effective radio." There was a universal view that broadcasting was primarily for entertainment and that a new nation should simply try to emulate what it observed in the United States or leading European countries. The author, on the other hand, started with the premise that the goal of effective radio should be to change behavior in the directions desired by local governments. Thus, if one goal of a nation were better health, effective radio could help persuade people to provide better sanitation in the home and to do other simple things that cut down on disease. If the goal were to raise more food, effective radio would help persuade farmers to obtain and use improved seed and fertilizer and to adopt better agricultural methods. If the government had a desire to reduce illiteracy, effective radio would help draw citizens into study centers and motivate them to learn reading, writing, and working with figures.

The concept of effective radio was very difficult to teach because there were so few examples to use. Some of the most effective political propaganda was associated with people like Hitler whose names were anathema throughout the world. In the United States the best examples of changing behavior came from advertising that the rest of the world looked down upon and that in political campaigns seemed to have little relevance for nations that had no experience with elections.

For more than two decades (until the change in political climate following the Vietnam war) the author and others travelled to the Third World trying to persuade new nations to develop effective radio, working on the scene with trainees and in American universities with students studying for baccalaureate and advanced degrees in communications. In the 1980s, there appears to be not a single country where radio or television has approached its potential in raising the quality of life or in stimulating national unity and stability. The only effective political use of broadcasting has been in attacking enemies (as with Radio Cairo versus Israel, and Radio Teheran versus the United States in the hostage crisis) rather than in nation building.

A look at the deterrents to effective use of broadcasting helps one understand much about the broadcasting problems in the Third World. (Some of the lessons are equally applicable to the United States.)

Deterrents to the Effective Use of Broadcasting

The failure to use radio (and later television) to raise the quality of life around the world can be largely attributed to four factors:

1. Failure to understand communication.

2. Expectation of easy answers.

3. Lack of organizational ability.

4. Lack of concern.

Understanding Communication

"Communication" is one of the most used and least understood concepts in the world. It is an ongoing process involving several elements. Take away any of its elements and it ceases to qualify for the term. It may be seen in five steps:

1. *A purpose to be accomplished:* This should relate to the behavioral response one wishes to achieve. For example, a program on health might have as its purpose getting villagers to boil water before using it for drinking and cooking.

2. *Articulation of the purpose:* If it is written communication, this step involves writing down the proper words. In broadcast communication, this step involves scripting and production.

3. *Transmission of what has been articulated:* Written communication is printed in large numbers and broadcast communication is sent out over the air.

4. *Reception of the message:* The written word is read, and a broadcast program is seen or heard, by an individual.

5. *Response to the original purpose:* The communication process is completed only when the hearer or viewer or reader changes his or her behavior to correspond with the concept that started the process. If there is no change in behavior, the process is as incomplete as if one of the other steps were missing.

Probably because most American programs have no purpose other than to attract individuals to receivers, very few here or overseas think of broadcasting in terms of changing behavior. Most so-called communicators are concerned only with articulation, transmission, and reception. If their peers praise the articulation, and the ratings prove extensive reception, a program is deemed successful. Only advertisers seem aware of the complete process, and they take advantage of extensive research and planning to incorporate into their commercials a clear-cut purpose and an evaluation in terms of changed behavior.

This discussion is not meant to fault American broadcasters for their failure to be concerned with behavior. This country has less need to be concerned with the quality of life in the material sense of the term and we are committed to the free enterprise system that achieves profits when large numbers of people choose a program. However, when Third World broadcasters look to this country as an example, they see very little that is pertinent to the needs of their people. Until they are able to devise communications systems especially geared to their own needs broadcasting can be expected to have little impact on how their people live.

Expectation of Easy Answers   The failure to understand communications has led to the expectation that there are easy answers to all broadcasting problems. America has for generations been a model of efficiency to much of the world. As foreign radio and television personnel have toured our country, their first and lasting impression of American broadcasting has been of extensive equipment in beautiful studios. Broadcasters from other countries have felt that if they had the same facilities they would be able to do as well as the Americans who seemed to work so effortlessly. This same preoccupation with technical mastery of facilities is also apparent in every American student who takes a broadcasting-production course in college.

There has been impatience with American advisors who talked about starting with a little equipment and concentrating on long-range training programs. Why not put in the best studios at the beginning, and why send a young person abroad for four years to learn to do what obviously required only a few months of practice? The expectation that competent broadcasting required only modern equipment has meant that solid training was never seriously considered in many countries to say nothing of being implemented.

Lack of Organizational Ability

It seems to be natural for Americans to organize whatever they do so that someone (individual or committee) takes responsibility for the overall effort. Clear lines of communication are attempted where a person in the middle has both responsibility and authority to make decisions. Until he or she fails, there is lack of interference with what is done. In many foreign government bureaucracies there is a failure to understand the principle of assigning responsibility and authority. Broadcasting is so visible that every official wants to play a role in its details. For example, in one country where AID was trying to help in broadcast training for use of a station that had been provided by the United States, newscasters received instructions from everyone who outranked them. They were on occasion directed by the king, his prime minister, the minister of information, the director general of broadcasting, and the station manager as well as the news director. This situation was most confusing and destructive to consistent newscasting. More important, it was wasteful of policy-making time and while the high officials concerned themselves with details, they were neglecting overall policy so it became nonexistent.

If a broadcast system is to be used to raise the quality of life, there must be a conscious decision to that effect by the leaders and considerable time must be devoted to planning the policies that will be implemented by the working personnel. That development is not likely to occur in many Third World countries.

A concomitant problem is the fear that many middle-level persons in a bureaucracy have of those who have been sent abroad for specialized training. Obviously they are better qualified than those who did not have the same opportunity and they are seen as a threat both to peers and superiors. As a consequence, they are rarely given the chance to use their training and gradually drift away from broadcasting entirely. In fact, many stations could be well staffed by the foreign-trained broadcasters who have gone into private business or some other branches of government because they were held back in their earlier efforts.

Lack of Concern

Finally and most serious of all is a characteristic of most officials and government employees in all nations—a lack of personal concern for the quality of life of those in their society who enjoy fewer material benefits than they do. There is an intellectual sympathy, but the gulf between the broadcaster in the capital city and the peasant in the village is so great that the needs of the latter are easily ignored. Most people are so concerned with their own problems that they have little time for those of others. In fact, they seldom even take notice.

As a consequence, few broadcasters in underdeveloped lands feel their jobs are related to a responsibility to somehow make their countries better places in which to live. Programs are prepared in the traditional western patterns whether they meet needs or not. When one is required to do something in the area of basic education, that person generates so little interest that he or she does not make the effort to prepare to do it well.

The presence of any one of the above deterrents would make it unlikely that an effective system of broadcasting could be built. When all these conditions are found, it should surprise no one that radio and television are not better used in the most important purpose they could possibly have—raising the quality of life.

Effect of the Political Climate

The extent of America's influence on broadcasting around the world has been dependent on the overall political climate. In the 1950s American television programs were readily accepted on many foreign stations and American advisors were welcomed. Their reports were solicited and students gladly started training programs both here and abroad. During the late 1960s the disaffection with the war in Vietnam and the growing nationalism in the Third World meant that fewer of American-government-sponsored programs were being broadcast and American advice was not sought. The tragedy of the past three decades is that while this country and others have successfully used broadcasting to entertain and spell out political positions, there seems to be little prospect of gain for the average Third World person who so desperately needs the benefits that could accrue from the reception and use of basic information.

GLOSSARY ITEMS

The following words and phrases used Chapter 14 are defined in the Glossary:

Government-Chartered Monopoly

Government-Licensed Free Enterprise

Government-Owned-and-Operated

Jamming

Run-of-Schedule

PREVIEW

As broadcasting (especially television) has monopolized more of people's time, it has become the subject of more controversy. The effects of most purposive programming—news, politics, and advertising for adults—are reasonably clear. It is entertainment and advertising for children that have led to most controversy. Minority groups are concerned about stereotyping. Parents worry about what television does to children. While there is no probability that controversy will be eliminated, it is to be hoped that dialogue will become more productive as broadcaster and consumer-critic try harder to understand each other. They must compromise since each has rights that conflict with the rights of others. The futures of both broadcasting and society will be bright when all approach controversy and differences of opinion as partners in search for workable answers.

CHAPTER 15

EPILOGUE: CONTROVERSY AND COMPROMISE

To this point, understanding broadcasting has included studying various controversies within the field. The reader has seen the great difference of opinion about the role of the FCC and about whether the Fairness Doctrine and other regulatory activities are compatible with a commitment to free speech. Little agreement has existed concerning how much pay cable should be permitted to compete with conventional television for popular programming (such as sports events). There is much confusion about the directions public broadcasting should take and the extent to which the CPB should be involved in programming.

In addition to these intra-media controversies, it is important that future broadcasters and consumers know about the controversies surrounding the roles the media do and should play in society and the effects they have on individuals. These controversies originate in charges brought by critics and other members of the public. Radio has been comparatively ignored in recent years, but television is subjected to more criticism than all the other mass media combined. Some imply that it is callously indifferent to the fate of American youth and that it is motivated by a greed matched only by Midas. In response, some broadcasters tend to become defensive and ask that their critics assume an impossible burden of proof. With rhetorical hyperbole, both critic and broadcaster overstate their cases and lose credibility among those who seek the truth. The reader should be concerned with understanding the points of view of both sides and the possibility that healthy dialogue might lead to better understanding between them, to compromise, and to better media in a better society.

15.1 BROADCASTING AND SOCIETY

The essence of the controversy about the role and influence of broadcasting is a question about broadcasting itself—is it an integral part of society? If broadcasting has been totally absorbed by society, it is able to move only as society moves it. If, on the other hand, it is to some degree separate, it can take actions independently of the rest of society and seek to exert an influence of its own.

It is a difficult question because in social relationships the neat separation of cause from effect is usually impossible. While an individual or institution seems to be reflecting the environment, he, she, or it may also be changing the environment. For example, when a baby is born, it is usually expected that he or she will to a degree absorb and then reflect some characteristics of its family. Yet, the family itself may have been so greatly changed by the introduction of the child that it becomes impossible to identify purely familial influences. In fact, family and child are inseparable.

Since broadcasting began in the early 1920s, people have raised questions about the influence of radio and television on this society. The answers have generally been inconclusive except to those who wanted to prove a prior judgment with whatever research and statistics they might find favoring their beliefs. Broadcasting has without question reflected many of society's characteristics. It has also changed society. The question is whether broadcasting by itself caused the change or whether society so shaped broadcasting that what the latter did was inevitable. Only to the extent that broadcasting is extrasocietal can it have a will and consequence of its own. Otherwise, it can no more change society than can our schools, churches, newspapers, banks, and other institutions. Although this book cannot clearly define the societal status of broadcasting, it will be helpful to bear the question in mind in seeking to understand the controversies rising from criticism of the media.

15.2 ENTERTAINMENT VS. PURPOSIVE BROADCASTING

Understanding the role of broadcasting in society is enhanced by a clarification of the purposes for which various materials are aired. As shown in Fig. 15.1 everything on radio and television can be divided into two

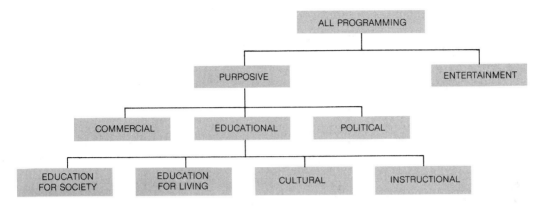

Fig. 15.1
Categories of broadcast materials

categories. This classification is not related to whether a program is on commercial or public stations—only the reason for putting it in the schedule and the goals the writers and producers are trying to accomplish are important.

Entertainment Broadcasting

"Entertainment" is presented only to attract people to their sets either so they will be exposed to the commercials of the advertisers who are paying the costs or so they will contribute to the upkeep of a station. There is no ostensible desire that people be any different at the end of an entertainment program than they were when it started. If people watch a sporting event or a typical evening of entertainment, the chances are the only effect on them is that they have grown two or three hours older and enjoyed the aging process.

Purposive Broadcasting

"Purposive" broadcasting, on the other hand, is presented because someone wants to change the listener-viewer in some way. A company presents commercials so potential customers will try its products or at least go to a showroom where personal salesmanship can be exercised. Political broadcasts are intended to make people more likely to vote for a candidate or party.

Within the category of purposive broadcasting is the classification of "educational broadcasting" whose purpose has two characteristics:

1. The desired change is significant. The producer is trying to do something more important than teach how to recite the alphabet backwards.

2. The desired change is noncontroversial. This is not to say the material must be noncontroversial. There might be a discussion on abortion, which is one of the most controversial topics in society today, with the purpose of inducing people to inform themselves on all aspects of the issue. Or, a program might concern politics but only aim to persuade people to go to the polls without urging them to vote for one party or another.

Within the category of educational broadcasting are four groups of material:

1. Education for Society.
2. Education for Living.
3. Cultural Exposure.
4. Instructional Materials.

Education for society is trying to change a person to make him or her a better citizen: 1) by understanding the issues facing this democracy (news programs can thus be considered educational), 2) by participating in democracy by voting or serving on jury when called and paying taxes honestly, and 3) by understanding and being tolerant of those who may differ in culture, race, religion, or other ways.

Education for living is trying to make an individual happier and more effective through encouraging such things as enhanced appreciation of his or her heritage and productive use of leisure time.

Cultural programming is exposing an individual to the best in our literature, music, dance and other arts.

Instructional material is designed to be part of the formal educational process: it may come under any of the above three subdivisions or be presented as preparation for further learning such as the teaching of spelling simple words as a step to more difficult ones.

In considering the role of radio and television in this society, the discussion will be organized around purposive and entertainment broadcasting.

15.3 CONTROVERSIES ABOUT PURPOSIVE BROADCASTING

Controversy about Television News

There is general agreement that television news coverage is significant. This has been especially true since 1963 when the networks expanded their evening newscasts from fifteen minutes to half an hour in length. Since

1940 Americans had used radio as a primary source of up-to-the-minute information about what they considered important. In the 1960s they began to accept from the television newscasts their perceptions of what was important. Although the half-hour was only sufficient to provide a few headlines, it seemed long enough to cover the major stories. Therefore, if television consistently covered a story night after night, viewers thought it must be important. Conversely, if television ignored a story, viewers assumed the item was not as significant as the ones that were included. In effect, television news editors were giving the viewers a rank order of importance for various news items of the day.

The controversy about news coverage derives from the differences of opinion about what is important enough to be included in the few stories television can present. For example, the Vietnam protest movement, which had started as a few skirmishes and picket lines in 1965, became much larger in 1967 and 1968. The networks considered the demonstrations newsworthy and covered them consistently. This coverage, in turn, reinforced the opinion of those who already had an antiwar leaning and caused sober questioning by people who had all their lives assumed that information from their government was to be trusted. As respectable citizens like Dr. Benjamin Spock and leaders of various religious faiths appeared in televised demonstrations, more and more who considered themselves part of the establishment began to ask questions for which the government had no satisfactory answers. Eventually, so many people were influenced that President Johnson first had to severely curtail his trips around the country and then to announce he would not be a candidate for reelection in 1968.

Television was criticized then (and later in 1969 by Vice President Agnew) on the ground that it should have ignored the protests that, unreported, would then have more quickly faded away. There was evidence that the demonstrators planned their activities and publicized them to the medium in such a way as to ensure maximum coverage. While the demonstrations would have been continued even without television coverage, there is little chance that as many people would have known about them or been affected by them. Many felt that television had set out to make the demonstrations more important than they actually were. Broadcasters responded that this was like the ancient king who killed the messenger who had brought bad news.

Controversy about Broadcasting in Politics

Political campaigning has changed greatly in the last fifty years, and much of the change is due to broadcasting. Candidates have relied more and more on the broadcast advertising techniques by which manufacturers sell soap, autos, cereals, and drugs. In 1964 one party prepared a political commercial showing a little girl picking daisies with a nuclear explosion in the background implying that the other candidate might get the country into war. A book on Richard Nixon's campaign by Joe McGinniss was titled *The Selling of the President, 1968*. Present campaigns rely heavily on commercials stressing slogans and superficial generalizations about personality and points of view on issues.

There is controversy about the degree to which broadcasting has degraded the political process. Critics bemoan the selling of political candidates and yearn for the days when issues seemed more important. One can question, however, whether the average voter in prebroadcast days was as well informed about the candidates as are the voters of today. Before broadcasting, voters could only read on the printed page what reporters, editors, and publishers wanted them to know. Today's voters can at least see the candidates and form impressions of their personalities and capacities.

WALTER CRONKITE b. 1916

Courtesy: CBS News Photo

In 1981 Walter Cronkite retired as managing editor and anchorman of the CBS Evening News, a position he had occupied for nearly two decades. In a poll of American leaders he was the only journalist to be voted among the top ten "most influential decision makers in America." In other polls of the general public he was found to have more credibility than any one else in the society. The recipient of practically every honor in the field, he was a worthy successor to Edward R. Murrow under whose leadership he became a CBS-TV correspondent in 1950.

Born in 1916, Cronkite attended the University of Texas where he was campus correspondent for the *Houston Post* and in his spare time was sports announcer for a local radio station. He became a full-time reporter for the *Houston Press* and worked for a year in Kansas City radio before joining the United Press in 1937.

As a correspondent in World War II he covered the battle of the North Atlantic and landed with Allied troops in North Africa and Normandy. He dropped with the 101st Airborne Division in Holland and was with the U.S. Third Army in the Battle of the Bulge when it broke through the German encirclement at Bastogne in December 1944.

After reporting the German surrender, Cronkite was chief United Press correspondent at the Nuremberg trials and spent two years in Moscow.

Returning home in 1948 he broadcast events in Washington, D.C. for midwestern radio stations before joining CBS in 1950.

In his thirty years with CBS Cronkite has been in on practically every major news story of national and international magnitude. His broadcasts themselves have also on occasion made news. In November 1977 his interviews with Egyptian President Sadat and Israeli Prime Minister Begin made headlines around the world and led directly to the first face-to-face contacts between the two heads of state.

It should also be noted that with regard to politics, broadcasting truly mirrors our society. Broadcasters did not set out to change the political process and would, indeed, be glad to devote less time to political campaigning than they do. They are, however, required to make their facilities available to candidates without any restrictions on material used. It is politicians who have decided to use circus techniques because they believe this society is one in which those techniques are the most effective way of getting votes.

Controversy about Television Advertising

Some of the criticism aimed at television advertising is equally appropriate to the other mass media. For example, some say that since a manufacturer obviously passes advertising costs on to consumers, every billion dollars spent on television commercials means that much more in costs to the American public. But at the same time it is theorized that advertising actually reduces the cost of individual units. As advertising creates demand, manufacturers can use mass production techniques that lower prices (even with advertising) far below the levels of goods made in smaller quantities and not advertised.

Along this same line, it is then remarked that in creating demand, advertising must lead to wasteful spending. If people were not induced to want so much, might they not all live more frugally and be better off? This view is a possibility. But that would require a curtailment of all advertising, and if that succeeded in substantially lowering demand, we would have to start subsidizing the living costs of those who are now making cosmetics, beer, drugs, autos, and the other products that people might use to a far lesser degree.

A criticism peculiar to broadcast advertising concerns the irritation factor. It is quite possible to ignore print advertising but some people resent the interruption of broadcast programs (especially serious drama) for "this important message." There is, however, little evidence that the majority of Americans object to commercials.

A more serious complaint concerns the degree to which broadcasters, because of advertising pressures, let themselves be dominated by the ratings. This complaint stems from the fact that there are two fairly distinct types of viewers during all parts of a broadcast day. The first type tunes in at a given time to see a particular program. It may be a show he or she watches regularly or one consciously selected from those listed in *TV Guide*. If the set is not on or if this type of viewer is not already tuned to the proper channel, he or she will adjust the receiver. For this selective viewer the broadcasters design programs they hope will be attractive.

The other type of viewer turns on the set out of habit, looking to television to provide companionship and to relieve monotony. He or she is "watching TV" rather than making conscious choices among programs. To explain these viewers, former NBC program executive Paul Klein formulated a "Least Objectionable Program (LOP) Theory" which hypothesizes that some people shift channels more to avoid the unusually dull than to find the especially attractive. Even if only five percent of the population are of this type (and the proportion is probably much higher), they are important to the ratings figures. In statistical calculations it makes no difference if a set is tuned to a program because a selective viewer really wants to see it or because the TV watcher was not sufficiently bored to change the dial.

No broadcaster expects to have the top rating in every time period of the week. Each is content with a share of audience approximately equal to that of the competition. But no broadcaster can afford to have even one time period so dull it will drive the audience to the other channels. That would be disastrous for the rest of the morning or afternoon or evening in which it occurred. It would take several hours to regain a fair share of those who just watch television and who are required for satisfactory rating figures.

For most, television is a very profitable business. The critics are quite correct in feeling the station can afford to give away a half-hour here and there to present an important program that will not be sponsored. The broadcasters' problem is that they see a half-hour allocated for an educational program driving away the audience and depriving the broadcasters of revenues for much more time than the critic would think of requesting. Thus, the ratings extend their influence to those who make reasonable requests for small amounts of time in which to present significant programming.

The most serious criticism of television advertising is directed at broadcasters not for something they do themselves but for what they permit others to do on their facilities. Since the mid-1920s when it became clear that America was committed to a broadcast system financed by sale of time for advertising, broadcasters have regulated advertisers only by limiting the amount of time for commercials in a program and by refusing to carry commercials for certain products. So long as the products were legitimate and not harmful and the advertising techniques were not proscribed by the Federal Trade Commission or the industry code, an advertiser was free to do as he or she pleased on the air.

As noted in Chapter 5 the major controversy of the 1970s revolved around whether a broadcaster should permit an advertiser to direct commercials to the children who have been drawn to home sets in such large numbers. Should the host who has become like a family member be permitted to act as a salesperson for products? Should advertisements for important items like vitamins and cereals be directed at children who will insist on something their parents may not consider best for them? In short, should the *caveat emptor* attitude taken toward advertising for adults be suspended when the viewers are preschoolers who have yet to develop defenses against sophisticated sales messages?

Broadcasters' first inclination might be to say that parents should direct their criticism and threats of retaliation against advertisers; stations and networks simply make their facilities available for the accepted practice of selling goods. Broadcasters might also be tempted to disclaim responsibility if parents are unable or unwilling to prevail over their children in important decisions of how the parents' money is to be spent for items affecting health. Neither answer will satisfy parents who feel that broadcasters are irresponsible if they permit their facilities to be used irresponsibly by others. Until some accommodation is reached, broadcasters must expect to be criticized for permitting misuse of their privileged status as guests in the home and members of the family.

15.4 CONTROVERSIES ABOUT ENTERTAINMENT BROADCASTING

The controversy surrounding purposive broadcasting is fairly simple because the material is overt and easy to describe. The controversy surrounding entertainment programming is much more difficult because the effects are apt to be unintentional and cannot be clearly defined.

Controversy about Entertainment Programming and Stereotypes

There is an inherent danger in entertainment because people come to it with their guards down and are susceptible to influences they would resist in other circumstances. This is demonstrated by the practice of some manufacturers who incur major expenses in order to have their products given away as prizes on game shows. Because the descriptions of the products are not obvious commercials, they are frequently more credible.

The danger arises if writers and producers either consciously or unconsciously cast certain roles so that members of a group are consistently portrayed in a particular way. This constitutes stereotyping, and it has been a problem for various ethnic minorities and for women over many years. For example, it was customary in the movies and in radio for blacks to be cast either as buffoons or in lazy, contented, subservient roles. The listener-viewer who perceived blacks only in such roles in entertainment tended to associate real-life blacks with the stereotypes. There was a concerted effort to keep off television the radio stereotypes of blacks personified by "Amos 'n Andy" and the servile buffoon Rochester in the Jack Benny programs. Broadcasters have responded by using blacks in a few more roles but there is still a valid complaint that blacks are not being portrayed on television in the variety of roles approximating real life or as fully as are whites.

As the women's movement grew stronger in the 1960s, there was an attempt to stop casting women as only secretaries, nurses, school teachers, and housewives. A program trend of the same decade was the detective series in which criminals were frequently associated with the Mafia or Cosa Nostra, a peculiarly Italian organization in the minds of most. In response to vigorous protests from Italian-Americans, television producers began refraining from giving criminals obvious Italian names and from referring to either the Mafia or the Cosa Nostra.

Stereotyping is one of the most vicious practices that can exist in a society and a broadcaster has one clear responsibility—to ensure there is never cause for criticism by being sure stereotyping does not occur. This policy includes having a sensitivity that stereotyping can also occur in commercials and working with advertisers, if necessary, to curb any tendencies in that direction.

Controversy about Violence on Television

Concern about violence on television began in the earliest days of the medium in the late 1940s. That the broadcasters were sensitive to the criticism was indicated in the first television code written in 1951. There was a paragraph on violence in the section on children's programming. There was to be no violence for the sake of violence and it was never to be shown in an attractive light.

The presence of violence in television in the early days was predictable. The network schedules were limited and the stations were forced to fill substantial amounts of time on their own. After scheduling some old theatrical films, the next readily available source of programming was antiquated cartoons that had long since completed their box office runs. A major source of the humor was slapstick violence to which children reacted as enthusiastically as their parents had years before in movie theaters. As the old cartoons proved to be successful programming during the "children's hours" (Saturday and Sunday mornings and weekdays after school), new ones were made in the old formula. Violence abounded.

Drawn for BROADCASTING by Sid Hix

"Violence on TV has nothing to do with it. They're fighting over me!"

Reprinted, with permission, from Broadcasting

When the networks began regular service, their programming for adults followed the proven formula of the morality story in which there was conflict between the "good guys" and the "bad guys"—the former were expected to win and punish the latter, and the more violent the punishment the better. There were cowboys and Indians, sheriffs and rustlers, policemen and crooks, and detectives and murderers. In the intense rivalry for ratings it was discovered that violence in itself was a popular ingredient, so violence multiplied. The factor that concerned many was that youngsters watched television much later in the evening than anyone would have predicted. Between the cartoon programs presented by the stations and the adult programming from the networks, children were seeing far more violence than their parents had experienced in their youth (see Fig. 15.2).

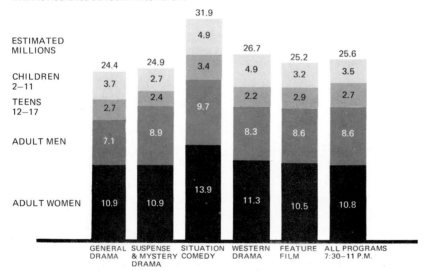

AUDIENCE COMPOSITION OF SELECTED PRIME-TIME PROGRAM TYPES

NIELSEN ESTIMATES
NTI/NAC AUDIENCE DEMOGRAPHICS REPORT

Fig. 15.2
Nielsen estimates show that children constitute an important part of the audiences to all types of prime-time programs between 7:30 and 11 P.M.
Used by permission. A. C. Nielsen Company

In 1954 and 1955 television was considered, among other factors, by a Senate Juvenile Delinquency Subcommittee chaired by Senator Estes Kefauver (D-Tenn.). The subcommittee reported (as would most of its successors in later years) that it had been unable to find a direct and causal relationship between viewing violence on television and subsequent criminal behavior. With great insight the report pointed out the difficulty of meaningful dialogue when broadcasters would only talk about the effect of an individual program on an individual child while critics wanted to discuss the cumulative effect of seemingly endless hours of viewing crime and violence. Broadcasters took the position that television (like an individual in court) should be considered innocent until proven guilty. Critics searched in vain for evidence that specific programs had caused specific antisocial behavior and still maintained that the overall result of so much violence on television must be harmful.

Many studies were conducted by social scientists with conflicting results. The most widely accepted statement on the effect of televised violence on children was made by Schramm, Lyle, and Parker in a 1961 study at Stanford University:

> For some *children, under* some *conditions,* some *television is harmful. For* other *children under the same conditions, or for the same children under* other *conditions, it may be beneficial. For* most *children, under* most *conditions,* most *television is probably neither harmful nor particularly beneficial.**

The Report of the Surgeon General's Committee

In 1969 Senator John O. Pastore (D-R.I.), chairman of the Senate Subcommittee on Communications, asked the surgeon general of the United States to appoint a committee to study what harmful effects, if any, televised crime and violence had on children. Unfortunately, the surgeon general wanted too much to ensure that his committee's report would have the backing of broadcasters. From a long list of nominees he chose forty potential committee members and submitted their names to the presidents of the National Association of Broadcasters and the networks asking them to indicate which would *not* be appropriate on the committee. Seven of the forty names were stricken and from the rest the final twelve were selected. In their report the committee members said they had not been aware of the veto power given to the broadcasters and they regretted it. The report was made in 1972 and, although there was generally good acceptance of it by most people, the method of selecting committee members convinced some critics in advance that the results would be tainted.

* Schramm, Lyle, and Parker, "Television in the Lives of our Children," p. 1.

The committee had a million dollars to cover its expenses in reviewing all past research and commissioning new studies. It worked about two-and-a-half years on the project. The report first considered the known facts about children's viewing:

1. Ninety-six percent of American homes had sets.

2. The average set was on for six hours a day.

3. The average child watched at least two hours a day.

4. Much of the viewing was with only partial attention to television as a child did other things at the same time.

5. The most frequent viewing is from the ages of three to twelve.

6. Most children develop individual program tastes by the time they enter the first grade.

It was then pointed out that violence was a major component of television and of the other media and was most prevalent in the cartoons. Violence seemed to be an attractive element that was used to raise ratings of programs.

After reviewing the evidence of both old and new studies, the committee concluded:

> *The studies reviewed in this chapter indicate that a modest relationship exists between the viewing of violence on television and aggressive tendencies.**

Since the committee members were all respected scientists (including the two who represented CBS and NBC), it is unfortunate that the results were found lacking in credibility. The report is a solid one. The competent personnel had money with which to review past research and commission new studies. There was ample time for considering the evidence. Had broadcasters not been permitted to veto membership, the chances are the results would have been identical and the report accepted as the nearly definitive effort it was with the research tools available.

Following the 1972 report of the surgeon general's committee, attention shifted from televised violence to the ACT petitions on advertising to children. However, there were three news stories in the mid-1970s that kept alive the issue of violence.

"Born Innocent"   In September 1974 NBC aired a television movie, "Born Innocent," about teenage girls in a reformatory. In one of the scenes a girl was held down by several others and "raped" with the wooden handle of a plumber's

---

* "Report of Surgeon General's Advisory Committee on Television and Social Behavior," p. 181.

plunger. Four days later a nine-year-old girl was accosted in a San Francisco park by three older girls and a boy who held her down and performed a similar act with a beer bottle. When apprehended, they said they had seen the movie and had emulated it in the attack.

The girl's mother brought suit for $11 million against NBC and its local affiliate charging negligence in airing the program at 8:00 P.M. when young people customarily watch television. The issue of television's culpability was not resolved, since the judge ruled that negligence was not a restriction on free speech unless the plaintiff could prove NBC intended to create a situation of clear and present danger in which such imitative acts were highly predictable.

The *Zamora* Case Three years later in Miami, Florida, fifteen-year-old Ronnie Zamora robbed the home of an eighty-two-year-old neighbor, but when she caught him in the act, he murdered her. During the trial the defense argued that Zamora had been brainwashed by his many hours of viewing television that had produced in him warped senses of morality and of the value of human life. It was argued he should be found innocent by reason of television-induced insanity and his lawyer tried to call as a witness Telly Savalas, star of "Kojak." The judge refused to subpoena Savalas or to permit psychiatrists to express their views that violence on television was responsible for the murder. The jury returned a verdict of guilty.

The Belson Report It was also in 1977 that Professor William Belson of North East London Polytechnic Institute issued the first report on a study funded by CBS. Working with 1,500 boys aged twelve to seventeen, he concluded that some televised violence may tend to encourage aggression in viewers. Rather than analyze the violence itself, he concentrated on the contexts in which it appeared. He found five types of situations in which violence would be most likely to stimulate undesirable behavior:

1. Violence involving close personal relationships.
2. Fortuitous violence not necessary to plot.
3. Violence in fiction presented with great realism.
4. Violence committed by the "good guys" on the "bad guys."
5. Violence in westerns.

On the other hand he could find no relationship between aggressive behavior and violence in sports, cartoons, science fiction, or slapstick comedy.

By the end of the 1970s it was obvious that those who felt televised violence was responsible for significant aggressive behavior would not be able to persuade broadcasters to change programming. The fact is that every individual is shaped by an extremely complex environment of which television is only one part. He or she is a product of parental influence, neighborhood, schools, peer pressure, presence of absence or religion, comic books, radio, and any number of other items. There are no tools capable of assigning responsibility to individual factors. Even in the "Born Innocent" case where the older girls said they had copied behavior from the program, psychiatrists argue there had to be earlier influences that predisposed them to such antisocial behavior and the program itself only suggested specific actions. It is also pointed out that millions of other young people saw the program without such reactions.

Television critics are still convinced too much televised violence must have an impact on individuals. Broadcasters continue to promise they will remove any specific programs that have proven deleterious effects. Several questions remain that should concern all of us:

1. Is desensitizing children toward violence an issue quite aside from encouraging aggressive behavior? Will society one day reap the whirlwind of bringing up several generations of children to whom the most extreme violence is a matter of course?

2. Is it in the public interest to use scarce broadcasting frequencies to make any contribution to aggression whether it be "modest" or not?

3. If, as study suggests, only a handful of children throughout the country are led by televised violence to extreme aggression that hurts others as well as themselves, would the damage done to those few and those they hurt be more than offset by the pleasure the rest of us receive from viewing the violence without any ill effects?

More General Effects on Children

It was clear from the beginning that television was an excellent babysitter. The moving images claimed the attention of even the youngest children and kept them quiet while parents could get work done. Some parents worried that television might supplant other desirable activities, such as outdoor exercise and reading books. At the same time, they acknowledged that children seemed to become better acquainted with the world outside the home and to grow faster intellectually as they watched television. The purposive programs like NBC's "Ding Dong School" in the 1950s and the later "Mr. Rogers' Neighborhood" on PBS assisted in the socialization of preschool children and furthered their ability to get along with their peers outside the home. Programs like "Sesame Street" aided in developing learning readiness for children starting school, especially in deprived neighborhoods, although there has been little evidence that the early advantage was carried over into later years.

On the other hand, it has been clear that children are becoming addicted to watching television and there was concern about the nonspecific effects this addiction might have on personality. Marshall McLuhan said the "medium is the message" and it really doesn't matter what children watch. Whether it be "Sesame Street," cartoons, or the "Gong Show," children watching television are developing a passivity that may be a handicap in the years ahead. If this is so, broadcasters will say that it is parents who have let children down. It would certainly be unreasonable (and many adults would complain bitterly) if stations were forced to go off the air so children would be forced to do something else.

15.5 UNDERSTANDING PEOPLE

Seeking to explain the media leads to the conclusion that problems will begin to be solved and controversy used when broadcasters and consumers better understand each other as well as the workings of the industry. Most broadcasters are intelligent, honest, and sincere persons who not only want to do well at their jobs but also want to feel that what they do makes a difference. They want to be more than the travelling medieval juggler who brought temporary surcease from misery but left each town exactly as he found it. Broadcasters are frequently frustrated by pressures from stockholders who insist that each year be more profitable than its predecessor, if possible. Most consumer-critics are also intelligent, honest, and sincere. They are frustrated by conditions generally and criticize the most visible media with the knowledge that even if all their demands were met, they still would not achieve all the desired changes in the world generally. Still, they are impelled to do what they can.

Both sides must be willing to put themselves in the other's position and to appreciate the points of view and motivations of the other. Consumer-critics must understand the pressures on well-meaning broadcasters. They should realize that some of the stockholder demands come from their own neighbors who happen to own some broadcast stock and are dependent on its increasing value to counter inflation. They must realize that the plethora of entertainment (including violence) is in response to the will of a majority of fellow citizens who may be less discerning than they. Once they understand the industry, they should confess that if they were broadcast executives they would probably do what is now being done in their desire to survive in the job.

Broadcasters must be willing to put themselves in the position of the consumer who lacks expertise about television but takes its influence on people and society very seriously. They must try to understand the parent whose child is developing undesirable traits while watching the television screen several hours a day. Broadcasters need to sympathize with minority groups who seek a better economic life but see themselves nearly invisible in the most visible of the media. They must remember that many who insist most loudly on the right to be heard do so because the law says that the airwaves really belong to the public and not to broadcasters.

15.6 RIGHTS AND RESPONSIBILITIES
Rights and Responsibilities of Free Enterprise

Nearly all criticism of American broadcasting arises from the consequences of this country's commitment to the free enterprise system in its communications media. Free enterprise must seek profits which are closely related to size of audience. Many might believe broadcasters themselves devised the system and foisted it on the American public. Yet, nothing is further from the truth. It was Herbert Hoover who shaped the system in the early 1920s and whose concepts were accepted by Congress when it passed the Radio Act of 1927. He felt that giving profit-seeking persons and companies the use of the public's frequencies was better than having government or a quasigovernmental organization decide what the American people might receive.

Although Hoover had early doubts about advertising, he never wavered in his support of the system. But, in his annual radio conferences he constantly sought to stimulate in broadcasters a sense of responsibility. Today he would be the first to ask them to face the question: to what extent is a public responsibility inherent in accepting the rights of free enterprise operation on the public airwaves? He would insist that so long as a broadcaster assumed only the minimum responsibility required by law and the FCC, the extent of accountability was at an unsatisfactory level.

Each broadcaster must decide how important it is that society improve rather than stand still or deteriorate. Since one cannot change the world alone, one can at least start to earn the confidence of consumer-critics by dealing with them in complete frankness and persuading them that one really is interested in their points of view. Second, broadcasters can go to as much effort to learn about other people's problems as they devote to their own problems with regulation and competition. Third, broadcasters can welcome rather than resist the pressures to make their profession more responsive to society in general. They can perceive the efforts of the FCC to involve stations in the discussion of public issues as a buffer between themselves and the stockholders who think broadcasters' only purpose should be returning greater profits. They can see that many of those they most resent are, in the final analysis, among their most valuable allies in giving them an opportunity to be more than the medieval juggler. Fourth, the many broadcasters who already have a lively concern for their responsibility can try to communicate it better to their employees. Too much of the consumer criticism of stations and networks is occasioned by second-

and third-echelon personnel who inaccurately understand what their employers value most highly.

Such preliminary steps may or may not lead to changes in programming and employment practices. But in this situation what a broadcaster actually does may be less important than that he or she has a concern that is made clear to the public.

The Rights and Responsibilities of Consumerism

The consumer has a right to enjoy the programming provided by broadcasters on the public's airwaves. There is a further right to protection from any broadcast that might have a demonstrable ill effect on persons, families, or society in general. There is a right to hope that broadcasters, as well as others, will accept a share of responsibility for keeping the society healthy. The consumer-critic has a responsibility to understand broadcasters and their problems as well as he or she wants them to understand the consumer's problems. There is a responsibility to make requests that are not totally inconsistent with broadcasters' right to make money in the free enterprise system.

Drawn for BROADCASTING by Bill Davey

"I liked it better as a vast wasteland."

Reprinted, with permission, from Broadcasting

There is a further responsibility to realize there are some 220 million consumers in this country and each has rights in making demands on stations. There are those who want only entertainment—for better or for worse, that is the way some people are. When the consumer-critic protests that certain matters of particular concern should be emphasized over entertainment, it is a criticism of some fellow consumers as much as it is of broadcasters. Even those who join in criticizing broadcasting may differ greatly about which concerns are most important. There needs to be more dialogue among various consumer groups so their efforts can be focused on the areas of greatest importance.

The Rights and Responsibilities of Free Speech

It is ironic that so much of the controversy between broadcasters and consumers stems from the one concept all endorse most enthusiastically—freedom of speech. This book has noted the conflict between the literalist and functionalist points of view—the right of individuals to express themselves and the right of the public to hear what it deems important. Although they appear at times to be diametrically opposed, the literalist and functionalist approaches are of equal importance in this society and equally deserving of respect.

Discussion of free speech is never simple—there are too many caveats and qualifications to be made. For example, the right to express one's self is never absolute. There are limits, usually relating to the welfare of others. The right to hear belongs to the public and not to an individual or small group. Until one can persuade a substantial part of the public to accept his or her appraisal of what is most important, no *right* to hear it on the air exists.

Broadcasters' right to express themselves must be accompanied by a desire to use at least part of their time for what they think the public has a right and need to hear. Consumers' right to hear must be accompanied by acknowledgment of the general public's right to determine what shall be demanded of the broadcaster.

Philosophically both broadcasters and consumers must face the fact that free speech is meaningless if it is not exercised in significant ways. The broadcaster with nothing to say is subverting the theory of using the public's airwaves in the public interest. The public that refuses to listen to significant ideas and information is doomed to mental deterioration.

15.7 THE NEED FOR COMPROMISE

In free enterprise and free speech there must be compromise. There are too many rights in conflict to expect that anyone can have everything to which he or she feels entitled. Broadcasters must be permitted to make money and willing to accept responsibility. Consumer-critics must be heard by the broadcaster yet willing to accept a judgment that other needs may be more important than theirs. Broadcasters must be permitted to control the broadcast schedule and willing to use wisely the power this control gives. Consumers must make constructive criticism and become partners rather than adversaries to others whose values are different from theirs.

Perhaps the greatest danger we face is that either side or any single group might gain indisputable control over the media. Broadcasters must be held accountable to others as well as to their stockholders. No group of consumer-critics can be in a position to dictate to broadcasters. If one consumer group can dictate today, another will have the same power tomorrow, and the second may be more indifferent to today's activist than were the broadcasters. It would be even more unfortunate if government in the form of the FCC were able to exert total control over radio and television. Power tends to corrupt and the members of government are as susceptible to its corrosive influence as is anyone else. The sharing of power is the ideal in this society. The danger comes when that sharing depends wholly on tests of strength among the participants and the knowledge that many, if they were able, would take all power for themselves.

15.8 IN RETROSPECT AND IN PROSPECT

In looking back, one sees that the American system has worked. Society absorbed and was changed by broadcasting. Just as none can claim all credit for the beneficial contributions broadcasting has made to this society, so none must bear all blame that radio and television have not done more.

As the blind men saw the elephant differently, so will people see broadcasting from different perspectives. Even with a common understanding of the media, there is room for differences of opinion on what broadcasting has done and should do to this society. There will always be different notions of how conflicting rights in free enterprise and free speech should be resolved. But the future appears bright. As more people are willing to take the time to understand broadcasting and to understand each other, everyone can continue to benefit from prosperous media in a healthy society.

APPENDIX A
EXCERPTS OF THE COMMUNICATIONS ACT OF 1934 AS ORIGINALLY ENACTED

Purpose of the Act

Sec. 1. For the purpose of regulating interstate and foreign commerce in communication by wire and radio so as to make available, so far as possible, to all the people of the United States a rapid, efficient, nation-wide, and world-wide wire and radio communication service with adequate facilities at reasonable charges, . . . there is hereby created a commission to be known as the "Federal Communications Commission," which shall be constituted as hereinafter provided, and which shall execute and enforce the provisions of this Act.

Definitions

Sec. 3. For the purposes of this Act, unless the context otherwise requires—

b) "Radio communication" or "communication by radio" means the transmission by radio of writing, signs, signals, pictures, and sounds of all kinds . . .

c) "Licensee" means the holder of a radio station license granted or continued in force under authority of this Act.

h) "Common Carrier" or "carrier" means any person engaged as a common carrier for hire, in interstate or foreign communication by wire or radio or in interstate or foreign radio transmission of energy, except where reference is made to common carriers not subject to this Act; but a person engaged in radio broadcasting shall not, insofar as such person is so engaged, be deemed a common carrier.

o) "Broadcasting" means the dissemination of radio communications intended to be received by the public, directly or by the intermediary of relay stations.

p) "Chain broadcasting" means simultaneous broadcasting of an identical program by two or more connected stations.

Provisions Relating to the Commission

Sec. 4.
a) The Federal Communications Commission (in this Act referred to as the "Commission") shall be composed of seven commissioners appointed by the President, by and with the advice and consent of the Senate, one of whom the President shall designate as chairman.

b) . . . Not more than four commissioners shall be members of the same political party.

c) . . . shall be appointed for terms of seven years . . .

i) The Commission may perform any and all acts, make such rules and regulations, and issue such orders, not inconsistent with this Act, as may be necessary in the execution of its functions.

License for Radio Communication or Transmission of Energy

Sec. 301.
It is the purpose of this Act, among other things, to maintain the control of the United States over all the channels of interstate and foreign radio transmission; and to provide for the use of such channels, but not the ownership thereof, by persons for limited periods of time, under licenses granted by federal authority, and no such license shall be construed to create any right beyond the terms, conditions, and periods of the license. No person shall use or operate any apparatus for the transmission of energy or communication or signals by radio . . . except under and in accordance with this Act and with a license in that behalf granted under the provisions of this Act.

General Powers of Commission

Sec. 303.   Except as otherwise provided in this Act, the Commission from time to time, as public convenience, interest, or necessity requires shall—

a) Classify radio stations;

b) Prescribe the nature of the service to be rendered by each class of licensed stations and each station within any class;

c) Assign bands of frequencies to the various classes of stations, and assign frequencies for each individual station and determine the power which each station shall use and the time during which it may operate;

d) Determine the location of classes of stations or individual stations;

g) Study new uses for radio, provide for experimental uses of frequencies, and generally encourage the larger and more effective use of radio in the public interest;

i) Have authority to make special regulations applicable to radio stations engaged in chain broadcasting;

o) Have authority to designate call letters of all stations;

Waiver by Licensee

Sec. 304.   No station license shall be granted by the Commission until the applicant therefor shall have signed a waiver of any claim to the use of any particular frequency or of the other as against the regulatory power of the United States because of the previous use of the same, whether by license or otherwise.

Allocation of Facilities; Term of Licenses

Sec. 307.   a) The Commission, if public convenience, interest, or necessity will be served thereby, subject to the limitations of this Act, shall grant to any applicant therefor a station license provided for by this Act.

c) The Commission shall study the proposal that Congress by statute allocate fixed percentages of radio broadcasting facilities to particular types or kinds of nonprofit radio programs or to persons identified with particular types or kinds of nonprofit activities, and shall report to Congress, not later than February 1, 1935, its recommendations together with the reasons for the same.

d) No license granted for the operation of a broadcasting station shall be for a longer term than three years . . .

Applications for Licenses

Sec. 308.   a) The Commission may grant licenses, renewal of licenses, and modification of licenses only upon written application therefor received by it . . .

Granting of Licenses

Sec. 309.   a) If upon examination of any application for a station license or for the renewal or modification of a station license the Commission shall determine that public interest, convenience, or necessity would be served by the granting thereof, it shall authorize the issuance, renewal, or modification thereof in accordance with said finding. In the event the Commission upon examination of any such application does not reach such decision with respect thereto, it shall notify the applicant thereof, shall fix and give notice of a time and place for hearing thereon, and shall afford such applicant an opportunity to be heard under such rules and regulations as it may prescribe.

b) 1) The station license shall not vest in the licensee any right to operate the station nor any right in the use of the frequencies designated in the license beyond the term thereof nor in any other manner than authorized therein.

2) Neither the license nor the right granted thereunder shall be assigned or otherwise transferred in violation of this Act.

Limitation on Holding Licenses

Sec. 310.   a) The station license required hereby shall not be granted to or held by—

1) Any alien or the representative of any alien;

2) Any foreign government or the representative thereof;

3) Any corporation organized under the laws of any foreign government.

b) The station license required hereby, the frequencies authorized to be used by the licensee, and the rights therein granted shall not be transferred, assigned, or in any manner either voluntarily or involuntarily disposed of, or indirectly by transfer of control of any corporation holding such license, to any person, unless the Commission shall, after securing full information, decide that said transfer is in the public interest, and shall give its consent in writing.

Revocation of Licenses

Sec. 312.   a) Any station license may be revoked for false statements either in the application or in the statement of fact which may be required by Section 308 hereof, or because of conditions revealed by such statements of fact as may be required from time to time which would warrant the Commission in refusing to grant a license on an original application, or for failure to operate substantially as set forth in the license . . .

Facilities for Candidates for Public Office

Sec. 315.   If any licensee shall permit any person who is a legally qualified candidate for any public office to use a broadcasting station, he shall afford equal opportunities to all other such candidates for that office in the use of such broadcasting station, and the Commission shall make rules and regulations to carry this provision into effect: *Provided*, that such licensee shall have no power of censorship over the material broadcast under the provisions of this section. No obligation is hereby imposed upon any licensee to allow the use of its station by any such candidates.

Announcement That Matter Is Paid for

Sec. 317.   All matter broadcast by any radio station for which service, money, or any other valuable consideration is directly or indirectly paid, or promised to or charged or accepted by, the station so broadcasting, from any person, shall, at the time the same is so broadcast, be announced as paid for or furnished, as the case may be, by such person.

Rebroadcasting

Sec. 325.   . . . nor shall any broadcasting station rebroadcast the program or any part thereof of another broadcasting station without the express authority of the originating station.

Censorship

Sec. 326.   Nothing in this Act shall be understood or construed to give the Commission the power of censorship over the radio communications or signals transmitted by any radio station, and no regulation or condition shall be promulgated or fixed by the Commission which shall interfere with the right of free speech by means of radio communication. No person within the jurisdiction of the United States shall utter any obscene, indecent, or profane language by means of radio communication.

Right of Appeal

Sec. 402.   b) An appeal may be taken, in the manner hereinafter provided, from decisions of the Commission to the Court of Appeals of the District of Columbia in any of the following cases:

1) By any applicant for a construction permit for a radio station, or for a radio-station license, or for renewal of an existing radio-station license, or for modification of an existing radio-station license, whose application is refused by the Commission.

2) By any other person aggrieved or whose interests are adversely affected by any decision of the Commission granting or refusing any such application.

e) At the earliest convenient time the court shall hear and determine the appeal upon the record before it, and shall have power, upon such record, to enter a judgment affirming or reversing the decision of the Commission, and in event the court shall render a decision and enter an order reversing the decision of the Commission, it shall remand the case to the Commission to carry out the judgment of the court: *Provided, however*, That the review by the court shall be limited to questions of law and that findings of fact by the Commission, if supported by substantial evidence, shall be conclusive unless it shall clearly appear that the findings of the Commission are arbitrary or capricious. The court's judgment shall be final, subject, however, to review by the Supreme Court of the United States . . .

War Emergency—Powers of the President

Sec. 606.   c) Upon proclamation by the President that there exists war or a threat of war or a state of public peril or disaster or other national emergency, or in order to preserve the neutrality of the United States, the President may suspend or amend, for such time as he may see fit, the rules and regulations applicable to any or all stations . . . and may cause the closing of any station for radio communication . . .

APPENDIX B
SELECTED AMENDMENTS TO THE COMMUNICATIONS ACT OF 1934

Sec. 303.   Except as otherwise provided in this Act, the Commission from time to time, as public convenience, interest, or necessity requires, shall—

(s) have authority to require that apparatus designed to receive television pictures broadcast simultaneously with sound be capable of adequately receiving all frequencies allocated by the Commission to television broadcasting when such apparatus is shipped in interstate commerce, or is imported from any foreign country into the United States, for sale or resale to the public.

Sec. 310.   . . . Any such application for transfer of license shall be disposed of as if the proposed transferee or assignee were making application under Section 308 for the permit or license in question; but in acting thereon the Commission may not consider whether the public interest, convenience, and necessity might be served by the transfer, assignment, or disposal of the permit or license to a person other than the proposed transferee or assignee.

Sec. 315.   . . . Appearance by a legally qualified candidate on any—

1) *bona fide* newscast,

2) *bona fide* news interview,

3) *bona fide* news documentary (if the appearance of the candidate is incidental to the presentation of the subject or subjects covered by the news documentary), or

4) on-the-spot coverage of *bona fide* news events (including but not limited to political conventions and activities incidental thereto),

shall not be deemed to be use of a broadcasting station within the meaning of this subsection. Nothing in the foregoing sentence shall be construed as relieving broadcasters, in connection with the presentation of newscasts, news interviews, news documentaries, and on-the-spot coverage of news events, from the obligation imposed upon them under this Act to operate in the public interest and to afford reasonable opportunity for the discussion of conflicting views on issues of public importance.

Sec. 508.   a) . . . any employee of a radio station who accepts or agrees to accept from any person (other than such station), or any person (other than such station) who pays or agrees to pay such employee, any money, service, or other valuable consideration for the broadcast of any matter over such station shall, in advance of such broadcast, disclose the fact of such acceptance or agreement to such station.

(g) Any person who violates any provision of this section shall, for each such violation, be fined not more than $10,000 or imprisoned not more than one year, or both.

Sec. 509.   a) It shall be unlawful for any person, with intent to deceive the listening or viewing public—

(1) To supply to any contestant in a purportedly *bona fide* contest of intellectual knowledge or intellectual skill any special and secret assistance whereby the outcome of such contest will be in whole or in part prearranged or predetermined.

(c) Whoever violates subsection (a) shall be fined not more than $10,000 or imprisoned not more than one year, or both.

GLOSSARY

Access Channels In cable, channels required by FCC and some franchisers, for use by public, education, and government; also leased.

Access Hour The hour between 7 P.M. and 11 P.M. local time in which affiliated and owned stations may not carry network feed or off-network programs.

Ad hoc Network A number of stations carrying a single program or series simultaneously with no other ongoing relationship among them.

Adjacent Channels Television channels which adjoin each other on the radio spectrum.

Administrative Law Judge (ALJ) FCC staff member who presides at hearings and recommends actions to the Commission. Formerly called "Hearing Examiner."

Advertising "Mix" Combination of time buys in an advertising campaign usually involving network and spot, different classes of time, and different programs (also different media).

All-Channel Receiver Television receiver capable of tuning in the UHF as well as the VHF broadcast channels.

Alternate Sponsor   An advertiser who shares with another the cost of time and program and uses half the commercial openings.

Amplitude Modulation (AM)   (1) Refers to method of imposing program on carrier wave by modulating amplitude or strength of signal. (2) Refers to medium wave or standard broadcasting between 535 and 1605 kHz.

AM-FM Combination   AM and FM stations operated by a single licensee in a community.

AM-FM Duplication   The same program schedule being simultaneously carried on commonly owned AM and FM stations in a community.

Antisiphoning Rules   FCC rules preventing both subscription TV and pay cable from purchasing certain program material which has been of great importance to conventional television.

Area of Dominant Influence (ADI)   Arbitron term for "market" or the area from which business tends to flow to a focal point. Cf. DMA.

Ascertainment   The procedure by which problems of the community are studied when preparing an application for a new station or license renewal.

Availability   Time spot in the schedule which is currently available for sale to an advertiser.

Barter   (1) A form of syndication in which the advertiser donates a program to a station in return for a specified number of free commercial minutes in the program. (2) An arrangement in which the station waives compensation for carrying a network program in return for commercial openings which are left open for sale by the affiliate.

Bicycle Network   Circulation of programs among affiliates by mail so individual episodes are seen in different weeks on different stations.

Billings   The total amount of bills to advertisers by broadcasting category, such as AM stations, FM stations, networks, national spot, etc.

Blacklisting   The practice of listing producers, writers, and performers who were unacceptable to certain groups in the 1940s and 1950s, presumably on the grounds of being alleged Communist sympathizers.

Blue Book   1946 document of the FCC entitled "Public Service Responsibility of Broadcast Licensees."

***Bona Fide* News**   In Section 315, news programming on which the appearance of a candidate is not considered "use" and therefore does not incur an equal-opportunity liability by the broadcaster.

Broadcast Channel   The segment of the radio spectrum assigned to a broadcast station.

Broadcasting   Transmission of radio and television programs to reach all or part of the general public. Contrast with point-to-point transmission intended for a limited number of receivers.

Cable Franchise   Document from the local community permitting a cable system to install its equipment along or under the streets and to sell its services to homes.

Cable Penetration   Percentage of homes on the cable route which have subscribed to the service.

Cable Pseudo Freeze   Period from 1965 to 1972 in which cable growth in the top 100 markets was virtually halted by refusal of the FCC to grant microwave licenses for importation without full hearings.

Cable Television   Delivery of television programs to homes by cable as opposed to over-the-air transmission. Cable service may include CATV, importation, origination, access channels, and pay cable.

Cable Three-Tiered Regulation   Reference to fact that three levels of government are involved in much cable regulation: local community gives franchise under guidelines of state commission and the FCC issued the Certificate of Compliance.

Carrier Wave   The broadcast signal on which program material is imposed.

Certificate of Compliance   An FCC document required for operation of cable television.

Chain Broadcasting   Term used in the Communications Act of 1934 to denote network broadcasting.

Chain Regulations   FCC rules pertaining to network-station relations. Originally eight were passed in 1941, followed by others (including three promulgated in 1970).

Channel Assignments   Assignment of commercial and educational TV channels to specific communities during the TV Freeze from 1948 to 1952.

Channel Separation Factor   The minimum mileage which must separate television stations: co-channel separation = miles required between stations on the same channel; adjacent-channel separation = miles required between stations on adjacent channels.

Class of Time   Division of broadcast schedule into segments with different prices: e.g., prime time vs. day time vs. "fringe time," etc.

Clear and Present Danger   A situation in which freedom of speech can be justifiably curtailed.

Closed Caption (CC)   Subtitles included in the television transmission available to the hard-of-hearing who have special attachments for their sets.

Closed-Circuit Television (CCTV)   Transmission of television signal by wire or radio waves not available to people with conventional over-the-air receivers.

Co-Axial Cable (co-ax)   Series of wires in a shield which can carry several television programs or thousands of telephone conversations.

Commercial Minute (or Thirty)   A unit of time sold for a commercial message in participating advertising. Contrast with sponsorship.

Community Antenna Television (CATV)   (1) Generic term for all cable television in the 1950s and 1960s. (2) A cable system's delivery to homes of programs picked up directly off the air as opposed to importation.

Compensation   Money stations receive for carrying network programs.

Compulsory License (copyright)   Right to use copyrighted material without negotiating with copyright holder. Includes payment of fee to a group which will distribute money to the owners of the material.

Construction Permit (CP)   FCC authorization to build a station with assurance that the license will be granted when final engineering data based on performance are satisfactory.

Continuity   (1) Nondramatic script for broadcasting. (2) Continuity writer— one who writes routine material for announcer and commercials and public service announcements. (3) Continuity acceptance—reviewing material to be broadcast to ensure maintenance of standards of good taste.

Cooperative Advertising (co-op)   Arrangement in which retailer buys local time to run manufacturer's commercial followed by local announcement of where product may be purchased. Cost is shared by retailer and manufacturer.

Cost per Point (CPP)   The cost to an advertiser or delivering a commercial to one percent of the homes or persons.

Cost per Thousand (CPM)   The cost to an advertiser of delivering a commercial to a thousand homes.

Counter Commercials   Airing of anticigarette public service announcements during period when cigarettes were being advertised on radio and television.

Cross-Ownership   The common ownership of different media, such as: (1) newspaper and broadcast stations (s) in a community, (2) broadcast station(s) and cable system in a community, (3) television network and cable system anywhere. It does not refer to common ownership of different broadcast services (AM, FM, TV) in a community.

Cumulative Audience (Cume)   The estimated percentage of homes which are tuned to part of a program during one or more episodes.

Deintermixture   FCC attempts in the 1950s to solve the UHF problem by changing "mixed markets" to either all VHF or all UHF.

Demographics   The characteristics of the audience in terms of age, sex, income, etc.

Designated Market Area (DMA)   Term used by A. C. Nielson Co. to indicate geographic area where a station is received. DMA is subdivided into the Metro Area, the local DMA, and the adjacent DMA, Cf. ADI.

Diary   Method of measuring the audience by asking respondents to keep a written record of viewing and listening during a week.

Digital Television   Use of pulse code modulation to translate video and sound signals into a binary computer code consisting of "ones" and "zeros."

Direct Broadcast Satellite (DBS)   A satellite transmission intended to be picked up directly by home receivers.

Direct Wave   Radio signal traveling by line-of-sight from the transmitter to the receiving antenna.

Directionalized Antenna   Transmitting antenna arrangement which causes more signal strength in some directions than in others.

Distress Sale   FCC authorization to sell for a reduced price a station whose license is in jeopardy.

Double Billing   An illegal practice in cooperative advertising when station receipts two bills for time purchased. Retailer pays the smaller bill and sends the larger to the manufacturer for partial reimbursement.

Drive Time   The early morning and late afternoon hours when many radio listeners are commuting by car.

Earth Station   An installation for transmitting signals to and receiving signals from a communications satellite.

Economic Injury   The harmful economic impact of a new station or a cable system on an existing station.

Educational Reservations   Setting aside FM and television channels for noncommercial use by educational institutions.

Educational Television   (1) Generic name of stations designated by the FCC as noncommercial. Currently called public television stations. (2) Broadcasting of educational material on either public or commercial stations. (3) Any broadcast activity by an educational institution.

Electromagnetic Spectrum   The range of all electromagnetic energy, including radio and visible light.

Electron Gun   Device which aims electrons at elements in the television camera. Reflected electons cause modulations of electrical energy.

Electronic News Gathering (ENG)   Recording news events on portable videotape recorders instead of film, or sending the signals directly back to the studio for recording and transmission.

Electronic Television   Television system in which neither studio nor receiving equipment has physically moving parts.

"Equal Time Law"   Popular misnomer for Section 315 of the Communications Act of 1934 which requires broadcaster to give equal opportunity to opposing candidates.

Exclusive Affiliation   Earlier practice where station agreed to carry no programs from a network other than the one with which it was affiliated.

Fairness Doctine   FCC rules and policies requiring stations to devote a reasonable amount of time to discussion of controversial issues and to see that opposing points of view are aired.

Fiber Optics   Distribution of television material, imposed on light waves, through a hair-thin glass core.

Fifty-Fifty (50–50) Rule   Proposed FCC rule in the 1960s which would have required networks to control no more than half of their prime-time programming.

Fixed Assignments   Assigning television channels to communities and accepting applications only on the basis of the prior assignments.

Fixed-Rate Price   Highest price for a commercial spot which is not subject to preemption for another advertiser.

Flight   A unit of the national spot campaign covering expenditures of specifice amounts in specific communities in a specific length of time.

Frequency Modulation (FM)   Imposing program on carrier wave by modulating the frequency of the wave within its channel.

FM Multiplexing   Transmission of more than one program on an FM channel, as in stereophonic broadcasting (two signals), and quadrophonic broadcasting (four signals).

Format Radio   Station schedules designed to attract one segment of the audience all day long with comparatively similar programming.

Fringe Time   Between day time and prime time in television rate card. Usually about 4:30 to 6:00 P.M.

Full-Network Station   In cable regulations, a network affiliate which carries at least 85 percent of its network's prime-time feed.

Government-Chartered Monopoly A system of broadcasting in which facilities are owned by a chartered organization of private citizens, e.g., British Broadcasting Corporation and the Independent Broadcasting Authority in England.

Government-Licensed Free Enterprise A system of broadcasting in which stations are licensed to private individuals or companies who seek to make a profit from the operations, e.g., United States.

Government-Owned and Operated A system of broadcasting in which the government owns all facilities and employs all broadcasters. Found in most countries of the world.

Grandfather Clause Provision that existing enterprises may for a period of time continue practices or conditions prohibited to new enterprises.

"Great Debates" The televised debates between presidential candidates Nixon and Kennedy in 1960.

Ground Wave Radio signal traveling along the contours of the earth.

Group Owner Single licensee of stations in two or more communities.

Headend The location from which the TV signals received directly off the air and the imported signals received by microwave are sent on to homes by cable.

Hearing Examiner Former title of the Administrative Law Judge (ALJ).

Hertz (Hz) One cycle per second (frequency with which wave crests pass a given point). The abbreviations kHz and mHz refer to thousands and millions of cycles per second, respectively.

High Fidelity Capacity of FM signal to carry the full range of sound which is audible to the human ear.

Homes Using Television (HUT) Estimated percentage of homes where the set is being used at a given time.

Importation Distribution by cable of broadcast signals taken off the air at a distant point and relayed to the headend by microwave relay or satellite.

Independent Station A station having no relationship with a network.

Institutional Advertising Commercials telling the good features of the advertiser without trying to sell specific products.

Instructional Television Fixed Services (ITFS) Use of frequencies in the 2500 mHz range for distributing instructional television among buildings which are reasonably close together.

Instructional Television Use of television programming in conjunction with the formal classroom.

Interactive Cable Use of the upstream capacity to send signals from a subscribing home back to the cable studio.

Interconnection In public broadcasting, the designation of PBS as simply distributing programs as opposed to being a network which would also control what it distributed.

Interim Operation Arrangement for joint operation of a new station by some or all of the applicants while the FCC determines which should eventually get the license.

Jamming Transmitting noise on a frequency being used by another party so the interference nullifies the program being jammed.

Kennelly-Heaviside Layer Layer of the ionosphere from which some sky waves will be reflected back to the earth.

Kilohertz (kHz) Thousands of cycles per second.

Kinescope (1) The picture tube in the receiver. (2) Kinescope recording is making a motion picture off the face of the kinescope tube.

Lead-in Audience The portion of the audience viewing the preceding program which remains for the next program.

Leapfrogging Cable importation of independent station signals from cities more distant than the two closest of the top 25 markets.

Licensee Individual or company licensed by the FCC to operate a broadcast station.

Line Charges The network payments to AT&T for distribution of programs to stations.

Local Carriage In cable, the requirement that cable systems carry all local stations.

Lowest Unit Charge In Section 315, the requirement that broadcasters not charge candidates more than the lowest rate advertisers are paying for the same class and amount of time.

Magazine Concept (1) Participation advertising where commercial time is purchased in program controlled by the broadcasters. (2) Programming format which includes unrelated sgements.

Magnetic Impression The alignment of magnetic particles on tape which, when played back, will recreate electrical modulations coming from the microphone or television camera.

Margin of Error The range around an estimated percentage in which there is confidence that the true figure lies.

Market An area from which business tends to flow to a central community. Cf. ADI, DMA.

Master Antenna   Receiving antenna which services a limited number of households in close proximity—usually requires no amplification of signals.

Mechanical Television   System of television where studio and receiving equipment have physically moving parts, such as a wheel with a concentric circle of holes which serves as a scanning device.

Megahertz (mHz)   Millions of cycles per second.

Merchandising   Relating advertising to the point of sales through use of store displays of sponsored products and of the programs on which they are advertised.

Microwave Relay   Distribution of television and other signals by beamed radio relay between points on mountains or high buildings.

Minimum Channel Capacity   FCC rule that cable systems in the top 100 markets must install a system with at least 20 channels and with an "upstream capacity."

Mixed Markets   Communities in which the FCC assigned both VHF and UHF stations during the Television Freeze.

Modulation   Encoding a program by altering or changing the amplitude, frequence or pulse code of the carrier wave.

Monitor   TV set on which the television program is seen in the studio and control rooms.

Multiple-Ownership Rules   FCC limitations on the number of broadcast stations which may be owned by a single licensee.

Multipoint Distribution Service (MDS)   Use of microwaves to transmit pay cable programs to apartment houses or homes not connected to a cable system.

National Spot Business   Station sale of time to nonlocal advertiser through the station representative: contrasts with network business.

Network   (1) Technically, two or more stations carrying the same program simultaneously. (2) A number of stations making an arrangement with a network organization to carry programming distributed by the network. (3) A number of stations carrying a single program or series simultaneously with no other ongoing relationship among them.

Network Affiliate   (1) Commercial station which signs a contract agreeing to carry network programs in return for compensation. (2) Noncommercial station which pays a membership fee in return for permission to carry network programs.

Network Cooperative Programming (co-op)   A program distributed by a network with openings for commercials to be sold locally. Stations reimburse network for program costs.

Network Feed   Programs distributed by networks to stations.

Network Owned and Operated Stations (O&O's)   Broadcast stations licensed to one of the national networks.

Network Primary Affiliate   Station which normally carries most programs from the network. Contrasts with secondary affiliate which carries from the network only some of those programs the primary affiliate rejects.

Noncommercial Television   The FCC designation of broadcast stations which are also called ''educational'' or ''public.'' May not accept money from sale of time for advertising.

Off-Network Syndication   Sale to stations of rerun rights to programs which have been on a network earlier.

Original syndication   Sale to stations of right to show television programs which were produced specifically for syndication and have not been shown on the networks.

Origination   In cable, distribution of program material not received from a broadcast station, but normally produced in the system's studio or generated on its film chain or videotape playback, or received by satellite relay.

Participating Advertiser   One who buys commercial spots within a program provided by and controlled by the broadcaster. Contrast with sponsor who had degree of ownership or control over program.

Patron Plan   Donation of program funds to public television by commercial company. Grant must be acknowledged at beginning and end of program.

Pay Cable   Distribution by cable of material for which viewer pays in additon to subscription fee for other basic services.

Payola   Illegal radio practice in which record companies surreptitiously pay disk jockeys to play certain tunes.

Penetration (FM, UHF, cable, etc.)   The percentage of homes equipped to receive a given type of service.

Persons Using Television (PUT)   The estimated percent of persons in a population segment who are watching television.

Petition to Deny Renewal   A request to the FCC that a station's license not be renewed.

Phonevision   System of Pay TV using telephone line to provide a synchronizing element to unscramble the broadcast picture.

Pilot Program   A program prepared as a sample for a proposed series.

Preemptible Rate   Less than the highest fixed price with the understanding that if another advertiser will pay the fixed rate, that commercial will be placed in the spot purchased.

Preemption   Cancellation of a regularly scheduled program for a special or a news event.

Pre-Freeze Station   Television station authorized by FCC prior to beginning of the TV Freeze in September 1948, although it might not have started broadcasting until two or three years later.

Prime Time   The highest priced time in the schedule. In television, from 7 to 11 P.M.; in radio, during drive time, 7 to 9 A.M. and 4:30 to 6 P.M.

Prime Time Access Rule (PTAR)   A 1970 FCC Chain Regulation ruling that affiliated television stations might not carry more than three hours of network programming between 7 and 11 P.M. local time.

Program Exclusivity   Cable regulation prohibiting importation of a program being aired by a local station.

Program Packager   Company other than station or network which delivers a program ready for airing.

Program Syndication   Sale of programs specifically produced for television to individual stations or to groups of stations.

Public Access Channels   Cable channels required by FCC and some franchises to be open to the public on a first-come, first-served basis without advertising and without censorship of content.

Public Affairs Programming   A term loosely applied to programming related to current events and discussion. Sometimes synonymous with "public service," although the latter implies absence of advertising.

Public Interest, Convenience, and Necessity   The criterion laid down in the Communications Act of 1934 as a guide to all actions by the FCC.

Public Service Announcement (PSA)   An announcement for an educational, charitable, or other nonprofit group carried by stations without charge.

Public Service Programming   A term loosely applied to sustaining programs which are other than entertainment. Sometimes interchangeable with "public affairs."

Public Television   Label for noncommercial television stations and related activities which, prior to 1967, were called educational television.

Pulse Code Modulation (PCM)   Modulating or altering the carrier wave by turning it "on" and "off" millions of times per second.

Quadraphonic Broadcasting   Transmission of four related signals on one FM carrier wave (see FM Multiplexing).

Quiz Scandals   Revelation in the late 1950s that some of the big-money television quiz programs had been "rigged."

Radio Schedule Syndication   Sale to a radio station of all material for the schedule except news and commercials.

Radio Spectrum   The frequency range of radio energy including portions used for broadcasting. Spectrum extends from under 10 kHz to over 100,000 mHz.

Radiotelephony   Use of radio to carry telephone conversations. A necessary prerequisite to the development of broadcasting.

Radio Wave Frequency   The number of cycles per second (hertz) or the number of wave crests passing a given point in a second. A measurement used to differentiate among radio waves, e.g., 600 kHz vs. 1200 kHz.

Radio Wave Length   The distance between the crests of individual waves. A measurement used to differentiate among radio waves, e.g., 10 meters vs. 20 meters.

Random Digital Dialing   Use of a computer to select telephone numbers at random.

Random Sample   A sample chosen so every member of the population has an equal chance of being selected.

Rate Card   List of prices charged by a station or network along with information on facilities and policies.

Rating   (1) In television, estimated percentage of television homes tuned to a given station at a given time. (2) In radio, estimated percentage of persons tuned to a given station at a given time.

Remote Unit   The equipment required to originate a radio or television program from a location outside the studio.

Renewal Challenge   Request that a license up for renewal be given to someone other than the incumbent.

Representative Sample   A sample chosen to include in proper proportions the characteristics of the population from which it is drawn. Normally accomplished by drawing a random sample.

Roster Recall   Audience measurement by asking the interviewee to recall listening activities for previous time period while consulting a roster of stations.

Run of Schedule (ROS)   Purchasing a quantity of commercial openings at low rates without specifying in advance when the commercials will be aired.

Sampling Making generalizations about a population based on information gathered from a small portion of the total.

Satellite Relay Distribution of television program via satellite which receives signal from one point and relays it to an earth station within the line-of-sight horizon.

Satellite Subscription Television (SSTV) Satellite transmission of subscription programming directly to home receivers.

Saturation Campaign Purchase of many commercial openings throughout a station's schedule with little attention to programs in which they will be aired.

Servicing the Account A wide range of activities making certain the advertising contract is fulfilled and that the advertiser is pleased enough to renew the contract.

Sets in Use Index (SIU) In radio, the estimated percentage of receivers being used at a given time.

Share Estimated percentage of viewing homes which are tuned to a program or to a station at a given time. In radio, percentage of listening persons.

Simulcast Broadcasting a program on both radio and television.

Sky Wave Radio signal traveling up from the transmitter and going out into space or being relfected back to earth by the Kennelly-Heaviside layer of the ionosphere.

Special (spectacular) Occasional nonseries program in place of series episode.

Sponsorship (1) Loosely applied to any broadcast advertising. (2) In traditional radio, the purchase of a time unit by an advertiser who provided the program and used all the commercial openings. (3) In modern times a radio or television advertiser who buys all the commercial spots in a program or program segment.

Station Program Cooperative (SPC) The mechanism whereby public television stations "vote" on the Public Broadcast Service schedule by telling for which programs they are willing to pay in proportional shares.

Station Representative (Rep) A company serving as a station's time sales organization in the national spot market.

Step Process An arrangement whereby the network provides money in successive steps for program development.

Stereophic Broadcasting Transmission of two related signals on one FM carrier wave (See FM Multiplexing).

Storage Instantaneous Audimeter (SIA)   The device used by the A. C. Nielsen Company to record tuning information about a television set and then to deliver it to a central computer on demand.

"Stripping" a Program   Scheduling a program at the same time five or more days a week ("across the board").

Subscription Television (STV)   Transmission over a conventional broadcast channel of a coded program for which the subscriber must pay by renting a decoding device.

Superstation   A conventional television station whose signal is relayed by satellite to cable systems as part of their importation services.

Sustaining Program   A program without commercials.

Sweep   A period during which television audiences are being measured in a market.

Syndication   Sale of program material directly to stations (see Program Syndication and Radio Schedule Syndication).

Tax Certificate   FCC document given to one who sells a station to minorities permitting deferment of capital gains taxes.

Telephone Coincidental   Audience measurement by telephone interview to ascertain viewing or listening at the moment.

Telephone Recall   Audience measurement by telephone interview to ascertain viewing or listening during an earlier period.

Teletext   Transmission of printed copy to a television screen by a broadcast signal.

Television Freeze   Period from September 1948 through June 1952 during which the FCC processed no license applications but sought to complete a blueprint for long-range development of national system.

Theatrical Film   Motion pictures produced primarily for exhibition in theaters.

Tiered Services   In cable, the offering of different levels of services at different costs.

Time Buyer   Advertising agency employee who purchases time on stations in a national spot campaign.

"Topless" ("Sex") Radio   Talk programs in the early 1970s emphasizing explicit telephone discussion of sexual topics.

Traffic   Reference to the second-by-second schedule of a station or network. Traffic manager prepares the schedule.

Transponder   Equipment (on a satellite, for example) which receives and retransmits signals.

Ultra High Frequencies (UHF)   Portion of the radio spectrum opened up to television stations during the Freeze. (Channels 14–83)

UHF Converter   A device attached to the VHF television receiver enabling it to receive UHF stations also.

Upstream Capacity   The ability of a cable system to carry signals from a subscribing home back to the headend.

Very High Frequencies (VHF)   Portion of the radio spectrum opened to television station in 1940. (Channels 2–13).

Video Disc (disk)   Recording a television program on a disc either by cutting grooves like audio records or by imposing a pattern which can be "read" by a laser beam.

Videotape Recording (VTR)   Recording a television program by imposing magnetic impressions on plastic tape.

Viewdata   Transmission of printed copy to a television screen by wire.

Waste Circulation   Persons in the audience who are neither potential purchasers of the product being advertised nor likely to influence those who will purchase.

Wire Services   Organizations delivering news by teletype to stations 24 hours a day. Also provide photo services for television stations.

Wireless Telegraphy   Early use of radio to send messages in "dot and dash" code.

Zapple Doctrine   Extension of the Fairness Doctrine to cover all aspects of political campaigning not covered by Section 315.

INDEX OF INITIALS

Asterisk (*) indicates inclusion of the item in the Glossary.

AOR   Album Oriented Rock

AP   Associated Press

ASCAP   American Society of Composers, Authors, and Publishers

AT&T   American Telephone and Telegraph Company

BBC   British Broadcasting Corporation

BEM   Business Executives Move for Peace in Vietnam

BEST   Black Efforts for Soul in Television

BMI   Broadcast Music Incorporated

BRC   Broadcast Rating Council

CATV*   Community Antenna Television

CBS   Columbia Broadcasting System

CC*   Closed Caption

CCTV*   Closed Circuit Television

C&W   Country and Western

CNN   Cable News Network

COMSAT Communications Satellite Corporation

CP*   Construction Permit

CPB   Corporation for Public Broadcasting

CPM*   Cost per Thousand

CPP*   Cost per Point

CRT   Copyright Royalty Tribunal

C-SPAN Cable Satellite Public Affairs Network

CTW   Children's Television Workshop

DBS*   Direct Broadcast Satellite

DJ   Disk Jockey

DMA*   Designated Market Area

DuM   Dumont Network

EHF   Extremely High Frequencies

ENG*   Electronic News Gathering

ESPN   Entertainment and Sports Programming Network

ET   Electrical Transcription

ETS   Educational Television Stations division of NAEB

ETV*   Educational Television

FCBA   Federal Communications Bar Association

FCC	Federal Communications Commission
FRC	Federal Radio Commission
FTC	Federal Trade Commission
HBO	Home Box Office
HUT*	Homes Using Television
IBA	Independent Broadcasting Authority (England)
INS	International News Service
ITA	Independent Television Authority (England)
ITFS*	Instructional Television Fixed Services
JCET	Joint Committee (later Council) for Educational Television
kHz	KiloHertz
MBS	Mutual Broadcasting System
MDS*	Multipoint Distribution Service
mHz	MegaHertz
MOR	Middle of the Road (radio format)
NAB	National Association of Broadcasters
NAEB	National Association of Educational Broadcasters
NBC	National Broadcasting Company
NAIPD	National Association of Independent Program Directors
NCCB	National Citizens Committee for Broadcasting
NCTA	National Cable Television Association
NET	National Educational Television
NPACT	National Public Affairs Center for Television
NPR	National Public Radio
NTIA	National Telecommunications and Information Agency
NTSC	National Television Systems Committee
O&O	(Network) Owned and Operated
OPT	Operation Prime Time
OTP	Office of Telecommunications Policy
OWI	Office of War Information
PAO	Public Affairs Officer
PBL	Public Broadcasting Laboratory
PCM*	Pulse Code Modulation
PD	Program Director

BIBLIOGRAPHY

Adler, Richard, and Carter, Douglass, eds. *Television as a Cultural Force*. New York: Praeger, 1976.

————. *Television as a Social Force: New Approaches to TV Criticism*. New York: Praeger, 1975.

Archer, Gleason L. *Big Business and Radio*. New York: The American Historical Society, Inc., 1939. Reprint. New York: Arno, 1971.

————. *History of Radio to 1926*. New York: The American Historical Society, Inc., 1938. Reprint. New York, Arno, 1971.

Arlen, Michael J. *Living Room War*. New York: Viking, 1969.

Armsey, James W., and Dahl, Norman C. *An Inquiry Into the Uses of Instructional Technology*. New York: The Ford Foundation, 1973.

Ashley, Paul P., and Hall, Camden M. *Say It Safely: Legal Limits in Publishing, Radio and Television*. 5th ed. Seattle: University of Washington Press, 1976.

Ashmore, Harry S. *Fear in the Air Broadcasting and the First Amendment*. New York: Norton, 1973.

Bagdikian, Ben H. *The Information Machines: Their Impact on Men and the Media*. New York: Harper & Row, 1970.

Baker, Robert K., and Ball, Sandra J. *Violence and the Media* (a staff report to the National Commission on the Causes and Prevention of Violence). Washington, D.C.: GPO, 1969.

Baker, Sam Sinclair. *The Permissible Lie: The Inside Truth about Advertising.* Cleveland: World, 1968.

Barcus, Francis E. *Concerned Parents Speak Out on Children's Television.* Newtonville, Massachusetts. Action for Children's Television, 1973.

Barnouw, Erik. *Tube of Plenty: The Development of American Television.* New York: Oxford University Press, 1975.

———. *The Image Empire.* New York: Oxford University Press, 1970.

———. *The Golden Web.* New York: Oxford University Press, 1968.

———. *A Tower in Babel.* New York: Oxford University Press, 1966.

Barron, Jerome A. *Freedom of the Press for Whom? The Rise of Access to Mass Media.* Bloomington: Indiana University Press, 1973.

Bartlett, Jonathan, ed. *The First Amendment in a Free Society.* New York: H. W. Wilson, 1979.

Belson, William A. *Television Violence and the Adolescent Boy.* Farnborough, Hants. Saxon House, 1978.

Berenson, Bernard, and Janowitz, Morris, eds. *Reader in Public Opinion and Communication.* 2d ed. New York: The Free Press, 1966.

Berner, Richard O. *Constraints on the Regulatory Process: A Case Study of Regulation of Cable Television.* Cambridge, Massachusetts: Ballinger Publishing, 1976.

Blakely, Robert J. *To Serve the Public Interest: Educational Broadcasting in the U.S.* Syracuse, New York: Syracuse University Press, 1979.

———. *The People's Instrument: A Philosophy for Public Television.* Washington, D.C.: Public Affairs Press, 1971.

Blanchard, Robert O., ed. *Congress and the News Media.* New York: Hastings House, 1974.

Bluem, A. William. *Documentary in American Television.* New York: Hastings House, 1965.

Blumler, Jay G., and Katz, Elihu, eds. *The Uses of Mass Communications: Current Perspectives on Gratifications Research.* Beverly Hills, California: Sage Publications, 1974.

Blumler, Jay G., and McQuail, Denis. *Television and Politics: Its Uses and Influences.* Chicago: University of Chicago Press, 1969.

Bogart, Leo. *The Age of Television.* 3d ed. New York: Frederick Ungar, 1972.

Bower, Robert T. *Television and the Public.* New York: Holt, 1973

Briggs, Asa A. *The War of Words: The History of Broadcasting in the United Kingdom.* Vol. 3. London: Oxford University Press, 1970.

———. *The Golden Age of Wireless: The History of Broadcasting in the United Kingdom.* Vol. 2. London: Oxford University Press, 1965.

————. *The Birth of Broadcasting: The History of Broadcasting in the United Kingdom.* Vol. 1. London: Oxford University Press, 1961.

Brown, Lee. *The Reluctant Reformation: On Criticizing the Press in America.* New York: David McKay, 1974.

Brown, Les. *Television: The Business Behind the Box.* New York: Harcourt, 1971.

Bunce, Richard. *Television In the Corporate Interest.* New York: Praeger, 1976.

Burke, Richard C., ed. *Instructional Television: Bold New Venture.* Bloomington: University of Indiana Press, 1971.

Burns, Tom. *The BBC: Public Institution and Private World.* London: MacMillan: New York: Holmes and Meier, 1977.

Cabinet Committee on Cable Communications. *Cable* (Report to the President.) Washington, D.C.: GPO, 1974.

Cater, Douglas, and Strickland, Stephen. *TV Violence and the Child: The Evolution and Fate of the Surgeon General's Report.* New York: Russell Sage, 1975.

Cater, Douglass, and Nyhan, Michael J., eds. *The Future of Public Broadcasting.* New York: Praeger, 1976.

Cantril, Hadley. *The Invasion from Mars.* Reprint. New York: Harper, 1966.

Carnegie Commission on Educational Television. *Public Television: A Program for Action.* New York: Harper, 1967.

Chappell, Mathew, N., and Hooper, C. E. *Radio Audience Measurement.* New York: Stephen Daye, 1944.

Charnley, Mitchell. *News by Radio.* New York: Macmillan, 1948.

Chase, Francis. *Sound and Fury.* New York: Harper, 1942.

Cherry, Colin. *World Communication—Threat or Promise? A Socio-Technical Approach.* New York: Wiley, 1971.

Chester, Edward W. *Radio, Television and American Politics.* New York: Sheed and Ward, 1969.

Chester, Giraud; Garrison, Garnet R.; and Willis, Edgar E. *Television and Radio.* 4th ed. New York: Appleton-Century-Crofts, 1971.

Cline, Victor B., ed. *Where Do You Draw the Line? An Exploration into Media Violence, Pornography and Censorship.* Provo, Utah: Brigham Young University Press, 1974.

Cogley, John. *Report on Blacklisting, Vol. II: Radio-Television.* New York: The Fund for the Republic, 1956. Reprint. New York: Arno, 1971.

Cole, Barry G. *Reluctant Regulators: The FCC and the Broadcast Aud.* Reading, Massachusetts: Addison-Wesley, 1978.

————. ed. *Television: A Selection of Readings from TV Guide Magazine.* New York: The Free Press, 1970.

Coleman, Howard W. *Case Studies in Broadcast Management.* New York: Hastings House, 1970.

Coleman, Howard W., ed. *Color Television: The Business of Colorcasting.* New York: Hastings House, 1968.

Collins, Robert J. *A Voice From Afar: The History of Telecommunications in Canada.* Toronto: New York McGraw-Hill Ryerson, 1977.

Commission on Freedom of the Press. *A Free and Responsible Press.* Chicago: University of Chicago Press, 1947.

Comstock, George, et al. *Television and Human Behavior.* 3 vols. Santa Monica, California: Rand Corporation, 1975.

Culbert, David Holbrook. *News for Everyman: Radio and Foreign Affairs in Thirties America.* Westport, Connecticut: Greenwood Press, 1976.

Davidson, W. Phillips, and Yu, Frederick T. C., eds. *Mass Communication Research: Major Issues and Future Directions.* New York: Praeger, 1974.

DeFleur, Melvin L. *Theories of Mass Communication.* 2d ed. New York: David McKay, 1970.

Denisoff, R. Serge. *Solid Gold: The Popular Record Industry.* Edison, New Jersey: Transaction, 1974.

Diamant, Lincoln. *The Anatomy of a Television Commercial.* New York: Hastings House, 1970.

Diamond, Edwin. *The Tin Kazoo: Television Politics and the News.* Cambridge, Massachusetts: M.I.T. Press, 1975.

Dizard, Wilson P. *Television: A World View.* Syracuse, New York: Syracuse University Press, 1966.

Dunlap, Orrin, E., Jr. *Communications in Space.* 3d ed. New York: Harper, 1970.

———. *Dunlap's Radio and Television Almanac.* New York: Harper, 1951.

———. *Radio's 100 Men of Science.* New York: Harper, 1944.

Edmondson, Madeleine, and Rounds, David. *From Mary Noble to Mary Hartman: The Complete Soap Opera Book.* New York: Stein and Day, 1976.

Efron, Edith, *The News Twisters.* Los Angeles: Nash, 1971.

Elder, Robert E. *The Information Machine: The U.S. Information Agency and American Foreign Policy.* Syracuse, New York: Syracuse University Press, 1968.

Ellens, J. Harold. *Models of Religious Broadcasting.* Grand Rapids, Michigan: Eerdmans, 1974.

Emery, Walter B. *Broadcasting and Government: Responsibilities and Regulations.* Rev. ed. East Lansing: Michigan State University Press, 1971.

———. *National and International Systems of Broadcasting: Their History, Operation and Control.* East Lansing: Michigan State University Press, 1969.

Epstein, Edward Jay. *News from Nowhere: Television and the News.* New York: Random House, 1973.

Erickson, Don, *Armstrong's Fight for FM Broadcasting.* University, Alabama: University of Alabama Press, 1974.

Fang, Irving. *Television News.* 2d ed. New York: Hastings House, 1972.

Farrar, Ronald T., and Stevens, John D., eds. *Mass Media and the National Experience*. New York: Harper, 1971.

Faulk, John H. *Fear on Trial*. New York: Simon & Schuster, 1964.

Feshbach, Seymour, and Singer. Robert D. *Television and Aggression: An Experimental Field Study*. San Francisco: Jossey-Bass, 1970.

Foote, A. Edward, ed. *CBS and Congress: "The Selling of the Pentagon" Papers* (a special issue of *Educational Broadcasting Review*). Washington, D.C.: National Association of Educational Broadcasters, 1971.

Fornatale, Peter, and Mills, Joshua E. *Radio in the Television Age*. Woodstock, New York: The Overlook Press, 1980.

Francois, William E. *Mass Media Law and Regulation*. Columbus, Ohio: Grid, 1975.

Frank, Ronald E., and Greenberg, Marshall C. *The Public's Use of Television*. Beverly Hills, California: Sage Publications, 1980.

Fraser, John. *Violence in the Arts*. New York: Cambridge University Press, 1974.

Friendly, Alfred. *The Good Guys, the Bad Guys and the First Amendment: Free Speech vs. Fairness in Broadcasting*. New York: Random House, 1976.

Friendly, Alfred, and Goldfarb, Ronald L. *Crime and Publicity*. New York: Twentieth Century Fund, 1967.

Friendly, Fred W. *Due to Circumstances Beyond Our Control . . .* New York: Random House, 1967.

Galloway, Jonathan F. *The Politics and Technology of Satellite Communications*. Lexington, Massachusetts: Lexington Books, 1972.

Geller, Henry. *The Fairness Doctrine in Broadcasting: Problems and Suggested Courses of Action*. Santa Monica, California: Rand, 1973.

Gilbert, Robert E. *Television and Presidential Politics*. North Quincy, Massachusetts: Christopher Publishing House, 1972.

Gillespie, Gilbert. *Public Access Cable Television in the United States and Canada*. New York: Praeger, 1975.

Gilmor, Donald M. *Free Press and Fair Trial*. Washington: Public Affairs Press, 1966.

Gilmor, Donald M., and Barron, Jerome A. *Mass Communication Law: Cases and Comment*. 2d ed. St. Paul: West Publishing Co., 1974.

Glut, Donald F., and Harmon, Jim. *The Great Television Heroes*. New York: Doubleday, 1975.

Goldmark, Peter C. *Maverick Inventor: My Turbulent Years at CBS*. New York: Saturday Review Press, 1973.

Gordon, Andrew C., and Heinz, John P. *Public Access to Information*. New Brunswick, New Jersey: Transaction Books, 1979.

Green, Maury. *Television News: Anatomy and Process*. Belmont, California: Wadsworth, 1969.

Green, Timothy. *The Universal Eye: The World of Television.* New York: Stein and Day, 1972.

Greenfield, Jeff. *Television: The First 50 Years.* New York: H. N. Abrams, 1977.

Gross, Ben. *I Looked and I Listened.* New York: Random House, 1954.

Grundfest, Joseph A. *Citizen Participation in Broadcast Licensing Before the FCC.* Santa Monica, California: Rand Corporation, 1976.

Guimary, Donald L. *Citizens' Groups and Broadcasting.* New York: Praeger, 1976.

Haak, Kees van der. *Broadcasting in the Netherlands.* London, Boston: Routledge and K. Paul, 1977.

Hachten, William A. *The Supreme Court on Freedom of the Press.* Ames, Iowa: Iowa State University Press, 1968.

Harris, Paul. *Broadcasting from the High Seas: The History of Offshore Radio in Europe, 1958–76.* Edinburgh: P. Harris Publishing, 1977.

Head, Sydney W. *Broadcasting in America.* 3d ed. Boston: Houghton Mifflin, 1976.

Head, Sydney W., ed. *Broadcasting in Africa.* Philadelphia: Temple University Press, 1974.

Heighton, Elizabeth J., and Cunningham, Don R. *Advertising in the Broadcast Media.* Belmont, Calif.: Wadsworth, 1976.

Henderson, John. *The United States Information Agency.* New York: Praeger, 1969.

Hilliard, Robert L., ed. *Radio Broadcasting: An Introduction to the Sound Medium.* 2d ed. New York: Hastings House, 1974.

Hohenberg, John. *Free Press/Free People: The Best Cause.* New York: Columbia University Press, 1971.

Howitt, Dennis, and Cumberbatch, Guy. *Mass Media Violence and Society.* New York: Wiley, 1975.

Jennings, Ralph M., and Richard, Pamela. *How to Protect Your Rights in Television and Radio.* New York: United Church of Christ, 1974.

Johnson, Joseph S., and Jones, Kenneth K. *Modern Radio Station Practices.* Belmont, California: Wadsworth, 1972.

Johnson, Leland L. *Cable Television and the Question of Protecting Local Broadcasting.* Santa Monica, California: Rand Corporation, 1970.

————. *The Future of Cable Television: Some Problems of Federal Regulation.* Santa Monica, California: Rand Corporation, 1970.

Johnson, Nicholas. *How to Talk Back to Your Television Set.* Boston: Atlantic-Little, Brown, 1970.

Kahn, Frank J., ed. *Documents of American Broadcasting.* 2d ed. New York: Appleton-Century-Crofts, 1973.

Kamen, Ira. *Questions and Answers About Pay TV.* Indianapolis: Howard W. Sams, 1973.

Katz, Elihu, and Wedell, George. *Broadcasting in the Third World: Promise and Performance.* Cambridge: Harvard University Press, 1977.

Kaye, Evelyn. *The Family Guide to Children's Television: What to Watch, What to Miss, What to Change.* New York: Pantheon Books, 1974.

Kendrick, Alexander. *Prime Time: The Life of Edward R. Murrow.* Boston: Little, Brown, 1969.

Keogh, James. *President Nixon and the Press.* New York: Funk & Wagnalls, 1972.

Kirschner, Allen, and Kirschner, Linda, eds. *Radio and Television: Readings in the Mass Media.* New York: Odyssey Press, 1971.

Kittross, John M., and Harwood, Kenneth, eds. *Free and Fair: Courtroom Access and the Fairness Doctrine.* Philadelphia: Broadcast Education Association, 1970.

Kittross, John M., ed. *Administration of American Telecommunications Policy.* New York: Arno Press, 1980.

Klapper, Joseph T. *The Effects of Mass Communication.* New York: The Free Press, 1960.

Kline, F. Gerald, and Tichenor, Phillip J., eds. *Current Perspectives in Mass Communication Research.* Beverly Hills, California: Sage, 1972.

Koch, Howard. *The Panic Broadcast: Portrait of an Event.* Boston: Little, Brown, 1970.

Koenig, Allen E., ed. *Broadcasting and Bargaining: Labor Relations in Radio and Television.* Madison: University of Wisconsin Press, 1970.

Koenig, Allen E., and Hill, Ruane B., eds. *The Farther Vision: Educational Television Today.* Madison: University of Wisconsin Press, 1967.

Krasnow, Erwin G. and Longley, Lawrence D. *The Politics of Broadcast Regulation.* New York: St. Martin's Press, 1978.

Kraus, Sidney, ed. *The Great Debates.* Bloomington: Indiana University Press, 1962.

Lacy, Dan. *Freedom and Communications.* 2d ed. Urbana: University of Illinois Press, 1965.

LaGuardia, Robert. *The Wonderful World of TV Soap Operas.* New York: Ballantine Books, 1974.

Lang, Kurt, and Lang, Gladys Engel. *Politics and Television.* Chicago: Quadrangle Books, 1968.

Larsen, Otto N., ed. *Violence and the Mass Media.* New York: Harper, 1968.

Lazarsfeld, Paul F., and Kendall, Patricia L. *Radio Listening in America,* New York: Prentice-Hall, 1948.

LeDuc, Don R. *Cable Television and the FCC: A Crisis in Media Control.* Philadelphia: Temple University Press, 1973.

Lee, S. Young. *Status Report on Public Broadcasting 1973.* Washington D.C.: GPO, 1975.

Legal Advisory Committee on Fair Trial and Free Press. *The Rights of Fair Trial and Free Press.* Chicago: American Bar Association, 1969.

Lent, John A., ed. *Broadcasting in Asia and the Pacific: A Continental Survey of Radio and Television.* Philadelphia: Temple University Press, 1978.

LeRoy, David J., and Sterling, Christopher H., eds. *Mass News: Controversies and Alternatives*. Englewood Cliffs, New Jersey: Prentice-Hall, 1973.

Lesser, Gerald A. *Children and Television: Lessons from Sesame Street*. New York: Random House, 1974.

Lessing, Lawrence. *Man of High Fidelity: Edwin Howard Armstrong*. New York: Bantam Books, 1969.

Levin, Harvey J. *The Invisible Resource: Use and Regulation of the Radio Spectrum*. Baltimore: Johns Hopkins Press, 1971.

Lichty, Lawrence W., and Topping, Malachi C., eds. *American Broadcasting: A Sourcebook on the History of Radio and Television*. New York: Hastings House, 1975.

Liebert, Robert M.; Neale, John M.; and Davidson, Emily S. *The Early Window: Effects of Television on Children and Youth*. Elmsford, New York: Pergamon, 1973.

Lisann, Maury. *Broadcasting to the Soviet Union: International Politics and Radio*. New York: Praeger, 1975.

Lucas, William A., and Posner, Karen B. *Television News and Local Awareness: A Retrospective Look*. Santa Monica, California: Rand Corporation, 1975.

Lujack, Larry, and Jedlicka, Danial A. *Superjock: The Loud, Frantic, Non-stop World of a Rock Radio DJ*. Chicago: Regnery, 1975.

Lyle, Jack. *The News in Megalopolis*. San Francisco: Chandler, 1967.

Lyons, Eugene. *David Sarnoff*. New York: Pyramid Books, 1967.

Maclaurin, William Rupert. *Invention and Innovation in the Radio Industry*. New York: Macmillan, 1949. Reprint. New York: Arno, 1971.

MacNeil, Robert. *The People Machine*. New York: Harper, 1968.

Macy, John Jr. *To Irrigate a Wasteland: The Struggle to Shape a Public Television System in the United States*. Berkeley: University of California Press, 1974.

Marconi, Degna. *My Father, Marconi*. New York: McGraw-Hill, 1962.

Martin, James. *Future Developments in Telecommunications*. Englewood Cliffs, New Jersey: Prentice-Hall, 1971.

Mayer, Martin, *About Television*. New York: Harper, 1972.

McCavitt, William E. *Radio and TV: A Selected Annotated Bibliography*. Metuchen, New Jersey: Scarecrow Press, 1978.

McGinniss, Joe. *The Selling of the President 1968*. New York: Trident, 1969.

McLuhan, Marshall. *Understanding Media: The Extensions of Man*. New York: McGraw-Hill, 1964.

Melody, William. *Children's Television: The Economics of Exploitation*. New Haven: Yale University Press, 1973.

Mendelsohn, Harold, and Crespi, Irving. *Polls, Television, and the New Politics*. Scranton, Pennsylvania: Chandler, 1970.

Metz, Robert. *CBS: Reflections in a Bloodshot Eye*. Chicago: Playboy Press, 1975.

Mickelson, Sig. *The Electric Mirror: Politics in an Age of Television*. New York: Dodd, Mead, 1972.

Midgley, Ned. *The Advertising and Business Side of Radio*. New York: Prentice-Hall, 1948.

Milgram, Stanley, and Shotland, R. Lance. *Television and Anti-Social Behavior: Field Experiments*. New York: Academic, 1973.

Miller, Merle, and Rhodes, Evan. *Only You, Dick Daring!* New York: William Sloane Associates, 1964.

Minow, Newton N. *Equal Time: The Private Broadcaster and the Public Interest*. Edited by Lawrence Laurent. New York: Atheneum, 1964.

Minow, Newton; Martin, John Bartlow; and Mitchell, Lee M. *Presidential Television*. New York: Basic Books, 1973.

Morgenstern, Steve, ed. *Inside the TV Business*. New York: Sterling Publishing, 1979.

Morriss, Norman S. *Television's Child*. Boston: Little, Brown, 1971.

Nelson, Harold L., and Teeter, Dwight L., Jr. *Law of Mass Communications: Freedom and Control of Print and Broadcast Media*. 2d ed. Mineola, N.Y.: Foundation Press, 1973.

Newcomb, Horace. *TV: The Most Popular Art*. New York: Anchor, 1974.

Noble, Grant. *Children in Front of the Small Screen*. Beverly Hills, California: Sage, 1975.

Noll, Roger G.; Peck, Merton J.; and McGowan, John J. *Economic Aspects of Television Regulation*. Washington, D.C.: The Brookings Institution, 1973.

Nye, Russel B. *The Unembarrassed Muse: The Popular Arts in America*. New York: Dial, 1970.

Owen, Bruce M.; Beebe, Jack H.; and Manning, Willard G., Jr. *Television Economics*. Lexington, Massachusetts: Lexington Books, 1974.

Packard, Vance. *The Hidden Persuaders*. New York: Pocket Books, 1958.

Paley, William S. *As It Happened: A Memoir*. Garden City, New York: Doubleday, 1979.

Passman, A. *The DJs*. New York: Macmillan, 1971.

Pelton, Joseph N., and Snow, Marcellus S. *Economic and Policy Problems in Satellite Communications*. New York: Praeger, 1977.

Pennybecker, John H., and Braden, Waldo W., eds. *Broadcasting and the Public Interest*. New York: Random House, 1969.

Phillips, Mary Alice Mayer. *CATV: A History of Community Antenna Television*. Evanston, Illinois: Northwestern University Press, 1972.

Polsky, Richard M. *Getting to Sesame Street: Origins of the Children's Television Workshop*. New York: Praeger, 1974.

Porter, William E. *Assault on the Media: The Nixon Years*. Ann Arbor: University of Michigan Press, 1976.

Posner, Richard A. *Cable Television: The Problem of Local Monopoly*. Santa Monica, California: Rand Corporation, 1970.

Post, Steve. *Playing in the FM Band: A Personal Account of Free Radio.* New York: Viking, 1974.

Price, Monroe E., and Wicklein, John. *Cable Television: A Guide for Citizen Action.* Philadelphia: Pilgrim, 1972.

Quaal, Ward L., and Martin, Leo A. *Broadcast Management.* New York: Hastings House, 1968.

Quinlan, Sterling. *The Hundred Million Dollar Lunch: The Broadcasting Industry's Own Watergate.* Chicago: Philip O'Hara, 1974.

Redd, Lawrence N. *Rock is Rhythm and Blues: The Impact of Mass Media.* East Lansing: Michigan State University Press, 1974.

The Report of the Commission on Obscenity and Pornography. New York: Bantam Books, 1970.

Rissover, Frederic, and Birch, David C., eds. *Mass Media and the Popular Arts.* New York: McGraw-Hill, 1971.

Rivers, William L., and Schramm, Wilbur. *Responsibility in Mass Communications.* Rev. ed. New York: Harper, 1969.

Rivers, William L. *The Opinion Makers: The Washington Press Corps.* 2d ed. Boston: Beacon, 1967.

Rivkin, Steven R. *Cable Television: A Guide to Federal Regulations.* New York: Crane, Russak, 1974.

Rogers, Everett H. *Modernization Among Peasants: Impact of Communications.* New York: Holt, 1971.

Rosenberg, Bernard, and White, David Manning, eds. *Mass Culture: The Popular Arts in America.* New York: The Free Press, 1957.

————. *Mass Culture Revisited.* New York: Van Nostrand/Reinhold, 1971.

Ross, Leonard. *Economic and Legal Foundations of Cable Television.* Beverly Hills, California: Sage, 1974.

Routt, Ed. *The Business of Radio Broadcasting.* Blue Ridge Summit, Pennsylvania: GL/Tab Books, 1972.

Routt, Ed: McGrath, James B.; and Weiss, Frederic, A. *The Radio Format Conundrum.* New York: Hastings House, 1978.

Rubin, Bernard. *Political Television.* Belmont, California: Wadsworth, 1967.

Rucker, Bryce W. *The First Freedom.* Carbondale, Illinois: Southern Illinois University Press, 1968.

Saldich, Anne Rawley. *Electronic Democracy: Television's Impact on the American Political Process.* New York: Praeger, 1979.

Sandage, C. G., and Fryberger, Vernon. *Advertising Theory and Practice.* 18th ed. Homewood, Illinois: Irwin, 1971.

Schiller, Herbert I. *Mass Communications and American Empire.* New York: Augustus A. Kelley, 1969.

Schmidt, Benno C., Jr. *Freedom of the Press vs. Public Access.* New York: Praeger, 1976.

Schramm, Wilbur. *Mass Media and National Development: The Role of Information in Developing Countries.* Stanford, California: Stanford University Press, 1964.

Schramm, Wilbur, and Roberts, Donald F., eds. The *Process and Effects of Mass Communication.* Rev. ed. Urbana: University of Illinois Press, 1971.

Schramm, Wilbur; Lyle, Jack; and Pool, Ithiel. *The People Look at Educational Television.* Stanford, California: Stanford University Press, 1963.

Schramm, Wilbur; Lyle, Jack; and Parker, Edwin B. *Television in the Lives of Our Children.* Stanford, California: Stanford University Press, 1961.

Seiden, Martin M. *Cable Television U.S.A.: An Analysis of Government Policy.* New York: Praeger, 1972.

Seldes, Gilbert. *The New Mass Media: Challenge to a Free Society.* Washington, D.C.: Public Affairs Press, 1968.

————. *The Public Arts.* New York: Simon & Schuster, 1956.

Serling, Rod. *Patterns.* New York: Simon & Schuster, 1957.

Servan-Schreiber, Jean-Louis. *The Power to Inform.* New York: McGraw-Hill, 1974.

Settel, Irving. *A Pictorial History of Radio.* New York: Citadel, 1960.

Shamberg, Michael. *Guerrilla Television.* New York: Holt, 1971.

Shanks, Bob. *The Cool Fire: How to Make it in Television.* New York: Norton, 1976.

Shapiro, Andrew O. *Media Access: Your Rights to Express Your Views on Radio and Television.* Boston: Little, Brown, 1976.

Shayon, Robert Lewis. *Open to Criticism.* Boston: Beacon, 1971.

Shulman, Arthur, and Youman, Roger. *The Television Years.* New York: Popular Library, 1973.

Siebert, Frederick S.; Peterson, Theodore; and Schramm, Wilbur. *Four Theories of the Press.* Urbana: University of Illinois Press, 1956.

Siebert, Fred, et al. *Free Press and Fair Trial.* Athens: University of Georgia Press, 1970.

Sipemann, Charles A. *Radio's Second Chance.* Boston: Little, Brown, 1946.

————. *Radio, Television, and Society.* New York: Oxford University Press, 1950.

Simmons, Steven J. *The Fairness Doctrine and the Media.* Berkeley: University of California Press, 1978.

Skornia, Harry J. *Television and Society.* New York: McGraw-Hill, 1965.

————. *Television and the News: A Critical Appraisal.* Palo Alto, California: Pacific Books, 1968.

Skornia, Harry, and Kitson, Jack William, eds. *Problems and Controversies in Television and Radio.* Palo Alto, California: Pacific Books, 1968.

Sloan Commission on Cable Communication. *On the Cable: The Television Abundance.* New York: McGraw-Hill, 1971.

Small, William. *To Kill a Messenger: Television News and the Real World.* New York: Hastings House, 1970.

Smead, Elmer E. *Freedom of Speech by Radio and Television.* Washington, D.C.: Public Affairs Press, 1959.

Smith, Anthony. *The Shadow in the Cave: The Broadcaster, His Audience, and the State.* Urbana: University of Illinois Press, 1974.

Smith, Ralph Lee. *The Wired Nation.* New York: Harper Colophon, 1972.

Smith, Robert F. *Edward R. Murrow: The War Years.* Kalamazoo, Mich.: New Issues Press, 1978.

Smith, Robert Rutherford. *Beyond the Wasteland: The Criticism of Broadcasting.* Falls Church, Virginia: Speech Communication Association, 1976.

Smythe, Ted C., and Mastroianni, George A., eds. *Issues in Broadcasting: Radio, Television, and Cable.* Palo Alto, California: Mayfield, 1975.

Stavins, Ralph L., ed. *Television Today: The End of Communication and the Death of Community.* Washington, D.C.: Communication Service Corporation, 1971.

Steinberg, Charles S. *The Creation of Consent: Public Relations in Practice.* New York: Hastings House, 1976.

Steiner, Gary A. *The People Look at Television: A Study of Audience Attitudes.* New York: Knopf, 1963.

Sterling, Christopher H., and Kittross, John M. *Stay Tuned.* Belmont, California: Wadsworth, 1978.

Stevens, Paul. *I Can Sell You Anything: How I Made Your Favorite TV Commercial with Minimum Truth and Maximum Consequences.* New York: Peter Wydeb, 1972.

Summers, Harrison B.; Summers, Robert E.; and Pennybacker, John H. *Broadcasting and the Public.* Belmont, California: Wadsworth, 1978.

Summers, Robert E., and Summers, Harrison B. *Broadcasting and the Public.* Belmont, California: Wadsworth, 1966.

Surgeon General's Scientific Advisory Committee on Television and Social Behavior. *Television and Growing Up: The Impact of Television Violence.* Washington, D.C.: GPO, 1972.

Tate, Charles, ed. *Cable Television in the Cities: Community Control, Public Access, and Minority Ownership.* Washington, D.C.: Urban Institute, 1971.

Taylor, Sherril W., ed. *Radio Programming in Action.* New York: Hastings House, 1967.

Thompson, A. H. *Television and Presidential Politics.* Washington, D.C.: Brookings, 1956.

Tressel, George W., et al. *The Future of Educational Telecommunication.* Lexington, Massachusetts: Lexington Books, 1975.

Tuchman, Gaye, ed. *The TV Establishment: Programming for Power and Profit.* Englewood Cliffs, New Jersey: Prentice-Hall, 1974.

Twentieth Century Fund Task Force. *A Free and Responsive Press.* New York: Twentieth Century Fund, 1973.

Tyrrell, Robert. *The Work of the Television Journalist.* New York: Hastings House, 1972.

Udell, Gilman G., comp. *Radio Laws of the United States.* Washington, D.C.: GPO, 1972.

Waller, Judith, *Radio, the Fifth Estate.* 2d ed. Boston: Houghton Mifflin, 1950.

Whale, J. *The Half-Shut Eye: Television and Politics in Britain and America.* London: Macmillan, 1969.

White, Llewellyn. *The American Radio.* Chicago: University of Chicago Press, 1947. Reprint. New York: Arno, 1971.

White, Paul. *News on the Air.* New York: Harcourt, 1947.

Winick, Charles, et al. *Children's Television Commercials.* New York: Praeger, 1973.

Wolf, Frank. *Television Programming for News and Public Affairs.* New York: Praeger, 1972.

Wright, Charles R. *Mass Communication: A Sociological Perspective.* 2d ed. New York: Random House, 1975.

Wyckoff, Gene. *The Image Candidates.* New York: MacMillan, 1968.

Recommended Periodicals

Access

Advertising Age

Broadcasting

Columbia Journalism Review

Federal Communications Bar Journal

Journal of Broadcasting

Journal of Communication

Journalism Quarterly

Marketing/Communication

New York Times

Panorama

Public Opinion Quarterly

Public Telecommunications Review (PTR)

TV Guide

Variety

INDEX

1967   Court of appeals upheld FCC in *Red Lion* case.
FCC raised Fairness Doctrine to level of rules.
RTNDA appealed Fairness Doctrine rules to court.
FCC required counter commercials for cigarette ads.
WLBT hearings held in Jackson, Miss.
Carnegie Commission on ETV submitted its report.
Congress passed the Public Broadcasting Act.
Ford Foundation funded two-year Public Broadcasting Laboratory.

1968   Chicago appeals court ruled Fairness Doctrine unconstitutional.
UCC protested three-year renewal of WLBT.
Southwestern case affirmed FCC cable authority.
Fortnightly case ruled out cable copyright liability.
Joan Ganz Cooney formed Children's Television Workshop.
ABC started four-network news services.
FCC approved pay TV and antisiphoning rules.

1969   Americans saw live television of man on moon.
Court of appeals vacated WLBT license.
KTAL-TV agreed to policy change and citizen petition dropped.
Blacks petitioned FCC to deny renewal to WMAL-TV in Washington.
Vice President Agnew attacked television in Des Moines, Iowa.
Supreme Court upheld Fairness Doctrine in *Red Lion* case.

1970   Congress approved Office of Telecommunications Policy.
ACT petitioned FCC for rules on TV advertising to children.
FCC passed three more Chain Regulations.
FCC extended Fairness Doctrine to political campaigns.
PBS formed as interconnection unit for CPB.
BEM appealed to FCC on WTOP refusal to carry anti-Vietnam spots.
FCC announced new renewal policy favoring incumbents.

1971   Congress required reasonable access to federal candidates.
Appeals court reversed FCC in *BEM-DNC* case.
FCC renewed license of WMAL-TV without a hearing.
OTP Director Whitehead proposed cable regulation compromise.
PBS started interconnection service for CPB.
Whitehead gave "localism" speech to NAEB.

1972   Surgeon General issued Committee report on TV violence.
Appeals court affirmed WMAL-TV renewal without a hearing.
Whitehead proposed longer licenses in "carrot and stick" speech.
FCC announced long-awaited cable regulations.
CPB won budget fight in Congress; lost to Nixon veto.
New leadership installed in CPB.

1973   Some radio stations broadcast "sex radio" dialogues.
Supreme Court reversed appeals court in *BEM-DNC* case.
Whitehead sent renewal proposal to Congress.
Trading in Teleprompter stock suspended by Exchange.
Cable banned in Boston.
PBS reorganized as representative for public stations.

1974   FCC failed to act in response to ACT petition.